*Engaging the Bible
in a Gendered World*

Katharine Doob Sakenfeld

Engaging the Bible in a Gendered World

An Introduction to Feminist Biblical Interpretation in Honor of Katharine Doob Sakenfeld

LINDA DAY
CAROLYN PRESSLER,
EDITORS

Westminster John Knox Press
LOUISVILLE • LONDON

Scripture quotations from the New Revised Standard Version of the Bible are copyright © 1989 by the Division of Christian Education of the National Council of the Churches of Christ in the U.S.A. and are used by permission.

Scripture quotations from *The New Jerusalem Bible,* copyright © 1985 by Darton, Longman & Todd, Ltd., and Doubleday & Co., Inc. Used by permission of the publishers.

Scripture translations not from the New Revised Standard Version of the Bible or *The New Jerusalem Bible* are those of the authors.

Book design by Drew Stevens
Cover design by Jennifer K. Cox

First edition
Published by Westminster John Knox Press
Louisville, Kentucky

This book is printed on acid-free paper that meets the American National Standards Institute Z39.48 standard. ♾

PRINTED IN THE UNITED STATES OF AMERICA

06 07 08 09 10 11 12 13 14 15 — 10 9 8 7 6 5 4 3 2 1

Library of Congress Cataloging-in-Publication Data

Engaging the Bible in a gendered world : an introduction to feminist biblical interpretation in honor of Katharine Doob Sakenfeld / Linda Day, Carolyn Pressler, editors. — 1st ed.
    p. cm.
Includes bibliographical references
ISBN-13: 978-0-664-22910-8 (alk. paper)
ISBN-10: 0-664-22910-7 (alk. paper)
1. Bible—Feminist criticism.   I. Sakenfeld, Katharine Doob.   II. Day, Linda.
III. Pressler, Carolyn
BS521.4.E55   2006
220.6082—dc22   2006041365

Contents

Contributors

PHYLLIS A. BIRD, Professor Emerita of Old Testament Interpretation, Garrett-Evangelical Theological Seminary

NANCY R. BOWEN, Associate Professor of Old Testament, Earlham School of Theology

L. JULIANA M. CLAASSENS, Associate Professor of Old Testament, Baptist Theological Seminary at Richmond

LINDA DAY, General Editor, *The Catholic Biblical Quarterly*

F. W. DOBBS-ALLSOPP, Associate Professor of Old Testament, Princeton Theological Seminary

FREDA A. GARDNER, Thomas W. Synnott Professor Emerita of Christian Education, Princeton Theological Seminary

ADA MARÍA ISASI-DÍAZ, Professor of Christian Ethics and Theology, Drew University

NYASHA JUNIOR, Ph.D. Candidate, Princeton Theological Seminary

JACQUELINE LAPSLEY, Associate Professor of Old Testament, Princeton Theological Seminary

EUNNY P. LEE, Assistant Professor of Old Testament, Princeton Theological Seminary

PATRICK D. MILLER, Charles T. Haley Professor Emeritus of Old Testament Theology, Princeton Theological Seminary

CHRISTIE COZAD NEUGER, Professor of Pastoral Theology and Pastoral Counseling, Brite Divinity School

KATHLEEN M. O'CONNOR, Professor of Old Testament, Columbia Theological Seminary

DENNIS T. OLSON, Charles T. Haley Professor of Old Testament Theology, Princeton Theological Seminary

CAROLYN PRESSLER, Harry C. Piper Professor of Biblical Interpretation, United Theological Seminary of the Twin Cities

J. J. M. ROBERTS, William Henry Green Professor Emeritus of Old Testament Literature, Princeton Theological Seminary

KATHRYN L. ROBERTS, Associate Professor of Old Testament, Austin Presbyterian Theological Seminary

ANNA MAY SAY PA, Principal, Myanmar Institute of Theology

C. L. SEOW, Henry Snyder Gehman Professor of Old Testament Language and Literature, Princeton Theological Seminary

BETH LANEEL TANNER, Assistant Professor of Old Testament, New Brunswick Theological Seminary

SARAH ZHANG, Ph.D. Candidate, Princeton Theological Seminary

Introduction

As its title implies, the purpose of this volume is twofold. First, we, the editors, have planned and prepared this work to honor a beloved colleague, the Reverend Doctor Katharine Doob Sakenfeld, on the occasion of her election to the presidency of the Society of Biblical Literature. At the same time that the essays honor Professor Sakenfeld, they have been selected and organized to introduce feminist approaches to biblical interpretation, and especially to the Older Testament,[1] to learners inside and outside of the classroom who may have had little previous exposure to biblical studies in general or feminist biblical scholarship in particular. We have sought to present essays that represent a range of cultural perspectives and methods, and that lift up texts and issues of importance to the discipline.

These two aims may seem strange bedfellows. Typically, the contributors to a festschrift (a volume of essays compiled to honor an esteemed scholar) represent the colleagues, students, and close friends of the honoree, while contributions for an introductory textbook are solicited from leaders in the various aspects of the academic field being explored. Moreover, authors of festschrift essays typically have a wide degree of freedom to choose the topics of their work, which often explores very narrowly focused and quite technical topics. In contrast, an introduction to a discipline requires essays that broadly cover representative aspects of the field and that are accessible to people who may not have previously studied the topic.

The nature of Professor Sakenfeld's career—and her character— makes such a combined aim not only possible but richly productive.

---

1. There is an ongoing discussion within biblical scholarship over what to call that part of the Bible shared by Jews and Christians. For many, the traditional Christian designation "Old Testament" suggests that the Pentateuch, Writings, and Prophets have been superseded by the Gospels, a view that in turn implies that the "new covenant" has rendered the first covenant, and therefore Judaism, null and void. Various efforts to address the implied supersessionism of the traditional terms have been proposed, including "First and Second Testaments," "Hebrew Scriptures and Greek Scriptures," "Older Testament and Newer Testament," or using "Old Testament" and "New Testament" when referring to the Bible within the context of the church and "Hebrew Scriptures/Hebrew Bible" and "Greek Scriptures" in academic or interfaith contexts. The reader will encounter varying terminology in this volume, depending on the choices of the various authors.

Kathie, as she is known to her colleagues and friends, is a rigorous scholar who is internationally known and respected, a committed woman of faith, and among the foremost feminist interpreters of the Bible for both the academy and the church. Not surprisingly, among her close colleagues, friends, and students are many leading feminist biblical scholars. A wide range of such persons is represented in those who have contributed essays to this volume, including present and past faculty colleagues (Miller, Gardner, J. Roberts, Seow, Olson, Neuger, Lapsley, Dobbs-Allsopp, Lee), past doctoral students (O'Connor, Anna May, Pressler, Day, Bowen, K. Roberts, Tanner, Claassens), present doctoral students (Junior, Zhang), and long-term colleagues in the field of feminist study (Bird, Isasi-Díaz). In this list are a few "firsts": Gardner was the first woman called to the faculty at Princeton Theological Seminary; O'Connor was the first woman to be awarded a Ph.D. in biblical studies from the institution. Some fall into more than one category, as students who later became faculty colleagues (Dobbs-Allsopp, Lapsley, Lee). Moreover, Kathie inspires the kind of affection and esteem that has led contributors to be willing to work within the tightly defined limits necessary for an introductory text. The generosity and flexibility of the authors of the essays in this collection have been essential to its compilation. Though not all carry out their primary research in the area of feminist study, the topics of their essays for this volume are directly relevant to and valuable for feminist probes of the Bible. Words cannot express our deep gratitude as editors for their efforts and our sheer delight in the creativity and wisdom of their insights.[2]

We can think of no more fitting type of work to honor Professor Sakenfeld than a textbook. Kathie is a superlative teacher. Unlike many other world-class scholars, she has always given as much of her talent and creative energy to her teaching as she has to her academic research. We speak firsthand of her abilities and her passions, for the two of us were once Kathie's students. Always humble and ready to listen, she is ever as eager to learn from others as she is to instruct them.[3] With this volume, we hope that Professor Sakenfeld's legacy will continue to inform, excite, and challenge future generations of students.

2. Phyllis Bird and Patrick Miller generously provided excellent advice during the planning stages of this project. We are immensely grateful for their conversation and ongoing support. We also express our gratitude to Pam Wynn, who served as our research assistant, and to Stephanie Egnotovich of Westminster John Knox Press, who enthusiastically shepherded this project.

3. See her comments in *Just Wives? Stories of Power and Survival in the Old Testament and Today* (Louisville, KY: Westminster John Knox, 2003), 1–5.

FEMINIST BIBLICAL INTERPRETATION:
SKETCHING THE PARAMETERS

Feminist and related approaches to biblical interpretation have emerged within the past few decades; the field is growing exponentially and in multiple directions. Less a single method than a perspective or set of interrelated perspectives, feminist interpretation "has become quite complex in the best sense of the term, that is, rich and varied, not narrow and predictable in its outcomes" (Miller, 244).

This complexity, however, is in no way new but part of the history of the discipline. Historically speaking, women's movements have never stood alone. Feminism is ultimately a democratic notion, concerned for the rights of all people, including women. Therefore, the struggle for women's emancipation has regularly been connected to other struggles for emancipation: for the abolition of slavery, for religious freedom, for civil rights, for safe labor conditions, for world peace. The legacy of this interrelatedness and complexity carries through as well to the modern academic discipline of feminism. Today, feminist theology exists as part of a web of what might be loosely categorized as "liberation theologies," including, for instance, Asian and Asian American theologies, African American and black theologies, postcolonialism, native theologies, ecological theology, and queer theology. All are together concerned with issues of oppression, justice, and equality. These movements are woven together, their participants and philosophies overlapping to the degree that it is impossible fully to separate them.

With regard to biblical studies in particular, the development of forms of biblical interpretation usually seen as closely related to and yet distinct from feminist biblical studies further complicates efforts to define the discipline. For example, womanist interpretation draws on African American women's experience to analyze biblical texts in terms of race/ethnicity and class as well as gender. *Mujerista* theology takes as its goal and theological criterion the survival and liberation of Latinas in North America. Asian American feminist biblical interpretation likewise views the Bible through the lens of the concerns of women of Asian heritage, which represents a very broad and diverse range of cultures from Indian to Thai to Japanese. "Masculist" study shares the feminist commitment to mutuality between genders and examines, from an explicitly male point of view, the ways biblical narratives construct masculinity. Therefore, within this wide scope of perspectives, some scholars choose to use the term "feminism" to refer to all of these approaches; others restrict the term to the work of European and Euro-American women. In this volume, we use the term in its broader sense, while seeking to acknowledge the specificity and integrity of differing perspectives.

So, then, what is "feminist biblical interpretation"?[4] In general, "feminist consciousness" can be seen as "an awareness of women's subordination as unnatural, wrong, and largely determined by society rather than written into our bodies by biology alone" (O'Connor, 11). Thus, as our basic starting point for delineating feminist biblical interpretation, we can say that it brings a feminist consciousness to analyzing biblical texts. At the risk of reductionism, we may further identify this widely—and even wildly—diverse discipline by naming some key assumptions held by many, if not all, interpreters who call themselves "feminist."

> Biblical interpretation, like all forms of knowledge, is thoroughly contextual. That is, it is shaped by the social location (race, class, gender, sexual orientation, age, etc.) and faith commitments of the interpreter. Simply put, what one sees in a text and how one construes its meaning depends on where one stands.

> Such particularity and diversity is not innocent. The Bible is vested with tremendous authority not only in synagogues and churches, but also in cultures within which biblical religions play significant roles. Determining which biblical texts are chosen to be emphasized in hymns, liturgies, newspapers, and courthouse monuments; what types of interpretation are deemed valid and what types invalid; and what meanings are derived from these texts is ultimately a matter of power.

> Thus, as Sakenfeld writes, "Biblical interpretation is a political act, an act with consequences for the church and the world."[5]

> Feminist interpretation is engaged. Eschewing the myth of disinterested, objective scholarship, feminists seek justice for all people and are "especially concerned for the fate of women—all women—in the midst of 'all people.'"[6]

---

4. The descriptions offered by various contributors to this volume demonstrate the lack of a single definition of the phrase. For example, Miller understands "feminist interpretation" as "a particular critical method, in some ways much richer and more complex than other critical methods," which entails "reading the Bible in a way that is attentive to the place of women in the text and the world of the text, what is said about them and by them, what is done to them and what they cannot do" (Miller, 247–48, 238–39). In contrast, Tanner observes that "from the very beginning, feminist criticism was not a strict method but a way of looking at the Bible. It was an endeavor that struggled with the text to provide a view from the perspective of women, but at the same time that considers any scholar's view to be one of many" (Tanner, 69–70).

5. "Feminist Biblical Interpretation," *Theology Today* 46 (1989): 164.

6. Sakenfeld, "Feminist Perspectives on the Bible and Theology: An Introduction to Selected Issues and Literature," *Interpretation* 42 (1988): 5.

SITUATING THIS VOLUME

Given the rich complexity of the discipline and its emphasis on the contextual nature of all acts of interpretation, it is important to situate this volume within the larger field of feminist biblical scholarship. Feminist interpretation may be analyzed and categorized according to numerous factors, including the social location of the interpreter; the methodology that the interpreter employs; the interpreter's assessment of the patriarchal use of the Bible and understanding of its authority in light of the way the Bible has been used against women; and whether and how the interpreter relates gender justice to racial, economic, and sexual justice.[7]

Social Location

The social locations of the contributors to this volume differ. We are baby boomers, retirees, and graduate students; straight and lesbian; Asian, African, Euro-American, African American, Latina, and Asian American; we are women and men. Nonetheless, there are key aspects of our social locations that contribute to the particular shape of this volume and its relationship to other feminist and related voices. Many of the characteristics of the volume can be traced to the social location of Katharine Sakenfeld, who has taught at Princeton Theological Seminary for the entirety of her career but who has also engaged extensively in study and dialogue with biblical interpreters worldwide, and who consistently seeks to find ways for silenced voices to gain a hearing in the academy and in the church.

Like Kathie, the contributors to this volume are Christian, and predominantly Protestant.[8] All of us have studied or taught at Protestant

---

7. Scholars have mapped feminist biblical interpretation in numerous ways. For an analysis of three hermeneutical approaches by early feminist biblical interpretation, see Sakenfeld, "Feminist Uses of Biblical Materials," in *Feminist Interpretation of the Bible* (ed. Letty M. Russell; Philadelphia: Westminster, 1985), 55–64; for a typology based on exegetical approaches, see her "Feminist Biblical Interpretation." Carolyn Osiek ("The Feminist and the Bible: Hermeneutical Alternatives," in *Feminist Perspectives on Biblical Scholarship* [ed. Adela Yarbro Collins; Chico, CA: Scholars, 1985], 93–105) considers the interplay of interpreters' understanding of gender, biblical authority or lack of authority, and goals to identify five types of feminist biblical interpretation. In the present volume, O'Connor uses Sakenfeld's outline of hermeneutical approaches to sketch the history of the discipline, then discusses some of the recent movements in the burgeoning field of feminist biblical studies that she finds most useful.

8. It is both unfortunate and telling that the adjective "Christian" has come for many people to connote a rather narrow, conservative slice of the broad spectrum of church members and has too often been used dogmatically to describe that small group of Christians over and against others who also confess Christ as the way in which God has encountered them. Reclaiming the term as descriptive of all who belong to the broad and varied communities of faith in Jesus the Christ is an important and ongoing task. We use it to claim our particular faith stance and invite persons of other beliefs into dialogue, not to define ourselves over and against others who are also Christian.

seminaries (most often, Princeton); almost all are active in local religious congregations. This volume belongs to the academy. The contributors are educated biblical scholars and committed teachers, and some of the essays are written primarily for an academic audience. This volume also belongs to the church. A significant number of the articles are shaped by an explicit faith perspective and written from and for the church.

Such commitment is inevitably particular. The fact that this volume represents the work of Christian scholars means that important voices —Jewish, Muslim, or postbiblical—are not included. Jewish feminist scholar Judith Plaskow, among others, has justly criticized Christian feminists for writing as if our perspectives are universal rather than particular.[9] We acknowledge the particular faith tradition out of which this volume has been written and express our appreciation of and desire for dialogue with feminist biblical scholars from other traditions. The reader is encouraged to explore the writings of Jewish and Muslim feminists as well as postbiblical feminist scholars.[10]

The contributors to this volume are both women and men. The choice to invite men to contribute to a book that introduces feminist interpretation is neither inevitable nor uncontroversial. Some feminist scholars define the discipline as biblical interpretation that uses as its primary interpretive lens the experience of women (either individually or in the communal struggle for liberation). By this definition, only women can be feminists. We, however, prefer a broader understanding of what can constitute "feminist" thought. We have intentionally included men in this volume not only because Kathie's closest colleagues include people of both sexes, but primarily because from the earliest days of feminist biblical studies there have been men interpreting Scriptures with an awareness of their privileged location and a conscious commitment to gender justice. Whether one calls them "feminist," "pro-feminist," "masculist," or "ally," some male scholars have been involved in early and

---

9. Absolutizing their perspectives is only one of the salient critiques that Plaskow makes of Christian feminist theologians. See her "Feminist Anti-Judaism and the Christian God," *Journal of Feminist Studies in Religion* 7 (1991): 99–108; also Amy-Jill Levine, "The Disease of Postcolonial New Testament Studies and the Hermeneutics of Healing," in "Roundtable Discussion: Anti-Judaism and Postcolonial Interpretation," *Journal of Feminist Studies in Religion* 20 (2004): 91–132.

10. For instance, see Judith Plaskow, *Standing Again at Sinai: Judaism from a Feminist Perspective* (New York: HarperCollins, 1990); Phyllis Trible and Letty M. Russell, eds., *Hagar, Sarah, and Their Children: Jewish, Christian, and Muslim Perspectives* (Louisville, KY: Westminster John Knox, 2006); Kristen E. Kvam, Linda S. Schearing, and Valerie H. Ziegler, *Eve and Adam: Jewish, Christian, and Muslim Readings on Genesis and Gender* (Bloomington: Indiana University Press, 1999); Ellen Frankel, *The Five Books of Miriam: A Woman's Commentary on the Torah* (New York: Putnam, 1996); Elyse Goldstein, ed., *The Women's Torah Commentary: New Insights from Women Rabbis on the Fifty-four Weekly Torah Portions* (Woodstock, VT: Jewish Lights, 2000); Mieke Bal, *Lethal Love: Feminist Literary Readings of Biblical Love Stories* (Bloomington: Indiana University Press, 1987); Carter Heyward, *Speaking of Christ: A Lesbian Feminist Voice* (ed. Ellen C. Davis; New York: Pilgrim, 1989).

ongoing efforts to make language more inclusive, support women's ordination, and recover and highlight neglected stories about women. Moreover, younger feminists are increasingly defining their goal as a transformed community of women and men, a goal that also underlies several of these essays.

We must name one more aspect of the social location of the contributors to this volume. That is, most of us study and teach the Older Testament. Isasi-Díaz is an ethicist who has written extensively on stories from both the Newer and the Older Testament; Gardner is a religious educator; Neuger's discipline is pastoral care. The rest of us, however, work in the discipline of Older Testament studies. The essays in this volume raise issues of importance to interpretation of both parts of the canon and can well serve to introduce feminist biblical interpretation generally. Moreover, one author (Isasi-Díaz) interprets a Newer Testament pericope (the transfiguration). Nonetheless, the volume is slanted toward the Hebrew Scriptures. This focus reflects in part the career of Katharine Sakenfeld, an Older Testament scholar. But it also responds to what we have seen as a gap in the literature. Although there are several edited volumes of feminist interpretation of the Newer Testament, of the Bible as a whole, or of the Torah, we are not aware of any other introduction to feminist interpretation of the Older Testament.[11]

Exegetical Method

In her article "Feminist Biblical Interpretation," Sakenfeld describes three major exegetical methods typically used by feminist biblical scholars. A formal literary approach "focuses on the narrative as it is received as text, with interpretive constraints provided by the perceived literary design and by grammatical and syntactical elements." A "culturally cued literary reading" "is also within the literary realm, but it concentrates much more on reading the text as a product of its own culture." The third method is historical; it "seeks to use data from other

11. Athalya Brenner and Carole Fontaine, eds., *A Feminist Companion to Reading the Bible: Approaches, Methods, and Strategies* (Sheffield: Sheffield Academic Press, 1997); Harold C. Washington, Susan Lochrie Graham, and Pamela Thimmes, eds., *Escaping Eden: New Feminist Perspectives on the Bible* (Biblical Seminar 65; Sheffield: Sheffield Academic Press, 1998); Elisabeth Schüssler Fiorenza, ed., *Searching the Scriptures*, vol. 1, *A Feminist Introduction* (New York: Crossroad, 1993); Luise Schrottroff, Silvia Schroer, and Marie-Theres Wacker, *Feminist Interpretation: The Bible in Women's Perspective* (trans. Martin and Barbara Rumscheidt; Minneapolis: Fortress, 1998). The sole collection concentrating on the Older Testament is Alice Bach, ed., *Women in the Hebrew Bible: A Reader* (New York/London: Routledge, 1999), but as its subtitle implies, its focus is not introductory. All of these works include intriguing and illuminating articles, however, and the reader is encouraged to consult them.

ancient Semitic cultures, as well as comparative sociological models and material remains found by archaeologists, in order to begin to reconstruct a clearer and more reliable picture of women's life in ancient Israel."[12] In the years since Sakenfeld developed her typology in 1989, the number of disciplines employed by feminist biblical scholars has "exploded," including anthropology, sociology, folklore studies, critical theory, legal history, and biology (see O'Connor, 19–23). Feminist interpreters place biblical texts in dialogue with stories and histories drawn from world literature and world religions, with every possible form of artistic representation, and with accounts of women's daily lives. Given the explosive proliferation of methods in biblical studies generally and in feminist biblical scholarship in particular, it is not possible for one volume to represent the ever-growing range of methods found in the discipline. Literary approaches, however, continue to predominate, and are most fully represented in this volume. Perhaps reflecting Kathie's preference for culturally cued literary readings, most of the essays here also incorporate the insights of historical criticism along with close attention to literary features of the text. In addition, social scientific (Olson), historical (Roberts, Pressler), and storytelling (Bowen) methods are also represented.[13]

Hermeneutical Framework: Patriarchy and Authority

How feminists define the problem of patriarchy in biblical interpretation and how they view the authority of the Bible comprise yet other, interrelated factors by which their interpretation may be mapped. Two overriding questions need to be asked by any feminist encountering the Bible: Is the Bible redemptive for women? Is the Bible redeemable for women?[14] On the one end of the spectrum, some believe that the Bible is irredeemably patriarchal. Scholars who hold this position may study the Scriptures in order to critique texts that wield authority within soci-

12. Sakenfeld, "Feminist Biblical Interpretation," 161–62.
13. A further area of primary feminist concern has been investigation of the everyday lives of ancient Israelite women. The reader is encouraged to examine reconstructions of women's lives in ancient Israel, Palestine, and Hellenistic cultures. Two now-classic studies are Carol Meyers, *Discovering Eve: Ancient Israelite Women in Context* (New York/Oxford: Oxford University Press, 1988); and Elisabeth Schüssler Fiorenza, *In Memory of Her: A Feminist Theological Reconstruction of Christian Origins* (New York: Crossroad, 1988); see also Tal Ilan, *Jewish Women in Greco-Roman Palestine* (Peabody, MA: Hendrickson, 1996).
14. Carolyn Osiek, "Reading the Bible as Women," in *The New Interpreter's Bible* (ed. Leander Keck et al.; Nashville: Abingdon, 1994), 1:183; see also see Phyllis A. Bird, "Biblical Authority in the Light of Feminist Critique," in *Missing Persons and Mistaken Identities: Women and Gender in Ancient Israel* (Overtures to Biblical Theology; Minneapolis: Fortress, 1997), 248–65.

ety or as a matter of academic interest, but reject any claims that the Newer or Older Testaments are authoritative. On the other end of the spectrum, some feminist Christians cherish the Bible as the unalloyed Word of God. These interpreters maintain that all biblical texts, properly understood, are salvific for women and men, and the ways the Bible has been used against women represent distorted interpretation. Within these two poles, a wide range of positions and approaches is found. The scholars who have contributed to this volume embrace the historical-critical understanding that all biblical texts are the products of the particular cultures that shaped them and the feminist awareness that those cultures were patriarchal. The biblical texts themselves encode—and thus support—patriarchy. Most of the contributors do not directly address the question of biblical authority. Those who do find in the Bible liberating as well as oppressive dynamics (Anna May, Bowen), turn to it as a memory of and inspiration for struggle (Isasi-Díaz), or acknowledge that the word of God is always spoken to and through human beings whose cultural perspectives and assumptions leave their marks on the texts (Miller, Pressler, Lapsley).

Because they experience the Bible as both patriarchal and liberating, many of the contributors to this volume engage in a twofold hermeneutic or interpretive approach, a "hermeneutics of suspicion" and a "hermeneutics of retrieval." A hermeneutics of suspicion expects that the Bible serves the interests of those who authored, edited, and canonized it: that is, males. The first task of feminist interpretation, therefore, is "questioning the text, identifying its patriarchy and oppression of women, resisting its power to effect such ways of being and acting in the contemporary culture and the church. . . . The hermeneutic of retrieval cannot come before the problems of the text have been identified" (Miller, 248).

A "hermeneutics of retrieval" seeks to identify "resistant voices and narrative strategies that complicate patriarchy" (O'Connor, 21). Such an enterprise lifts up texts that relate women's agency, that represent the deity with feminine images or attributes, that can be used to reconstruct women's history, and in general, texts that refuse to accept the inevitability of suffering or powerlessness. There are a variety of possible strategies to retrieve a meaningful word from the biblical texts.[15] One such approach involves investigating the significance of female characters and God imagery (Day). Early feminists especially sought to

---

15. Our discussion of ways in which contributors have sought to retrieve a word for themselves is indebted to Carol Lakey Hess's enumeration of "strategies for dealing with difficult texts" in her *Caretakers of Our Common House: Women's Development in Communities of Faith* (Nashville: Abingdon, 1997), 195–206.

identify stories about women and divine imagery that had been largely ignored throughout the centuries-long history of biblical interpretation. Yet the difficulty remains that there are too few positive stories about women in the Bible; moreover, most of them express men's views of women rather than women's views of their own lives. A solution is to consider how characters and phrases not highlighted in the texts themselves can still prove to be quite significant (Claassens, Seow).

A further feminist strategy for reclaiming biblical texts has been to identify in them female voices (Dobbs-Allsopp). This does not necessarily mean that the texts were authored by women, but instead that a woman's point of view can be at least partially discerned in them.[16] Setting biblical texts in conversation with one another has been yet another way in which interpreters committed to gender justice respond to biblical patriarchy, to let "Scripture interpret Scripture" (Olson, Lapsley). Viewing a difficult text in the light of texts that present more egalitarian and positive ideas can often prove affirming. Similarly, feminists have long identified liberating principles or dynamics in the Bible with which to critique sexism in both the biblical texts and in contemporary society (Pressler).

Gender Injustice in Relationship to Other Types of Injustice

One additional way of situating the volume is to ask how broadly or narrowly the contributors define the goal of feminist biblical interpretation. How does the goal of gender justice relate to racial, economic, and/or sexual justice in their analyses? At least in its early form, European and Euro-American women, who were typically middle- and upper-middle-class, spoke about our experience as if it were somehow representative of the experience of all women (Junior, 40–41). White feminists' early exclusive focus on gender was harshly criticized by womanist, *mujerista,* and Asian American feminists, who insisted that race/ethnicity, class, and gender (and today we would also add sexual orientation, age, nationality, and physical abilities) intersect, mutually defining what each means.[17] Some of the essays in this book focus

---

16. See Athalya Brenner and Fokkelien van Dijk-Hemmes, *On Gendering Texts: Female and Male Voices in the Hebrew Bible* (Leiden: Brill, 1993).

17. One might ask, if feminist commitment to justice extends beyond gender to include freedom from all forms of oppression, why is feminism necessary at all? Why not fold gender concerns into more general liberationist approaches to biblical interpretation? In our view, as a practical matter there need to be some people for whom gender justice is the primary (though not exclusive) focus, others who concentrate their efforts on racial justice work, and so forth. Generic discussions of "human liberation" too often serve to remove the focus from challenging the status quo.

primarily on gender, while others reflect an awareness of the interlocking nature of structures of dominance and a commitment to resist these multiple forms of oppression. For example, the concerns of gender can rarely fully be separated from the concerns of ethnicity when appraising biblical texts (Lee), nor from the concerns of social status (Tanner); cultural expectations can affect whether we see female biblical characters as positive or negative examples (Anna May); or the Bible can be used to critique modern cultural norms for other oppressed minority populations as well as women (Pressler).

THE ORGANIZATION OF THE VOLUME

The essays that form this volume are divided into four main parts. An overview of feminist biblical interpretation is followed by essays that highlight varying perspectives from which to view the Bible (part 1), interpretations of pertinent texts (part 2), selected issues that have been of particular importance to feminist biblical scholarship (part 3), and intersections of feminist biblical interpretation with other disciplines (part 4). As is often the case, these divisions are somewhat arbitrary. As discussed earlier, an essential tenet of feminist thought is that all interpretations are contextual; every interpreter brings a particular perspective to the texts. Therefore, the reader will note that essays that concentrate on specific biblical texts also raise numerous issues of importance to feminist, womanist, *mujerista,* and masculist interpretation. In similar fashion, none of the particular issues addressed can be isolated from the specific biblical texts that render such concerns significant for feminist interpreters, be they either beneficial or problematic. Readers will also clearly see how the social locations and experiential perspectives of the authors in the final section (the academy, the church) influence what they choose to place in conversation with feminist interpretation. Nonetheless, these four categories introduce the reader to what we see as major foci and directions in the academic field of feminist biblical interpretation.

An overview essay by Kathleen O'Connor introduces the field of feminist biblical interpretation, and it should be read first. Locating the origins and impetus of feminist biblical scholarship firmly in the women's movement of the 1960s and 1970s, she sets out the history of the discipline, identifies its primary approaches, and maps avenues for its future growth. O'Connor views these issues through the lens of the story of the impoverished widow (2 Kgs 4:1–7) and weaves into her essay reflections of her own experience of feminism as both life-giving and challenging.

Perspectives

One of the basic assumptions of feminist biblical interpretation is that every reading of a biblical text is shaped by the interpreter's perspective(s), including an individual's social location and life experiences. A collection of essays concentrating on a range of perspectives follows the introductory overview, which we hope will give the reader a sense of the rich and varied conversation that is currently a part of feminist hermeneutics.

Ada María Isasi-Díaz writes from a *mujerista* perspective, emphasizing the importance of communication and friendship in the daily lived experiences of Latinas. Turning to the Bible, she lifts up the key role of speech and conversation partners in the story of Jesus' transfiguration. Nyasha Junior describes and problematizes womanist biblical interpretation. Tracing its origins to African American women's critique of Euro-American feminism, she identifies key aspects of womanist scholarship. Junior observes, however, that relatively few African American women have entered the field of biblical studies, and she cautions us against imposing the designation "womanist" on all African American female scholars. Anna May Say Pa writes from the perspective of Asian feminism. After highlighting important aspects of the story of Ruth, she questions the adequacy of Ruth as a role model for Asian women. Beth LaNeel Tanner points out that, rather than its assumed universality, the early feminist movement was in actuality monolithic and exclusionary, representing a perspective that was primarily North American or European, Caucasian, and Christian. She creatively engages in conversation with the biblical character Sarah to explore ways in which both of their stories reflect their vulnerability and powerlessness as women—and how their privileged economic and ethnic status implicates them both. Finally, Dennis Olson writes from the particularity of a self-conscious male interpreter as he examines the dynamics of the first family in Gen 2–4. The social-scientific research on masculinities he utilizes represents a second wave in gender studies; after female scholars began to articulate the uniqueness of a woman's perspective, some men began to consider what components constitute a male, or masculist, perspective.

Texts

Though all parts of the biblical canon have been subject to feminist inquiry, certain portions have received greater attention than others. These have been passages that include female characters or images of God or that provide evidence helpful for reconstructing women's lives in ancient Israel and Palestine. Many of these important texts are taken up in essays in other parts of the volume: for instance, the narratives about the women surrounding David (Miller), Hagar and Sarah (Tanner), Tamar (Bowen), and the numerous instances of feminine imagery for God (Claassens). To render this textbook more complete, we have solicited essays that concentrate on a few texts that have been of especial and perennial interest to feminist scholarship over the years.

The book of Ruth is one such text. Many feminist scholars have lifted up the relationship between Naomi and Ruth as a rare biblical example of women's friendships and of female agents working out their own survival; moreover, some lesbian interpreters have embraced the book as a story of women whose primary commitment is to one another. Yet other feminist interpreters find problematic the story's insistence on cultural assimilation and its emphasis on obedience to one's elders. In addition to Anna May's assessment of Ruth as a potential role model for Asian women, in this volume Eunny P. Lee and Jacqueline Lapsley provide multiple interpretations of the story. Lee examines the ways in which Ruth negotiates ethnic differences and kinship ties, raising the concern of how we relate to those who are "other." Lapsley reflects on the history of interpretation of the book, asking why attention has focused on the more docile younger woman rather than on the older Naomi, whose protests about her losses parallel those of Job. These three essays on the book of Ruth, we believe, present the reader with an opportunity to see the diversity of feminist scholars' methods and conclusions in action.[18]

Two characters of intense interest to feminists are the subject of Linda Day's essay: Eve and Woman Wisdom (*Hokmah* in Hebrew, *Sophia* in Greek). Tradition has been harsh on Eve. Created after Adam and thus supposedly his inferior, the first to eat the forbidden fruit and thus held responsible for sin, Eve has long been used to legitimize the subjugation of women.[19] Phyllis Trible's groundbreaking book *God and the*

---

18. Their inclusion also reflects Katharine Sakenfeld's long-standing research interest in the book of Ruth.
19. See, for instance, Kvam, Schearing, and Ziegler, *Eve and Adam.*

Rhetoric of Sexuality has become an influential feminist reinterpretation of Gen 2–3, demonstrating how aspects of the creation story are at least as plausibly interpreted as depicting the woman Eve's equality to the man.[20] Reading Olson's analysis of the construction of masculinities in Gen 2–4 in conjunction with Day's treatment of the same stories allows the reader to note the commonalities and differences between a feminist and a masculist approach.

The paucity of female metaphors for God in the Bible has generated much interest in one prevalent image: "Woman Wisdom," which is promulgated in the biblical books of Proverbs and Wisdom of Solomon. A complex and elusive metaphor, Woman Wisdom functions on several levels of meaning, mediating between God and humankind, "calling humanity to herself and through herself to God . . . She is the wisdom of God; she is the name Israel gave to the One God."[21] Moreover, some scholars find this female wisdom tradition continuing into the New Testament's portrayal of Jesus. Day articulates the strong connection between the attributes of wisdom and female characters in the biblical literature.

The Song of Songs has been the focus of many feminist interpreters, who often extol its joyous celebration of romantic, even frankly erotic, love that is based on mutuality rather than subordination and dominance, or find in it the presence and even predominance of a female voice. Renita J. Weems has made a compelling case that the lovers in the Song face social opposition; theirs is a resistant love.[22] Athalya Brenner and Fokkelien van Dijk-Hemmes, in a study of the gender of the discourse of texts (and not necessarily of their authors), has identified the Song as a "female" text.[23] Other scholars caution readers, however, that the Song is not free of patriarchal ideology; it may reflect men's desire more than it expresses the actual voices of women.[24] F. W. Dobbs-Allsopp, in his essay, employs the theories of Algerian Jewish feminist

20. *God and the Rhetoric of Sexuality* (Overtures to Biblical Theology; Philadelphia: Fortress, 1978).

21. Carolyn Pressler, "Faithful Yet Free: God Talk and the Old Testament," *Theological Markings* 2, no. 2 (1994): 11–15. The description of Woman Wisdom draws on the work of Kathleen O'Connor, *The Wisdom Literature* (Message of Biblical Spirituality 5; Wilmington, DE: Michael Glazier, 1988), 82–85.

22. Renita J. Weems, "The Song of Songs," in *The New Interpreter's Bible* (ed. Leander Keck et al.; Nashville: Abingdon, 1997), 5:361–434.

23. Brenner and van Dijk-Hemmes, *On Gendering Texts.*

24. See David J. A. Clines, "Why Is There a Song of Songs, and What Does It Do to You If You Read It?" in *Interested Parties: The Ideologies of Writers and Readers of the Hebrew Bible* (Journal for the Study of the Old Testament Supplement Series 205; Gender, Culture, Theory 1; Sheffield: Sheffield Academic Press, 1995), 94–121; J. Cheryl Exum, "Ten Things Every Feminist Should Know about the Song of Songs," in *The Song of Songs: A Feminist Companion to the Bible (Second Series)* (ed. Athalya Brenner and Carole Fontaine; Sheffield: Sheffield Academic Press, 2000), 24–35.

philosopher Hélène Cixous to open up intriguing new interpretive pathways into this often-studied book. He argues that the woman's playful spirit, affirmative view on life, and self-assertiveness reflect the text as a "feminine writing."

Most of the female characters in the Bible are bit players, given few actions and even fewer lines. We readers have to fill in the gaps in our attempt to understand them. C. L. Seow takes up one of these minor characters, the unnamed wife of Job. Even with its predominant interest in a male character, Carol A. Newsom has demonstrated that the book of Job does offer feminists some positive resources. It elevates experience—even over and against tradition—as a theological resource and offers a model of faith that refuses to be passive in the face of unjust suffering.[25] Seow's choice to compare two paintings to the biblical text reflects the emerging trajectory of visual imagery in biblical interpretation.[26] Not dissimilarly from Lapsley's articulation of the distortion in traditional interpretation of Naomi, he demonstrates how distortions have prevented scholars from recognizing that these paintings actually depict the wife of Job quite positively.

Issues

This section begins with essays about gender-inclusive language and female imagery for God, topics that have generated great passion in both feminists and their opponents. Feminist scholars join others in arguing that the language and images we humans choose to use not only reflect but also construct our reality. As Miller maintains in his essay, speech that uses male terms generically conveys the idea that women are subsumed within, and therefore subordinate to, men. Similarly, the use of exclusively or predominantly male language for God in theology and worship implicitly suggests that the deity more closely resembles men than women. Both forms of gender-exclusive language have been at the forefront of feminist scholarship since its earliest days (see O'Connor's comments). In this section, Christie Cozad Neuger

25. "Job," in *Women's Bible Commentary,* rev. ed. (ed. Carol A. Newson and Sharon H. Ringe; Louisville, KY: Westminster John Knox Press, 1998), 138–44.

26. See, for instance, J. Cheryl Exum, *Plotted, Shot, and Painted: Cultural Representations of Biblical Women* (Journal for the Study of the Old Testament Supplement Series 215; Gender, Culture, Theory 3; Sheffield: Sheffield Academic Press, 1996); Margarita Stocker, *Judith, Sexual Warrior: Women and Power in Western Culture* (New Haven, CT/London: Yale University Press, 1998).

discusses the political, social, ecclesiological, and pastoral importance of inclusive language and imagery. Neuger, a pioneer in feminist approaches to pastoral care, has researched extensively the role that image and theological imagination play in psychological and spiritual health. She shows how exclusively male theological language becomes a form of idolatry, equating the Creator with a creature, and how it legitimates male dominance in faith communities and in society. L. Juliana M. Claassens investigates the depictions of God as mother and midwife in Psalm 22. Using the literary theory of Mikhail Bakhtin, Claassens shows that the female metaphors—precisely because they "rupture" traditional God language—are uniquely able to open up new meanings and new possibilities for healing.

Biblical images of Yahweh are not the only divine images of concern, however. Feminist biblical interpreters, historians, and archaeologists have long been at work to determine the goddesses worshiped by persons in the ancient Near East, and even possibly in ancient Israel.[27] The biblical text contains hints of allegiance to goddesses, and the question is to what degree such worship complemented or competed with worship of Yahweh. J. J. M. and Kathryn L. Roberts enter into this discussion, as they consider the possibility of ancient Israelite belief in the goddess Asherah, fueled in part by archaeological discoveries of inscriptions referring to "Yahweh and his Asherah." They conclude that by the time the biblical materials were written, Asherah, originally a Canaanite goddess, had been absorbed into Israel's God under the influence of militant Yahwism. The Robertses' conclusions may disappoint feminists who seek more permanent signs of the goddess. Yet their argument demonstrates that ancient Israel at one time did honor a feminine expression of their God, Yahweh's Asherah, thus suggesting a female dimension of the biblical deity akin, perhaps, to Woman Wisdom or to Shekinah, the female personification of God in later Jewish tradition.

Another issue that has been the focus of much feminist discussion is the Bible's portrayal of violence against women.[28] The biblical tradition is far from a "safe space" for women. Rather, it abounds with stories of physical and sexual violence perpetrated against women, laws that sanc-

---

27. See, for instance, Tikva Frymer-Kensky, *In the Wake of the Goddesses: Women, Culture, and the Biblical Transformation of Pagan Myth* (New York: Free Press, 1992); Susan Ackerman, *Under Every Green Tree: Popular Religion in Sixth-Century Judah* (Atlanta: Scholars, 1992).

28. See, for instance, Renita J. Weems, *Battered Love: Marriage, Sex, and Violence in the Hebrew Prophets* (Overtures to Biblical Theology; Minneapolis: Fortress, 1995); J. Cheryl Exum, *Fragmented Women: Feminist (Sub)versions of Biblical Narratives* (Journal for the Study of the Old Testament Supplement Series 163; Sheffield: Sheffield Academic Press, 1993); Phyllis Trible, *Texts of Terror: Literary-Feminist Readings of Biblical Narratives* (Overtures to Biblical Theology; Philadelphia: Fortress, 1984).

tion such actions, and even prophecies that present God as acting in such ways. Moreover, patriarchal silencing and distorted depictions of women can be considered to constitute violence by the biblical texts. Nancy R. Bowen charts the numerous intersections of women, violence, and the Bible. She concludes by identifying strategies, including the reconceiving and retelling of stories (midrash), that feminists have used to counter the potential harm of such texts.[29]

Women's roles within the family and within marriage, as well as stories that depict relationships among mothers, daughters, sisters, and other family members, have obvious significance for interpreters committed to gender justice. Carolyn Pressler takes up a specific aspect of that larger issue, that is, the multiple views of marriage found in the Older and Newer Testaments. Her argument challenges the myth, beloved of conservative Christians, that the Bible contains a single, monolithic attitude toward marriage, and she concludes that the various patterns it does contain are shaped by cultures whose needs were vastly different from those of twenty-first-century North America. In that her argument has implications for the debate around same-sex marriage, Pressler also touches on the issues of sexual orientation.

We have been able to include only a sampling of the myriad issues that feminist biblical interpreters address. Some of the essays in other parts of the volume attend to other frequently addressed topics. For instance, as is inevitable in a discussion of either the Song of Songs or Cixous's work, sexuality and embodiment weave their way into Dobbs-Allsopp's essay. Sexual exploitation and trafficking form a menacing background to the essays by Anna May, Bowen, and Tanner. Lapsley's discussion of Naomi touches on the problem of ageism in biblical interpretation, a justice issue that deserves more exploration than feminists have yet undertaken. Tanner, Bowen, and Isasi-Díaz model how telling and retelling women's stories can create new understandings. Most prominently, numerous essays highlight the theme of community. The Latina community is central to Isasi-Díaz's method and goal. Olson, Miller, Anna May, and others envision a transformed community of women and men in mutual, egalitarian relationship. O'Connor and Bird lift up sisterhood as a key aspect of feminism in general and feminist biblical interpretation in particular. All of these issues, plus many

---

29. Missing from Bowen's otherwise comprehensive discussion of violence is any reference to possible biblical resources for women who have been victims of violence. For such a discussion, see Susan Brooks Thistlethwaite, "Every Two Minutes: Battered Women and Feminist Interpretation," in *Feminist Interpretation of the Bible* (ed. Letty M. Russell; Philadelphia: Westminster, 1985), 96–107.

more, demonstrate the richness of the maturing discipline of feminist interpretation.

Intersections

The final section of the book explores what might well be described as feminist interpretation facing outward, the intersection of feminist biblical interpretation and other disciplines. Our hope is that the topics selected will provide the reader with some sense of both the possibilities and the difficulties that feminist interpreters face as they seek to influence the academy and the church. They represent places of current and continuing conversations between feminism and other entities that bring their own contexts and criteria. Phyllis A. Bird, an early and highly respected feminist biblical scholar, investigates the intersection of feminist biblical interpretation with biblical theology, another subdiscipline of biblical studies. After considering the origins and issues of biblical theology, she documents the lack of women engaged in the field and explores the reasons that feminist scholars have chosen not to engage this discipline.

Freda A. Gardner's focus on education reminds us that feminism was never envisioned as self-serving, a conversation among only academics, but has always had as one of its purposes to help the general population, the persons in the pews. She writes from the perspective of a religious educator about the challenges of introducing feminist interpretation to the laity. Utilizing the work of Parker Palmer, Gardner reminds educators that introducing ideas that challenge the learners' worldviews requires openness, boundaries, and hospitality, and that the challenge is especially great when teaching about the Bible.

The final essay, by Patrick D. Miller, should be read as a counterpart to the very first essay, that of O'Connor. Both represent the experiences of senior scholars—female and male—speaking from the vantage point of watching the discipline of biblical studies change over the past few decades. Miller writes that though feminism does not constitute the center of his work, he considers how "the ways into the text arising out of feminist interpretation belong to any serious effort to read and interpret Scripture" (247). Miller's reflections on what he has "learned from his sisters" serve as an overview of the contributions of feminist biblical interpretation to biblical studies and to the church, a contribution not yet fully embraced but of enormous transformative potential. Vital to this ongoing work is his insistence that the interpretive community becomes valid and complete only when women and men work together in mutual respect.

We, as the volume's editors, envision no possible greater purpose for this book than to facilitate its female and male readers to come into conversation and community with one another around the concerns raised throughout its pages.

Overview

1

The Feminist Movement Meets the Old Testament

One Woman's Perspective

KATHLEEN M. O'CONNOR

The feminist movement came as an electrifying summons for me and many of my contemporaries in the last half of the twentieth century. It seemed like the voice of the Spirit beckoning our spirits to rise[1] and directing us to think and live differently. From the beginning the movement was a call to conversion. Feminist ideas broke in upon us all as a troubling disruption of the way things were and as an exhilarating revelation of how they might be. They gave us new understandings of ourselves, of our relationships, and of the lives of our mothers and our grandmothers before us. They stirred up vital energy to work for the well-being of future generations, and ultimately for the earth itself. For those of us committed to our religious faith, they also compelled us to rethink our beliefs about God, the Bible, and our religious institutions.

A SYMBOLIC NARRATIVE

The biblical story of the indebted widow about to lose her children in 2 Kgs 4:1–7 seems a riveting, if imperfect, tale for reflecting on the rise

Professor Katharine Sakenfeld was my teacher and is now my colleague and friend. She and I were part of a small group of women faculty and Ph.D. students at Princeton Theological Seminary who, during my years of study, met regularly to read feminist literature and to discuss our lives and our vocations as theologians and biblical scholars. It is a pleasure to write this essay in her honor.

1. With apologies to Carol P. Christ and Judith Plaskow for borrowing from the title of their important book *Womanspirit Rising: A Feminist Reader in Religion* (San Francisco: Harper & Row, 1979).

3

of the women's movement and its impact on biblical studies. In this story of enslavement escaped, of power gained, and of abundant life poured out upon women with too little of the world's goods, I see many analogies with the feminist movement of the late twentieth century.

A threatening world underlies the widow's story in 2 Kgs 4:1–7. The widow lives in extreme poverty. The text portrays her by what she does not have: no name, no food, and no way to protect her children from creditors coming to take them as payment for her dead husband's debt. Like all biblical stories, this one takes place in a social world much different from postindustrial societies familiar to us in the West. In the economic system of ancient Israel, there was no protection from creditors. They could come anytime to call in their loans, and they could charge any amount of interest on money or goods loaned to debtors. Sometimes to pay debts, families had to sell their property, their children (most often daughters), or even themselves into slavery or indentured servitude.

That the woman is a widow adds to the precariousness of her existence. A widow in the ancient world faced danger, hardship, and even death, particularly if she did not have adult sons to support her.[2] She was forced either to return to her father's house, where she would become a financial burden, or to make a living on her own. Perhaps like Ruth she might become a "day laborer" in the fields—a migrant worker, in our terms—or she might sell her daughters and sons, or even herself, into slavery of one kind or another. Facing the most dire circumstances, she might become a prostitute.

What sets this biblical story in motion is the widow's cry for help to the prophet Elisha. "Your servant my husband is dead; and you know that your servant feared YHWH, but a creditor has come to take my two children as slaves" (v. 1). Like her dead husband, Elisha is a member of a company of prophets. An exceptional character, he neither dismisses her plea nor treats her as if she were invisible. Instead, he honors the widow by hearing her, acknowledging her plight, and taking her appeal for help seriously. His questions continue to show respect to her even as they further reveal the danger in which she and her children reside. "What shall I do for you? What do you have in the house?" he asks. She replies to only the second question. All she has is "a jar of oil," and there is nothing to cook in it. But the little that belongs to her, her jar of oil, becomes the key to her survival and that of her children.

---

2. Paula S. Hiebert, "'Whence Shall Help Come to Me?': The Biblical Widow," in *Gender and Difference in Ancient Israel* (ed. Peggy L. Day; Minneapolis: Fortress, 1989), 125–41.

Elisha sends the widow to find help among members of her community. "Go outside, borrow vessels from all your neighbors, empty vessels and not just a few" (v. 3). Since it was women who did the cooking, I imagine these vessel-gathering neighbors to be women as poor and hungry as the widow herself. With generosity sometimes stunningly evident among the poor, these neighbors start bringing empty vessels and then keep bringing them. Next Elisha urges the widow to pour out the meager oil she has. We can imagine her as doubtful at first, unable to think how anything could happen from such a simple action of daily life. Her mind must expand to see the possibilities of new life. When she pours from her oil, she keeps pouring until all the vessels are filled and there is no emptiness left. After she reports this miracle to Elisha, he tells her to "Go sell the oil and pay your debts, and you and your children can live on the rest" (v. 7).

PARALLELS

It would be stretching the text way too much, of course, to say that this story fits the modern women's movement with any precision, especially since one of its main characters is a man who orders the woman around. Nonetheless, I find certain common elements.

Socioeconomic systems afflict women in antiquity as well as, of course, women in many parts of the world today, though in vastly different ways. Both modern and ancient women suffer from social and economic arrangements designed to benefit men and to exclude women. In this story, the widowed woman and her children face the double threat of starvation and enslavement by aggressive creditors. When modern feminist women began to analyze our common predicament, we realized that we, too, were excluded and demeaned simply because we were female. It seemed as if a multiarmed octopus kept us in our place with a set of tentacles that were economic, legal, spiritual, sexual, psychological, and theological.

The situation begins to change when the widow and modern feminist women seize the initiative and act for their own sake and the sake of their children. In order to survive, both behave with a boldness that society discourages in women. The widow calls out to a man for help, and her initiative transforms her from a passive victim of fate into an active figure. Similarly, modern feminists began to act on our own, as independent agents, participants in the wider world for the benefit of society.

For both the widow in 2 Kings and feminist women, new life appears because they gather in community. The widow's request for help from her neighbors invites their generosity and support, even though they seem to have as little as she. Her appeal to her neighbors turns the community of poor women into the sacred space in which God generously nourishes all. Something like the widow and her neighbors, modern women formed communities to share our emptiness and to rethink our difficulties in terms larger than our personal failures and inadequacies. In "consciousness-raising groups," women told of their hungers, fears, and self-doubts—and began also to discover strength and hope, to share our small jars of oil. Initially, at least, many feminists were bound together in a community of sisters coming back to life from partial or complete emptiness.

Both the widow and feminist women draw upon their own resources. When the widow begins to pour from the little oil she has, it flows and flows and flows. From that outpouring comes new life for her, her children, and perhaps even her neighbors. What she already has multiplies and becomes the space wherein God is the Pourer of divine generosity. Feminists, too, began to draw from our own lives, our inner resources, and our hidden strengths. We began to see our experiences as women to be different from, but of equal importance with, the experience of men. We realized that society promoted male experience as "normative," the ideal of the human, the model in nearly all avenues of thinking and acting. Instead of accepting a dualism that maintained sharp lines of demarcation between the sexes, we began to understand women's lives for their own sake, as a vast, barely explored arena for interpreting and re-imagining life in family, society, and church. We reflected on the contributions that women were already making to home, family, and society in the upbringing of children, care for the sick and elderly, and support for husbands. We realized painfully that society often ignored or belittled "women's work" and failed to compensate it justly.

The widow and modern feminists garnered cooperation from some men. In Elisha, the widow encounters a man who respects her and takes her distress seriously. When he asks her how he can help, he neither patronizes her nor fixes things for her. Instead, he acts as a wise friend and encourages her to act on her own. Even though, initially, many men were greatly threatened and perturbed by "uppity women," some modern men "got it." They saw the suffering of women and their hunger for a better world and, like Elisha, became allies in the effort to change society. Sadly, only a few such men were to be found in the churches.

At the beginning of the twenty-first century, we realize that it is very difficult to generalize about women's present economic and social conditions because they vary greatly. One result of the women's movement was the distressing discovery that white middle-class women, the dominant feminist voices of the late 1960s and 1970s, wrongly understood their experiences as the norm for all women. Many of us unwittingly acted like those men who had diminished us by making their worlds and their experience the center of life and treating everyone else as invisible or deviant. It did not take long for African American, Latina, and Asian American women, and later women from the Two-Thirds World, to name their different situations and relationships also as places of feminist struggle, creativity, and theological reflection. Not only were their insights clearly equal to ours, but they were also necessary for our conversion from our cultural arrogance, as this book hopes to show. Still in its first flush, the feminist movement among mostly middle-class white women set out important themes that would later develop, drop out, or be rethought among many and varied groups of women around the world.

WOMEN'S WORLDS AND SEXISM

Sexism is a way of thinking and acting, as well as a set of social and economic arrangements, that benefit one sex and harm the other. Because we are all embedded in the way things are—that is, our worldviews seem like absolute truths rather than socially formed ideas—most people accepted the way things were before the women's movement brought them to light. The following are a few ways sexism diminished women's lives in the middle of the last century.

> Women were second-class citizens of political, social, and religious institutions. We were excluded from many educational institutions, from professions, from sports training and competition, and from leadership roles everywhere, except within female organizations and sometimes the home.

> Women who did work outside the home typically made half the wages for the same work as a comparably educated and experienced man, and women were routinely passed over for promotions and advancement.

Women and girls were too often perceived as "sex objects," valued primarily for their bodies and the satisfaction they gave to men. (I leave it to you to decide whether this has changed.)

Teachers, and also frequently parents, gave boys more attention and encouragement than girls, even in classrooms and homes run by women.

Women disappeared into marriages where they became subordinate to their husbands' finances and decision making, and sometimes became victims of physical violence at their husbands' hands.

Women had difficulty opening bank accounts separate from their husbands or fathers, establishing credit apart from their husbands, opening businesses, and protecting themselves economically in divorce in which women's household labor went unrecognized and uncompensated.

Society judged all women to be less strong, capable, and responsible than men. We were seen as more emotional, fickle, dependent, and in need of protection by men, by the law, and by religious institutions. Women's bodies were largely under the control of these institutions.

Economically deprived women were invisible.

But these examples from the recent past reveal only part of the story. The deeper cost of sexism for many Caucasian middle-class women was crippled personhood. Too often, we believed that we were less able, less talented, less suited for leadership roles, less adequate for contributing to the world than the men in our lives. Self-hatred and disdain for other women was one way women collaborated in sexism and misogyny. From girlhood on, many of us silenced ourselves to keep safe; we lost our voices and the courage to live our dreams. These inner attitudes are called "internalized sexism," akin to internalized racism. Both terms mean that the subordinate group absorbs and believes myths about itself that harm it and benefit the dominant group.

For many women, the feminist movement called us to conversion, to spiritual transformation, by shaking up what we thought to be true. It challenged our identities as women, producing critical thinking about relationships between the sexes and among women and about gender roles assigned to us because we are female. (The term "gender" usually signifies roles assigned to us by society because of our sex, whereas the term "sex" refers to biological reality.) And the feminist movement also illuminated who we might become. A growing body of thought, it provided the theory necessary to analyze how society, culture, and church both defined and constrained us, and it created vision to work for a world more hospitable to women and children.

THE RISE OF FEMINISM IN THE GENERAL CULTURE

Feminism did not arise from discoveries in church and synagogue that half the world's population was oppressed, discriminated against, or excluded because of their sex. Nor did religious institutions notice biblical texts or religious traditions that actually challenge this sorry state of affairs—texts, for example, about God making humans in the divine image, or about Jesus' instruction to love your neighbor as yourself, or Paul's claim that in Christ there is neither Greek nor Jew, slave nor free, male or female. Rather, the call for change came from the general culture. The contradictions within the world of religion regarding women came into view only when women who had discovered feminism in the general culture began to emerge as teachers, ministers, lay leaders, and scholars.

Nor did the women's movement or feminist biblical criticism actually begin in the twentieth century. Throughout history, resistance to sexism appeared in brief, repetitive bursts that were quickly suppressed and forgotten.[3] Hildegard of Bingen and Christine de Pizan were early commentators on the Bible from a "woman-focused" perspective.[4] As early as the eighteenth century, Judith Sargent Murray cited a nonsexist interpretation of Genesis 2–3 in support of her efforts to establish schools for girls in the newly founded United States. In the nineteenth century in the United States, the women's movement had affinities and alliances with the movement to emancipate slaves. Both movements strove to recognize human dignity and to free people from various forms of oppression. Abolitionists like the Grimké sisters were drawn to the women's movement because their male colleagues belittled their views, even as they worked with them to free black slaves.[5] African American women, such as Sojourner Truth and Anna Julia Cooper, focused on the emancipatory message of the biblical text as they challenged both racism and

---

3. Gerda Lerner, *The Creation of Feminist Consciousness: From the Middle Ages to Eighteen-seventy* (New York: Oxford University Press, 1993).

4. Ibid., 142–46.

5. See Alice Ogden Bellis, "Feminist Biblical Scholarship," in *Women in Scripture: A Dictionary of Named and Unnamed Women in the Hebrew Bible, the Apocryphal/Deuterocanonical Books, and the New Testament* (ed. Carol Meyers; Boston: Houghton Mifflin, 2000), 24–32.

sexism. In 1895, Elizabeth Cady Stanton and a group of women produced *The Woman's Bible*.[6] This shocking and clearheaded book surveyed each book of the Bible to expose its treatment of women—the ways it demeaned them or offered them hope. But it was ahead of its time, considered irreverent and too radical for most women and men, and so fell into general cultural forgetfulness.

My first encounter with feminist thinking was not with *The Woman's Bible* but with the eye-opening work of Simone de Beauvoir, aptly titled *The Second Sex*.[7] A French philosopher, Beauvoir argued that women were secondary citizens of the world. Most lived what she called "imminent" lives within repetitive cycles of caregiving, more or less in the same fashion as their mothers, grandmothers, and great-grandmothers before them—washing, cleaning, tending to others' bodily and emotional needs. She noted that women engaged the broader world only vicariously through the exploits and adventures of the men in their lives.

Men, by contrast, said Beauvoir, lived "transcendent" lives, outstripping or "transcending" accomplishments of their fathers before them, going out into the world, doing and discovering that which was not yet known or done. Despite later recognition that some men lived as repetitive and cyclical existences as women, Beauvoir showed how society inhibited and constrained even the most talented women. Women and girls had little opportunity to explore the world in their youth, undertake careers suited to their talents, or even imagine themselves in roles other than the traditional ones of wife and mother. For Beauvoir, men defined women, and women, in turn, displaced themselves to meet those definitions.

Virginia Woolf's compelling work *A Room of One's Own*, written in 1927, was rediscovered in the middle of the last century.[8] Woolf proposed that every woman needs a room of her own and five hundred pounds a year, that is, enough money to be financially independent and able to pursue her own creative talents. In a similar vein, Betty Friedan, in her influential *The Feminine Mystique*, argued that women had forfeited their identity in a progressive dehumanization for a "comfortable concentration camp" of marriage and homemaking, where their own talents, yearnings, and hopes were persistently denied.[9] The central

---

6. Elizabeth Cady Stanton and the Revising Committee, *The Woman's Bible* (New York European Publishing Co., 1895–1898; reprint, Seattle: Coalition Task Force on Women and Religion, 1974).

7. Simone de Beauvoir, *The Second Sex* (New York: Knopf, 1953).

8. Virginia Woolf, *A Room of One's Own* (London: Hogarth, 1938).

9. Betty Friedan, *The Feminine Mystique* (New York: Dell, 1963).

idea of these and other writings is that women are persons in their own right, entitled to independence and self-determination.

Among women, notions like these were life-altering and institution-changing, and the churches could not escape their influences, try though they did. Feminism spread like fire in a dry field because it named what many of us already knew about our lives but had neither language nor theoretical framework to name. Of course, these ideas plunged us into conflict with some women and men who believed that feminists were elitist (cut off from the lives of real women), antifamily, and antifemale. But despite vociferous backlash, social change was under way.

Mary Daly brilliantly applied Beauvoir's thinking to the church.[10] She noted that even though women make up the majority of members in the churches and do massive amounts of work to keep the churches afloat, they tend to be accorded only second-class status. In most religious communities, women could not preach, lead worship, or serve in leadership roles that were not concerned exclusively with children. This is still the case in many churches, where—despite flowery rhetoric about women's dignity—women remain second-class citizens. The work of the liberation of women is still an ongoing battle around the world.

FEMINIST BIBLICAL SCHOLARSHIP

Feminist biblical interpretation emerges from these large societal changes and cannot be understood apart from them. Critical feminist scholarship is also born of the Enlightenment, the triumph of scientific thinking that moved from acceptance of the world as given to critical testing of truth according to scientific principles. Although contemporary feminists are frequently critical of forms of scientific thinking, the capacity to evaluate evidence, to locate it in historical context, and to subject literature to doubt are scientific tools used also in feminist biblical criticism

Women began to read the Bible with feminist consciousness. The designation "feminist consciousness" refers to an awareness of women's subordination as unnatural, wrong, and largely determined by society rather than written into our bodies by biology alone.[11] Feminist women have some sense of sisterhood with girls and other women. They have

10. Mary Daly, *The Church and the Second Sex* (Boston: Beacon, 1985).
11. Lerner, *Creation of Feminist Consciousness*, 274.

learned strategies for self-determination and have begun to create alternative visions of the future. When feminist women began to study the Bible with such consciousness, many difficulties about reading it appeared that had previously not been apparent. The discovery of these problems was deeply disturbing for many believing women, but the problems themselves set out the initial agenda of feminist biblical scholarship.

Problems for Feminists Reading the Bible

1. The first problem women faced is that female characters are scarce in the Bible. Feminist women searched biblical texts for examples of women of faith, but soon discovered that female figures who might serve as models of faith are in short supply. Women appear rarely; they have been "disappeared," to use a term from Latin America to describe the forceful removal of people from a society. When women do appear in the text, as New Testament scholar Elisabeth Schüssler Fiorenza frequently noted, they often emerge as glorified male versions of womanhood or as troublemakers who disturb "the history of salvation."[12] Frequently, women who are included in the text are nameless—unlike their male counterparts—as if the women did not matter to the writers and editors of the texts.

2. The Bible is androcentric. The term "androcentric" means "male centered." Women's experience, women's history, and women's spiritual struggles are either pushed to the corners of biblical pages or are altogether invisible, subsumed into androcentric texts. The Bible is written largely from male viewpoints—by men, about men, and, yes, largely for men. The result is that even when women do appear, they are portrayed through male eyes, and their images and behavior are filtered through male experience and bias.

3. Sexist language for people and for God excludes women. The androcentrism of the Bible remains the source of many bruising modern battles over sexist language. The concept of sexist language in biblical studies refers to way the Bible speaks about humans and God in male terms. Both testaments use predominantly male language to speak of the community of faith and of Jesus' disciples, as if they included

12. See Elisabeth Schüssler Fiorenza, *In Memory of Her: A Feminist Theological Reconstruction of Christian Origins* (New York: Crossroad, 1983).

only men—sons of Israel, brothers, or other male roles that hide the presence of women. The original biblical languages generally exclude women from the communities of Israel and the church, but English translations were even worse, sometimes translating more generic words for "human" or "humankind" with male terms.

Biblical language for God is equally androcentric. The Bible usually speaks of God with male pronouns ("he," "him," "his") or in male roles like lord, king, judge, or father. But as Mary Daly so aptly put it, "If God is male, then the male is god."[13] That means the biblical languages buttress male authority when they associate only men with God, making men God's stand-in on earth. Exceptions to this welter of male terms—for example, gender-neutral imagery for God in terms drawn from nature or in terms drawn from women's lives—were rarely noted by interpreters nor used in worship.

4. The texts encourage violence toward women. Even worse than its androcentrism, some biblical texts actually command the subordination of women, convey hatred of women (misogyny), or put God in the role as the abuser of women. Some texts appear to support and condone physical abuse of women and wives, and in some of the prophetic texts, God participates in and authorizes it (cf. Jer 13:22–27). Such texts have been used to condone domestic violence against women and children similarly to the way biblical texts were once used to support slavery.

5. The societies that produced the Bible were patriarchal and hierarchical. When feminist scholars delved more deeply into the social and cultural worlds of ancient Israel and early Christianity, other interpretive problems appeared. Not only are biblical texts androcentric and biblical languages sexist, but the social, economic, and political systems of the ancient world were patriarchal and hierarchical. The term "patriarchy" refers to social arrangements in which the *pater*, the father of the household, holds power over those in his extended family and household. In the ancient world, that included his sons, his wife, his daughters, freeborn men and their wives who worked for the household, and finally male and female slaves.

The way this authority is ordered is called "hierarchy." Hierarchy involves a top-down distribution of power. The man at the top can determine the fate of the ones below him, and his sons make decisions for their wives and slaves, and so on. In these arrangements, men always had power over women, even among slaves. In the story of the widow

---

13. Mary Daly, *Beyond God the Father: Toward a Philosophy of Women's Liberation* (Boston: Beacon, 1973), 9.

in 2 Kgs 4, no physical violence is perpetrated against the woman (though perhaps potentially against her children), but the social economic system is already treating her violently. The patriarchal world is economically, socially, and politically arranged to benefit men directly and to benefit their families only at the father's pleasure.

6. The history of interpretation is biased against women. The history of biblical interpretation did not fare well under the feminist gaze either. Interpretations usually overlooked women completely and accepted the Bible's treatment of them without question. Interpretation of the story of the widow in 2 Kgs 4 illustrates my point. Prefeminist commentaries barely notice the widowed woman at all, except as the object of the prophet's attention. Elisha, the male prophet and ally of the dead husband, was alone the important character for these interpreters. He shows concern for the widow not for her sake, but in fellowship with his deceased colleague, and only by extension for the husband's bereaved family. According to these earlier views, God's generous, miraculous care finds expression entirely through the work of the prophet and not by any action of the woman herself.[14] The widow's actions go unnoticed.

7. These many problems faced by women raised the question of how the Bible can be theologically and spiritually authoritative for women. With all these issues confronting feminists who turn to the Bible for life and hope, the question of biblical authority jumped to the center of their theological conversation. If the Bible was used throughout history to maintain the oppression of both women and slaves, how can the Bible now be a word of God for women or for descendants of slaves? Must women leave biblical religion and look elsewhere for spiritual life?

Questions of the Bible's authority divided feminists. Some left biblical faith and religious institutions behind altogether, deeming them hopelessly mired in sexism and misogyny. Others shifted their interest to treat the Bible as reflective of ancient religion, holding little spiritual value for modern feminists but worth studying because of its historic and cultural import in Western culture. Still others pursued ancient goddess traditions in search of female images for the divine. But some feminist biblical scholars began the quest for new meaning, for new life, and for innovative ways of interpreting the Bible and claiming it for women of faith. With this sense of commitment, feminists began to change biblical studies from a male bastion oblivious to women's lives to a set of disciplines alive with power, authority, and insight. Through

---

14. See, for instance, John Gray, *I and II Kings: A Commentary,* rev. ed. (London: SCM, 1970), 491–95.

feminist labor and in conversation with other disciplines, feminist biblical study has produced an amazing flowering of creativity in feminist interpretation, criticism, and publication that is still in process.

Feminist Interpretation of the Old Testament

At first, feminist ideas came slowly into biblical studies in general and Old Testament studies in particular. Virginia Ramey Mollenkott, for example, began to speak very gently of the biblical God as having feminine qualities, a point that won her much strife, for this was the beginning of cultural transgression, no matter how mildly stated.[15] Phyllis Trible broke things open in biblical studies with her rhetorical-critical study of key Old Testament texts featuring women. In her book *God and the Rhetoric of Sexuality,* she defined her work "not as a narrow focus on women but as a critique of culture in light of misogyny."[16] This analysis even in these early days critiqued racism, ecological terrorism, class systems, and stereotypical notions of human sexuality.

Trible writes a feminist hermeneutic. The term "hermeneutic" means "interpretation" and derives from the name of the Greek god Hermes, the winged-footed messenger of Zeus. Hermes' task in the Greek Pantheon is to translate the mind of the high god into language understandable by humans. Biblical hermeneutics has the analogous task of "translating" the text's ancient linguistic, cultural, and literary worlds into terms understandable and useful to modern readers. Feminist hermeneutics of the Old Testament "translates" texts through women's multifaceted perspectives. It seeks both to discover meaning in texts and to create meaning from texts for the benefit of women. But feminist hermeneutics were not merely affirmations of the text. Since they began from a posture of suspicion in relation to women's lives, feminist interpreters engaged in a "hermeneutics of suspicion" that challenged, critiqued, and refused to accept some biblical literature at face value.

Katharine Doob Sakenfeld, whose career as scholar and teacher this book honors, mapped feminist efforts in the 1970s and early 1980s to interpret biblical texts.[17] She named three directions or methodological

---

15. Virginia Ramey Mollenkott, *Women, Men, and the Bible* (Nashville: Abingdon, 1977).

16. Phyllis Trible, *God and the Rhetoric of Sexuality* (Overtures to Biblical Theology; Philadelphia: Fortress, 1978), 7.

17. Katharine Doob Sakenfeld, "Feminist Uses of Biblical Materials," in *Feminist Interpretation of the Bible* (ed. Letty Russell; Philadelphia: Westminster, 1985), 55–64.

approaches then being used in feminist hermeneutics.[18] These approaches are: literary readings in search of women in the text, readings that seek liberating themes in the text for the benefit of women, and historical/cultural readings that investigate the lives of women behind the text in their historical conditions.

The first efforts of biblical feminists to read the texts with feminist consciousness were to find stories and images of biblical women to serve as models of faith and inspiration for contemporary women. Literary critic Carolyn Heilbrun once wrote that women need stories of women's lives even more than they need exemplary women in the flesh.[19] This is because uninterpreted human life is inchoate and chaotic; life requires ordering. Stories and poems, written or oral, organize experience and give meaning to our otherwise swirling existence. They interpret life, tell what is important, and provide grids for imagining our own lives differently. Modern biblical feminists searched precisely for such stories. They trolled the Scriptures, looking for women who had long been neglected as minor supporting characters in male-dominated narratives. Such studies retrieved biblical women, named and unnamed, and showed their struggles, their faithfulness, and their suffering.

To pay attention to Sarah and Hagar, Leah, Rachel, Bilhah and Zilpah, Naomi and Ruth, to Rahab the prostitute and to Athalaya the Queen was to discover that women had some significant place in the story of Israel. Their oppression and resistance, their survival and faith, and their particular heroic actions inspired and encouraged women to keep struggling. Recovery of these stories gave many women a sense of being included, albeit marginally, in the central texts of the faith, provided women with role models, and inspired us to keep looking for other women's stories.

It is partly this approach I used to tell the story of the nameless widow in 2 Kgs 4. I focus on her as the main character, seeing in her a model of courage, fidelity, and community building. I discover, in the concrete exertions of her daily life to feed and protect her family, the power of God made manifest.

But the good-women-in-the-Bible approach soon proved inadequate to address larger problems women encountered in turning to the Bible for insight and nourishment. For one thing, there are not that many biblical women to be found in major or even minor roles. But more impor-

18. See also her article published a year later, in which she applies the three approaches to the story of the daughters of Zelophehad (Num 27:1–11): "Feminist Biblical Interpretation," *Theology Today* 46 (1986): 154–68.
19. Carolyn Heilbrun, *Writing a Woman's Life* (New York: W. W. Norton, 1988), 37.

tant, inspiring stories of women did nothing to undercut other stories that Trible would memorably call "texts of terror."[20] These horrifying texts include accounts of violence against women raped, murdered, and sacrificed. Trible studied the story of the priest's concubine (Judg 19), the sacrifice of Jephthah's daughter to fulfill her father's foolish vow (Judg 11:29–40), and the double enslavement of Hagar as a sex worker in Abraham's family (Gen 16, 21), but "texts of terror" became a catch-phrase for many other passages that express violence toward women and others, and to which the pro-biblical-woman approach cannot mount a strong response.

It soon became clear that the labor of biblical feminists must include critical analysis of the ways the Bible teaches misogyny and sexism to keep women in place. In response to these problems, feminists began to look for biblical teachings to counter women's oppression. Sakenfeld labeled the second approach, "Looking to the Bible Generally for a Theological Perspective Offering a Critique of Patriarchy," which refers to searches for texts and interpretations that, whether they mention women or not, could be used to construct feminist theology. "It approaches the Bible in the hope of recognizing what the gospel is really all about." Using Christian language, she declared this to be a search for themes "that bear witness to the incarnate Word of God."[21]

This second approach differs from the previous one in the attention it gives to biblical passages with liberating claims that can be appropriated for women. These themes might serve as important antidotes to, or cancellations of, texts that harm women: for example, the command to "love your neighbor as yourself" includes women as both agents and recipients of love, or the Genesis claim that God created all humans in the divine image is to assert an inherent equality and acceptance of everyone, regardless of their sex. Women turned this text into a claim for equality of opportunity, talent, and dignity for all people. Or one might think of exodus from slavery as women's movement toward liberation from bondage.

From this vantage point, the story of the widow in 2 Kgs 4 appears as a text about God's special care for women, children, and the poor. Through the actions of the widow, the prophet, and the community, God not only provides food to a needy woman and her children, but also encourages her to negotiate her way bravely and freely in the world, set-

---

20. Phyllis Trible, *Texts of Terror: Literary Feminist Readings of Biblical Narratives* (Overtures to Biblical Theology; Philadelphia: Fortress, 1984).

21. Sakenfeld, "Feminist Uses of Biblical Materials," 59.

ting her up in business in accord with the biblical theme of *koinonia* (the New Testament word for fellowship or community). Letty Russell interprets *koinonia* as partnership in God's liberating action in the world.[22]

Sakenfeld labeled the third approach of early feminist biblical scholarship "Looking to Texts about Women to Learn from the History and Stories of Ancient and Modern Women Living in Patriarchal Cultures." Rather than highlighting only texts viewing women in a positive light or looking for texts that support human liberation in general, this approach explores the realities of women's lives in antiquity as they illuminate texts. It attempts to reconstruct women's lost history. Such an approach draws on archaeological, anthropological, and cultural studies.

Working in both testaments, women scholars began a systematic investigation into the status and roles of women in antiquity. What was the actual historical situation of women behind the text, in the real lives of Israelite women or followers of Jesus? Could women's history be recovered, and how? What were the clues to women's actual lives to be found in the text? What were cultural, economic, political, and historical realities behind the text? Schüssler Fiorenza, for example, did extremely important work in New Testament studies in attempting to re-create the role of women who were followers of Jesus and early leaders in the community.[23] Some later examples of this approach include efforts to probe historical circumstances that produced the account of women as childbearers and men as agriculturalists (Gen 2–3),[24] or to investigate the historical lives of women in relation to Israelite law.[25] Phyllis Bird has studied historical conditions of women's roles as wives, as poor, as participants in worship, and as harlots. Her work uncovers bias not only in the text but equally among modern interpreters.[26]

My account of the widow in 2 Kgs 4 draws briefly on this approach with its information about widows in ancient Israel and about the socioeconomic system that kept the widow and her children trapped as the consequence of the father's debt. Using this feminist approach means that no matter how terrible a text may be for women, it can provide a window into culture, bias, and misogyny useful for analysis and critique, and for knowing our past. But it soon became clear to feminist

---

22. Letty Russell, *Growth in Partnership* (Philadelphia: Westminster, 1981).

23. Schüssler Fiorenza, *In Memory of Her.*

24. See Carol Meyers, *Discovering Eve: Ancient Israelite Women in Context* (New York: Oxford University Press, 1988).

25. See Carolyn Pressler, *The View of Women Found in the Deuteronomic Family Laws* (New York: Walter de Gruyter, 1993).

26. Phyllis A. Bird, *Missing Persons and Mistaken Identities: Women and Gender in Ancient Israel* (Overtures to Biblical Theology; Minneapolis: Fortress, 1997).

biblical scholars that reinterpretation, study of women's historical location, and the recovery of redemptive traditions for women in the texts were not enough.

Newer Approaches

Since Sakenfeld's early articles, the field of feminist biblical studies in general has exploded beyond our early imaginings. These three root approaches have burgeoned into a lush garden of publication and creative new approaches, changing along with the general field of biblical studies.

In accord with changes in gendered language occurring in the broader society, the Bible's use of sexist language for humans both in the original languages and in translations became a hot spot in the struggle for women's lives in the academy and in the churches. The New Revised Standard Version, with its gender-inclusive translation, was a response to these interpretive changes. For male terminology in the biblical text, it substituted more inclusive language for humans and avoided exclusively male terms, except where translating texts about specific males. Gradually, in many, but not all, synagogues and churches, inclusive language became normative for public worship and for proclamation.

Language for God has been a far thornier problem. Even though most believers hold that God transcends all human categories, including sex and gender roles, tampering with names like Father, Judge, King, and Lord, or even supplementing them with female or nongendered language, became a most disruptive matter among religious communities.[27] What is at stake for women in this argument is not only the supremacy of maleness implied by exclusive use of male terms, but also the absence of female representation in images of God. How could women find themselves in the Bible at all if it was an exclusively male domain?

I think the most important developments in feminist biblical studies correspond with movements called postmodernism and postcolonialism. "Postmodernism" is a slippery term in philosophy and cultural studies, but, at the very least, it means that our grasp on truth is inevitably shaped by our context. Feminist postmodern biblical studies includes many literary and sociological approaches, including reader-response analysis. My interest, though, is in its recognition that truth is always expressed

---

27. See Rosemary Radford Ruether's classic study, *Sexism and God-Talk: Toward a Feminist Theology* (Boston: Beacon, 1983).

from a particular perspective, which means that the interpreters' social-economic contexts both limit and illuminate their understanding of texts. This recognition grew among feminists in the face of accusations within the feminist movement that our new and liberating discourse was liberating for white elite women who either ignored or dominated other women: poor women, women of color, women in other countries. Postmodern feminism continues the call to conversion; we need to be in conversation with, and to struggle with, many different interpretations at once so that the immense richness of texts might emerge.

African American women were among the first I heard resisting naïve assumptions underlying feminism. The question of women's experience did not yield the uniform picture that Caucasian middle-class women had assumed. Feminists initially overlooked African American women's history of slavery, their resistance to white supremacy, their historical awareness of power relations among the races and the sexes, and their dedication and concern for their men and for the poor in general. Novelist Alice Walker is credited with inventing the designation "womanist" for African American feminists. Some women's conferences became places of deep struggle as women sometimes argued bitterly with each other. But the call to conversion was the invitation to see the world through eyes of others so that God could be found among us all. Womanism undermines white supremacy and hidden prejudice, and often exhibits unflinching confidence in the Bible's power to call African American women and men forth from cultural slavery just as God rescued Israel from the chain gangs of Egypt.[28]

Feminist biblical conversation expanded further in the United States as Latina women named their approach to feminist theology with the term *mujerista,* from the Spanish term for women. Latina women introduced to the larger feminist conversation their cultural appreciation of motherhood, and their sense that men, despite *machismo* attitudes, were linked closely with them in the United States, where most Hispanics were objects of bias, jokes, and exclusion and where their distinct cultural identities such as Mexican, Peruvian, or Puerto Rican were lumped together into one stereotype. Yet the cultural richness of these communities in which people are often bilingual and able to bridge two cultural worlds, often called "hybridity," brought new insight to biblical texts,

---

28. See, for example, Renita J. Weems, *Just a Sister Away: A Womanist Vision of Woman's Relationships in the Bible* (San Diego: LuraMedia, 1988); and *Battered Love: Marriage, Sex, and Violence in the Hebrew Prophets* (Overtures to Biblical Theology; Minneapolis: Fortress, 1995); and Delores S. Williams, *Sisters in the Wilderness: The Challenge of Womanist God-Talk* (Maryknoll, NY: Orbis, 1993).

often noting how texts replayed the lives of women and spoke to their realities.[29]

Jacqueline Lapsley might be called a postmodern feminist theologian of the Old Testament.[30] Her work challenges dismissal of faith-oriented feminist approaches as naïve or impossible, a point of view frequently expressed by feminist biblical scholars working in nonreligious university settings. Lapsley urges women and men to learn how to read Old Testament texts with more subtlety, with critical awareness, and with willingness to enter the text emotionally and find there an encounter with a complex moral world created by the artistry of narratives. Lapsley knows that texts are patriarchal and driven by patriarchal values, but she refuses to reduce them to ideology or to monolithic power systems. Instead, she argues, the Old Testament texts contain resistant voices and narrative strategies that complicate patriarchy because they are too rich in literary and theological meaning to be exhausted by sociological analysis. Because the text is patriarchal, sexist, and androcentric does not mean that it cannot also be a word of God for us when studied from other angles.

Katharine Sakenfeld embraced the many voices emerging in feminist interpretation, quickly recognizing the place of social setting in interpretation but also bringing in such voices to illuminate and challenge her own efforts. Her travels across several Asian countries in pursuit of women's ways of engaging and reflecting on Scripture created important themes in her commentary on the book of Ruth. She finds in it the story of displacement and survival, of struggles with motherhood and mothers-in-law, and of women's friendship across barriers of age and culture.[31] Her work attends to the importance of class and cultural differences among women. Sakenfeld's travels taught her what many Western scholars are still learning, that the Bible is a word of fire and freedom in other parts of the world, especially among the poor and the excluded. The context of the readers' lives profoundly shapes interpretation, and poverty, exclusion, and suffering provide a most acute lens for discovering meaning in texts and for constructing new meanings. Her recent work *Just Wives?* reads stories of biblical women in an

29. See writings of Ada María Isasi-Díaz, especially "'By the Rivers of Babylon': Exile as a Way of Life," in *Social Location and Biblical Interpretation in the United States*, vol. 1, *Reading from This Place* (ed. Fernando F. Segovia and Mary Ann Tolbert; Minneapolis: Fortress, 1995), 149–63.

30. Jacqueline Lapsley, *Whispering the Word: Strategies for Reading Women's Stories in the Old Testament Theologically* (Louisville, KY: Westminster John Knox, 2005).

31. Katharine Doob Sakenfeld, *Ruth: A Bible Commentary for Teaching and Preaching* (Interpretation; Louisville, KY: Westminster John Knox, 1999).

effort to include "voices of women different from my own predominantly white, upper-middle-class, North American setting."[32] She intends
in this work to create new levels of empathy and understanding among
women from diverse worlds and to show how these worlds inform readings of the text.

It has long become clear through such postmodern approaches that
honor many voices and multiple ways of interpreting that there is no
single correct reading of a biblical text, nor is there one right, feminist
interpretation helpful to all women. This recognition highlights the call
to conversion I continue to find inherent in the feminist movement. In
its multifaceted, many-voiced expressions, feminist biblical criticism not
only calls men, churches, and societies to new openness to the Spirit
pulsing through the lives of women, but it calls women to the same radical willingness to hear ourselves critiqued, to learn from the pain and
struggles of other women, and to step aside from dominant centers of
power for the sake of the flourishing of all.

The designation "postcolonial" refers to an increasingly strong critical response to Western imperialism and globalization in its cultural
and economic domination of non-Western peoples. Postcolonial feminist biblical studies, which arise from lives of women who are from
communities subjected to Western imperialism, expand feminist biblical studies yet again. Postcolonial feminists note that earlier feminists
have shown little or no recognition of how they too are imperial subjects, that is, colonized by the imperialist culture of the West and, often
despite the best of intentions, still working with inadequate self-
understanding about their location in the world. Even those strong
feminist theorists like Schüssler Fiorenza, who argue that patriarchy is
the principal oppression and that imperialism is only one of its expressions, miss the larger point. As Musa W. Dube insists, for women of the
Two-Thirds World "imperial oppression remains as real and persistent
as the patriarchal one."[33]

Gale A. Yee uses such an interdisciplinary postcolonial approach in
her recent study, in which she investigates ways the Bible symbolizes
women as figures of evil.[34] Yee insists that it is not enough merely to see

32. Katharine Doob Sakenfeld, *Just Wives? Stories of Power and Survival in the Old Testament and Today* (Louisville,
KY: Westminster John Knox, 2003).
33. Musa W. Dube, *Postcolonial Feminist Interpretation of the Bible* (St. Louis: Chalice, 2000), 112. See also Kwok
Pui-lan, *Postcolonial Imagination and Feminist Theology* (Louisville, KY: Westminster John Knox, 2005).
34. Gale A. Yee, *Poor Banished Children of Eve: Women as Evil in the Hebrew Bible* (Minneapolis: Fortress, 2003).

how patriarchy presents women as incarnations of the sinful; it is also necessary to see how these literary figures serve economic, class, and imperialist agendas. Such an approach emphasizes the need not only to study gender in regard to biblical texts but also to analyze matters of class, race, and power both in the text and in the interpreters. This, it seems to me, is a very difficult state of affairs, but it is also a promising one, not only for others but for ourselves as well.

The question about how the Bible can be a saving word for women remains a central one in the present global feminist enterprise. Surely, one of the firmest conclusions of modern critical biblical studies is that the Bible itself is thoroughly enmeshed in the social, political, cultural, imperialist, and religious worlds that produced it. Hence, God's word comes wrapped, shaped, and formed by its various cultures. It is the study of, the critique of, and the discovery of that word ever anew, under the power of the Spirit at work among the community, that drives feminist biblical studies among believers. It is an ever-thrilling and creative process.

This essay omits more about modern biblical feminism than it includes, but it expresses my perspective on feminist biblical interpretation as a continual opening out to broader arenas of meaning, self-knowledge, and struggle. At first, feminism seemed to explain my life completely in both its riches and its meagerness. But I later discovered that I needed other interpretive lenses to come to grips with my life as woman and as biblical interpreter. I needed family systems theory. I needed voices of women different from me to see how benefits came to me simply because I am Caucasian with a privileged education, with the securities afforded to middle- and upper-middle-class people. Later because of a teaching position in a school of foreign mission where the students represented some of the world's economically poor yet culturally rich nations, my eyes were opened to the realities of women and men in the Two-Thirds World and to immensely powerful, original, and challenging readings of texts that emerged from them.

Now I am grappling with the ethical questions of how to interpret Old Testament texts in light of current global imperialist realities. Can the saving presence of God, the forgiving and reconciling grace of God, and the life-enhancing, body-freeing, and spirit-enlivening power of God be known among us? How? Answering these questions remains the task of feminist hermeneutics in the twenty-first century. I invite readers of this book to join in the struggle.

FOR FURTHER STUDY

Bellis, Alice Ogden. *Helpmates, Harlots, Heroes: Women's Stories in the Hebrew Bible*. Louisville, KY: Westminster John Knox, 1994.

Bird, Phyllis A. *Missing Persons and Mistaken Identities: Women and Gender in Ancient Israel*. Overtures to Biblical Theology. Minneapolis: Fortress, 1997.

Brenner, Athalya, ed. A Feminist Companion Series. Sheffield: Sheffield Academic Press.

Dube, Musa W. *Postcolonial Feminist Interpretation of the Bible*. St. Louis: Chalice, 2000.

Meyers, Carol. *Discovering Eve: Ancient Israelite Women in Context*. New York: Oxford University Press, 1988.

———. *Women in Scripture: A Dictionary of Named and Unnamed Women in the Hebrew Bible, the Apocryphal/Deuterocanonical Books, and the New Testament*. Boston: Houghton Mifflin, 2000.

Newsom, Carol A., and Sharon H. Ringe, eds. *The Women's Bible Commentary*. Rev. ed. Louisville, KY: Westminster John Knox, 1998.

Schüssler Fiorenza, Elisabeth. *Wisdom's Ways: Introducing Feminist Biblical Interpretation*. Maryknoll, NY: Orbis, 2001.

Weems, Renita J. *Just a Sister Away: Understanding the Timeless Connection between Women of Today and Women in the Bible*. Rev. ed. New York/Boston: Warner, 2005.

PART ONE

Perspectives

2

Communication as Communion

Elements in a Hermeneutic of *Lo Cotidiano*

ADA MARÍA ISASI-DÍAZ

Mujerista biblical interpretation is grounded in Latinas' struggle for survival and the conviction that reading the Bible must contribute to our liberation/fullness of life. Such interpretation grows out of *mujerista* theology, which is a liberation theology that uses as its theological source the lived experiences of Latinas living in the United States for whom Christian faith is central to their struggle for survival. *Mujerista* theology has as its goal the holistic liberation of Latinas and our communities—a social and personal liberation that takes into consideration the psychological as well as the religious and spiritual. *Mujerista* theology brings liberation, feminist, and cultural considerations to the reflection of Latinas' religious beliefs and practices.

A *mujerista* interpretation is therefore rooted in Latinas' religious faith and the role it plays in our lives, in *lo cotidiano,* our daily lived experiences. Such an interpretation demands a critical cultural, sociohistorical, political, and economic analysis of our reality. In turn, a *mujerista* interpretation starts with this same thorough study of every biblical pericope, following a cultural-critical, much more than a historical-critical, paradigm that focuses particularly on the daily reality of the biblical characters. Their relationship with, and understanding of, Yahweh grows out of their daily lives, just as it grows out of *lo cotidiano* of Latinas. The importance of the Bible's message lies in how its revelation about the divine is used by and helps the struggle for survival of those to whom it refers and those who embrace it now as the word of God.

The goal of *mujerista* theology is the liberation/fullness of life—first of Latinas living in the United States and then of all poor and oppressed people. This is also the main criterion of the *mujerista* theo-ethical school of thought. Therefore, any interpretation of the Bible that does not contribute positively to this goal is not accepted as valid, and any biblical text that impedes this goal is denounced.

A *mujerista* interpretation listens to grassroots Latinas whose readings may not be scholarly but are valid insofar as they are life-giving to them and to their communities. This recognition of the authority of Latinas to interpret the Bible is intrinsic to a *mujerista* praxis of liberation that seeks to contribute to the strengthening of these women's moral agency and self-definition. Our interpretations point to the dissonance that exists between Latinas' experiences and values, on the one hand, and traditional interpretations of biblical texts, on the other. This dissonance gives rise to the suspicion that all reading and interpretation of the Bible is ideological and, siding with grassroots Latinas, *mujerista* interpretation privileges their worldview.

In this article I look for *lo cotidiano* in a text that has not been interpreted from that perspective, Luke 9:28–36. Using Latinas' understanding of the importance of "words" and the centrality of relationships—friends, family, community—in our culture, I seek to understand how Jesus has to share with others what he is beginning to sense, that his mission would lead him to death. The focus is not psychological but rather social-anthropological, exploring the role of words in creating and maintaining community and solidarity.

COMMUNICATION-COMMUNION AS A KEY ELEMENT OF *LO COTIDIANO*

Lo cotidiano is a complex concept, easier to describe than to define. It constitutes the immediate space of our lives, the first horizon of our experiences, experiences that in turn are constitutive elements of our reality.[1] *Lo cotidiano* is where we first meet and relate to the material world, made up not only of physical realities but also of our relationship to that reality (culture) and our understanding and evaluation of it (history). *Lo cotidiano* is necessarily enmeshed in the material reality of

---

1. For an extensive elaboration of *lo cotidiano* as a category of meaning, interpretation, and praxis, see my book *La Lucha Continues: Mujerista Theology* (Maryknoll, NY: Orbis, 2004), 92–106.

life and is a key element of the structuring of social relations and their limits. *Lo cotidiano* situates us in our experiences. It has to do with the practices and beliefs that we have inherited, and with our habitual judgments, including the tactics we use to deal with daily reality. By *lo cotidiano*, however, we do not refer to an acritical reproduction or repetition of all we have been taught or to which we have become habituated. On the contrary, we understand by *lo cotidiano* that which is reproduced or repeated consciously by the majority of people in the world as part of their struggles for survival and liberation.[2] *Lo cotidiano* has much to do with the experiences that we have lived, with experiences that have been analyzed and integrated into our understandings and behaviors. It is what makes the world of each and every one specific, and, therefore, it is in *lo cotidiano* and starting with *lo cotidiano* that we live the multiple relations that constitute our humanity. It is the sphere in which our struggle for life is most immediate, most vigorous, most vibrant.

Lo cotidiano is what we face every day; it includes also how we face it. In no way should *lo cotidiano* be seen as belonging mostly to the private world, for it interacts at all times with social systems, impacting their structures and mechanisms. *Lo cotidiano* refers to the way we think and express ourselves, as well as to the impact that class, gender, poverty, and work have on our routines and expectations. It has to do with relations within families and among friends and neighbors in a community. It extends to our experience with authority and encompasses our central religious beliefs and celebrations.[3]

Taking *lo cotidiano* seriously in *mujerista* biblical interpretation, we follow a line of inquiry called cultural criticism that has as its focus "the text as means, as evidence from and for the time of composition."[4] The emphasis is on the text "as a product and reflection of its context or world, with specific social and cultural codes inscribed, and hence a means for reconstructing the sociocultural situation presupposed, reflected, and addressed."[5] In *mujerista* biblical interpretation we search for the meaning of the text by looking at the "world behind it, with analysis of text, author, and readers undertaken in terms of their

2. In other words, we are not suggesting that a conscienticized *cotidiano* is one that supports this or that ideology, but one that describes, relates to, and identifies the reality of grassroots people.

3. Daniel Levine, *Popular Voices in Latin American Catholicism* (Princeton, NJ: Princeton University Press, 1992), 317.

4. Fernando F. Segovia, "And They Began to Speak in Tongues," in *Social Location and Biblical Interpretation in the United States*, vol. 1, *Reading from This Place* (ed. Fernando F. Segovia and Mary Ann Tolbert; Minneapolis: Fortress, 1995), 22.

5. Ibid.

relationship to and participation in that world."[6] We are particularly interested in *lo cotidiano* of that world, with emphasis on the personal both in the private and in the political spheres, on issues of gender, ethnicity-culture, anthropological understandings, and ideologies. Readers who use *mujerista* biblical interpretation are not innocent but rather critically thinking Latinas who come to the text from a specific location, with a specific intention. The reader may be academically untrained, but never unsophisticated.

THE MEANING AND IMPORTANCE OF WORDS[7]

"Tu palabra me basta"—a frequently heard phrase among Latinas and Latinos—highlights what it means to give our word. The mystery of the human word! Words make it possible for us to explain ourselves. And since there is no way of explaining what one does not understand, it is words that make it possible for us to construct our thoughts, our thinking. But there is more. Our words make our very selves present; they embody us. Our words "contain" us and contain also our dignity. "Your word is enough for me" is all I need to say to assure you that I will do all in my power to make happen what I have said.

As we weave together our words, as we narrate what we do, what we see, what we think, what we desire, and for what we hope, we create a story that makes us present not only to others, but also to our own selves. As we create our own account—our own history—we come to understand ourselves and begin to realize that we have not lived a series of individual, separate moments, but that we have lived a life imbued with meaning and importance based on our values and beliefs. Listening to ourselves, we hear how we share what we have done and what has happened to us, and this is how we come to realize that we indeed have a specific approach to life, a particular way of thinking, of facing reality, and of relating to others that identifies and defines us. When we pay attention to what we say about ourselves and our lives, we realize that there is an organizing principle, a vision of life, a worldview, often developed since we were very young without our realizing it.

Precisely because words make present what they mean, it is so difficult, even impossible, to go back on what we have said. This is what

6. Ibid.

7. Though indeed influenced by reading widely on the meaning and role of the written as well as the oral word, my reflection on how words are valued in Latino/a culture grounds my approach in this article.

happens with the blessing Jacob receives, though it is intended for Esau: there is no possibility of Isaac withdrawing it (Gen 27:1–40). This is what often happens with little ones. Once we say to children that we are going to do this or that, they understand the promise as a fact, as a reality. They refuse to understand that there is a long way between what is said and what is done; for children, not to keep one's word is a deep betrayal.

For Christians, the Eucharist is the best example of the efficacy of words, the best example of words bringing forth the reality they announce. We believe that, when we repeat the words in the Gospels uttered by Jesus at the Last Supper, what they express becomes a reality: Jesus becomes present at the eucharistic celebration. This sense of the efficacy of words in Christian rituals today is the same as the belief of the people of Israel that the word of Yahweh accomplishes what it says: "Yes, as the rain and the snow come down from the heavens and do not return without watering the earth, making it yield and giving growth to provide seed for the sower and bread for the eating, so the word that goes from my mouth does not return to me empty, without carrying out my will and succeeding in what it was sent to do" (Isa 55:10–11).[8]

The long hours friends and lovers spend talking may seem to others extravagant. Yet in conversation they not only come to know each other and share who they are. The time spent this way also shapes their friendship, their relationship, and their love for each other. Their conversations bond them inextricably, for as they put into words how much they love each other, the relationship they are creating is strengthened and grows more solid. Expressing their emotions repeatedly makes those emotions a stronger reality. We cannot imagine that someone loves us if she or he never tells us so. We cannot believe anyone is interested in us personally if he or she does not express it through words and gestures. The more those who love tell each other about their love, the deeper the communication becomes. It is only when we have deep communication that we can speak of communion, that is, of being with, of, and in the other in such a way that without the other one is not fully oneself.

For true communion, human beings need not only words spoken, but also someone willing to listen, someone to receive with reverence and honesty the words into which we pour ourselves. So many times we are silent, without really communicating, simply because we have no one to listen to us, no one to embrace our words! So many times I have

---

8. All biblical quotations in this article are from *The New Jerusalem Bible* (New York: Doubleday, 1985).

been with Latinas to whom no one had ever paid attention. When I have asked them to speak about themselves, they simply cannot believe that I would be interested, that I would take time to listen to them. Then, as they begin to share, they come to know themselves, to see their values, and to discover their worldview. They come to understand their lives—lives of unbelievable struggle. These relationships, created through the sharing of our lives, form, strengthen, and maintain family and community, realties so central to our Latina culture.

THE IMPORTANCE OF WORDS
IN THE TRANSFIGURATION

The importance of words is central to a *mujerista* interpretation of the event we know as the transfiguration of Jesus. If we concentrate on what the event means for Jesus and pay attention to the role of words in this text, we see how Jesus needs to talk in order to understand himself and his mission. He needs to disclose to his friends what he is thinking, sensing, feeling. The transfiguration gives us the opportunity to see the importance of words for Jesus, the importance of conversation and communication.[9]

In the passages about the transfiguration we find three sets of words, or three moments in which the action as well as the intent and meaning of the pericope is carried by spoken words. First, we see Moses and Elijah talking with Jesus about what is going to happen to him in Jerusalem or, as some translations put it, what Jesus is to accomplish in Jerusalem (see Luke 9:31). In this first mention of words, we sense Jesus' need to talk about the risks he is taking and the difficulties that he will have to face. He needs to talk about all of this so as to under-

---

9. Besides being guided by the explanations of cultural criticism published by my fellow Cuban, colleague, and friend Fernando F. Segovia, I am influenced in this study of the transfiguration by Elizabeth A. Johnson's approach to Mary in her book *Truly Our Sister: A Theology of Mary in the Communion of Saints* (New York: Continuum, 2003), 209–16. Her method, it seems to me, brings together cultural criticism (though she does not use this term but rather talks about "the world behind the text") and "the world ahead of the text, or the ongoing struggle of women today for full participation in every dimension of life."

I am also influenced by the uncovering of the world behind Mary and the creative reading of Mary of Lesley Hazelton, *Mary: A Flesh and Blood Biography of the Virgin Mother* (New York: Bloomsbury, 2004).

I am deeply indebted to the work of fellow Cubans José Ignacio and María López Vigil. They have written a book that has been published in English in Philippines, but here in North America I have not been able to acquire it. I know only the Spanish edition, *Un Tal JESÚS* (La Habana: Editorial Caminos, 2000). The book consists of transcripts of 144 radio episodes, fifteen minutes each, on the life of Jesus, based on distinct New Testament pericopes. When they compiled the episodes into a book, the authors added the pertinent biblical references as well as scholarly endnotes after each episode. Their creativity in dealing with texts has urged me to affirm vehemently the right of grassroots Latinas to their way of reading and valuing the Bible.

stand and embrace what he is living and what he is going to undergo. Given the reactions of the leaders of the community to Jesus' insistence on justice, on the importance of being part of the kin-dom of God, of course Jesus and the disciples know that the confrontations with the authorities would continue and would become more and more serious.[10] Jesus knows that he is preaching a social revolution and that, as a consequence, he could indeed be put to death.[11]

Shortly before the transfiguration in the accounts in Matthew (16:21–23) and Mark (8:31–33), Jesus wants to talk with the disciples about what is going to happen, but they do not allow him to do so. Perhaps afraid that what he said might come to pass, they do not want Jesus to say it. Jesus answers them with some of the sharpest words we hear from him, scolding the disciples for not letting him talk with them about what he has to do. As a fully human person, in order to be able to understand what he needs to do and to have the courage to do it, he needs to share it with his friends.[12] His answer when they refuse to allow him to converse with them—"Get behind me, Satan!"—shows Jesus' exasperation and disappointment. If he does not share with them what he has to face, how will he have the strength and courage to do it?

If the disciples do not want to talk about the impending future, then Moses and Elijah will have to be the friends with whom he discusses it. In talking to Moses, the leader of the people during the exodus, the first great liberation of his people, Jesus begins to see how his life would be a new exodus, a new liberation for the people. In talking to Elijah, whom the people of Israel are expecting to return before the coming of the Messiah, Jesus begins to understand that what is going to happen to him—being jailed, tortured, and executed—will be a consequence of his life's mission. This is the result of preaching love of neighbor and justice for the poor and the oppressed. Jesus' imprisonment, torture, and execution will become for his disciples his passion and death, events with profound religious meaning. From his conversation with Moses and Elijah, he begins to understand the significance of what he

---

10. The "kin-dom of God," or *la familia de Dios* (the family of God), seems to us to be a much more relevant metaphor for what the Gospels proclaim as the goal of Jesus and his teaching. There are hardly any kingdoms left in the world in the twenty-first century, and those left are not necessarily forms of government that are in keeping with the ethical considerations of justice and self-determination central to the Christian message. The term "kin-dom," instead of kingdom, not only avoids sexist and classist-elitist considerations inherent in this word, but also taps into an important value in Latina culture, i.e., family.

11. John Dominic Crossan, *Jesus: A Revolutionary Biography* (San Francisco: HarperCollins, 1994), 123–33.

12. Of course, how do I know what Jesus needed? This is a valid question. I can only extrapolate from what I know about the way human beings act, about our need to put into words what we think in order to understand it fully, and about the need for the support of our friends. And, of course, I could indeed ask the question the other way around, that is, how do we know that he did *not* need to share with others about his future actions?

is to undergo in Jerusalem. With words and through words Jesus discovers the deepest meaning of his life and mission: liberation and salvation for his followers.[13] Having understood what he has to endure in order to be faithful to his mission, Jesus "resolutely turned his face towards Jerusalem" (Luke 9:51), even if "the people would not receive him because he was making for Jerusalem" (Luke 9:53). Many who previously welcomed him now evade him. But Jesus is able to handle such hurtful treatment, for the conversation with Moses and Elijah gives him the self-assurance he needs to carry on with his life.

The second reference to words in the episode of the transfiguration has to do with a theophany, a perceivable manifestation of God. This one occurs through words. A voice comes out from the clouds, "This is my Son, the Chosen One" (Luke 9:35). Or, as the version in Mark and Matthew says, "This is my Son, the Beloved," Matthew adding, "He enjoys my favor."

Jesus heard these words at the beginning of his public life. When he was baptized by John, these words made clear that he had a mission, that his life had a purpose: to establish the kin-dom of God. Hearing himself called "beloved" by God gives him the strength of conviction needed to move ahead with what he believes he is called to do. The same happens now at the time of the transfiguration. Faced with imminent danger, to know himself to be God's beloved, to know that he is pleasing to God, can only be helpful. Jesus may not doubt that God loves him, but, being fully human, he needs to hear it, to know it through his senses, in his body. If he does not need to hear again that he is beloved of God, why then this repetition of what we have already been told at the beginning of the Gospels? The purest and strongest commitment seems not to be enough for Jesus. He also needs love expressed through words, the tenderness of a response to his need.

The third group of words in the transfiguration refers to the human need to share what we have experienced, even as we realize that those without the same or similar experiences will most probably not be able to understand. This is why Jesus tells the disciples not to tell the others about what has happened. It is not a matter of keeping a secret; it is because people will not be able to comprehend. Later on, after the others have experienced similar events, little by little they too will be able to understand what happened on the mountain.

---

13. I am here guided by the work of John Dominic Crossan. It is not what he says in his writings but his method of deducing what we can say about Jesus that guides me in this article.

Sometimes our words find no echo in others and come back to us empty. When what we say has no resonance in our friends, how painful that is! We feel alone and not understood when what we share falls into a vacuum. Only through the intimacy of relationships can one bridge the distance between varied experiences. Only in the solidarity born of our commitment to justice and peace can we bridge the distance between our very different lived experiences.

MUJERISTA LEARNINGS

The transfiguration of Jesus teaches us the significant role that words play in our lives and the importance of having someone with whom to share them. As followers of Jesus, we have to take time to put into words what we have done, to thread the different stories of our lives into narratives that show us and others the values and commitments that have guided us, that have been woven together to constitute our worldview. We, first of all, have to "talk" to ourselves, to better understand ourselves: Who am I called to be, and what am I to do with my life? This is the kind of conversation that takes time and requires silence. If we have not paid attention to these questions, the answers are buried deep within us and only with attentive patience will they surface. We also have to give ourselves time for these questions and answers to make an impression on us. They can affect us and help us to understand the meaning of our lives.

Even more, we have to find a Moses and an Elijah with whom we can share deeply and intimately. We have to find someone who can gather what we say, like one who picks up the slivers of a broken mirror and puts them back together so we can see ourselves reflected in our own words. We need a friend.[14] "You can never be fully visually present to your own self. The one you love, your *anam cara,* your soul-friend, is the truest mirror to reflect your soul. The honesty and clarity of true friendship also brings out the real contour of your spirit."[15] We need a friend. Friendship is one of life's most beautiful treasures! Friendship is a deep mutual relationship in which we constantly give and receive. A

14. Books on friendship are many and varied. Here I mention four that I have reviewed for this article. A classic is C. S. Lewis, *The Four Loves* (New York: Harcourt Brace, 1960). Three contemporary books are bell hooks, *All about Love: New Visions* (New York: Harper Collins, 2000); Joan Chittister, *The Friendship of Women: A Spiritual Tradition* (Erie, PA: Benetvision, 2000); and John O'Donohue, *Anam Cara: A Book of Celtic Wisdom* (New York: Harper Collins, 1997).

15. O'Donohue, *Anam Cara,* 21.

friend is someone who is interested in us, whom we can trust totally, who will remain with us and be faithful to us no matter what happens. Friendship makes it possible to go deep within oneself to learn about and embrace the tenderness of God. With the help of a real friend, we can come to understand that God is more intimate to us than our own selves, that God embraces us and delights in us.

The transfiguration teaches us the importance of shared experiences. It teaches us that, without such experiences, words alone are not able to communicate what we want to share with others. When our experiences differ widely, we have to turn to solidarity—a solidarity so strong that it makes us understand the need to dialogue in order to find common interests that can tie us together as a human community. The gospel's "love one another" goes hand in hand with "you shall love your neighbor as yourself." This commandment does not point to superficial relationships but to relationships that count. Not every relationship is worthy of such trust. It is when we have a "soul friend," however, that we can go beyond ourselves and be in solidarity with others, particularly with the poor and the oppressed whom the Scriptures privilege.

The transfiguration of Jesus, then, shows us the very personal need all humans have to be in relationship and to share themselves with others. This reality impacts our *cotidiano* and signals to us the importance of self-esteem and of valuing others that is needed in our struggles for justice and peace. From the perspective of *lo cotidiano,* the transfiguration of Jesus makes it possible for us to sense the importance of the tenderness of God's love. It is no less important for us than it was for Jesus to hear from God, through the lips of friends, "I delight in you."

FOR FURTHER STUDY

Chittister, Joan. *The Friendship of Women: A Spiritual Tradition.* Erie, PA: Benetvision, 2000.

hooks, bell. *All about Love: New Visions.* New York: William Morrow, 2000.

Isasi-Díaz, Ada María. En La Lucha: *A Hispanic Women's Liberation Theology.* Minneapolis: Fortress, 1993.

———. "*La Palabra de Dios en Nosotras*—The Word of God in Us." In *Searching the Scriptures.* Vol. 1, *A Feminist Introduction*, 86–97. Edited by Elisabeth Schüssler Fiorenza. New York: Crossroad, 1993.

O'Donohue, John. *Anam Cara: A Book of Celtic Wisdom.* New York: Harper-Collins, 1997.

3

Womanist Biblical Interpretation

NYASHA JUNIOR

WOMANIST SCHOLARSHIP

In this essay I discuss the emergence of womanist scholarship and womanist biblical interpretation. Womanist scholarship developed, in part, from critiques of feminist scholarship. Some scholars in a variety of disciplines have argued that feminist criticism concentrates on gender as a singular category without addressing the interplay of gender, race/ethnicity, and class. African American women have provided some of the most strident critiques of feminist criticism. For example, African American writer bell hooks contends, "Privileged feminists have largely been unable to speak to, with, and for diverse groups of women because they either do not understand fully the inter-relatedness of sex, race, and class oppression or refuse to take this inter-relatedness seriously."[1] Although some feminists focus on patriarchy as a primary form of oppression, others, especially African American women, treat oppression as multidimensional.

A number of African American women began to appropriate Alice Walker's definition of "womanist," rather than using the term "feminist." Though the archaic usage of the term "womanist" meant a "womanizer," African American writer Alice Walker redefines the term in her collection of nonfiction essays, *In Search of Our Mothers' Gardens:*

---

1. bell hooks, *Feminist Theory from Margin to Center* (Boston: South End, 1984), 14.

Womanist Prose. In her four-part definition, she describes a "womanist" as "a black feminist or feminist of color" and explains that "womanist is to feminist as purple is to lavender."[2] Walker's definition has evoked a number of responses from African American women.

Some African American women find that Walker's definition provides a useful way to identify themselves and their work, while distancing themselves from feminism, which they equate with the experiences and interests of white women.[3] Yet not all African American women self-identify as "womanists." Of those who regard themselves as feminists, some choose to call themselves African American or black feminists, although they may share the concerns of "womanists."[4] Still others prefer to self-identify simply as feminists.[5]

The second part of Walker's four-part definition, "a woman who loves other women, sexually and/or nonsexually,"[6] has stimulated the greatest controversy regarding the adoption of the term "womanist," especially within fields that are related to religious thought. For example, social ethicist Cheryl Sanders argues, "In my view there is a fundamental discrepancy between the womanist criteria that would affirm and/or advocate homosexual practice, and the ethical norms the black church might employ to promote the survival and wholeness of black families."[7] Other African American women find this condemnation of homosexuality to be particularly disheartening, given the oppression faced by African Americans. Responding to Sanders, theologian M. Shawn Copeland writes, "It seems to me that black feminists and/or womanists seek a new common ground from which all women and men may vigorously oppose racism, sexism, homophobia, ageism, class exploitation, intentional limitation of the disabled, and—I add, as Christians must—anti-Semitism."[8] Although some African American

---

2. Alice Walker, *In Search of Our Mothers' Gardens: Womanist Prose* (San Diego: Harcourt Brace Jovanovich, 1983), xi–xii.

3. Sherley Ann Williams explains her reasons for identifying as a womanist in "Some Implications of Womanist Theory," in *Reading Black, Reading Feminist: A Critical Anthology* (ed. Henry Louis Gates; New York: Meridian, 1990), 68–75.

4. Michele Wallace describes her development as a black feminist in "A Black Feminist's Search for Sisterhood," in *All the Women Are White, All the Blacks Are Men, But Some of Us Are Brave: Black Women's Studies* (ed. Gloria T. Hull, Patricia Bell Scott, and Barbara Smith; Old Westbury, NY: Feminist Press, 1982), 5–12.

5. bell hooks explains her self-identification as a feminist in "Black Women and Feminism," in *Talking Back: Thinking Feminist, Thinking Black* (Boston: South End, 1989), 181–82.

6. Walker, *In Search of Our Mothers' Gardens*, xi.

7. "Roundtable Discussion: Christian Ethics and Theology in Womanist Perspective," *Journal of Feminist Studies in Religion* 5 (1989): 90. For responses by Katie G. Cannon, Emilie M. Townes, M. Shawn Copeland, bell hooks, and Cheryl Townsend Gilkes, see 92–112; see also Sanders's response, 109–12.

8. Ibid., 99–100. On homophobia within African American communities, see Kelly Brown Douglas, "Homophobia and Heterosexism in the Black Church and Community," in *Sexuality and the Black Church: A Womanist Perspective* (Maryknoll, NY: Orbis, 1999), 87–108.

women reject the term "womanist" because of the inclusion of lesbian sexuality within Walker's definition and presumably within womanist thought, others remain troubled by this inclusion but choose to focus on other elements of the definition, including its support of "survival and wholeness of entire people, male *and* female."[9]

Despite Walker's description, womanist approaches remain difficult to define.[10] In general, womanist scholarship utilizes the gains of feminist scholarship but attempts to move beyond gender-focused analysis. Womanist approaches stress the concept of intersectionality. "Intersectionality" refers to interlocking forms of oppression and underscores the importance of treating oppression not as universal or exclusive but as multidimensional.[11] In addition, it refers to overlapping dimensions of experience, particularly regarding gender, race/ethnicity, and class. For instance, African American women are both African Americans and women, but they do not belong to one group more than another. African American feminist, lesbian, mother, cancer-survivor, and poet Audre Lorde describes her frustration at limitations that others attempt to place on the complexity of her experience. She writes, "I find I am constantly being encouraged to pluck out some one aspect of myself and present this as the meaningful whole, eclipsing or denying the other parts of self. But this is a destructive and fragmenting way to live."[12] Intersectionality highlights the interdependence of one's various positions in life rather than their fragmentation.

Another key feature of womanist scholarship involves its engagement with the lived experiences of African American women, which remain largely untreated within the academy. Thus, womanist scholarship includes the social, cultural, and religious experiences of African American women within scholarly discourse and draws on the artistic, literary, and intellectual production of these women as resources. For example, aided by Alice Walker's "rediscovery," the work of Harlem Renaissance writer Zora Neale Hurston has received renewed attention and interest from scholars in various fields.[13]

9. Walker, *In Search of Our Mothers' Gardens*, xi.

10. On characteristics of black feminism/womanism, see Patricia Hill Collins, "Distinguishing Features of Black Feminist Thought," in *Black Feminist Thought: Knowledge, Consciousness, and the Politics of Empowerment* (New York: Routledge, 2000), 21–43.

11. On intersectionality, see Kimberle Crenshaw, "Mapping the Margins: Intersectionality, Identity Politics, and Violence against Women of Color," *Stanford Law Review* 43 (1991): 1241–99.

12. Audre Lorde, "Age, Race, Class, and Sex: Women Redefining Difference," in *Sister Outsider: Essays and Speeches* (Freedom, CA: Crossing, 1984), 120.

13. Alice Walker, "In Search of Zora Neale Hurston," *Ms. Magazine,* March 1975, 74–79, 84–89.

WOMANIST BIBLICAL INTERPRETATION

Like feminist scholarship in other fields, feminist biblical interpretation has faced harsh criticism, especially for its focus on the experiences and concerns of white Christian women. For example, Chinese theologian Kwok Pui-Lan highlights the absence of Third World and non-Christian voices in feminist biblical interpretation.[14] As a Jewish woman, Judith Plaskow discusses the ways in which many Christian feminists have maligned Jewish traditions.[15] Similarly, some African American women critique the lack of attention to issues of race/ethnicity and class within feminist biblical interpretation that gives primary focus to gender issues.

Biblical and religious studies literature often links feminist and womanist biblical interpretation very closely, which creates some confusion. Given that some African American female scholars do not identify themselves as womanists, womanist biblical interpretation is not simply feminist biblical interpretation carried out by African American women. Instead, womanist biblical interpretation has the above-mentioned features of womanist scholarship, and it involves engagement with biblical texts by scholars who identify themselves and their work as womanist. It includes the work of African American scholars in nonbiblical fields and those educated in biblical studies.

Yet, in contrast to feminist biblical scholarship, in womanist biblical interpretation those outside of biblical studies have generated the preponderance of material. Although scholars continue to debate what constitutes a feminist approach to biblical texts, feminist biblical interpretation has a diverse, well-developed, and growing body of literature created by a critical mass of feminist biblical scholars. Despite the use of biblical texts in conjunction with feminist approaches in other fields (e.g., feminist theology, feminist ethics), these fields remain distinct from feminist biblical interpretation. Those outside of biblical studies (e.g., literary theorist Mieke Bal) have made substantial contributions to feminist biblical interpretation, but their work complements that of biblical scholars. It does not constitute the majority of such scholarship.

In spite of the lack of clarity regarding terminology, womanist scholars in nonbiblical fields have provided notable readings of biblical

---

14. Kwok Pui-Lan, "Racism and Ethnocentrism in Feminist Biblical Interpretation," in *A Feminist Introduction*, vol. 1, *Searching the Scriptures* (ed. Elisabeth Schüssler Fiorenza; New York: Crossroad, 1993), 101–16.

15. Judith Plaskow, "Anti-Judaism in Feminist Christian Interpretation," in *A Feminist Introduction*, 1:117–29.

texts. For instance, in her construction of womanist god-talk (theology), African American womanist theologian Delores S. Williams rereads Gen 16 and 21 from the perspective of Hagar, an Egyptian slave woman. Williams draws parallels between the lives of African American women and the experiences of Hagar.[16] In addition, the scholarship of African American womanist ethicists such as Katie Geneva Cannon involves considerable interaction with biblical texts.[17]

Womanist biblical interpretation by biblical scholars is rare in part because of the limited numbers of African American biblical scholars. In 2001, an unofficial count of African Americans with doctoral degrees in biblical studies (e.g., Ancient Christianity, Christian Origins, Early Christianity, Hebrew Bible, Near Eastern Languages and Civilizations, New Testament, Religions of Late Antiquity, and Semitics) includes forty-five persons. Of those forty-five, twenty-one specialize in Hebrew Bible and twenty-four in New Testament. Also, eleven of the forty-five are women. Of those eleven women, eight specialize in Hebrew Bible and three in New Testament.[18]

Clarice J. Martin, in 1985, was the first African American woman to receive a doctoral degree in New Testament, a Ph.D. from Duke University. Renita J. Weems, in 1989, was the first African American woman to receive a doctoral degree in Old Testament, a Ph.D. from Princeton Theological Seminary. Treatments of womanist biblical interpretation tend to include Martin and Weems as prime examples of womanist interpreters, since they are trained biblical scholars. Yet discussions of their work within biblical and religious studies may mislead the reader unknowingly, insofar as scholars frequently describe Martin and Weems as if they provide representative examples of womanist biblical interpretation rather than being just two of the very few available cases.

The work of Martin and Weems illustrates some of the difficulties in defining womanist biblical interpretation. Martin argues for a womanist approach in the translation and interpretation of biblical texts in her article "Womanist Interpretations of the New Testament: The Quest

16. Delores S. Williams, *Sisters in the Wilderness: The Challenge of Womanist God-Talk* (Maryknoll, NY: Orbis, 1993).

17. For example, see Katie Geneva Cannon, *Katie's Canon: Womanism and the Soul of the Black Community* (New York: Continuum, 1995).

18. Randall C. Bailey, "Academic Biblical Interpretation among African Americans in the United States," in *African Americans and the Bible: Sacred Texts and Social Textures* (ed. Vincent L. Wimbush; New York: Continuum, 2001), 707. Since the publication of this article, other African American men and women have received degrees in biblical studies, but no official data are available.

for Holistic and Inclusive Translation and Interpretation."[19] She investigates translations of the Greek *doulos* as "servant" or "slave" and surveys the history of interpretation of texts that include the term *doulos* in U.S. debates regarding slavery. Martin argues that a womanist approach to translation and interpretation goes beyond the feminist concern to lift up the voices of women in biblical texts and also includes the concern "to amplify the voices of *all* persons who are marginalized in the text."[20]

Martin expands her work on translation and interpretation in an article on the household codes (Col 3:18–41; Eph 5:21–6:9; 1 Pet 2:18–3:7), "The *Haustafeln* (Household Codes) in African American Biblical Interpretation: 'Free Slave' and 'Subordinate Women.'"[21] Martin questions why many African Americans have taken a critical approach to literal interpretations of the slave codes without a similarly critical evaluation of texts supporting women's subordination. She uses a womanist perspective to argue for the elimination of sexism and to support "the need to create and implement responsible ethical guidelines for the dismantling of the gender hierarchy of African American men and women."[22]

Weems's *Just a Sister Away* provides one of the earliest and most popular books utilizing a womanist approach. Designed for African American Christian women, *Just a Sister Away* draws parallels between the experiences of modern African American women and women in selected biblical texts. Weems combines aspects of feminist biblical criticism with African American oral tradition in order to provide "creative reconstructions" of the relationships between female biblical characters, such as Hagar and Sarah (Gen 16:1–16 and 21:1–21) and Mary and Martha (Luke 10:38–42).[23]

Weems identifies herself as a "feminist biblical scholar" and as a "black and womanist biblical scholar."[24] She describes womanist biblical interpretation most clearly in "Womanist Reflections on Biblical Hermeneutics."[25] In this work, she critiques the historical-critical method for its

---

19. Clarice J. Martin, "Womanist Interpretations of the New Testament: The Quest for Holistic and Inclusive Translation and Interpretation," *Journal of Feminist Studies in Religion* 6 (1990): 41–61. See also the responses to Martin and to Elizabeth Castelli ("*Les belles infideles*/Fidelity or Feminism? The Meaning of Feminist Biblical Translation") by Joanna Dewey, Peggy Hutaff, and Jane Schaberg, in "Responses to Castelli and Martin," 63–85.

20. Martin, "Womanist Interpretations of the New Testament," 53.

21. Clarice J. Martin, "The *Haustafeln* (Household Codes) in African American Biblical Interpretation: 'Free Slave' and 'Subordinate Women,'" in *Stony the Road We Trod: African American Biblical Interpretation* (ed. Cain Hope Felder; Minneapolis: Fortress, 1991).

22. Ibid., 228.

23. Renita J. Weems, *Just a Sister Away: A Womanist Vision of Women's Relationships in the Bible* (San Diego: Lura-Media, 1988), x.

24. Renita J. Weems, "Gomer: Victim of Violence or Victim of Metaphor?" *Semeia* 47 (1989): 90 n. 10.

25. Renita J. Weems, "Womanist Reflections on Biblical Hermeneutics," in *Black Theology: A Documentary History* (ed. James H. Cone and Gayraud S. Wilmore; Maryknoll, NY: Orbis, 1993), 2:216–25.

attempts at objectivity, and feminist biblical scholarship for its focus on the experiences of Anglo-American women. Weems has written scholarly and popular articles, as well as personal memoirs and books directed toward laypersons. Nevertheless, Weems's only monograph-length critical exegetical work is *Battered Love: Marriage, Sex, and Violence in the Hebrew Prophets*, in which she uses an interdisciplinary approach to examine images and metaphors in prophetic literature. Though Weems acknowledges that her identity as an African American woman has influenced her interest in this project, she does not construct or use an explicitly womanist approach.[26]

The limited numbers of African American scholars educated in biblical studies provide a significant barrier to the development of womanist biblical interpretation generated by biblical scholars, as opposed to theologians or ethicists. As greater numbers of African Americans earn degrees in biblical studies, some of them may provide more overt treatments of gender, race, and class, and label their work as "womanist." For example, recent dissertations by Valerie Bridgeman Davis ("A Womanist Reading of the Book of Micah") and Raquel St. Clair ("Call and Consequences: Markan Discipleship through a Womanist Cultural Lens") interpret biblical texts from an explicitly womanist perspective.[27]

Other African American biblical scholars may build on feminist and womanist insights without explicitly situating their scholarship as womanist biblical interpretation. For instance, African American New Testament scholar Gay L. Byron uses an interdisciplinary approach to investigate color and ethnic differences in early Christian writings.[28] African American Hebrew Bible scholar Cheryl B. Anderson writes on issues of gender and law, and describes herself as a "Christian (Protestant) and feminist/womanist African-American female."[29] Although neither Byron nor Anderson identify their work as explicitly "womanist," both incorporate concerns of womanists, including sustained attention to gender, race, and class.

26. Renita J. Weems, *Battered Love: Marriage, Sex, and Violence in the Hebrew Prophets* (Overtures to Biblical Theology; Minneapolis: Fortress, 1995).

27. Valerie Bridgeman Davis, "A Womanist Reading of the Book of Micah" (Ph.D. diss., Baylor University, 2002); Raquel St. Clair, "Call and Consequences: Markan Discipleship through a Womanist Cultural Lens" (Ph.D. diss., Princeton Theological Seminary, 2005).

28. Gay L. Byron, *Symbolic Blackness and Ethnic Difference in Early Christian Literature* (New York: Routledge, 2002).

29. Cheryl B. Anderson, *Women, Ideology, and Violence: Critical Theory and the Construction of Gender in the Book of the Covenant and the Deuteronomic Law* (Journal for the Study of the Old Testament Supplement Series 394; New York: Clark, 2004), 19.

Nevertheless, increased numbers alone may not affect the development of womanist biblical interpretation, since not all African American scholars choose to employ feminist and/or womanist perspectives in their research. For example, African American Hebrew Bible scholar Madeline Gay McClenney-Sadler uses social-scientific methods to investigate biblical kinship systems and incest prohibitions.[30] Also, African American New Testament scholar Monya Stubbs investigates the economic, political, and social power dynamics at work in Rom 13.[31] One can describe the work of all of these scholars as biblical interpretation by African American biblical scholars, but it would be unfair to their scholarship to group them together as womanist biblical scholars.

Womanist biblical interpretation has been largely absent from feminist biblical literature. A brief survey of key works in that field attests to the lack of substantive impact that womanist approaches have had on the discipline of biblical studies. The volume edited by Adela Yarbro Collins, *Feminist Perspectives on Biblical Scholarship* (1985), does not include an article on black feminist or womanist thought.[32] In Letty Russell's edited volume, *Feminist Interpretation of the Bible* (1985), Cannon, an ethicist, contributes an article on black feminist consciousness.[33] In addition, Cannon writes "Womanist Interpretation and Preaching in the Black Church," in Elisabeth Schüssler Fiorenza's *Searching the Scriptures* (1993).[34] In the seventeen volumes of the Feminist Companion to the Bible series, edited by Athalya Brenner, only one article has an explicitly womanist approach.[35] Brenner's overview volume, *A Feminist Companion to Reading the Bible* (1997), does not include an article on womanist biblical interpretation.[36] In the nine volumes of the Feminist Companion to the New Testament and Early Christian Writings series, edited by Amy-Jill Levine, there are no articles from a womanist perspective. Moreover, to date there is no full-length monograph on womanist biblical interpretation or edited volume utilizing womanist approaches.

---

30. Madeline Gay McClenney-Sadler, "Re-Covering the Daughter's Nakedness: A Formal Analysis of Israelite Kinship Terminology and the Internal Logic of Leviticus 18" (Ph.D. diss., Duke University, 2001).

31. Monya Stubbs, "Romans 13 and the Market Economy: Subjection, Reflection, Resistance" (Ph.D. diss., Vanderbilt University, 2005).

32. Adela Yarbro Collins, ed., *Feminist Perspectives on Biblical Scholarship* (SBL Biblical Scholarship in North America 10; Chico, CA: Scholars, 1985).

33. Katie Geneva Cannon, "The Emergence of Black Feminist Consciousness," in *Feminist Interpretation of the Bible* (ed. Letty M. Russell; Louisville, KY: Westminster/John Knox, 1985), 30–40.

34. Katie Geneva Cannon, "Womanist Interpretation and Preaching in the Black Church," in *A Feminist Introduction*, 1:326–37.

35. Koala Warsaw-Jones, "Toward a Womanist Hermeneutic: A Reading of Judges 19–21," in *A Feminist Companion to Judges* (ed. Athalya Brenner; Sheffield: Sheffield Academic Press, 1993), 172–86.

36. Athalya Brenner and Carole Fontaine, eds., *A Feminist Companion to Reading the Bible: Approaches, Methods, and Strategies* (Sheffield: Sheffield Academic Press, 1997).

FUTURE DIRECTIONS

This discussion has concentrated on academic biblical interpretation, but biblical texts have provided significant resources for theological and ethical reflection by African Americans outside of the academy. African American women, including pastors, preachers, and laypersons, have a history of meaningful engagement with biblical texts.[37] I anticipate that African American women will continue to make use of their experiences as part of their reading strategies. Although these strategies may include some elements of womanist thought, I would not describe their reading as "womanist biblical interpretation," as it is unlikely that many of these women would identify as "womanists."

Given the progress of womanist scholarship in nonbiblical fields, I foresee its continued growth and development in theology, ethics, and other fields. Some of this work will include engagement with biblical texts. Yet labeling such scholarship as "womanist biblical interpretation" is somewhat misleading since it draws comparisons to feminist biblical interpretation, which typically presumes scholarship by biblical scholars.

In the future, I imagine that some African American biblical scholars will use feminist and womanist insights in their work, but not all will do so explicitly. Although their work could be termed "womanist biblical interpretation," these scholars should be permitted to position themselves and their research within the field as they see fit. One should not assume that female scholars are feminists, nor should one assume that African American female scholars are womanists. As increased numbers of African American men and women earn degrees in biblical studies, I expect that they will further broaden the range of interests and methods used by African American biblical scholars. I hope that the guild will welcome their contributions without limiting its expectations regarding what should constitute biblical scholarship by African Americans.[38]

FOR FURTHER STUDY

Bailey, Randall C., ed. *Yet with a Steady Beat: Contemporary U.S. Afrocentric Biblical Interpretation.* Society of Biblical Literature Semeia Studies 42. Atlanta: Society of Biblical Literature, 2003.

37. On African American women's relationship to biblical texts, see Renita J. Weems, "Reading Her Way through the Struggle: African American Women and the Bible," in *Stony the Road We Trod,* 57–77.
38. On African American biblical interpretation, see Bailey, "Academic Biblical Interpretation among African Americans in the United States," 696–711.

Brown, Michael Joseph. *Blackening of the Bible: The Aims of African American Biblical Scholarship.* African American Religious Thought and Life. Harrisburg, PA: Trinity Press International, 2004.

Collins, Patricia Hill. *Black Feminist Thought: Knowledge, Consciousness, and the Politics of Empowerment.* Rev. ed. New York: Routledge, 2000.

Felder, Cain Hope, ed. *Stony the Road We Trod: African American Biblical Interpretation.* Minneapolis: Fortress, 1991.

Gates, Henry Louis, ed. *Reading Black, Reading Feminist: A Critical Anthology.* New York: Meridian, 1990.

Wimbush, Vincent L., ed. *African Americans and the Bible: Sacred Texts and Social Textures.* New York: Continuum, 2000.

4

Reading Ruth 3:1–5 from an Asian Woman's Perspective

ANNA MAY SAY PA

For Burmese women growing up in a Bama Buddhist culture,[1] the ideal Burmese woman is said to be:

> As beautiful as Onmar Dani,
> As clever as Amaya,
> As loyal as Madi.

These three women are prominent in Bama Buddhist literature as consorts of the Lord Buddha in his previous incarnations. For the last named, Madi, her role was to be the "fulfiller of the destiny" of her husband, Waythandaya, in his quest for enlightenment. She submitted herself totally to her husband's will, even to the extent of acquiescing to his giving her away to another person.[2]

In a similar vein, Burmese Christian girls and young women are told to be:

> As brave as Deborah,
> As resourceful as Esther,
> As obedient as Ruth.

---

1. The term "Burmese" is used for all ethnic groups living in Burma (Myanmar), and "Bama" is used for the ethnic majority.

2. Waythandaya was the last incarnation of the Lord Buddha before being born as Prince Siddartha. To gain merit, he needed to do charitable deeds. Earlier he had given away his two children. See Maung Htin Aung, *Burmese Drama* (Oxford: Oxford University Press, 1956), 94–97.

In fact, in most Bible studies used with Burmese women's groups, Ruth is held up as being brave and resourceful as well. She is perceived as an exemplary "good woman," loyal, loving, and obedient, a perfect role model for Burmese Christian young women. The ideal wife of Prov 31 is seen to be embodied in the figure of Ruth.

ASIAN FEMINIST READINGS OF THE BIBLE

Asian feminists and church women have taken strength from the Bible, and in recent times they have added their own Asian perspectives to the reading of the Bible. As Asian women they have experienced exclusion from the circles of power and decision making, and are often marginalized in society and church. The Bible is seen both as legitimizing this kind of exclusion and as liberating women to be the "new woman in Christ." Women read the Bible to counteract its negative impact on church and community. Feminist liberative readings are being carried out in magazines such as *In God's Image* and through workshops sponsored by the Christian Conference of Asia, the Asia Women's Resource Centre for Culture and Theology, and other women's organizations.

In such biblical readings, women's stories and experiences form the context. This reading is often done from the underside, that is, from the place of those who have undergone rejection and marginalization. Asian women's reading is also transformative. Believing that women and men are created in the image of God, such interpretation emphasizes equality and mutuality. These readings empower women to move beyond hierarchical structures of violence toward new ways of being community. Moreover, Asian women's reading of the Bible is innovative and creative. Utilizing myths, legends, songs, poetry, and art, Asian women retell the biblical stories in their own voices. For instance, Esther Danpongpee uses Karen myths to make the Bible more meaningful to the Karen women of Thailand, and Yuko Yuasa uses Noh drama to present biblical stories, such as that of Mary Magdalene.[3] Through such readings the Bible becomes the liberating and transforming word.

The story of Ruth and Naomi especially resonates in the hearts of Asian women. Asian societies, like ancient Israelite society, are patriarchal and the lives of women continue to be struggles for survival. Issues

---

3. Esther Danpongpee, "Karen Stories of Creation," *Programme for Theology and Culture in Asia Bulletin* 13 (2000): 69–77; Yuko Yuasa, "Magdalene Dancing in Crimson: A Biblical Noh Drama," *Japan Christian Activity News,* Spring/Summer 1996, 2–3.

concerning women, such as refugee conditions, migrant labor practices, sexual harassment, and oppressive traditions and customs, are still
very much alive in today's Asia. In Burma particularly, political insta-
bility, ethnic conflicts, militarism, misguided economic policies and
globalization have led to violence against women, including the trafficking of women, rape, and prostitution. Burmese Christian women
see their lives mirrored in the story of the struggles of Ruth and Naomi.

Ruth and Naomi are two women who, in spite of differences in ethnicity, religion, and age, bond together in their search for security. Both
are widows and foreigners (Naomi in Moab and Ruth in Judah), with no
man around to support them. Ruth is admired for her loyalty to Naomi.
Angela Wong Wai-Ching considers Ruth to be the outsider who, by her
words and action, moves Boaz to perform acts of faithfulness and loyalty
(ḥesed in Hebrew). This foreign woman becomes a model for doing
ḥesed.[4] For Hisako Kinukawa, "Ruth is challenging us through her
openness to other faiths and her courage to cross borders. She should be
remembered not because she gave birth to David's grandfather, but for
risking her own religious identity to support another woman's faith."[5]
The bonding of two very different women and their reliance on each
other for their very physical existence is empowering for women.

Yet Naomi's and Ruth's dependence on marriage to a rich man for
security, the questionable means the women use to secure a husband,
and Ruth's obedience and submission to her mother-in-law are some of
the concerns that Asian women raise when reading the story. This paper
attempts to find out whether the story of Ruth is a truly liberative
model for Asian women or whether it is a model that perpetuates and
reaffirms the oppressive patriarchal idea of the submissive woman. By
concentrating on Ruth 3:1–5 from the perspective of Asian women, the
figure of Ruth is explored as an ideal for Asian women.

THE BACKGROUND

The family of Elimelech, comprising his wife (Naomi) and sons (Chilion and Mahlon), leave Bethlehem in Judah for Moab because of

---

4. Angela Wong Wai-Ching, "History, Identity and a Community in Ruth 1:1–17," *Asia Journal of Theology* 13 (1999): 11.

5. Hisako Kinukawa, "'And Your God My God': How We Can Nurture Openness to Other Faiths; Ruth 1:1–19 Read from a Feminist Perspective of a Multi-Faith Community," *Scripture, Community, and Mission: Essays in Honor of D. Preman Niles* (ed. Philip Wickeri; Hong Kong: Christian Conference of Asia, 2002), 202.

famine. While in Moab, Elimelech dies, and the sons marry Moabite women, Chilion to Orpah and Mahlon to Ruth. The marriages are barren, and the two sons also die. When the famine is over, Naomi decides to return to Bethlehem (1:6). The two Moabite daughters-in-law seem to fall in with her plans. On the way, however, Naomi thanks her daughters-in-law for their loyalty (ḥesed) to her and her deceased sons, and then urges them to go back to their homes to find husbands among their own people (1:8–9). Orpah heeds Naomi's words and returns, but Ruth throws in her lot with Naomi. She commits herself fully to her mother-in-law, her God, her people, and her country (1:16–17). Ruth's decision is as radical as Abraham's actions; they both leave their own people, land, and God for the unknown (Gen 12:1–4). Ruth's decision, however, unlike that of Abraham, is based not on a call and a promise but rather on her ḥesed to Naomi. With no divine promise or hope of security, and against Naomi's attempted dissuasion (1:15), Ruth sticks firmly to her decision.

Back in Bethlehem, Naomi tells the townspeople no longer to call her Naomi ("pleasant") but Mara ("bitter"), because she experiences God's hand as bitter against her. She had gone out full, but now she returns empty (1:20–21). Naomi seems not to take notice of her Moabite daughter-in-law Ruth, who followed her to a strange land.

It is up to Ruth, as the younger woman, to find a way for the two women to live. As it is the time of the barley harvest, Ruth takes the initiative by gleaning in the field of Boaz, a near kinsman of Elimelech and a "man of substance," in Hebrew, ʾîš gibbôr ḥayil (2:1).[6] Boaz shows kindness to Ruth by inviting her to glean in only his field and to stick close to his young women. He instructs his young men to draw water for her and not to molest her (2:8–9). He speaks words of praise for her loyalty to her mother-in-law and even invokes God's blessing for her (2:11–12). He shares the midday meal with her, providing enough for Ruth to save some for Naomi (2:14). Boaz tells the workers to deliberately drop sheaves for her to pick (2:15–16). At the end of the day, Ruth shows Naomi the barley she had gleaned and reports all that had happened. Naomi concurs with Boaz that, for her safety, Ruth should stick close to Boaz's young women (2:22). Throughout the barley and wheat harvests, Ruth gleans in Boaz's fields, obeying Boaz's and Naomi's injunction to stay close to the female workers (2:23).

---

6. Since the phrase ʾîš gibbôr ḥayil can signify a man of strength, power, wealth, or ability, the exact meaning of ḥayil in this context can be only inferred. A man with fields and laborers working for him, Boaz is presented as a man of substance with standing in the community. Ruth is later designated as ʾēšet ḥayil, a "woman of worth," by Boaz (3:11).

Although Boaz is kind and helpful to Naomi and Ruth, at the end of the harvests, the two are no closer to finding a permanent solution to their problem of sustainable livelihood. Apparently Boaz does not feel compelled to go beyond what he had already done for the two widows.

One reason that Boaz does not take any further action may be that, as Naomi indicated, he is a kinsman, of the family of Elimelech, but not the next-of-kin, the *gōʾēl*. There is another kinsman nearer than he, a fact he later reveals to Ruth (3:12). As the *gōʾēl*, Boaz would have had the responsibility of caring for the welfare of the two women in a more substantial way. The next-of-kin, or redeemer, was the one responsible for rescuing or redeeming the relative who was in difficulty. It was his duty to buy back and restore property that had been sold because of poverty (Lev 25:25; cf. Jer 32:6–15). He also had to buy back and set free a relative sold into slavery (Lev 25:47–49). Furthermore, avenging a murdered man was the responsibility of the next-of-kin.[7]

Was it also required of the next-of-kin to marry the widow of the dead man? This is what the book of Ruth seems to suggest. In the story of Tamar (Gen 38), it is under the levirate marriage law (Deut 25:5–10) that Judah, her father-in-law, arranges for her marriage with his second son. In a levirate marriage, the widow's future was secured and the continuation of her dead husband's line ensured. As Katharine Doob Sakenfeld notes, "Only in the book of Ruth do the two spheres of marriage among kin and land redemption among kin come together."[8] Boaz probably does not consider himself as either Ruth's *gōʾēl* or her levirate husband, and so takes no further steps to act on behalf of the women.

Another reason for Boaz's reticence could be the very foreignness of Ruth. Ruth is identified in the narrative several times as "the Moabite" (1:22; 2:2, 6, 21; 4:5, 10). She is a foreign woman. Foreign or strange women were thought to be seducers, like Potiphar's wife (Gen 39:7–18).[9] They were blamed for causing men to worship other gods, like Solomon's wives and Jezebel (1 Kgs 11:1–8; 16:31–33). Injunctions forbade marriage to foreign women (Deut 7:1–5), and in the time of Nehemiah and Ezra, mixed marriages were condemned (Ezra 9:1–15; Neh 10:28–30; 13:23–30). Worse, Ruth is a Moabite, from a nation born out of an incestuous relationship (Gen 19:30–38) who had been hostile to Israel

---

7. Katharine Doob Sakenfeld, *Ruth* (Interpretation; Louisville, KY: John Knox, 1999), 59. See also E. John Hamlin, *Ruth: Surely There Is a Future* (Grand Rapids: Eerdmans, 1996), 25–26.

8. Sakenfeld, *Ruth*, 59.

9. See Gail Corrington Steele, *The Strange Woman: Power and Sex in the Bible* (Louisville, KY: Westminster John Knox, 1997), 52–54.

on their journey to Canaan (Num 22). Their women had tried to seduce and lead the Israelite men to apostasy (Num 25:1–2). Moab was prohibited from ever being part of the covenant community (Deut 23:3–6). Ruth the Moabite, therefore, embodies all the foreignness against which Israel had been warned.

Ruth is also a widow. In some Asian cultures, marriage with widows is not encouraged. It is thought that a widow will bring bad luck and that the marriage will not be auspicious.[10] In India, widows used to commit *sati,* self-immolation, on their husbands' funeral pyres. Widows were assured that the heroic act of self-immolation would deify them. If they did not perform *sati,* they were expected to remain widows until their deaths. In the Hebrew Bible, though, there are no laws against the remarriage of widows. Although under Hebrew law a widow's rights of inheritance were ignored, along with the orphan and the sojourner she was under special consideration (Deut 14:28, 29; 16:11, 14; 24:17; 24:19–22).[11] In any case, a widow would not be the first choice of a wife for an upright citizen like Boaz. The bride of choice would be a virgin who had never known a man. Virginity was so highly prized that if a bride could not provide proof of virginity, she could be stoned to death (Deut 22:20–21). In such a society, then, Ruth the Moabite widow would have little attraction for such a worthy person as Boaz. Therefore, there are strong reasons for Boaz to do nothing further for the two widows.

In this situation of "no action" on the part of the kinsmen of Elimelech, Naomi proposes to act for Ruth and herself. Earlier Ruth had taken the first steps for survival. Now Naomi must put forward a bold and daring plan for their future.

NAOMI'S PURPOSE

Naomi begins by revealing her plan for Ruth's welfare: "My daughter, I need to seek some security for you, so that it may be well with you" (3:1). Earlier Naomi had expressed concern for the future of her daughters-in-law when she had urged both of them to go back to their mothers' houses, "YHWH grant that you may find security, each of you in the house of your husband" (1:9). In that she herself can no longer bear children for them to wed, Naomi knows of only one way to gain

---

10. In Burmese culture widows are sometimes called *yawkkya sa,* meaning "eater of husband," inferring that they are responsible for their husbands' deaths, directly or indirectly.

11. See Theophile James Meek, *Hebrew Origins* (New York: Harper, 1960), 77–78.

security for her daughters-in-law—marriage to a husband who could provide a home. Like most Asian parents, Naomi is anxious to settle the future of her daughters-in-law. In Bama Buddhist homes, the five duties of a parent include the arranging of a suitable match for one's son or daughter.[12] If a child remains single, it reflects badly on the parents. As Orpah had heeded Naomi's words, she is no longer Naomi's concern. Ruth, however, still remains with her. Naomi's widowhood means she is dependent on the charity of others. Ruth, on her own initiative and with the goodwill of Boaz, had managed to meet their immediate basic needs. Yet Ruth's future without a husband was too uncertain.

According to Frederic Bush, "In the light of what will ensue, let us note here that Naomi's whole concern is her responsibility to see that the destitute state and reproach that widowhood represented in Israelite society is resolved for Ruth."[13] Beyond that, Naomi desires well-being for Ruth. E. John Hamlin explains, "This meant finding a partner who would care for, be kind to, and respect the dignity of his foreign, vulnerable wife and their children, and be concerned with the welfare of the entire community."[14]

There is also the problem of two women living alone. The basic unit of an Israelite community was the father's house, where protection was ensured for the members. In contrast, Naomi and Ruth appear to be outside such a communal unit. They are fending for themselves. Not only is there no economic security, as outsiders in the social units of the community they are vulnerable to sexual harassment, assault, and rape. This danger had already been pointed out by Boaz to Ruth (2:8–9). In an Asian society of that period, a woman was either under the protection of her father, husband, son, or another male relative.

With those concerns Naomi takes the first step by speaking of her concern for Ruth's future. For Naomi, the solution to these problems is marriage.

NAOMI'S STRATEGY

Naomi goes on to reveal how this is to be accomplished. She divulges that it is not just marriage in general but marriage with a particular man

---

12. The other duties of a parent are to prevent children from doing evil, to teach them to do good, to provide an education and skills for a livelihood, and to give them a start in life with financial help.

13. Frederic Bush, *Ruth/Esther* (Word Biblical Commentary; Waco, TX: Word, 1996), 147.

14. Hamlin, *Ruth*, 40.

that she has in mind. And who better to marry than Boaz, the upstanding man of the community who has already displayed a measure of concern for Ruth and Naomi? Boaz had tried to protect Ruth by advising her to stick close to his young women and admonishing his young men not to molest her (2:8–9). This, indeed, is how Naomi identifies him, "our kinsman Boaz, with whose young women you have been working" (3:2a). The intended husband will not be a stranger but a kinsman who had previously shown kindness to Ruth.

Naomi is well aware of the activities of harvest time and, more to the point, what Boaz would be doing. She informs Ruth that Boaz would be winnowing barley that night at the threshing floor. This accurate information about Boaz's activities points to the fact that, although she speaks to Ruth of "now," Naomi has been planning for this night.

Her instructions to Ruth are very specific. "Wash and anoint yourself, and put on your best clothes and go down to the threshing floor; but do not make yourself known to the man until he has finished eating and drinking. When he lies down, observe the place where he lies; then, go and uncover his feet and lie down; and he will tell you what to do" (3:3–4). Naomi, who had earlier advised Ruth to stick close to Boaz's young women lest she be molested, now suggests that she embark on a dangerous undertaking. As Phyllis Trible describes it, it is an undertaking that may lead to life or to death.[15]

Harvest time was a joyful time, a time of eating, drinking, and merrymaking after the hard work of the day (Judg 9:27; Isa 9:3; Ps 126:5–6). But it could also be a time fraught with danger for young women (Judg 21:20–21). It was a time when young men and young women, under cover of darkness, could engage in sexual acts. Nighttime was the time for lovers' trysts. Yet evil deeds, such as the gang rape of the Levite's concubine, could also occur at night (Judg 19:10–26; cf. Gen 19:1–11). The threshing floor itself was a dangerous place. It was used not only for agricultural purposes but also for sexual licentiousness of the fertility cult. For instance, Hosea warns Israel not to rejoice,

> for you have played the whore, departing from your God.
> You have loved a prostitute's pay on all threshing floors.
> (Hos 9:1b)

---

15. Phyllis Trible, *God and the Rhetoric of Sexuality* (Overtures to Biblical Theology; Philadelphia: Fortress, 1978), 183.

Ruth is told in not so subtle ways to make herself attractive. She is instructed to wash, anoint herself, and put on her best clothes. Anointing with oils and scents is how Esther prepares herself to be attractive for a night with King Ahasuerus (Esth 2:12). An unfaithful wife lures a foolish young man by promising him a night of love on a bed perfumed with scents (Prov 7:10–20). In Ezek 16:8–12, similar preparations are carried out for Israel the bride. For Naomi's plan to succeed, therefore, Ruth must approach Boaz and arouse his romantic interest.

After Boaz is in a merry mood from feasting and drinking and falls asleep, Ruth is to "uncover his feet and lie down" (3:4). Commentators have noted that the term "feet" is a euphemism for a man's private parts (Exod 4:25; Isa 7:20) and "to uncover the feet" has connotations of revealing nakedness for sexual purposes (Deut 27:20; Isa 47:1–3). Thus there are sexual overtones to the actions Ruth is to perform. Ruth is to act in a provocative manner toward a man in the middle of the night. It seems as if Naomi is asking Ruth to go beyond the boundaries of accepted female behavior and to act out the stereotype of the strange woman who leads on Israelite men.

RUTH'S RESPONSE

If we are surprised at the extent to which Naomi goes to further her ends, we are doubly surprised at Ruth's reply, "All that you tell me I will do" (3:5). The woman who had refused her mother-in-law's injunction for security with a Moabite husband now acquiesces to her scheme. What is going on here?

Ruth and Naomi both work for their survival. In the beginning Ruth had initiated the action of gleaning so the two could have food for physical survival. In this next venture, Naomi becomes the main initiator for security and well-being. She is aware of the precarious nature of their existence and desires a more permanent solution. Ruth, more than Naomi, had risked everything by leaving her family and country to throw in her lot with Naomi. Now she is challenged to undertake another daring act. A Burmese proverb states, "As the topknot follows the head, so does the woman follow the man." Men are the decision makers, and women abide by their decisions. In this situation, however, Naomi and Ruth are to lead and Boaz is to respond, either negatively or positively.

Earlier Naomi had praised Ruth and Orpah for their *ḥesed*, actions of faithfulness and loyalty, to her family and to her (1:8). No explanation is given of what this entailed. We might imagine that all the daily deeds of kindness and loyalty that dutiful daughters-in-law perform in the course of family living must have been encompassed in this doing of *ḥesed*. When he comes upon her in his field, again Ruth is given words of approbation, this time by Boaz, for all she has done for her mother-in-law (2:11–12). Although the word *ḥesed* is not used, the acts of Ruth in leaving her home and country to be with Naomi are most certainly meant. For Ruth, does doing *ḥesed* also mean obedience to the will of her mother-in-law?

According to Sakenfeld, the doing of *ḥesed* must meet three criteria. First, the act must be essential for the survival or well-being of the recipient. Second, the act may be done only by that particular person. Third, the act of *ḥesed* is done within an already existing relationship.[16] Ruth's response to Naomi's request can be noted as such an act. Boaz, in his response to Ruth's request, seems to underscore this aspect, "May you be blessed by YHWH, my daughter; this last instance of your loyalty (*ḥesed*) is better than the first; you have not gone after young men, whether poor or rich" (3:10). In this last act of *ḥesed* to Naomi, Ruth portrays herself as the faithful and loyal daughter-in-law.

Ruth's loyalty to Naomi could also extend to her deceased husband, brother-in-law, and father-in-law. It could include providing an heir for Naomi within the structure of levirate marriage.[17] According to Hamlin, "Ruth showed that her primary motivation was not self-gratification, but rather the desire to help rescue Naomi and the family of Elimelech from extinction."[18] According to Athalya Brenner, Ruth is motivated neither by pleasure seeking nor by financial or social ambitions in seeking to marry Boaz. She is willing to take risks "in order to perpetuate the continuity of Judahite leaderstock."[19] Although Bush argues against this as the motivation for Naomi's and Ruth's action, the possibility exists that Ruth remains loyal to her husband's family.[20]

Ruth's obedience to the words of her mother-in-law is the expected response of younger to older, daughter to mother, in an Asian culture.

---

16. Sakenfeld, *Ruth*, 24.

17. Katharine Doob Sakenfeld, *Faithfulness in Action: Loyalty in Biblical Perspective* (Overtures to Biblical Theology; Philadelphia: Fortress, 1985), 32.

18. Hamlin, *Ruth*, 46.

19. Althalya Brenner, *The Israelite Woman: Social Role and Literary Type in a Biblical Narrative* (Sheffield: JSOT, 1985), 108.

20. Bush, *Ruth/Esther*, 170–71. See also Sakenfeld, *Ruth*, 61–62.

Ruth's promise to Naomi, "Where you go, I will go" (1:16), has led her to this stage in their journey together.

ASIAN WOMEN'S EXPERIENCES

The story of Ruth may be read as a novelette about loyalty and commitment. Ruth may be held up as the model Asian woman: brave, resourceful, and loyal. And that is how Burmese Christian women usually conceptualize her. There is a dark side, however, to this image of a devoted daughter-in-law.

Sakenfeld notes a feminist objection to this story:

> Ruth's behavior . . . encourages women to follow cultural expectations by serving others at the expense of their own needs, by sacrificing themselves for the sake of family or friends or workplace colleagues. The danger of such an interpretation may be especially acute in some Asian cultures, where some church leaders are reported to have used the example of Ruth to insist that young Christian women maintain a traditional cultural practice of serving their mothers-in-law rather than choosing to live as a nuclear family or work outside the home.[21]

Ellen Bruno, in her video *Sacrifice,* follows the lives of four Burmese prostitutes in Thailand. The most poignant story is that of a young Shan Buddhist girl, who states, "My uncle brought me to Thailand and sold me to a brothel. He said that I owe my life to my parents and as a dutiful daughter I should repay my debts to my parents."[22]

For Khin Thitsa, a Burmese scholar, it is the low status accorded to women in Buddhism and the Buddhist view of karma that makes young girls and women accept prostitution as their fate. This culture of obedience teaches daughters to sacrifice themselves for their parents and their family. Daughters are born with a debt to their parents that can only be repaid by filial obedience. A mother from the Mae Hong Son area says, "There is nothing wrong in sending out teenaged girls to be prostitutes. I am satisfied with the 2000–4000 baht my daughter sends home monthly. I can afford to buy a color TV, refrigerator and

---

21. Sakenfeld, *Ruth*, 13.
22. Ellen Bruno, *Sacrifice* (private production, 1998).

other electronic appliances because my daughter shows her gratitude to me by sending home money."[23]

Kuo Siu May does not see Ruth as a liberating model for women. She points out that as "[k]ind and considerate to her daughter-in-law as Naomi is made out to be, she made all the arrangements (for Ruth's marriage to the middle-aged Boaz) without her leave. Her [Ruth's] submissiveness, at best, is negative in nature."[24] Commenting on this aspect of the Ruth story, Wenh-In Ng says, "To have 'Whither thou goest, I will go' held up as one's model from the pulpit when one's culture already demands that you do, is far from liberating."[25] Furthermore, Chinese women have been socialized into accepting Confucian values: obeying one's elders, letting men make the decisions, supporting sons over daughters, and giving power to mothers-in-law over her daughters-in-law.

Comparable use of Scripture in support of unreflective self-sacrifice is familiar to many women in many cultures, and in many spheres of life beyond the family. In certain ways, then, Ruth and Madi, the consort of Waythandaya, the Buddha-to-be, are sisters in their submission and obedience. Just as Ruth is pliant and submissive to the will of Naomi, so is Madi to her husband. She is ready to sacrifice her chastity and wifely virtue to help fulfill her husband's destiny.[26]

In traditional Asian cultures, heroines such as Ruth and Madi are held up as models for young women. But for women to develop self-esteem and self-affirmation, they must look beyond Ruth. In spite of the empowering message of female bonding and solidarity, the story of Ruth and Naomi has too often been used to put down women's struggle for self-fulfillment. We need to reexamine the concept of loyalty and obedience in familial relationships. We must map out new ways to relate to each other, ways that respect and affirm the human dignity of each one of us.

FOR FURTHER STUDY

Antone, Hope S., and Yong Tin Jin, eds. *Re-Living Our Faith Today: A Bible Study Resource Book*. Hong Kong: World Student Christian Federation, Asia-Pacific Region, 1992.

23. Khin Thitsa, *Providence and Prostitution: Women in Buddhist Thailand* (London: Change International, 1990), 11.

24. Kuo Siu May, *Venturing into the Bible* (Nanjing: University Press, 1989), 420.

25. Wenh-In Ng, "'Whither Thou Goest': In-Law and Other Relationships in Contemporary Chinese Family Networks," *In God's Image* 17 (1998): 13.

26. Htin Aung, *Burmese Drama*, 97. Madi may also be compared to Sarah, who acquiesces to Abraham's request that she be presented to Pharoah as his sister rather than his wife to save his life (Gen 12:10–16; cf. Gen 20; 26:1–11).

Kinukawa, Hisako. *Women and Jesus in Mark: A Japanese Feminist Perspective.* Maryknoll, NY: Orbis, 1994.

Kwok Pui-lan. *Introducing Asian Feminist Theology.* Cleveland: Pilgrim, 2000.

Lee, Oo Chung, et al., eds. *Women of Courage: Asian Women Reading the Bible.* Seoul: Asian Women's Resource Center for Culture and Theology, 1992.

Longkumer, Limatula, and Talijungla Longkumer, eds. *Side by Side: Naga Women Doing Theology in Search of Justice and Partnership.* Jorhat, India: Christian Conference of Asia–Education, Gender, and Youth Unit and Naga Women Theological Forum, 2004.

Ralte, Lalrinawma, and Evangeline Anderson-Rajkumar. *Feminist Hermeneutics.* Delhi: India Women in Theology/SPCK, 2002.

Say Pa, Anna May. "Chorus of Voices: Reading the Bible from Many Perspectives." *Committee for Theological Concerns Bulletin* 21, no. 3 (December 2005): 59–70.

5

My Sister Sarah

On Being a Woman in the First World

BETH LANEEL TANNER

Long ago, in seminary, a classmate asked me a question that haunts me to this day. Years later, I do not remember the exact context, but I do remember that the question was raised not in anger but in a spirit of growth and discovery. She asked, "What is it like to be white?" Now, I had been asked what it was like to be a girl, and to have red hair, and to be left-handed—but I had never been asked to define what is considered the cultural norm of the place in which I reside. What I discovered in that moment is that there is no answer to her question, because from a Euro–North American perspective there is not even a reason for her question.[1] The problem goes further than skin color, for to be a Euro–North American, a "Westerner," encompasses more than my skin color; my whole life and lifestyle needs no definition because it simply *is*.[2] As a feminist who is also of Euro–North American heritage and one who lives as a "Westerner," this is the reality in which I live and do my work. I must recognize that I am a child of privilege just by the color of my skin and the location of my birth. I did nothing to earn this position. It is simply where and from whom I was born.

---

1. This blindness of whiteness continues to be an issue in our cultures today. For example, Patricia Williams notes, "Perhaps one reason that conversations about race are so often doomed to frustration is that the notion of whiteness as race is almost never implicated" (*Seeing a Color-Blind Future: The Paradox of Race* [London: Virago, 1997], 4–5).

2. Musa W. Dube notes clearly that this issue is broader than the color of one's skin. She writes, "This approach maintains the West as the center of all cultural good, one with a supposedly redemptive impulse, but one that always proceeds by placing other cultures at the periphery" (*Postcolonial Feminist Interpretation of the Bible* [St. Louis: Chalice, 2000], 25).

It is this recognition of my status and for the reasons that unfold below that I feel a connection with the matriarch Sarah. I am aware that thousands of years have passed between her life and mine. I am also aware that we are from two very different cultures. Yet in the events of her life recorded in the Bible I find a sister, for her story describes the blessings and pitfalls of being a "First World"[3] daughter. This essay represents a conversation with my ancient sister, as her story intertwines with the realities I am called to see as a scholar and a woman. As such, I invite you to listen to my conversation with Sarah, as the story of her life encourages me to think about my own life in new ways.[4]

A CONVERSATION WITH SARAH

Your story begins much like the accident of my birth in North America. God picked Abram without giving a reason. That act of God seemed as random as the place of my birth. I had no choice in the matter. Sarah, you did not have any choice in the matter, either. As a wife[5] of Abram when I first encounter your story (Gen 11:29), you are also affected by God's call. Indeed, even though you are not addressed directly by God in the call in Gen 12:1–3 or in the subsequent covenants (Gen 15:1–21; 17:1–27), I learn in Gen 17:15–20 that it is you, Sarah, who will be the essential mother in God's plan.[6] The promises belonged to you as much as to Abraham. The narrative does not include you in the covenant ceremonies, but it is clear that you are chosen nonetheless. I must remember that I, too, was chosen by God to be in this place and to live at this time. I, like you, Sarah, must follow the call of God in the journeys of my life. We were both placed in the First World by the God who created and called us.

3. The terms "First World" and "Third World" are very descriptive of the inequalities in our world today. "Third World" is a term first used by the French economist Alfred Sauvy in 1952, but the definition has grown subsequently. The term first designated countries not aligned with either NATO or the USSR. Now the term has evolved to serve as a grouping phrase for countries that do not have the economic and social resources that the First World experiences (www.en.wikipedia.org).

4. This essay is a conversation dedicated to Katharine Doob Sakenfeld. Through her listening to women from all over the world, she has taught me the power of story, the joy of conversation, and the importance of honor for all whom God places before you. I owe her a debt of gratitude for all she has taught me over the years as my mentor, colleague, friend, and copresbyter. I am better as a scholar and as a person because she has shared her work and her friendship with me.

5. Or "woman" (ʾiššâ) in Hebrew. Unlike modern languages, there is no distinction in Hebrew for a married versus a single woman. The English word "wife" is assigned only by a translator.

6. Abram has other children who are not of the promise. Gordon J. Wenham notes that Abram adopts Lot after the death of his father (*Genesis 1–15* [Word Biblical Commentary; Waco, TX: Word, 1987], 272). Abraham also fathers Ishmael with Hagar (16:4) and six additional sons with Keturah after Sarah's death (25:1). In other words, Abram has many other children, but Sarah's child will be the child of the covenant promise (Gen 17:21).

Your First World status also seems to have much in common with my life. Your name gives a powerful clue as to your status. The name "Sarah" signifies a woman of rank or a princess. You are also a woman of means (Gen 12:5; 13:2, 5), but the narrative certainly does not depict you as a princess.[7] You are not found living in the lap of luxury, but in the kitchen taking orders from Abraham (Gen 18:6). I can relate. From a whole-world perspective, I too am a princess, but that fact is often hard to remember. I do not come from a wealthy family by First World standards, yet I have never known a time without food or shelter. As a professor, I do not make "big bucks," but I live comfortably. I am the first person in my family to graduate from college, but I also had access to the best schools in the First World and felt limited by little except my own abilities and choices. By First World standards, I am far from a "princess." From a global perspective, however, I stand in the top 5 percent. I have an education and a job that provide me with more than a large majority of the world's people have. Sarah, you remind me of the two worlds that I must see. With the question, "What is it like to be white and Euro–North American?" I should add, "What is it like to be wealthy?" I may feel like the Sarah in the kitchen, but your story reminds me that I must also remember that I have a kitchen in a sturdy house with electricity and plumbing—and that very fact makes me a princess. It reminds me that I cannot and must not speak as if my view is normative. My view of the world is definitely colored by my life in the First World.

The next thing I learn about you, Sarai, is all too familiar for women in the Euro–North American context, or at least its negativity is familiar.[8] "Now Sarai was barren, she had no child" (Gen 11:30). Before I learn much about your life, I learn of your greatest heartache and pain, for to be without a child, or more specifically a male child, was a mark of great shame in ancient cultures. One of the disadvantages of being a First World woman is that we are bombarded by our presumed inadequacies. Women today still struggle with barrenness, and we are still seen as incomplete if we cannot, or choose not to, have husbands and children. Yet all the while, the advertising world tells us that we need to fix our bodies, our clothes, and our families, preferably by buying expensive items that presumably make us happy. We may have too much of everything,

---

7. See Judg 5:29; 1 Kgs 11:3; and Isa 49:23, each of which indicates either a queen or a woman or royal rank. Claus Westermann sees "Sarai" as a title, instead of a proper name, that indicates her elevated status in the ancient world (*Genesis 12–36: A Commentary* [trans. J. Scallion; Minneapolis: Augsburg, 1985], 138).

8. The more familiar names "Sarah" and "Abraham" will not be given by God until the second covenant in Gen 17. For clarity, if the narrative is prior to Gen 17 I use the names "Sarai" and "Abram" in the discussion of the biblically recorded event. If I am referring to Sarah or Abraham in a more general sense, however, I use their God-given names.

but the message we are continually told is that nothing is ever enough because our worth is still measured by our greatest flaws. I can say to my ancient sister Sarah, "I know how you feel." Even women who "have it all" are sent daily messages that there is more perfection out there to chase. We are taught to worry constantly about what we are not, instead of see-ing what we are and what we have. It seems to me, Sarah, that this is one characteristic that each generation continues to teach the next.

From your story, I learn a valuable lesson about my own life and cul-ture; if I worry about only my own inadequacies, then I am only react-ing to the culture around me instead of proactively questioning that very culture's values. This focus on the negative aspects of my life serves to keep me in my place, just as your focus on your barrenness kept you in your place and even encouraged you to oppress others.[9] Your story reminds me that to focus on what I do not have can lead to serious con-sequences not only for me, but for the world.

The next scene in your life, Sarai (Gen 12:10–20, and again in 20:1–17), is one that also reflects a painful reality in the lives of women ancient and modern. Our bodies and our sexuality are at risk by those with more power. In these two parallel narratives, you are given to another man for Abram's protection. Then, to make matters even worse, these dangerous acts of being given away result in wealth for your husband, but nothing for you (Gen 12:16; 20:14–15)![10] Unfortu-nately, Sarah, all women are still vulnerable to sexual attack or exploita-tion.[11] In the United States today, one in six women is sexually molested or raped.[12] Sarah, we still are at risk just because we are born women. Granted, as a First World daughter, I have better protection from violent crime because of my middle-class address, but 66 percent of women who are attacked in this country are attacked by men they know, and in these cases the address of the victim is irrelevant.[13] Sarah,

9. For a complete explanation, see the section below on Sarah's treatment of Hagar.

10. Fokkelien van Dijk-Hemmes notes that she does not read this narrative as "history" but as culture: "The way Sarai is treated in Genesis 12 shows what sort of actions were *thinkable*—thus perhaps also possible or desirable—in the author's (or authors') perception of this particular story" ("Sarai's Exile: A Gender-Motivated Reading of Genesis 12.10–13.2," in *A Feminist Companion to Genesis* [ed. Athalya Brenner; Sheffield: Sheffield Academic Press, 1993], 225).

11. There is no language of "attack" or "violence" indicated in the biblical text. But in today's language, that is how a husband selling a wife to another would be viewed. Sarah does not protest here; indeed, she never speaks. This act of silence Wenham interprets as consent (*Genesis 1–15*, 287), although Trevor Dennis sees it as reflecting that Sarah is "taken" by Pharaoh in the same way that she is "taken" to a new land by her husband. Silence reflects that she has no personal control over her own body (*Sarah Laughed: Women's Voices in the Old Testament* [Nashville: Abingdon, 1994], 40).

12. According to the Rape, Abuse, and Incest National Network (RAINN) statistics (www.rainn.org).

13. According to RAINN statistics. The biblical saga of the rape of Tamar (2 Sam 13) also demonstrates that "princesses" were in danger in the home as well. Tamar is literally a princess, a daughter of David, who is raped by her half-brother Ammon.

it may be thousands of years later, but sexual control and violence are still a reality. Just as I must learn to carry the title of "princess," I also must carry the title of "victim." Sarah, women are still not safe, even in our own homes and families. Women around the world still face sexual exploitation and violence. Sadly, it may be one of the factors that all women through all ages share in common.

Oh, Sarah, the next account of your life is so painful to read, but to a First World sister, it may be the most important. The last time you appeared in the Genesis narrative, Abram was giving you away for his protection and profit. Did you not remember how you felt? Did you not remember the humiliation when your body was used by another? Or was the emptiness of your womb just too much to take?[14] Did the looks of pity and contempt from other women drive you to this deed? Or were slaves simply not considered people?[15]

Here in the story of you and Hagar (Gen 16:1–16; 21:9–21), you, Sarai, used the power of your First World status. It is here that the question from my seminary days—"What is it like to be white?"—thunders in my head, for this narrative has long represented the struggle of African American women under the yoke of slavery. As Delores S. Williams writes, "For more than a hundred years, Hagar—the African slave of the Hebrew woman Sarah—has appeared in the deposits of African-American culture. Sculptors, writers, poets, scholars, preachers, and just plain folks have passed along the biblical figure of Hagar to generation after generation of black folks."[16] Indeed, the story of Hagar has become paradigmatic in expressing the realities of slavery and the situation of racism in the Western world today. Yet Renita J. Weems reminds us that it is not only the issue of race that is part of the reality of slavery: "The differences between the two women, therefore, went beyond ethnic identities, beyond their reproductive capabilities. Their disparities were centered in their contrasting economic conditions."[17]

14. Sharon Pace Jeansonne argues that this fear and desperation is what drives Sarai to abuse Hagar (*The Women of Genesis* [Minneapolis: Fortress, 1990], 20, 28).

15. Renita J. Weems rightly reminds modern readers that this is not a paradigm of racism as we know it in modern-day North America, but that it does have similarities to "the realities of the relationships across racial lines among women today" (*Just a Sister Away: A Womanist Vision of Women's Relationships in the Bible* [San Diego: LuraMedia, 1988], 2). "It is also not a moral tale about slavery, since slavery was a cultural custom in the ancient world." Weems continues, "Theirs is a story of ethnic prejudice exacerbated by economic and sexual exploitation. . . . Theirs is a story of social rivalry."

16. Delores S. Williams, *Sisters in the Wilderness: The Challenge of Womanist God-Talk* (Maryknoll, NY: Orbis, 1993), 2.

17. Weems, *Just a Sister Away*, 3. Also see Elsa Tamez, "The Woman Who Complicated the History of Salvation," in *New Eyes for Reading: Biblical and Theological Reflections by Women from the Third World* (ed. J. Pobee and B. von Wartenberg-Potter; Geneva: World Council of Churches, 1986), 5–17.

Sarai is a "have" and Hagar a "have-not," yet these two women share a common powerlessness in the face of patriarchy.

The difference, my sister Sarai, is that although both of you knew the pain, you had more power than Hagar, and in those moments, for a multitude of reasons, you decided to use Hagar to achieve your most desired dream. Granted, as far as your culture was concerned, you did nothing wrong. This practice of using the womb of your maid was standard operating procedure for a wealthy but barren woman.[18] But Sarai, did you look in Hagar's eyes when she realized that she was to be forcefully impregnated? Did you think that you were helping God out by taking matters into your own hands before it was too late, or did you believe that God had forsaken you and the promise of children as numerous as the stars (Gen 15:5)?[19] Did you know that this birth would become representative of the division of much of the religious world into Jews and Christians, on the one hand, and Muslims, on the other? Did you know that the conflict represented by these half-brothers would still be causing tremors of fear and hatred in my world?[20] Did you know that you were not as powerless as you thought, since the ramifications of your actions have been much more numerous than all the stars in heaven? Is the recognition that "household" decisions can have worldwide impact part of the lesson of your story?[21]

With these questions in mind, your act, Sarai, seems far removed from the reality of my world. Certainly we don't own handmaidens, nor do we give others over to rape and unwanted pregnancy. Indeed, women of our age have fought hard for a woman's right to choose in matters of reproductive rights. We are outraged by your action and are quite convinced that we would not act as you do!

Yet if we look to our history, it has not been that long, Sarai, since white slave owners acted just as you did. Only a century and a half ago,

18. Wenham notes, "The practice of surrogate motherhood is attested throughout the ancient Orient from the third to the first millennium B.C. from Babylon to Egypt" (*Genesis 16–50*, 7). Unfortunately, this act of forced surrogacy also goes hand in hand with slavery in the modern world (see Williams, *Sisters in the Wilderness*, 62–71).

19. From a narrative perspective, the promise is given to Abram alone. The text does not indicate whether or not he tells Sarai of the promise. What we can surmise is that, whether or not she is aware of the specific promise, Sarai is desperate for a child. We are left only to guess whether her desire for a child is because of cultural expectations or because she knows about her promised role and decides to help it come about.

20. Although the Bible presents one of Abraham's sons as favored, the same is not true for the Qur'an, in which both sons are recognized equally: "We believe in Allah, what has been revealed to us, what was revealed to Abraham, Ishmael, Isaac, Jacob, and the tribes, and what was given to Moses, Jesus, and the prophets from their Lord. We do not make a distinction among any of them and to Him we submit" (Qur'an 3:84). Centuries of animosity and violence, however, provided the environment in which a shift has taken place, so that Ishmael has become the (almost) sacrificed and the preferred son in Muslim tradition today. The tradition, then, is to make this story of division within the family of Abraham as paradigmatic for the division between two religious traditions. For more information, see John Kaltner, "Abraham's Sons: How the Bible and the Qur'an See the Same Story Differently," *Bible Review* 18 (2002): 16–23.

21. Virginia Woolf asserts that the personal is indeed political! See *A Room of One's Own* (London: Harcourt, 1929).

black slaves were forced to serve as surrogate partners in the master's bed to free the mistress from further childbearing. Even after the end of slavery, surrogacy has been one of the ways that poor women have borne the burdens of the more powerful, wealthy women of the First World: cleaning our houses, cooking our food, nursing our children, and sometimes even providing a womb for a wealthy barren one. I personally may not have used another woman in this way, but I live in a world where, just as in yours, less powerful women carry an unequal portion of the burdens of daily life.[22]

And what if we look beyond the actual act to the result of using another for our own desires? Sarai, you did exactly what your culture said you could, and you did not stop to look beyond that yes to the no of Hagar or to the no of the consequences of your actions. You did not see Hagar as a full-fledged person. Welcome to the First World, my sister. There are millions whom we do not see, and our Euro–North American culture aids our blindness through its myopic focus on itself. There are those who work in sweatshop conditions all over the world to make the clothes we wear and the sheets between which we sleep. There are those who are forced into the sex trade that provides men with the victims they desire. There are thousands of women whom our First World claims to "liberate" by blowing up their homes and killing their husbands and sons. There are tens of thousands of men and women who cannot work for legal wages in this country, so they do the landscaping we enjoy on our walks, clean the buildings in which we shop, and build the houses we see on our way to church, but they are invisible to most First World daughters, even though they walk the same streets that we drive.

Oh, Sarah! This painful story of yours is really *my* story, too. I too am an oppressor of those I do not see, and even if I do not actively entrap others, I live in a culture that does not see these women and men. I live in a system that makes me not only a princess but an oppressor. Sarah, your decision to oppress changed the world. Will my decisions have such far-reaching consequences? Your story teaches me that these seemingly unimportant daily decisions may cause pain and violence for hundreds, even thousands, of years. Must I add the question to my list, "Why are you an oppressor of others?" Yes, if I am going to be faithful to the God who called me and made me a First World

22. Williams, *Sisters in the Wilderness*, 60–83.

daughter, then I have no choice but to claim the question and keep it before me with all the others.

Sarai, when you noticed Hagar and her growing belly, you did not respond as if you thought your plan was going well. Like King Midas, your grandest wish became a source of anger and rage. Not only did you oppress your weaker sister, but when her plight became visible, you drove her away. You sent her into the desert to starve—and that would have been the end of it, had God not intervened. You removed her from your sight because your own error was just too difficult to watch.

My world does the same with the people of Africa. The starving and AIDS-afflicted people of Darfur thought that, as soon as the media arrived, the First World would come to their aid. These hopes were dashed when media reports stopped neither the violence nor the starvation.[23] Unfortunately, this is simply one of many examples of how the First World has ignored and continues to ignore others. Our world does not want to see outstretched hands begging through the television into our spacious family rooms, so we "send them away." We did not wish to see their pleading eyes become, like Hagar's, eyes "full of contempt." To leave the protection of my First World, Sarah, I am called to see the very actions of my world and even my own self that hurt others. The list of questions grows, for now I must add, "Why do you ignore the suffering of the rest of the world?"

But it is not as simple as that, for God has also entered here. God found the lost Hagar and then tells her to "return and submit" (Gen 16:9). Sakenfeld writes, "Why isn't the slave Hagar offered the same liberation from her personal oppression that God gives to the Israelites later on? It is hard to understand how the God we know from so many parts of the Bible as the God of justice and deliverance could deny such liberation to Hagar."[24] Feminist study involves not only struggling with humans, but struggling with God. We know that Hagar's plight also occurs over and over in our world. Women in horrific situations remain in those places. As we struggle, we must add this picture to our portrait of God. God is intimately involved with those who suffer, but often not

23. David Nabarro, a World Health Organization official, criticized the First World nations for their refusal to respond to the crisis in Darfur, a region in Sudan. "It [the crisis] is covered in French newspapers, in Japanese newspapers, and other countries in Europe and the United States. But the conversion of information reaching the politicians into resources is not adequate and the price is measured in death" (article for the Agence France Press, October 15, 2004).

24. Katharine Doob Sakenfeld, *Just Wives? Stories of Power and Survival in the Old Testament and Today* (Louisville, KY: Westminster John Knox, 2003), 19.

in a cataclysmic way. We, as First World daughters, must be careful not to equate God's seeming inaction to an affirmation of what is "right." As members of God's kingdom,[25] we are called not only to see, but also to speak out against, oppression. Sakenfeld reminds us that "[t]he angel of God directed Hagar toward survival, but our discomfort with that command requires us to work for liberation."[26]

It seems like a rough jolt to move on with your story, Sarah, for what comes next is the fulfillment of the promise that, after your actions toward Hagar, seems completely undeserved. Sarah! YHWH appears live and "in person" to deliver the news (Gen 18:1–15). God will give you your dream! You are finally to give birth, but you are still in the kitchen for the great announcement. You might be a woman in the First World, but you are not invited to the dinner. You keep your ear to the door and overhear the wonderful news, and your response is not just a smile or a chuckle but a full-blown laugh! Commentators have offered a plethora of reasons for your laughter: your age, your doubt, your amazement.[27] Yet I have to wonder if you laugh for another reason, a deeply ironic one. Could it be that you have seen what your feeble human attempts have done to Hagar and to Ishmael and to you and to Abraham? Do you laugh because what you have received is unmitigated, undeserved grace? God has overlooked your failures and brought forth the promise to an oppressor who deserves no such gift. Is the child's name of "laughter" given because God fulfills God's promises even to the undeserving, yet broken, you?[28] Even in the First World, there is grace. Sarah, my sister, you saw grace in its proper context, for that is the story told again and again in the Bible, in the history of the church, and in all of our lives. Grace is given as a gift to an undeserving humanity—and the only response is to laugh with a glee that is given back as thanksgiving.

Yet the truth is that even grace will not protect us from oppressing or oppression. We still live in the human world. You sent Hagar away again (Gen 21), just as the First World goes on oppressing all others.

25. I am a feminist who cannot, in good conscience, change the word "kingdom" to something more gender neutral, not because I support male dominance but because I claim and hold at the center of my belief that God is the complete sovereign of the world and my life. I want, indeed demand, that readers see the connection to the "kingdom of God" spoken of in this essay and the "kingdom of God" explained in the Torah, the Psalms, Isaiah, the New Testament, and the language of Christian faith. If I change the kingdom language to something more gender neutral, this important connection is severed. Until the language of the English Scriptures changes, I must continue to use "kingdom," for that connection is more important than making my language gender neutral.

26. Sakenfeld, *Just Wives?* 20.

27. As noted by Dennis, *Sarah Laughed*, 51.

28. The name Isaac is derived from the Hebrew verb *ṣāḥaq*, which means "to laugh."

We all remain both corporately and personally responsible for oppressing others around the world.

Well, Sarah, that's how I see our journey together, in all of its light and darkness. You have taught me a great deal about who I am and who I should be. God called both of us to live in the First World, but from a close look at our journeys I have learned that this placement does not guarantee that all will be perfect. You and I still have the capacity to be oppressor and victim. After looking at your story, I know that I must approach my work as a feminist scholar not from a place of power but from a place of great responsibility. I must keep these haunting questions before my own eyes so that I can throw them at myself and my world. I must be careful not to speak for those whose lives I do not live. I am not my sister's keeper, but I must strive to be her advocate and to demand that she be allowed to speak on her own to the Powers of the world.[29] I cannot wait for my own oppression to end before I turn my concern to the much greater oppression of others. I am called to remember that God has placed me here to speak of a kingdom that is beyond my reality as a First World daughter.

REFLECTIONS ON FEMINIST WRITINGS
FROM A EURO-AMERICAN PERSPECTIVE

What is a feminist hermeneutic or reading? The question was posed in the classic 1985 volume *Feminist Interpretation of the Bible*.[30] Even in this early work, two realities become clear. First, feminist interpretation, at least as an academic pursuit, was primarily a Euro–North American enterprise led by brave and esteemed women who worked hard to get feminist ways of reading on the map of biblical studies.[31] The second reality was that, from the very beginning, feminist criticism was not a strict method but a way of looking at the Bible. It was an

---

29. It is here in this act of transferring understanding from "keeping" or caring to advocacy that allows all women to become full persons. By not offering "care" as if other women are less than I am and need my First World "hand-me-downs," I can offer advocacy so that they can have a voice and live into their own power. As my colleague Professor Warren Dennis reminds the faculty and the students at New Brunswick Theological Seminary, "Do not do for others what they are able to do for themselves."

30. This volume, edited by Letty M. Russell, was one of the first comprehensive works that reflected on the ten years of scholarship done to this point (Philadelphia: Westminster, 1985).

31. This does not mean that these women were the only ones "doing" feminist work in the Bible. Dorothy Bass notes, "Until the 1970s, it was necessary to seek feminist hermeneutics outside of the Society of Biblical Literature" ("Women's Studies and Biblical Studies: A Historical Perspective," *Journal for the Study of the Old Testament* 22 [1982]: 10). These women and the male scholars who encouraged them provided the first models of feminist interpretation.

endeavor that struggled[32] with the text to provide a view from the perspective of women, but at the same time that considers any scholar's view to be one of many, as the articles in this volume exhibit. Yet even though there were a variety of perspectives on how one looks at the Bible as a feminist, its social location was Euro–North American and primarily Christian. The movement had no desire to replace patriarchy with matriarchy, but, as Sakenfeld notes, "[it] need[s] to be alert not only for explicit patriarchal bias [in biblical texts] but also for evidence of more subtle androcentrism in the world view of the biblical authors."[33] Much of this early work was to "redeem" the picture of women in the Bible and to note the patriarchal view of both the Scriptures and its interpretation. Though the articles and books written for a period of time tended to be myopic in working on these issues, feminist biblical scholars also recognized that their interpretation should not be the only word on reading Scripture. A fledgling feminist way to read Scripture slowly emerged, and although it was applauded by many women for its focus, it also underwent scrutiny that demonstrated its unintended, but nevertheless problematic, cultural biases.[34]

At first, two areas of criticism were raised by women who lived, worked, and were educated within the Euro–North American culture but still sat at its margins. These women brought their critique to the feminist enterprise and showed that "woman" is not a universal category that can erase all issues of religion, class, and race. The Jewish feminist Judith Plaskow, among others, faulted Christian feminist scholarship as anti-Judaic, arguing that Christian feminists must break free of the old Christian paradigms that set Christianity against Judaism.[35] She also noted that, because she is from a minority in Euro–North American culture, her task as a feminist is even more complex. Plaskow writes, "It is very difficult for Jewish feminists to critique Judaism in a non-Jewish context when we know that what we say as internal criticism may appear

---

32. In this way, feminist hermeneutics shares a perspective with the ones who handed down these stories. Israel's very name means "to strive or struggle with God."

33. Katharine Doob Sakenfeld, "Feminist Uses of Biblical Materials," in *Feminist Interpretation of the Bible*, 56.

34. Judith Plaskow, a Jewish feminist scholar, writes, "The dream we had in the heady, early days of the feminist movement, that the bonds of sisterhood would annul or eradicate traditional divisions of religion, race, and class, and that we could formulate an analysis of women's situation . . . was based not on engagement with the particularities of women's experience but on a wave of a magic wand that made differences invisible ("Feminist Anti-Judaism and the Christian God," *Journal of Feminist Studies in Religion* 7 [1991]: 100).

35. Plaskow notes that Christian feminist scholarship is anti-Judaic in three ways: the contrasting view of God in the Old and New Testaments, the blaming of the Jews (or more specifically the God of the Jews) for the death of the goddess, and the ways Jesus has been portrayed as a "feminist" over and against his Jewish culture (ibid., 99–108). Also see Katharina von Kellenbach, *Anti-Judaism in Feminist Religious Writings* (Atlanta: Scholars, 1994).

against us in Christian work."[36] From her, we learn that our unintentional biases make the work of women at the margins of Western culture more difficult.

Women of color added their voices as well. Williams noted how, instead of speaking with womanist scholars, white feminist scholars spoke to and with white male scholars. In addition, they adopted no new paradigms for speaking and presenting their concerns. Therefore, to women of color it looked like the old racist, oppressive patriarchal system.[37] She, like Plaskow, challenged feminists to think outside the boxes of their Euro–North American education.

A few years after the women from the margins in Euro–North American culture voiced their concerns about feminist interpretation, women from other countries added their concerns. These also had much in common with the earlier observations. Ivone Gebara, a Latin American scholar, noted that if we continue to do scholarship in the same old ways, "We continue to live under masculine power, softened by a few feminist victories."[38] Musa W. Dube has also challenged feminist thinking. She writes, "Any feminist endeavor that seeks to recognize inclusivity, solidarity, and equality in the hermeneutical center should question why Christianity has been unique in imperial sponsorship."[39]

These women are just a few of the voices that have aided Euro–North American feminist scholars to rethink the feminist endeavor. Yet there is still much work to be done. The hurricane that devastated New Orleans in 2005 demonstrated very clearly that classism and racism are still standard operating procedures within the Euro–North American culture, and Dube reminds us all that we must confront the imperialistic forms of our culture and of our ways of being that continue to harm the whole world. What the critiques have stressed most of all is the need for different ways of doing the business of biblical interpretation, ways that are not dependent on Western paradigms of thinking.

This conversation with Sarah, in which the literary Sarah and the modern-day feminist Christian scholar share their lives as "haves," is one attempt at a new way of doing business. It does not focus on theological issues as much as cultural ones, yet the cultural conversation of

36. Plaskow, "Feminist Anti-Judaism," 107.

37. Delores S. Williams, "Womanist/Feminist Dialogue: Problems and Possibilities," *Journal of Feminist Studies in Religion* 9 (1993): 67–73. Cecil Cone made the same critique of African American theologians who use old Western paradigms (*The Identity Crisis in Black Theology* [Nashville: Henry Berlin, 1975]).

38. Ivone Gebara, "A Feminist Theology of Liberation: A Latin American Perspective with a View Toward the Future," in *Toward a New Heaven and a New Earth: Essays in Honor of Elisabeth Schüssler Fiorenza* (ed. F. Segovia; Maryknoll, NY: Orbis, 2003), 252.

39. Dube, *Postcolonial Feminist Interpretation of the Bible*, 33.

honestly speaking of what it means to be of the First World is essential if new paradigms are to be forged. Although the issues here are primarily ones of social location, this endeavor is ultimately theological because it sees Sarah as a complex character who is both oppressed and oppressor. By understanding the complexity of Sarah and her life, I now see God's grace in this ancient narrative in a new way, and thus I can see the same unmitigated grace operating in my First World as well.

These necessary new paradigms will come from naming as much cultural bias, as well as patriarchal bias, as we can. All the while we must listen to others on whom we depend to show us biases that we cannot see because of our own particular locations in the world. It must be a global conversation in which feminists from all cultures are not afraid to have honest and open dialogue, even if that dialogue is frightening. This is one path to a new way of doing biblical interpretation.

FOR FURTHER STUDY

Dube, Musa W. *Postcolonial Feminist Interpretation of the Bible*. St. Louis: Chalice, 2000.

Schroer, Silva, and Sophia Biethenhard, eds. *Feminist Interpretation of the Bible and the Hermeneutics of Liberation*. Sheffield: Sheffield Academic Press, 2003.

Sakenfeld, Katharine Doob. *Just Wives? Stories of Power and Survival in the Old Testament and Today*. Louisville, KY: Westminster John Knox, 2003.

Weems, Renita J. *Just A Sister Away: Understanding the Timeless Connection between Women of Today and Women in the Bible*. Rev. ed. New York/Boston: Warner, 2005.

Williams, Delores S. "Womanist/Feminist Dialogue: Problems and Possibilities." *Journal of Feminist Studies in Religion* 9 (1993): 67–76.

6

Untying the Knot?

Masculinity, Violence, and the Creation-Fall Story of Genesis 2–4

DENNIS T. OLSON

A coach yells to his male athletes, "You guys are a bunch of sissies!" A drill sergeant growls at new recruits huffing and puffing their way through an obstacle course, "Let's see who the real men in this group are!" A father hugs his son and says, "I'm proud of the man you've become." A yoga instructor meditates as he sits quietly on a hillside. A husband serves his wife breakfast in bed. Two gay men stroll hand in hand down the street. What different images of men and masculinity coexist in our culture? Is there one normative image of what a man should be? Are men biologically determined to think, speak, and act in ways different from women? Can men change their behavior in positive directions, or will boys always be boys? To answer such questions we may consider the results of recent social-scientific research on masculinity. In addition, the images of masculinity and men in the ancient book of Genesis may well have something to contribute in dialogue with this recent research on masculinity.

I begin with a brief survey of scholarly conclusions drawn from research on masculinity from contemporary social sciences. I then turn to the biblical book of Genesis and give attention to the chapters in

It is a great pleasure and honor to dedicate this article to my dear colleague and friend, Kathie Sakenfeld. Kathie's wisdom, scholarship, kindness, good humor, and wonderful friendship over nearly two decades of teaching together on the same faculty have enriched my life and the lives of all her colleagues at Princeton Theological Seminary. Among many other talents, she is a model teacher, a scholarly mentor in matters of gender and the Bible, and a gifted administrator. I am deeply thankful for the quality of her presence and work among us.

Genesis that are most often raised in discussions of gender and the Bible, Gen 2–3 and the story of Adam and Eve in the garden of Eden. But I argue that in addition to these chapters, Gen 4 (Cain's violent murder of his brother Abel) ought to be included as an integral part of the story of human sin and disobedience. Reading all of Gen 2–4 together as one interrelated story has implications for understanding the male images and masculinities that we encounter in the book of Genesis.

THE KNOTTY COMPLEXITY OF BEING A MAN: MASCULINITIES ACROSS DIFFERENT CULTURES

Two men's movements in the United States and elsewhere in the 1990s focused attention on the identity of men and masculinity, along with their particular problems and struggles. One of the movements, called Promise Keepers, was rooted in conservative Christian evangelicalism. The other movement was grounded in pop psychology and a simplified view that men generally suffer from a deep psychological wound of being cut off from a singular and universal deep image of masculinity, believed to be common to all men of all cultures. Books like Robert Bly's *Iron John* and Sam Keen's *Fire in the Belly* argued that men needed to reestablish bonds with other men through initiation rituals, retreats, and primal reattachments to this ancient and universally shared sense of manhood.[1]

Such popular men's movements often cobbled together rituals ripped out of context from other non-Western cultures, or simply invented rituals or stories to support their singular view of what it is to be a "man." Although these movements did some good things in bringing men together and getting men in better touch with their emotional and spiritual lives, R. W. Connell, who is a social-scientific researcher on masculinity, points to an overall assumption shared by many in these movements:

> The biggest problem of all in the pop-psychology approach to masculinity is its nostalgia, a persistent belief that solutions to the problem of men can be found by looking backwards. Pop psychology idealizes a pre-industrial past (a mythical one, in fact), when men knew how to be men, women know how to be mothers, and there was no homosexuality or equal opportunity legislation to muddy the

---

1. Robert Bly, *Iron John: A Book about Men* (New York: Random House, 1990); Sam Keen, *Fire in the Belly: On Being a Man* (New York: Bantam, 1991).

waters. Hence the weird result that pop psychologists' solution to the current problems of alienation and misunderstanding between men and women is often to argue for *more* gender segregation.[2]

Connell points instead to a body of scholarly social-scientific research on masculinities that has been building up over the last two decades that involves close ethnographic studies of men and the social construction of masculinity in many different cultures and settings around the world. It points to the need for more gender integration, not gender segregation.[3]

Connell notes that research reveals that multiple masculinities exist among diverse cultures, nations, and even within single communities or settings. Rather than one universally shared notion of masculinity, we should speak in the plural of "masculinities." Competing notions of masculinity often coexist within one society or community, with some being dominant and others subordinated or marginalized. This is true also at the level of the individual, as a number of studies reveal that individual men often identify contradictory desires and conduct related to conflicting images of masculinity that they hold within themselves. Inclinations to be nurturing fathers or husbands coexist in males who are also involved in acts of aggression or violence against others. In addition, the ways men act and relate with others are defined and maintained not only by individuals but also collectively by various powerful cultural institutions. Schools, military organizations, or competitive sports are examples of institutions that sustain certain understandings of masculinity. Masculinities are produced through a complex human interplay of male bodies, social structures, and social interactions. Therefore, masculinities are often in tension, both within individuals and within groups and societies.

Moreover, the dynamics of masculinities change over time, both in terms of an individual's life cycle and in different historical and cultural contexts. Research suggests that individual men and a culture's views concerning masculinity are not eternally fixed or predetermined. Men and cultures can change, whether for better or worse. That possibility of change offers hope that the gender order of balance or imbalance between men and women need not always remain the same. The historically privileged status of men in positions of power and wealth in modern societies is not unalterable. Yet, Connell notes, "The gender

2. R. W. Connell, *The Men and the Boys* (Berkeley: University of California Press, 2000), 6.
3. Ibid., 9–14.

order does not blow away at a breath. Donaldson's (1998) study of ruling-class men shows a major reason why—the persistence of power and wealth, and the active defense of privilege."[4]

ANDROCENTRIC, FEMINIST, AND "MASCULIST" READINGS OF GENESIS 2–4

If we take these insights into masculinity and place them alongside an ancient biblical text like Gen 2–4, what results might emerge? These chapters, especially Gen 2–3, have long been a site of contention and debate in regard to issues of gender and power. Some androcentric, or male-centered, readings of Gen 2–3 see the woman, Eve, as an inferior "helper" to the man. Moreover, in these interpretations Eve is viewed as the one primarily responsible for the origins of human sin because she manipulates an innocent and unknowing Adam to eat the forbidden fruit (see, for example, the New Testament text of 1 Tim 2:12–14). In contrast, many feminist or egalitarian readings argue that Adam and Eve are portrayed in Gen 2–3 as equal partners. Calling the woman a "helper" in Hebrew does not connote inferiority, since the Bible often uses the same word, "helper," to describe God, who is inferior to no one (e.g., Gen 49:25; Deut 33:7, 26, 29; Ps 115:9). Adam and Eve, feminists argue, are equally responsible for the act of disobedience in Gen 3, and the prediction that the man "will rule over" the woman (Gen 3:16) is a reality that is contrary to God's will for the equal partnership between men and women that God initially created and desired in Gen 2.[5]

But what if we come to the early chapters of Genesis in light of some of the questions and insights about masculinity that emerge from contemporary social research on masculinities? Rather than using a feminist approach, what if we read the early chapters of Genesis through what one scholar has called a "masculist" approach to the Bible?

By masculist interpretation I mean something different from male interpretation, which is simply what everyone did until twenty years

---

4. Ibid., 14. The study to which Connell refers is M. Donaldson, "Growing Up Very Rich: The Masculinity of the Hegemonic," *Journal of Interdisciplinary Gender Studies* 3 (1998): 95–112.

5. A helpful collection of both ancient and modern interpretations of the relationship of Adam and Eve as related to gender relations (both hierarchical and more egalitarian) in Gen 1–3 is Kristen Kvam, Linda Schearing, and Valarie Ziegler, *Eve and Adam: Jewish, Christian, and Muslim Readings on Genesis and Gender* (Bloomington: Indiana University Press, 1999). See also Gary A. Anderson, "Is Eve the Problem?" in *Theological Exegesis: Essays in Honor of Brevard S. Childs* (ed. Christopher Seitz and Kathryn Greene-McCreight; Grand Rapids: Eerdmans, 1999), 96–123.

ago. That is interpretation undertaken mostly by males of texts which were written mostly by males, without the possibility occurring to anyone that this might limit or skew what the interpreter saw. Feminist interpretation drew attention to all that and asked what might become visible in texts when women read them as women rather than as honorary men. Masculist interpretation is parasitic on feminist interpretation; it is by definition post-feminist. It asks what might become visible in texts when they are read in conscious awareness of maleness.[6]

Such a reading would take account of past feminist readings and would be generally pro-feminist in its orientation. But a masculist reading would shift the lens from a focus on the feminine to a focus on the masculine. Just as there are many different masculinities and just as there are many different feminist approaches and methods to biblical texts, so a masculist perspective in interpreting the Bible may use any number of different methods and may be shaped by the various contexts in which the interpretation is done. My own inclinations are to use a hybrid of historical-critical and close literary methods, coupled with a confessional commitment to a theological interpretation of Scripture in light of the larger biblical context and story.[7] When interpreting the biblical text, I assume that a better reading than another is one that takes account of more of the data and details of the text that emerge from the use of these methods when compared to alternative readings of the same text.

Genesis 2: It's Not Good for the Man to Be Alone— A Biblical Creation and Love Story

Already in Gen 2, we see various dimensions of the masculinity attached to the man whom God creates. The man is nothing but dust until God creates him and breathes into him the breath of life (v. 7). His primary vocation is to serve God and God's creation as a caretaker of the garden God has planted—"to till it and keep it" (v. 15). At the same time, the

---

6. John Goldingay, "Hosea 1–3, Genesis 1–4, and Masculist Interpretation," *Horizons in Biblical Theology* 17 (1995): 37–44, here 37.

7. With regard to Gen 1–5, most historical-critical scholars would agree that chaps. 2–4 are the product of what is usually called the Yahwist (J) tradition, while chap. 1 and chap. 5 bracket this Yahwist tradition with texts from a later Priestly (P) tradition. For our purposes, it is enough to realize that Gen 2–4 fits together as a cohesive narrative and probably stems from one author or tradition.

human is invited and elevated to the status of a co-creator with God who participates in naming the animals (vv. 19–20). Naming is a significant act in the ancient biblical world. It involves shaping and defining the character of the one named. The man is also portrayed as a passive and sleeping object, as God anesthetizes the man and surgically creates the woman out of the man's rib (vv. 21–22). The man is incomplete without an intimate relationship with another human being ("it is not good that the *adam* should be alone," v. 18) and celebrates with enthusiasm an intimate bond with the woman ("This at last is bone of my bones and flesh of my flesh," v. 23). As the biblical scholar Phyllis Trible and others have demonstrated, the Hebrew phrase used to describe the woman, "a helper (Hebrew *ʿēzer*) as his partner (*kᵉnegdô*)" does not connote inferior status but rather "identity, mutuality, and equality."[8] Thus, already in Gen 2, we see hints of multiple and complex masculinities—humble, subservient, and passive, as well as lifted up, active, and empowered. The man is created to be not a Lone Ranger or a solitary Marlboro Man, but a human embedded in a community of intimate companionship. The relationship between the man and woman is one of mutual help and interdependence.

Genesis 3: It's Not Good for the Woman to Be Alone— The First Half of a Biblical Story of Human Sin

Genesis 3 marks one of the most drastic and unexplained disjunctions in the whole Bible. We suddenly shift from the divinely intended and positive portrait of the human couple that emerges from the end of Gen 2 to a dramatic shattering and distortion of what God hoped for in these relationships. Shame, suspicion, distrust, conflict, and oppressive hierarchy flow out as the negative consequences of the human disobedience of God's command in Gen 2:17 not to eat from the tree of the knowledge of good and evil. Every relationship becomes distorted or shattered in some way. The humans hide from God. Enmity and conflict between the human and the serpent (vv. 14–15) join with the resistance of the land to produce its bounty; this signifies a rupture and distortion in the previously intimate bond of man (*adam*) and land (*adamah*) (vv. 17–19; cf. Gen 2:7). Moreover, the previous relationship of mutuality and inter-

---

8. Phyllis Trible, *God and the Rhetoric of Sexuality* (Overtures to Biblical Theology; Minneapolis: Fortress, 1978), 90. Trible's close literary-feminist reading of Gen 2–3 remains a standard; see 72–143. See also Phyllis Trible, "Depatriarchalizing in Biblical Interpretation," *Journal of the American Academy of Religion* 41 (1973): 30–48.

dependence between the man and the woman is distorted and replaced by a relationship of one "ruling over" the other (v. 16).

We must leave many issues aside for the moment. Our focus here is on the portrait of masculinity. In this case, verses 1–7 opens with the woman moving forward into the spotlight while the man remains silently alongside her ("her [man], who was with her," v. 6). It is the woman and not the man who speaks throughout verses 1–7. In the next verse, verse 8 portrays both the man and woman together hiding from God, paired together in their shame. The next section in verses 9–19 depicts God speaking first to the man (vv. 9–12), then the woman (v. 13), then the serpent (vv. 14–15), then the woman again (v. 16), and finally the man (vv. 17–19). The reader notes a kind of movement back and forth in terms of narrative focus. Sometimes the woman is in the forefront, at other times the man. Just as in the previous scene (Gen 2), Gen 3 presents masculinity as at times involving taking initiative and primary responsibility, and at other times stepping back and allowing the woman or someone else to take the lead.

But something has gone wrong in Gen 3. Some interpreters argue that what has gone wrong is indicated in God's words to the man in verse 17: "Because you have listened to the voice of your wife." However, the reader must pay attention to the whole of what God says, "Because you have listened to the voice of your wife *and have eaten of the tree about which I commanded you, 'You shall not eat of it'*" (emphasis added). The problem is a human one, shared by both the woman and the man. They both know God's command. They both heard the serpent's speech. They both could have told the serpent that he is dead wrong and to get lost. They both, in the end, act in willful disobedience. They both suffer severe consequences to their action. The root problem is the act of disobedience itself. Saying "the devil made me do it," the serpent made me do it, or the woman made me do it—none of that exonerates or excuses the man from full responsibility for his act of disobedience.

So what does go wrong? One key omission in the man's action in Gen 3 is that the man does not join and support the woman as an active dialogue partner in resisting the verbal sparring with the serpent. He does not speak up. Just as in Gen 2 it was "not good that the *man* should be alone" and just as the *man* needed "a helper as his partner," so too it is not good that the *woman* is alone in speaking and debating with the serpent in Gen 3. Like the man in Gen 2, the *woman* needs a mutually supportive and active helper as her partner to speak up and join her in resisting the serpent. Instead, the man stands silently "with her" (Hebrew ʿimmāh). He does not give voice or resist the serpent when the woman is under verbal attack.

Of course, it is not that the man should have simply taken over the conversation with the serpent ("Step aside, woman, I will take it from here"). Rather, if we are to take our cues from the mutuality envisioned in Gen 2, the man should have joined together in a human community of dialogue with the woman in order more effectively to resist the temptation. And if the narrative roles had been reversed in Gen 3 and the serpent had been talking to the man alone, it would have been just as much an error for the woman to have remained silent and allowed the man to be alone in conversation with the serpent. Without the mutual hearing and speaking with one another together in a gender-integrated community, the man and the woman become susceptible to temptation, error, self-deception, and distorted judgment. There may well be appropriate and helpful occasions for men and women to gather separately for mutual support and community in men's and women's groups. But men and women also need regularly to be with each other in community in order to discover the fullness of what it means to be male and female as faithful people of God.

Genesis 4: It's Not Good for a Brother to Be Alone— The Second Half of a Biblical Story of Human Sin

In the history of biblical interpretation, the focus on the garden of Eden story in Gen 3 as the definitive account of human sin has at times obscured the intimate connection between the garden of Eden story in Gen 3 and Cain's murder of Abel in Gen 4. As in Gen 3, the narrative of Gen 4 portrays the back-and-forth character of alternating between the male and the female characters as the primary protagonists. The chapter begins with Eve conceiving and giving birth to a male child. Just as the man named the animals as an act of co-creation with God (Gen 2:20), so Eve as a woman now moves into the narrative spotlight and names her son in an act of co-creation with God. She relates the name "Cain" to the Hebrew word "to produce/create" (qanâ) and says, "I have produced/created a man with the help of YHWH" (v. 2). Eve then bears a second son, Abel. With that, mother Eve recedes from the narrative, and the focus falls on her two sons, Cain and Abel.

Cain and Abel are two males, related as brothers but divided by vocation. Abel is a keeper of sheep, and Cain is a tiller of the ground.

The vocational differences function in part as ciphers for the sociological realities of the ancient world, in which shepherds and farmers as social groups traditionally clashed with one another. But the focus of the narrative is on the conflict that emerges when God accepts Abel's sacrifice of animals but not Cain's sacrifice of grain. The reason that God accepts one but not the other is not stated, and the narrative does not seem interested in addressing this issue. The focus of the story lies elsewhere: how will Cain respond to God's preference for Abel's sacrifice over his own? If the narrative experience of his mother and father would be any guide, Cain ought to expect that he and his brother will alternate in being brought into the foreground at some times and pushed to the background at other times ("Why are you angry? . . . If you do well, will you not be accepted?" vv. 6–7). Cain's time for acceptance and lifting up will come with effort and resolve. "Sin is lurking at the door . . . but you must master it" (v. 7). As was true for his father Adam in Gen 3, primary responsibility for Cain's actions does not lie outside himself. Rather, the primary responsibility for wrestling with his inner anger lies in himself; it is for him to master. But like his father and his mother, Cain externalizes the problem. Instead of looking inward at himself, resolving his anger and seeking to master it, Cain directs his anger at his brother Abel and kills him. The shame, distrust, suspicion, conflict, and distortions in power relationships begun in Gen 3 now spill over into bodily violence and bloodshed in Gen 4.

In response to God's question to Cain concerning the whereabouts of his brother Abel, Cain replies, "I do not know; am I my brother's keeper?" (v. 9). Looking elsewhere in the Bible at who typically "keeps" or "protects" other humans, we discover that it is often God who is said to "keep" or "protect" human individuals or communities (e.g., Exod 23:20; Josh 24:17; Pss 41:2; 121:3–5). In other words, Cain is saying that if anything happens to his brother Abel, it is God's responsibility: "Am I my brother's keeper? No, God, you are. And if anything has happened to Abel, it's your fault, not mine." Again Cain refuses to accept his own responsibility. He is unwilling to step forward and admit his guilt. He blames Abel and kills him. He also blames God and verbally assaults God. In Cain's response we hear echoes of father Adam's words to God, "The woman whom *you* gave to be with me" (Gen 3:12, emphasis added).

"Eye for eye, tooth for tooth, . . . life for life" (Exod 21:23–25; Deut 19:21). This was the ancient biblical norm that functioned in the ancient world to put limits on revenge and retaliation. It served to limit the potentially endless and escalating spiral of violence between individuals, families, and communities. As applied to Cain, the law should have meant the death of Cain because of his taking the life of Abel: a life for a life. But just as God mitigated the death sentence for Adam and Eve after their disobedience ("for in the day that you eat of it you shall die," Gen 2:17), so God mitigates the death sentence on Cain and allows him to live, but as a wanderer and exile. God protects Cain against revenge killing by placing a mark of divine protection "so that no one who came upon him would kill him" (v. 15). Whoever tried to kill Cain would suffer a sevenfold vengeance. God's mercy and God's justice are held together in a balance of divine leniency and divine judgment.

Michael Fishbane, in his book *Text and Texture*, has summarized the significant parallels that interpreters have noticed between Gen 3 and Gen 4 that bind them together as a matched pair. For instance, sin is associated with a crafty coiled serpent and an animal lurking at the door (3:1–5; 4:7); the woman's "desire" for the man is paralleled by sin's "desire" for Cain (3:16; 4:7); YHWH twice asks of the humans "where?" (3:9; 4:9); and words and phrases such as "cursed is/from the ground" (3:17; 4:11), "east (of the garden) of Eden" (3:24; 4:16), "send forth/drive away" (3:23; 4:14), and "rule over/master" (3:16; 4:7) are repeated.[9]

These numerous verbal parallels, along with deeper structural resonances in theme and plot, suggest that Gen 3 and Gen 4 should be taken together as a joint exploration of the topic of human sin and obedience. Adam and Cain, the two central male figures in the two chapters, exhibit family resemblances between them as father and son. They both give in to temptation and sin. They both seek to shift their guilt and shame away to someone else (the woman Eve, Abel) and even to God (Adam: "the woman whom you gave to be with me;" Cain: "Am I my brother's keeper?"). The one major difference between Adam and Cain is the contrast between Adam's passivity and silence (Gen 3) and Cain's aggressive action in violently killing Abel (Gen 4).

The fact that Gen 4 is so closely tied to Gen 3 provides a strong objection against any androcentric reading of Gen 3 that assumes that the woman, and not the man, bears primary responsibility for human sin. Genesis 3 by itself portrays the man and woman as equally culpable. But the pairing of Gen 4 as necessary to understand Gen 3 means that the story in the end tilts even more toward a condemnation of specifically

9. Michael Fishbane, *Text and Texture: Close Readings of Selected Biblical Texts* (New York: Schocken, 1979), 26–27.

male sin and the violence that flows from it. This is highlighted even further in the latter section of Gen 4, in which a male descendant of Cain named Lamech boasts to his wives about having killed a man for wounding him (vv. 23–24). The tendency for violence and revenge to spiral out of control among males—whether in families, gangs, communities, or nations—finds its first biblical expression here as Lamech pledges, "If Cain is avenged sevenfold, truly Lamech seventy-sevenfold" (Gen 4:24; cf. v. 15). In the Bible the number seven symbolizes wholeness or completeness, and so to pledge revenge seventy-seven times is equivalent to claiming a right to unending and limitless retaliation in response to any attack. Such a claim leads down a slippery slope to abuse, torture, and recurring cycles of violence and counterviolence, with no end in sight.

This predominant (though not exclusive) link between masculinities and violence has marked human experience throughout its history with disastrous results, ranging from domestic violence to world wars. Connell devotes a chapter in his survey of studies in masculinity to the topic of the relationship between masculinity and violence. He writes:

> It is not hard to show that there is some connection between gender and violence. This is obvious in the institutions which are dedicated to the techniques of violence, state agencies of force. The twenty million members of the world's armed forces today are overwhelmingly men. . . . Men also dominate other branches of enforcement, both in the public sector as police officers and prison guards, and in the private sector as security agents. Further, the targets of enforcement are mainly men. For instance, in 1999 no less than 94 percent of the prisoners in Australian gaols were men; in the United States in 1996, 89 percent of prison inmates were men. . . . [In the United States,] private gun ownership runs four times as high among men as among women. . . . Official statistics for 1996 show men accounting for 90 percent of those arrested for murder and manslaughter (US Bureau of the Census 1998). . . . It is clear that many women are capable of violence (e.g., in punishing children). The weight of evidence, however, indicates that major domestic violence is overwhelmingly by husbands toward wives, in wealthy countries at least (Dobash et al. 1992). Rape is overwhelmingly by men on women. . . . Further, men predominate in warlike conduct in other spheres of life. Body-contact sports, such as boxing and football, involve ritualized combat and often physical injury.[10]

---

10. Connell, *Men and the Boys*, 213–14. The Dobash study that is cited is R. P. Dobash, E. R. Dobash, and M. Wilson, "The Myth of Sexual Symmetry in Marital Violence," *Social Problems* 39 (1992): 71–91.

There is a widespread belief that males are biologically determined to be more aggressive and violent than women, with the male hormone testosterone often cited as the major culprit. Connell argues, however, that this popular belief does not conform to cross-cultural studies which have shown that very different masculinities do not correlate either with testosterone levels or with any biologically determined and universal pattern of masculinity.[11] The implication is that there is hope and a possibility for changing what are predominantly male patterns of violence in many societies. Violence and aggression need not be inevitably associated with men's behavior and instincts in an essentialist way.

UNTYING THE KNOT? MEN, VIOLENCE, AND GLIMPSES OF HOPE IN GENESIS

Does the Bible confirm this possibility and hope of untying this tight knot between masculinity and violence? Already in Gen 4, we find some hints that men and violence need not remain forever linked. Descendants of Adam and Eve and of Cain and his wife become the first biblical generation to create a city, a community of men and women existing together in interdependence (Gen 4:17). The city bears the promise of enhanced life in community, even though humans later will build a city for the wrong purposes (see the tower of Babel story in Gen 11). The creation of a city is followed by the creation of civilization and culture, of music and the arts, of trades and tools, all with the potential to enhance life in community (Gen 4:19–22). Adam and Eve continue to bear children with the help and blessing of God. And just as Eve named Cain at the beginning of Gen 4, so she names her son Seth at the end of the chapter. Her presence and influence continues to be felt in the back-and-forth interdependence of men and women in the book of Genesis, even as patriarchy predominates. The final note of hope in Gen 4 is its last sentence: "At that time people began to invoke the name of YHWH" (Gen 4:26). This is the beginning of men and women coming together for worship, confession, forgiveness, reconciliation, praise, thanksgiving, lament, theological debate, and community action in order to resist the idolatries, temptations, and acts of violence that diminish life together with one another and with God.

---

11. Connell, *Men and the Boys*, 215. Connell cites studies by T. D. Kemper, *Social Structure and Testosterone* (New Brunswick, NJ: Rutgers University Press, 1990), and A. Cornwall and N. Lindisfarne, eds., *Dislocating Masculinity: Comparative Ethnographies* (London: Routledge, 1994), in support of his claim that masculinity is not biologically or inherently linked to violence and aggression.

Images of men killing and committing violence continue in the stories that follow (Gen 6:11; 14; 25:23; 27:41; 34; 37:20). Glimpses of alternative masculinities, however, also appear, offering hope of another and better way. The feuding twin brothers, Jacob and Esau, symbolize two nations in conflict, Israel and Edom (Gen 25:23). Esau plotted to kill his conniving brother Jacob years earlier. But when they come together after a long separation, there is forgiveness, gift giving, and reconciliation: "But Esau ran to meet him, and embraced him, and fell on his neck and kissed him, and they wept" (Gen 33:4).

Similarly, although Joseph was threatened years earlier with death and then sold into slavery in Egypt by his own brothers, Joseph forgives his brothers when they confess their misdeeds to him. Joseph assures them, "Even though you intended to do harm to me, God intended it for good, in order to preserve a numerous people, as he is doing today" (Gen 50:20). Unlike Cain, Joseph's faith in God and God's larger purposes help him to master the sin lurking at his door, the sinful urge to take revenge.

From beginning to end, the images of males in Genesis are marked by this continual seesaw between violence and reconciliation, community building and community disintegration, hope and despair, harsh realities and glimmers of a new and more peaceful way. Realism about the pervasiveness of male violence coexists with periodic moments of reconciliation and peace that point to the possibility that the complex knot that has bound masculinity and violence so tightly together from biblical times to our own day is not forever resistant to untying. The vision remains hopeful and powerful, even if partial and distant. In the words of a male prophet, someday . . .

> They shall beat their swords into plowshares.
>   and their spears into pruning hooks;
> nation shall not lift up sword against nation,
>   neither shall they learn war any more.
>
> (Isa 2:4)

FOR FURTHER STUDY

Anderson, Gary A. "Is Eve the Problem?" In *Theological Exegesis: Essays in Honor of Brevard S. Childs*, 96–123. Edited by Christopher Seitz and Kathryn Greene-McCreight. Grand Rapids: Eerdmans, 1999.

Connell, R. W. *The Men and the Boys*. Berkeley: University of California Press, 2000.

Goldingay, John. "Hosea 1–3, Genesis 1–4, and Masculist Interpretation." *Horizons in Biblical Theology* 17 (1995): 37–44.

Gunn, David, and Danna Nolan Fewell. "Varieties of Interpretation: Genesis 4 through 2000 Years." In *Narrative in the Hebrew Bible*, 12–33. Oxford: Oxford University Press, 1993.

Kvam, Kristen, Linda Schearing, and Valarie Ziegler. *Eve and Adam: Jewish, Christian, and Muslim Readings on Genesis and Gender.* Bloomington: Indiana University Press, 1999.

PART TWO

Texts

7

Ruth the Moabite

Identity, Kinship, and Otherness

EUNNY P. LEE

Old Testament reflections on Israel's relationship with the nations are marked by a tension between inclusionary and exclusionary attitudes toward the foreigner. Israel moved between two opposing tendencies: relating to the nations in hospitality or radically separating itself from the nations in xenophobia, particularly when its own self-identity was embattled. The book of Ruth is often hailed as a premier model of the former. A Moabite woman journeys to Israel. She and a prominent man of Bethlehem take steps to meet one another, overcoming the barriers posed by their ethnic and class differences. Intermarriage is not excoriated but celebrated. Katharine Doob Sakenfeld has elegantly described the book's portrait of community as a microcosm of "the peaceable kingdom" envisioned in the prophetic tradition. "It is a human community in which the marginalized person has dared to insist upon full participation, in which the one in the center has reached out beyond societal norms to include the marginalized."[1] Native and foreigner, young and old, men and women—all receive the continuing sustenance and respect basic to a just community.

Indeed, the inclusion of the marginalized is an important theme of the book. But Ruth's journey to full inclusion is not an easy or straightforward one. Even in this most hospitable of tales, her efforts to make

It is a pleasure and honor to present this essay to Kathie Sakenfeld—teacher, colleague, and friend—whose life and work have modeled for me the meaning of hospitality toward the other.
1. Katharine Doob Sakenfeld, *Ruth* (Interpretation; Louisville, KY: John Knox, 1999), 10.

a home in her adopted land are impeded by the resistance and indecision of the people of Bethlehem. The ambivalence concerning Ruth is signaled by two features of the narrative. The first is a recurring emphasis on her Moabite ethnicity (1:22; 2:2, 6, 21; 4:5, 10). The repetition itself is suggestive, but the strategic manner in which the narrative registers Ruth's ethnicity in the story underscores the tension between kinship and otherness. Second, Ruth's identity is repeatedly contested and interrogated by other characters in the narrative (2:5; 3:9, 16; cf. 1:19), opening up the possibility of a dialogical reconstruction of identity—both of Ruth and those who would engage her. In the end, both the foreigner and her Israelite kin undergo profound changes in their self-understanding. The story's depiction of the "peaceable community" thus relies on and, at the same time, subverts its constructions of identity, kinship, and otherness.

MOAB, THE FAMILIAR OTHER

For most commentators, the portrayal of the relationship between Israelites and Moabites in the book of Ruth is a welcome counterpoint to the largely negative picture found elsewhere in the Old Testament. Indeed, the most memorable narratives concerning Moab are marked by scandal and animosity. The first mention of Moab appears in Gen 19:30–38, an unflattering account that traces the nation's origins to incest and duplicity. A deep-seated antipathy is further reflected in several texts that recount Israel's journey from Egypt to the promised land. King Balak of Moab hires Balaam to put a curse on the Israelites and is foiled only by divine intervention (Num 22–24). As the Israelites remain encamped in Moab, their men consort with Moabite women, leading the people to religious apostasy (Num 25:1–3; cf. 1 Kgs 11:1, 7, 33). Deuteronomy 23:3–6 strictly forbids Moabites from entering Israel's religious assembly because of this ancient hostility, and this prohibition later provides the rationale for the forced dissolution of foreign marriages in Ezra and Nehemiah.

But the Old Testament is not univocal in its treatment of Moabites. Multiple perspectives are present, pointing to shifting relations between the neighboring peoples and the ambiguous place that Moab occupies in Israel's genealogical imagination. Despite the pejorative tone of the story in Gen 19, Moabites are nevertheless regarded as relatives. The tradition preserved in Deut 2:1–25 traces a peaceful procession through the territories of the Edomites, Moabites, and Ammonites, and acknowledges that these kindred peoples also were recipients of a "promised land" (see 2:9). The biblical evidence suggests that there was continuous exchange between the two peoples, including intermarriage (cf. 1 Chr 4:22; 8:8–10). Traditions that report religious apostasy at Beth-Peor may reflect the ongoing experiences of Israelites who settled down among Moabites, intermarried with non-Israelites, and worshiped local deities. There would also have been counter-efforts to preserve ethnic and religious distinctiveness.[2] Thus Moab represents the familiar "other." And often in the Old Testament, danger lies not in the foreign "other" but in the alterity of the familiar and the threat of assimilation.[3]

This ambiguity concerning Moab is evident also in the book of Ruth. The tension between kinship and ethnic difference is brought to special focus in the character of Ruth and her hybrid identity. She is a Moabite woman, but she is also insistent on identifying herself with her Israelite mother-in-law. This devotion causes her to undergo a radical reorientation, yielding the odd notion of a Moabite who returns to Bethlehem from Moab (1:22; 2:6; cf. 4:3). The duality is fraught with conflict for Ruth and for the people of Bethlehem. She is ever a reminder that social, cultural, and ethnic boundaries are not altogether impermeable. She represents a destabilizing force, whose presence in the Israelite town undermines rigid constructions of identity and otherness.[4]

The theme of ethnic difference and the challenge it poses to kinship is foregrounded immediately in the opening verse: "A certain man of Bethlehem in Judah went to sojourn in the territory of Moab, he and his wife and two sons." Only after this initial setup are the names of the man and his family given, as if their individual identities are ancillary to their ethnic identity. Indeed, the latter is reiterated in the next verse: "[They were] Ephrathites from Bethlehem in Judah." Similarly, when Ruth and Orpah are introduced, it is first as Moabites and then by name. Famine leads to migration and the crossing of geographic and social boundaries. Ephrathite men marry Moabite women, yielding a hybrid family.

---

2. J. Maxwell Miller, "Moab and the Moabites," in *Studies in the Mesha Inscription and Moab* (ed. Andrew Dearman; Atlanta: Scholars, 1989), 18–19.

3. See Bruce Routledge, *Moab in the Iron Age: Hegemony, Polity, Archaeology* (Philadelphia: University of Pennsylvania Press, 2004), 42; Frank Crüsemann, "Human Solidarity and Ethnic Identity: Israel's Self-Definition in the Genealogical System of Genesis," in *Ethnicity and the Bible* (ed. Mark G. Brett; Leiden/New York/Cologne: Brill, 1996), 70–71.

4. For a discussion of the destabilizing force of the hybrid in postcolonial discourse, see Homi K. Bhabha, *The Location of Culture* (London: Routledge, 1994).

From this prologue Ruth and Naomi will emerge as characters in their own right, but in ways that highlight the tension between ethnicity and familiality. The story begins in earnest with Naomi's journey homeward (1:6–18). Initially her Moabite daughters-in-law travel with her. But in the absence of the men who had joined them together as family, the women must decide whether to continue their lives together or return to their respective families of origin. On the road between Moab and Judah, the women engage in a heated negotiation of kinship ties. Identities and relationships must be constructed anew in this in-between space. While the narrative frame emphasizes the opposing destinations of Moab and Judah (1:6, 19, 22), the women's speech is replete with kinship terminology: mother's house (v. 8), husband's house (v. 9), daughters (v. 11), sons (vv. 11–12), husbands (vv. 11–12), sister-in-law (v. 15). There are also references to two "peoples" ("your people," vv. 10, 16; "her people," v. 15; "my people," v. 16). Familial ties and ethnic difference are in tension, raising the question of which will prevail.[5]

Despite Ruth's radical identification with her Israelite mother-in-law (1:16), she remains "Ruth the Moabite" throughout most of the narrative. According to Adele Berlin, the title serves as an "objective token of identification," since it is natural for Ruth to bear this label among the natives of Bethlehem. She notes, however, that when the narrator names Ruth as such in the context of private conversations between Ruth and Naomi (2:2, 21), it points to an underlying opposition in the story between kinship and otherness.[6] This opposition seems all the more apparent when one considers that the narrator slips in the title precisely at those junctures when kinship ties are being emphasized. In 2:2, the narrator refers to Ruth as "Ruth the Moabite" immediately after reporting that Naomi has "a kinsman on her husband's side . . . of the family of Elimelech" (2:1). The next occurrence follows immediately after Naomi discloses to Ruth that Boaz is indeed a relative and kinsman-redeemer (2:20–21). In fact, one may argue against Berlin that the title is never used as an "objective token of identification." Ruth is never simply "the Moabite." Whenever the narrative refers to her by that label, it goes on to complicate the identification by asserting her familial ties with Naomi. She is "Ruth the Moabite, her daughter-in-law" (1:22; cf. 2:6) or "Ruth the Moabite, the widow of Mahlon" (4:10; cf. 4:5). The use of the title thus reflects the uneasy ambivalence

---

5. Naomi ironically exploits the power of kinship ties in an attempt to sever the ties between her and her Moabite daughters-in-law. Similarly, Phyllis Trible, *God and the Rhetoric of Sexuality* (Philadelphia: Fortress, 1978), 169.

6. Adele Berlin, *Poetics and Interpretation of Biblical Narrative* (Winona Lake, IN: Eisenbrauns, 1994), 88.

of the Bethlehem community toward this foreigner-kinswoman. It calls attention to Ruth's hybridity, and to the attendant tension between her foreignness and familiality.

INTERROGATION OF IDENTITY

A crucial feature of human life is its fundamentally dialogical character. It is universally recognized—by developmental psychologists, social scientists, and philosophers alike—that identity is dialogically formed. People define their identity always in dialogue with, and sometimes in struggle against, the things that others see in them. They become full human agents, capable of understanding and defining themselves, through the acquisition of rich languages of expression. Related to this idea is the importance of recognition in identity formation. The notion that nonrecognition or misrecognition may inflict harm (leading to self-depreciation and even self-hatred) has animated the debate in multiculturalism and identity politics.[7] One ought not impose modern categories of multiculturalism onto this ancient story, but the relationship between recognition and identity is raised by the narrative itself, as we see below.

The book of Ruth is composed largely of dialogues,[8] and these dialogues become an ideal vehicle for the deconstruction and reconstruction of identity and otherness. As discussed above, the first extended exchange occurs in 1:6–18, where Ruth's attempts to identify herself with Naomi are strenuously contested. Naomi acquiesces at the end of that initial dialogue, but once in Bethlehem, the resistance and negotiation resume. Three times in the book there is an explicit interrogation of Ruth's identity. At first glance, these questions may seem mundane and matter of course to the story. But there is more to the questions than the obvious. The repeated pressing of Ruth's identity is indicative of the indecision of the Israelite community concerning the Moabite woman. It is notable, moreover, that these questions are posed by the two characters who are most closely connected to her. Boaz and Naomi, relatives of Ruth by marriage, are most invested in and destabilized by the identity of this "familiar other." But the questions also signal the potential for mutual transformation. Whether intended or not, they invite a dialogical reconstruction of identity to take place.

7. See, for example, Charles Taylor, "The Politics of Recognition," in *Multiculturalism: Examining the Politics of Recognition* (ed. Amy Gutmann; Princeton, NJ: Princeton University Press, 1994), 25–74.

8. Fifty-six of its eighty-five verses are taken up in dialogue.

"Is this Naomi?" (1:19)

Before considering each of these encounters in turn, there is another "interrogation" of identity—and a glaring lack thereof—that merits attention. When Ruth and Naomi first appear together in Bethlehem, the women of the town greet them with the exclamation "Is this Naomi?" (1:19). The words communicate a mixture of delight and dismay. After more than ten years of living in a foreign land, Naomi is almost unrecognizable. Moreover, she is accompanied not by her menfolk but by an unknown woman. The women's query is thus provoked, in part, by Ruth's presence with Naomi. The Moabite Ruth signifies Naomi's changed circumstances, her estrangement from Israel. Naomi is not the same woman who left Bethlehem with her family fully intact; she is bereaved, widowed, uprooted from her land.[9] Indeed, Naomi disavows her former identity: she is no longer Naomi ("pleasant") but Mara ("bitter"). And in her bitterness, she declares herself to be utterly "empty," even with her devoted companion resolutely standing beside her. This reticence concerning Ruth is mirrored in Naomi's countrywomen, who neither speak to nor inquire about the Moabite woman. Hence, Ruth's initial reception in Bethlehem is marked by nonrecognition. No one—including her mother-in-law—acknowledges her.

"To whom does this woman belong?" (2:5)

Despite this initial silence, people soon begin to talk about Ruth. The first character to inquire explicitly about her is Boaz. When he notices the stranger gleaning in his field, he immediately questions the overseer of his reapers: "To whom does this young woman belong?" (2:5). The question as Boaz formulates it is indicative of unequal power relations (cf. Gen 32:18; 1 Sam 30:13, where a similar question is addressed to male household servants), but it is also intended to probe the woman's circumstances and her possible connections to the community. Whose servant is she? To what people does she belong? Of what family is she—whose wife or whose daughter? From the overseer's point of view, the most significant aspect of her identity is her foreignness: "she is a Moabite woman" (2:6). But she is not entirely a stranger, because he

---

9. Ilana Pardes observes astutely that the sudden emergence of her plot of land in 4:3 signals that Naomi has finally found her way back home. Its initial absence coincides with her sense of homelessness (*Countertraditions in the Bible: A Feminist Approach* [Cambridge, MA: Harvard University Press, 1992], 114–15).

immediately qualifies that she is "the one who returned with Naomi from the territory of Moab." The narrator has already informed us of Boaz's familial ties with Naomi; indeed, this aspect of his identity was emphasized even before his arrival on the scene (2:1, 3). Hence, it is not entirely surprising that Boaz next speaks to Ruth directly, addressing her as "my daughter," after the fashion of Naomi. But his actions toward her are markedly different from those of Naomi. His first words to her ("do not go . . . do not leave," 2:8) seem to reverse Naomi's first words to Ruth in the book ("go, turn back," 1:8).[10] He urges her to "stay close" (2:8, 21, 23; cf. 1:14) to his servants. If Naomi was intent on distancing herself from Moab and Ruth, Boaz draws her near with his solicitous concern.

Moreover, his addressing her gives her the opportunity to speak for herself. Like Boaz's worker, Ruth initially describes herself as a foreigner. But this self-designation is embedded in a question of her own: "Why have I found favor in your eyes that you should acknowledge me (*lĕ-hakkîrēnî*), though I am a foreigner (*nokriyyâ*)?" (2:10). The wordplay exploits the Hebrew verb *nākar* used in both phrases, which may mean either "to treat/act as a stranger" or "to recognize/acknowledge."[11] Ruth's carefully crafted question subtly confronts Boaz with a moral choice: will he regard her as a stranger or as one of his own? What began as an interrogation of Ruth's identity thus becomes a moment of critical self-evaluation for Boaz. If her words constitute a challenge to Boaz, her humble gesture—falling on her face before him—evokes his compassion (2:10). He is a wealthy landowner, and she is a destitute foreigner, with no power or privilege on her side. Her subtle rhetoric and sub-servient posture remind him, gently yet forcefully, that she is utterly dependent on those who would favorably take notice (*nākar*) of her.

Boaz replies that he has good reason to treat her with kindness. He is fully aware of her willingness to sever all of her previous ties for the sake of her mother-in-law (2:11). The heaping up of kinship terms ("your husband," "your father," "your mother," "your native land") poignantly captures the extent of Ruth's loss. Indeed, Boaz's account of Ruth's loyalty recalls what transpired on the road between Moab and Judah. Whereas Naomi had responded to Ruth with silence, now one of Naomi's relatives recognizes and fully appreciates the extent of her

---

10. Compare also Naomi's terse and perhaps detached "go, my daughter" at the beginning of this episode (2:3).

11. The noun "stranger" (*nokriyyâ*) and the verb "to recognize/acknowledge" (*nākar*, in the causative mode) likely derive from the same Hebrew root word, reflecting a contrary semantic development in the varied treatments of the strange and the extraordinary.

sacrifice. It also communicates Boaz's sympathy for Ruth's vulnerable position as an outsider with no legal, social, or emotional ties to the community (except to another widow). Deeply touched and emboldened by his kindness, Ruth dares to identify herself as "your maidservant" (*šipḥōtêkā*), a servant within the protective circle of an Israelite household, albeit on the lowest level of inclusion (2:13). She quickly retracts even this deferential term lest she has overstepped her bounds, but she has begun to imagine herself in a category other than "foreigner."

Boaz responds admirably to Ruth's implicit challenge. He invites her to the "table" at mealtime and serves her himself; he extends her gleaning privileges far beyond the norm; he protects her from the potential contempt of the other workers (2:14–16). Moreover, this hospitality is practiced in a public setting, where he, as the owner of the field, exercises considerable influence and authority. His words and actions thus function as an important moral witness to his community. Nevertheless, there is one thing that Boaz fails to do. His extraordinary hospitality notwithstanding, he refrains from identifying himself as Naomi's relative. The narrator has disclosed—indeed, emphasized—this aspect of Boaz's identity to the reader, but Boaz does not divulge it to Ruth. She will have to wait until Naomi informs her of the full significance of Boaz's kindness. Perhaps the delay is intended to build suspense and heighten delight when a newly animated Naomi excitedly tells Ruth that Boaz is "our relative . . . one of our redeemers" (2:20). But perhaps it is also indicative of a deep-seated ambivalence in Boaz. The power of human constructions of difference may exert itself even on this generous man. When Ruth "happens upon" the portion of the field that belongs to Naomi's kinsman (2:3) and he "recognizes" her (2:10), it all seems very promising. Yet, as the day comes to an end, he refrains—for whatever reason—from claiming the Moabite woman as kin. Instead, he lets her self-definition as "stranger" and "your maidservant, though not one of your maidservants" stand.

"Who are you?" (3:9)

Boaz's inaction continues throughout the harvest season—until another encounter with Ruth wrenches him from his slumber (quite literally!). When the man fails to make a move, Naomi decides that she must take initiative in order to secure a home for Ruth and devises a risky plan to send Ruth to Boaz while he sleeps at the threshing floor. The atmosphere is heavy with secrecy, ambiguity, and danger. It is night, with identities hidden behind the veil of darkness. But the night becomes a moment of uncovering and disclosure (3:4, 7; cf. 4:4). The scene repeatedly employs words related to "knowing/not knowing" and "recognizing/not recognizing" (*yādaʿ, nākar;* 3:2, 3, 4, 11, 14, 18) to suggest the interplay between concealment and disclosure. Ruth especially must not let herself be known until the critical moment of revelation (3:3).

She moves stealthily toward an unsuspecting Boaz and "uncovers" him. This moment is radically destabilizing for Boaz. The verb used to describe his reaction (*ḥārad,* "to tremble" or "to startle") often communicates fear and alarm (e.g., 1 Sam 14:15; Isa 19:16; Ezek 32:10), leading some commentators to speculate that Boaz's trembling is occasioned by the fear of female night-demons who were believed to attack sleeping men.[12] When Boaz startles awake to discover a mysterious figure lying at his feet, he demands that the intruder identify herself. In a moment of high drama, he poses the question directly and urgently: "Who are you?" The woman gives a decisive answer: "I am Ruth, your handmaid" (3:9). Not only does she identify herself by name—the first time anyone has done so in the story—she also boldly proposes marriage, using the very language that Boaz invoked earlier to bless her (*kānāp,* "cloak" or "wing"; 3:9; cf. 2:12).[13]

The episode is reminiscent of other "bride in the night" stories in the Old Testament, especially that of Tamar (Gen 38:1–30) and Leah and Rachel (Gen 29:21–30).[14] These narratives depict women who must overcome socially constructed obstacles in order to secure a future for themselves. They do so through an ethics of deception, relying upon the power of unanticipated disclosure. Ruth's own "repair in the night" suggests that she and Boaz too must overcome significant barriers. Perhaps a barrier is the personal insecurity of a bungling old man before an attractive younger woman (cf. 3:10). Or perhaps a barrier is an abiding ambivalence about her Moabite ethnicity. Notably, this scene occurs in

12. Jack M. Sasson, *Ruth: A New Translation with a Philological Commentary and a Formalist-Folklorist Interpretation* (Sheffield: Sheffield Academic Press, 1989), 74–78; Erich Zenger, *Das Buch Ruth* (Zurich: Theologischer Verlag, 1992), 70–71.

13. The word for "handmaid" that Ruth uses here (ʾāmâ) is different from the one in 2:13 (šipḥâ). Since the two are used almost synonymously elsewhere in the Old Testament, too much should not be made of the distinction, but it is possible that the term ʾāmâ indicates a social rank higher than that of šipḥâ, suggesting a servant who could aspire to marriage with her master. See the discussion in Edward F. Campbell, *Ruth: A New Translation with Introduction, Notes, and Commentary* (Garden City, NY: Doubleday, 1975), 101. The possibility, in this context, is heightened by Ruth's subsequent words. Her request, "spread your cloak over your handmaid," is an idiom for espousal (cf. Ezek 16:8; Deut 22:30 [Heb 23:1]; 27:20).

14. See especially Ellen van Wolde, "Texts in Dialogue with Texts: Intertextuality in the Ruth and Tamar Narratives," *Biblical Interpretation* 5 (1997): 1–28; Pardes, *Countertraditions in the Bible,* 98–117.

the only chapter of the book that does not identify Ruth as a Moabite. It is as if the darkness allows her ethnic identity to be concealed so that other dimensions of her character may emerge more fully. Indeed, the encounter leads Boaz to acknowledge her as "a woman of worth" (ʾēšet ḥayil, 3:11). As the narrative earlier referred to him with the parallel designation "a man of worth (ʾîš gibbôr ḥayil, 2:1), Ruth is presented as equal to Boaz in strength of character. Yet the moment discloses not only of Ruth's identity but also Boaz's identity. As a basis for her actions, Ruth confronts Boaz with a neglected dimension of his own identity: "You are a kinsman-redeemer." Her bold initiative and direct confrontation shocks him into recognition, forcing upon him a new apprehension of who she is and who he is in relationship to her. The comparison with Tamar and Judah (see Gen 38:24–26) suggests that this is indeed an epiphany for Boaz. She wrenches Boaz out of his ethnocentricity, his insecurity, his passivity, and dramatically alters his self-understanding.

"Who are you, my daughter?" (3:16)

The final interrogation of Ruth's identity comes from her companion of over ten years. The question is somewhat odd. Simple identification is obviously not the issue, since Naomi addresses the question to "my daughter."[15] Most translations therefore interpret the interrogative pronoun as an "accusative of condition," yielding "How is it with you?" or the like.[16] This is most likely the correct sense of the question. Anxious about what may or may not have transpired in the night, Naomi inquires about Ruth's state of being. How did she fare with Boaz? Did anything happen that may have altered her identity?

The grammatical explanation, however, must not obscure the rhetorical force of Naomi's query. Note that Naomi's words echo Boaz's question in 3:9. The tone of uncertainty and fear from the previous scene is thus mirrored in Naomi's speech. On one level, Naomi is genuinely anxious about Ruth's safety, especially after having sent her on the questionable assignment. On another level, however, Naomi's ques-

---

15. The proposal that Naomi is only verifying Ruth's identity, as in "Is that you, my daughter?" is unlikely, given Ruth's subsequent reply.

16. Wilhelm Rudolph, *Das Buch Ruth, Das Hohe Lied, Die Klagelieder* (Gütersloh: Mohn, 1962), 57. See the similar usage of the interrogative pronoun *mî* in Amos 7:2, 5 (*mî yāqûm yaʿăqōb*, "How can Jacob stand?") and Isa 51:19 (*mî ʾănaḥămēk*, "how shall I comfort you?").

tion may reflect an anxiety about her own well-being. Security for Ruth—even if achieved through marriage to Boaz—does not necessarily mean security for herself. The awkward tension in Naomi's question (she calls Ruth "daughter," but still needs to ask who she is) suggests that the older woman is not entirely free of her misgivings about Ruth's relationship to her.

The question of who Ruth is for Naomi will not be fully answered for Naomi until the story's end, when the women of Bethlehem declare that "your daughter-in-law who loves you . . . is more to you than seven sons" (4:15). For now, Ruth's response seems intended to address Naomi's fears. The night's events are summarized in a few words. The narrative then quickly shifts attention to Boaz's gift of grain. As Ruth presents it to Naomi, she elaborates: "For he said, 'Do not go back to your mother-in-law empty-handed'" (3:17). Boaz's concern for Naomi was not made so explicit in the scene at the threshing floor, and it is impossible to determine if the man actually spoke these words. Whether he did or not is less important than the care that Ruth exercises to reassure Naomi that she too is included in Boaz's care. Also significant is the literary impact of placing these words in the mouth of Ruth. The language of "empty-handed" (*rêqām*) recalls Naomi's lament in 1:21 that YHWH had brought her back "empty" (*rêqām*) from Moab. Then, Ruth remained silent and unacknowledged. Now, in response to that earlier judgment, the narrative allows Ruth to articulate her own worth to Naomi. It highlights the irony that Naomi's emptiness has been overturned through the agency of the Moabite woman whom she had so easily dismissed. In these final words spoken by the two women, Ruth is given voice to claim the importance of her role in Naomi's restoration.

With the marriage and blessing in the denouement of the story, Ruth appears to be fully integrated into her adopted community. When she is named for the last time, she is simply "Ruth" (4:13). The story that belabored her ethnic identity does so no longer. She is now the wife of a prominent Israelite citizen; she is likened to the matriarchs of Israel. One commentator concludes, "She is now an Israelite woman." She blends in unnoticeably, and there is no greater assurance for a foreigner.[17] But the silence concerning Ruth's Moabite origins also raises the question: Does her inclusion come at the expense of a vital element

---

17. Ellen Davis, *Who Are You, My Daughter? Reading Ruth through Image and Text* (Louisville, KY: Westminster John Knox, 2003), 117.

of her identity? Perhaps the ambivalence about Ruth can be settled only by erasing her foreignness. Indeed, she seems almost absent when Naomi takes Ruth's child into her bosom and the women of Bethlehem declare that a son has been born to the elderly woman. The image may be troubling, especially to modern readers, but it is tempered by two considerations. First, one must keep in mind that the story is just as much about Naomi's reintegration into the community as it is about Ruth's inclusion. Indeed, one may argue that the book is more Naomi's story than Ruth's story.[18] The focus on Naomi's restoration at the end is intended to bring to resolution the problem of her loss at the start. Second, despite the final silence concerning Ruth the Moabite, her otherness is not so easily expunged; it has already been deeply inscribed in the story. Indeed, the narrative's earlier propensity to name her as "Ruth the Moabite" preserves and honors that aspect of her identity, even as it signals the Israelite ambivalence toward it. Ruth's otherness, too, has been incorporated into Israel, generating an ongoing self-interrogation and transformation on the part of Israel.[19] The self-interrogation becomes all the more pressing, because the genealogy concluding the book implies her pride of place in the lineage of Israel's ideal king.[20] In the words of Julia Kristeva, "If David is *also* Ruth, if the sovereign is *also* a Moabite, peace of mind will never be his lot, but a constant quest for welcoming and going beyond the other in himself."[21]

The story of Ruth the Moabite challenges our narrow exclusivism, a perennial issue in human history. Perhaps it is all the more important for us to attend to this book in an age when the global community is so deeply riven with difference. Even societies that pride themselves for their multiculturalism find that identity politics often fail to ensure the recognition and dignity for all citizens. The emphasis on narrow special interests may in fact lead to division rather than mutuality and the promotion of the common good. Ruth teaches both the moral significance of difference and the possibility of kinship with the "other." It broadens our understanding of who is neighbor, who is family, who is welcome in our midst.

18. Berlin, *Poetics and Interpretation of Biblical Narrative*, 83–84; Frederic W. Bush, *Ruth/Esther* (Word Biblical Commentary 9; Dallas: Word, 1996), 49; Jacqueline E. Lapsley, *Whispering the Word: Hearing Women's Stories in the Old Testament* (Louisville, KY: Westminster John Knox, 2005), 89–108.

19. See Taylor, "The Politics of Recognition," in which he argues that any attempt to account for and understand another culture inevitably leads to a transformed self-understanding.

20. Indeed, in early Jewish interpretation of the book, David's Moabite origins posed a scandal that had to be addressed exegetically and theologically. Jacob Neusner argues that this is the primary purpose of *Ruth Rabbah* in *The Mother of the Messiah in Judaism: The Book of Ruth* (Valley Forge, PA: Trinity Press International, 1993).

21. Julia Kristeva, *Strangers to Ourselves* (trans. Leon S. Roudiez; New York: Columbia University Press), 75–76.

FOR FURTHER STUDY

Honig, Bonnie. "Ruth, the Model Emigrée: Mourning and the Symbolic Politics of Immigration." In *Ruth and Esther: A Feminist Companion to the Bible (Second Series)*, ed. Athalya Brenner, 50–74. Sheffield: Sheffield Academic Press, 1999.

Kwok Pui-lan. "Finding Ruth a Home: Gender, Sexuality, and the Politics of Otherness." Chap. 4 in *Postcolonial Imagination and Feminist Theology.* Louisville, KY: Westminster John Knox, 2005.

Sakenfeld, Katharine Doob. *Ruth.* Interpretation. Louisville, KY: John Knox, 1999.

Trible, Phyllis. "A Human Comedy." Chap. 6 in *God and the Rhetoric of Sexuality.* Overtures to Biblical Theology. Philadelphia: Fortress, 1978.

8

Seeing the Older Woman

Naomi in High Definition

JACQUELINE LAPSLEY

I can recall only one of the half-dozen or so essay questions I answered when I was applying to colleges many years ago. At the top of the page the application asked for extended reflection on the question, "What must we unlearn?" There may have been a few more words in the question, but that was basically it. I remember my seventeen-year-old self reacting initially with puzzlement to this query, perched at the top of the blanket of white space that seemed to go on forever on the blank page below. I had spent most of my years on the planet learning, so the idea that somehow some of that learning needed to be undone was both novel and disturbing. Yet the more I have reflected on the question since that time, the more I realize that there is much in the world to unlearn.

Thinking about the world through a feminist lens can be a disorienting experience at first. It is disorienting because one of the main things feminist hermeneutics asks of people is to make visible what the dominant hermeneutic—that is, the way most of us have learned to read—has made invisible. A simple example from the visual arts might help to illustrate what I mean. When one looks at the famous illustration below, one sees an older woman if the mind arranges the features in one way, but a younger woman if the mind arranges the features in a different way. The dominant culture in which most of us have been formed has trained us to see the world in a particular way, unconsciously eliminating those features that do not fit that picture. Obviously, our perception of reality is much more complex than deciding

whether ink on a page yields one picture (the older woman) or another (a younger woman). But the principle is similar. This is how ideology works, by training us to see, quite unconsciously, what fits in with its own values and interests, and by training us not to see, or oftentimes to reframe, what does not fit those values and interests.

We are trained to see and read and interpret our world in certain ways, and some of these ways of seeing are intimately bound up with how power operates in our society. This combination of ways of seeing and power is sometimes called "ideology" by literary and cultural critics. Terry Eagleton, a noted literary critic, defines ideology as "those modes of feeling, valuing, perceiving and believing which have some kind of relation to the maintenance and reproduction of social power."[1] Such "modes of feeling, valuing, perceiving," and so on, are usually almost entirely unconscious, just as we are not initially aware that we screen out one picture in order to see another—that the picture of the older woman must be rendered invisible for the picture of the younger woman to appear, and vice versa. In order to "see" the other picture, we have to bring to consciousness the act of seeing the picture, and therefore to reflect explicitly on what it means to see and interpret. We have to "reframe" what we are seeing so that we see it in a new way.

An example from English literary criticism may illumine the unconsciousness of dominant ways of interpreting, and the necessity of stepping back to ask what else is present in the picture that might not be immediately obvious. Thomas Hardy's novel *The Mayor of Casterbridge* begins with the drunk Michael Henchard selling his wife and infant daughter at a country fair. The well-known and respected political, social, and literary critic Irving Howe, in his 1967 work on Hardy, lauds this scene for its power and brilliance:

> To shake loose from one's wife; to discard that drooping rag of a woman, with her mute complaints and maddening passivity; to escape not by a slinking abandonment but through the public sale of her body to a stranger . . . and thus to wrest, through sheer amoral willfulness, a second chance out of life—it is with this stroke, so insidiously attractive to male fantasy, that *The Mayor of Casterbridge* begins.[2]

Feminist literary critic Elaine Showalter observes the way in which Howe's own unconscious ideological commitments (beliefs, values, ways of thinking) affect the way he interprets this scene, the way that the "fantasies of the male critic distort the text." She also lays out another view of this same passage which attends to the symbolic function in this scene of Henchard's rejection of the world of women, a reading that works integrally with Henchard's growing realization that he has chosen to live by the male values of paternity, money, and legal

---

1. Terry Eagleton, *Literary Theory: An Introduction*, 2nd ed. (Minneapolis: University of Minnesota Press, 1996), 13.
2. Irving Howe, *Thomas Hardy* (New York: MacMillan, 1967), 84.

contracts, and that his rejection of the female world of relational bonds has irremediably crippled him.[3]

Showalter does two things: (1) she observes the way Howe's interpretation is affected by his male bias, and (2) she offers her own interpretation that accounts for the features of the text without asking her to identify against her own interests and identity as a woman. Although Howe's explication is an extreme example from an earlier era, it is the kind of interpretation that presents itself as universal, since he declares that in "the entire history of European fiction there are few more brilliant openings."[4] Most women readers will resist such an overt display of misogyny. Yet embedded and unconscious ideologies function this way all the time, albeit usually much more subtly, obscuring as much as they disclose about the world around us.

The task of this essay is to reflect on what we might need to unlearn in order to hear Scripture better, and specifically to hear the book of Ruth in a slightly different way than is commonly done. The reading I propose here is not an attempt to supplant other compelling readings of the book. To the contrary, I urge the reader not only to read the other essays in this volume on Ruth by Anna May Say Pa and Eunny P. Lee, but also to move quickly to lay hands on Katharine Doob Sakenfeld's commentary on Ruth as well as her more recent book, *Just Wives?*[5] In these volumes Sakenfeld offers beautiful, insightful interpretation of the book of Ruth, and in the latter book she artfully and movingly interweaves her reading of Ruth with contemporary women's stories from around the globe. Sakenfeld rightly conveys the urgency of hearing Ruth through these women's stories, many of them achingly tragic.

In this essay I consider the book of Ruth with a different set of questions in mind, proposing the idea that there may be another picture to see in the "figure" of the book of Ruth that we presently do not see because it is obscured by the beauty of the dominant picture. In order to make visible the features of reality that have been hitherto invisible, or at best, distantly visible as a fuzzy, unfocused background, we must ask questions that might seem too obvious to be worth asking. Why, for example, is the

---

3. The passage is discussed in Elaine Showalter, "Toward a Feminist Poetics," in *The New Feminist Criticism: Essays on Women, Literature, and Theory* (ed. idem; New York: Pantheon, 1985), 129–30.

4. Interestingly, it is also one of the relatively few books on the work of Thomas Hardy in my local public library. Although written nearly forty years ago, the unreflected male values inherent in the book, which exemplify mainstream interpretation of a certain era, are still much in the public realm.

5. Katharine Doob Sakenfeld, *Ruth* (Interpretation; Louisville, KY: John Knox, 1999), and *Just Wives? Stories of Power and Survival in the Old Testament and Today* (Louisville, KY: Westminster John Knox, 2003).

book of Ruth named "Ruth" and not "Naomi," or "Naomi and Ruth," or something else? How does the title interpret the book for us before we have even begun to read it? The title tells us that the book is about Ruth. She is the central focus of this story; it is *her* story. Yet are we seeing only the picture of the younger woman? A closer look at Naomi reveals that if we bring some other features of the text to the fore, features usually backgrounded by the focus on Ruth, then it is Naomi's predicament, *her* story that appears central to the tale as a whole.[6]

SEEING AND HEARING NAOMI[7]

It is Naomi's speech, her complaint, that sets the plot of the book in motion. And it is specifically Naomi's situation that is addressed by the happy ending of the conclusion, for by then Ruth has faded into the background of the story. It is, then, worth attending to Naomi and the central problematic that surrounds her at the beginning of the story and that sets the plot in motion.

Within the first five verses of the book, Naomi is stripped of all her male kin (husband, sons) and is left utterly bereft, with no children or grandchildren. These losses and absences that change the composition of Naomi's family go to the heart of the story itself. In order to survive and prosper, a family in ancient Israel needed to be composed of men, women, and children. The absence of men or children seriously jeopardized both the family's economic survival and its social status. A woman who was unattached to a man was often destitute, dependent on the generosity of the community (hence the numerous prophetic calls to care for the widow and the orphan). The loss of her two sons in addition to her husband is thus a shattering turn of events for Naomi. Her daughters-in-law are the only remaining members of her family. Yet under normal circumstances their presence would be little consolation, since most young women in such a situation would return to their father's house, which would, in turn, effectively ensure the death of Naomi's family.[8]

6. Such a focus has not gone unremarked by some commentators, as this unequivocal statement by Frederic Bush attests: "Unquestionably the most important character in the book is Naomi" (Frederic W. Bush, *Ruth, Esther* [Word Biblical Commentary 9; Dallas: Word, 1996], 49).

7. This section is a much-abbreviated version of a longer discussion of Naomi in my *Whispering the Word: Hearing Women's Stories in the Old Testament* (Louisville, KY: Westminster John Knox, 2005), 89–108.

8. Surprisingly, Naomi encourages each young woman to return to her mother's house. See Carol Meyers, "Returning Home: Ruth 1:8 and the Gendering of the Book of Ruth," in *A Feminist Companion to Ruth* (ed. Athalya Brenner; Sheffield: Sheffield University Press, 1993), 85–114.

The straightforward narrative simplicity by which these events are recounted in verses 1–5 belies the catastrophe that has befallen Naomi. With the death of all her menfolk and the absence of children to carry on the line, Naomi's life has been effectively deprived of meaning and her very survival is in question. The rest of the story takes up these problems.

Naomi's Speech

Of particular interest for our purposes is the way in which Naomi herself articulates her experience of these events. Throughout the book the invocation of divine blessing on others, along with the embodiment of *ḥesed* (covenantal faithfulness) in the attitudes and actions of Ruth and Boaz, function to underscore the way in which the characters' deep faithfulness to God funds their faithfulness to the people around them. As Sakenfeld puts it, "God is at work through the everyday actions of faithful people seeking to manifest divine loyalty in their loyal interactions with those around them."[9] Because so much *ḥesed* permeates the book, it seems perfectly appropriate to this story that Naomi's first uttered words are, "May YHWH do with you *ḥesed*, just as you have done with the dead, and with me" (v. 8). An invocation of blessing on someone else, along with acts of *ḥesed*, loyal acts of kindness, make up the main themes of the whole story—how asking YHWH's blessing on others and engaging in acts of human *ḥesed* embodies and expresses divine *ḥesed* for God's people.

And yet, Naomi's invocation of divine blessing on her daughters-in-law hits the note rather flat. After all, she does not say, "May YHWH bless you as he has blessed me," but rather, "May YHWH be faithful to you just as you have been faithful with the dead and with me." To the reader's surprise, God does not set the example for human faithfulness, as one might expect; rather, the young women set the example of faithfulness that the deity would do well to follow![10] Given Naomi's own experience of famine and the death of all her menfolk, one may wonder even in this first speech how she understands the faithfulness of God, for she seems to be expressing, through the conventional form of an

---

9. Sakenfeld, *Ruth*, 15–16.

10. This point is observed by several commentators, including Phyllis Trible, *God and the Rhetoric of Sexuality* (Overtures to Biblical Theology; Minneapolis: Fortress, 1978), 169–70; Sakenfeld, *Ruth*, 25; Danna Nolan Fewell and David Miller Gunn, *Compromising Redemption: Relating Characters in the Book of Ruth* (Louisville, KY: Westminster John Knox, 1990), 71.

invoked blessing, her hope that her daughters-in-law receive better treatment from the deity than she herself has experienced.

Naomi's next remark confirms her sense of the disparity between what one might hope to receive from YHWH and what she in fact has received: "May YHWH give to you—and may you find—rest/security, each in the house of her husband" (v. 9). Again we note the discrepancy between what YHWH has given to Naomi—no security in the house of her husband—and what she hopes for Orpah and Ruth. Without ascribing any insincerity to Naomi here, for surely she does wish for her daughters-in-law a better future, her remarks nonetheless convey an undertone of bitterness that becomes increasingly explicit as the story progresses.[11]

In her next several statements, Naomi conjures a bizarre fantasy of a new family for herself, the strangeness of which only underscores her sense of hopelessness (vv. 11–13). Throughout this scene Naomi is surrounded by and associated with famine, emptiness, barrenness, old age, and death. Moreover, all of this sorrow and emptiness and death is seen as God's fault. Naomi finally blurts out her conviction that God is responsible for her afflictions, "It is much more bitter for me than for you, for the hand of YHWH has gone forth against me" (v. 13b).[12] Her grief is not the result of bad luck (hardly a prominent biblical concept), nor does the narrative suggest that Naomi has done anything to deserve so much personal catastrophe. Rather, Naomi believes that it is the will of the deity that she should suffer in this way; the "hand of YHWH" has actively struck out against her. Later, Naomi again identifies YHWH as the source of her bitterness: "Call me Mara, for Shaddai has caused me extreme bitterness. I went away full, but empty YHWH caused me to return" (vv. 20–21). The theme of emptiness and fullness that pervades the whole story is explicitly introduced here, as Naomi reiterates her understanding not only of her present situation but also of the trajectory of her life.

Naomi and Job

How are we as readers to hear Naomi's complaint and especially her assessment that God is responsible for so much grief, death, and suffer-

---

11. This view is further supported by Brent A. Strawn's analysis of the Kethib/Qere in Ruth 1:8 ("y'śh in the Kethib of Ruth 1:8: Historical, Orthographical, or Characterological?" unpublished paper). I am grateful to him for sharing his paper with me.

12. The confession confirms the reader's earlier suspicion that Naomi's invocation of divine blessing on her daughters-in-law in vv. 8–9 might not be entirely transparent.

ing? Attentive readers of the Bible will hear in Naomi's story an echo of Job's grief and subsequent railing against God as the author of that grief.[13] Everything that gave meaning to Job's life is stripped away, and he too lays the blame on the deity. Both his grief and his accusation against God live in the history of interpretation as unforgettable expressions of the human condition. The story of Job constitutes some of the most profound thinking about what it means to be human, and has also served as a catalyst for others' reflections on the human condition. So why, in contrast, is Naomi's story of divinely authored loss, death, and sorrow not perceived as parallel to that of Job?

At least three reasons are immediately apparent. First, although in Job the reader is aware of God's involvement in Job's misfortunes, we are not sure that God is the instigator of Naomi's misfortune. A second and more important reason for the failure to see parallels between the stories lies in the way the characters verbalize their suffering. Naomi's accusation against God does not soar to the heights of eloquence that Job's speech does. She offers us neither the same quantity nor quality of articulate reflection on loss, justice, and human integrity. Finally, as I noted earlier, the title tells us that the story is not really about Naomi; it is about Ruth. After all, it is the book of *Ruth*. Naomi, therefore, is easier to ignore. Yet it is precisely here, in the question of how the title of the book orients us to read the story in a particular way, that I see a connection to the visual illusion of the two women. The title of the book helps us see Ruth as the main character in the story, and in so doing, pushes Naomi to the background so that we do not see her as clearly.

In order to see Naomi more distinctly, let us consider Naomi in light of Job for a moment. The similarities between their stories are quite pronounced. Like Job, Naomi explicitly and repeatedly blames God for the tragic reversals in her life.[14] Therefore, one of the central theological issues that unfolds in the book of Ruth, as in the book of Job, is the problem of human suffering and how God responds to that suffering. Though the volume of Naomi's complaint against God does not approach Job's

13. The connection is observed as early as the *Midrash Ruth Rabbah* (2:10) and is often made in passing by modern commentators. Kirsten Nielsen notes the parallel to Job, remarking, "We are tempted to ask whether in fact Naomi is yet another example of the innocent sufferer" (*Ruth* [Old Testament Library; Louisville, KY: Westminster John Knox, 1997], 52). André LaCocque devotes a couple of paragraphs to the parallel, mainly observing their common concern with distributive divine justice (*Ruth: A Continental Commentary* [Minneapolis: Fortress, 2004], 49). In other recent work, three essays in *Reading Ruth: Contemporary Women Reclaim a Sacred Story* (ed. Judith A. Kates and Gail Twersky Reimer; New York: Ballantine, 1994) examine the connections between Job and Naomi explicitly, those by Nehama Aschkenasy, "Language as Female Empowerment in Ruth" (111–24); Patricia Karlin-Neumann, "The Journey Toward Life" (125–30); and Lois C. Dubin, "Naomi's Tale in the Book of Ruth" (131–44).

14. Alicia Ostriker states the parallel explicitly: "Naomi . . . is a female version of Job" ("The Book of Ruth and the Love of the Land," *Biblical Interpretation* 10 [2002]: 348).

speeches, her accusations are as harsh, and she does not hold back from repeating them. As Sakenfeld observes, Naomi's speech here is striking for its "anti-caring picture of God," in contrast to the backdrop of blessing in the rest of the book.[15] Her indictment of God accounts for much of her speech in the first chapter, and indeed in the book as a whole.

Numerous linguistic as well as thematic parallels link Naomi with Job. Here I explore only one linguistic similarity to give a sense of how alike these two characters are in their accusations against God. Naomi's claim that Shaddai has made her life bitter finds similar expression in Job. Specifically, Naomi's language in verse 20 ("Shaddai has made [it] exceedingly bitter for me" [*hēmar šadday lî mĕ'ōd*]) is echoed in the introduction to Job's oath in 27:2–4 that his integrity requires him to speak the truth about God, "As God lives, who has taken away my right, Shaddai who has made my life bitter" [*wĕšadday hēmar napšî*]. These are strikingly similar assertions, both employing the appellation "Shaddai" for God, a relatively rare occurrence outside of Genesis and Job.[16] As Sakenfeld comments, "Like the action of God in the life of Job, divine action in the life of Naomi is bitter and yields bitterness precisely because it is so utterly inexplicable."[17]

ASSESSING NAOMI

Out of closely parallel circumstances, Naomi and Job articulate remarkably similar assessments of their situation. Yet the history of interpreta-

---

15. Katharine Doob Sakenfeld, "Naomi's Cry: Reflections on Ruth 1:20–21," in *A God So Near: Essays on Old Testament Theology in Honor of Patrick D. Miller* (ed. Brent A. Strawn and Nancy R. Bowen; Winona Lake, IN: Eisenbrauns, 2003), 129–43, here 131). Sakenfeld's essay moves in similar directions to my reading here, though her focus is on reading Naomi's cry as a prayer of lament or complaint. Tod Linafelt is even more direct than Sakenfeld's gentler "anti-caring": "it seems more likely that Naomi is flat out attributing evil or wicked actions to God" (*Ruth* [Berit Olam; Collegeville, MN: Liturgical Press, 1999], 20).

16. On the connections to Genesis and Job, see J. Gerald Janzen, "Lust for Life and the Bitterness of Job," *Theology Today* 55 (1998): 152–62. On other connections to Jeremiah and Job, see Edward F. Campbell, *Ruth* (Anchor Bible 7; Garden City, NY: Doubleday, 1975), 77, 83; and especially Sakenfeld, "Naomi's Cry," 132–40.

17. Sakenfeld, "Naomi's Cry," 136. Aschkenasy makes a similar observation: "By couching her grievances in the language of the Jobian predicament, Naomi powerfully suggests that she calls God to task, that she sees herself as having been singled out by God for persecution" ("Language as Female Empowerment in Ruth," 114). With most modern interpreters, I do not see in the text any assignation of blame to Naomi for her losses, nor does the text suggest that Naomi understands herself to be at fault (but for a more ambivalent reading, see Fewell and Gunn, *Compromising Redemption*, 72, 121). Some ancient and medieval interpreters, on the other hand, follow the Targum's lead in assigning guilt to Naomi: "my sin has been testified against me" (*The Targum of Ruth* [trans. D. R. G. Beattie; The Aramaic Bible 19; Collegeville, MN: Liturgical Press, 1987]; see also the commentaries of Rashi and ibn Ezra, among others, in D. R. G. Beattie's *Jewish Exegesis of the Book of Ruth* (Journal for the Study of the Old Testament Supplement Series 2; Sheffield: JSOT Press, 1977), 60, 105, 138. Although Nicholas of Lyra follows in this same tradition, most Christian medieval interpreters read the book allegorically and thus paid little or no attention to Naomi's speech. For a sampling, see *Medieval Exegesis in Translation: Commentaries on the Book of Ruth* (trans. Lesley Smith; Kalamazoo, MI: Western Michigan University Press, 1996).

tion treats them quite differently. Job is held up as one who articulates par excellence the passion and striving and tragedy of the human condition, while Naomi's complaints are largely passed over in silence by major traditions. It is not that Naomi herself has been perceived negatively in the history of interpretation. On the contrary, the Jewish exegetical tradition views Naomi as strong, courageous, faithful, and as a role model for Ruth. D. R. G. Beattie's observation is an apt summary of traditional Jewish understandings of Naomi: "She was a woman of noble character who, by her advice and example, had led Ruth to the way of virtue and modesty."[18] Naomi achieves this positive evaluation partly as a result of her decision to return to Judah once the famine has abated.[19] Despite such a positive assessment of her character, however, Jewish as well as Christian interpreters largely ignored Naomi's assertions that God is to blame for her problems. When commentators made note of her complaints, they typically asserted that the devastating tragedies in Naomi's life must have been the result of her own sin.[20]

The sharp difference in the evaluation of Naomi and Job may suggest, among other things, that interpreters invoke different gender expectations in their perceptions of the two characters. In the history of the West and in Western interpretation of the Bible, it has been considered noble for a man to shake his fist at God, to rail against his lot, to question the justice of God. Extolling Job's virtues, William Safire describes Job as "one of the most towering figures of the Bible, daring to question God's fairness," and avers that "Job reaches across the millennia to express modern Man's [sic] outrage at today's inequities."[21] Expressing anger without reserve and aggressively challenging the powerful to respond to injustice in the world are commonly considered to be masculine behaviors. Indeed, as is often the case with behaviors that are associated positively with men but negatively with women,[22] in Naomi's mouth a Joban anger against the deity may be condemned because she is a woman. It can appear unseemly for a woman to rail at

18. Beattie, *Jewish Exegesis*, 189.

19. Jewish interpreters typically cast a suspicious eye on Elimelech for his decision to leave Judah for Moab in the first place. According to this line of interpretation, it is not really surprising that he ends up dead early on in the story; indeed, his death is often interpreted as punishment for this faithless act. See ibid., 188.

20. See the references in n. 17. Because of their allegorizing tendencies, most Christian interpreters also tended to ignore Naomi's complaints.

21. William Safire, *The First Dissident: The Book of Job in Today's Politics* (New York: Random House, 1992), xiii–xiv.

22. This discrepancy has been well-documented among anthropologists (for discussion and bibliography, see my *Can These Bones Live? The Problem of the Moral Self in the Book of Ezekiel* [Beihefte zur Zeitschrift für die alttestamentliche Wissenschaft 301; Berlin/New York: de Gruyter, 2000], 130–35). It is perhaps most obvious in the realm of sexuality; assertive sexuality is valued in men, but highly suspect in women.

the deity, and with this comes the idea that she should accept meekly the hand she has been dealt.

Indeed, those ancient interpreters who lauded Naomi for her desire to return to Judah also placed a pronounced value on "modesty" in women, and therefore found much to appreciate in Ruth's self-effacing humility.[23] Cultures in many different times and places, including North America in the twenty-first century, embrace an ideology in which self-sacrifice in women is very highly valued, and many would say excessively so.[24] To interpreters who value feminine meekness, Naomi's complaint may appear to be whining, especially as she is contrasted with the stalwart Ruth who does not complain (though her situation is almost as dire). Ruth acts instead to rectify her situation, in a quiet, unobtrusive, "feminine" way. Not wishing to besmirch the otherwise laudable Naomi by accusing her of unfeminine behavior, interpreters over the centuries have largely ignored her complaints, even though they are the pivot upon which the entire narrative hangs. An additional bias may be at work as well. In some interpretive contexts, and certainly in the modern West, older women are nearly invisible in the culture; in such contexts it is not surprising that the younger, more desirable Ruth is the focus of interest. Cultural biases against both assertive women and older women—ideology at work!—combine to silence the cry of Naomi.

The discussion brings us back to a question I posed earlier: Why is the book of Ruth named the book of Ruth, and not the book of Naomi? The reasons are assuredly complex, but peering at this question through the lens of gender offers some potentially helpful insights. Perhaps the culture prevalent at the time these books were written (and titled) shared our modern, Western view that when turmoil afflicts women, they are not supposed to complain about it but "bear up" or suffer in silence (thus the rabbis' commendation of Ruth's "mod-

23. "Ruth's modesty is pointed out by the sages and given great emphasis, as this is a quality they consider very important, especially in a woman" (Leila Leah Bronner, "A Thematic Approach to Ruth in Rabbinic Literature," in *A Feminist Companion to Ruth*, 157). For many interpreters, "modesty" seems to be a code word for self-effacing submissiveness, especially since Ruth can hardly be characterized as modest in the sexual sense, given her behavior on the threshing floor (chap. 3).

24. Both the broader feminist movement and feminist theology have sharply criticized the high value that most modern societies place on female self-effacement. Specifically, Christian feminist theology repudiates self-effacement as a violation of the created order; it denies the full dignity ascribed to all human beings created in the image of God. The issue is not merely an academic one, nor is it restricted to feminist theologians by any means. In her *New Yorker* column, television critic Nancy Franklin articulates the problem with her characteristic humor: "it just happens to be a fact, and a diamond-hard one, that boys aren't subject to the depredations of the Four Horsemen of Appropriateness—Received Notions About Femininity, Fear of Not Being Perceived as Nice, No Boy Will Ever Want You If You Act/Look/Talk Like That, and Caring Too Much What Other People Think of You. These soul killers, having been loosed on the world by all the manufacturers of pink toys and spaghetti-strap toddlerwear, and sometimes by well-meaning, anxious mothers, come after girls before they even start elementary school" (Nancy Franklin, "American Idiots: Seth MacFarlane's Animated Empire," *The New Yorker,* January 16, 2006, 86–87).

esty").[25] In the same way, according to this view, when turmoil afflicts men, it can raise them to the heights of eloquence and the expression of the profoundest truths concerning the human condition (Camus's existentialist novels come to mind). It is not that Ruth does not deserve the book's title; on the contrary, her faithfulness is exemplary in every way. It is just that one cannot help but observe how the difference in the way Naomi and Job are understood throughout the history of interpretation correlates with Naomi's absence in the title of the book that narrates her turmoil and the resolution to it.

I began with the idea that unlearning is sometimes an important step to new learning. To hear Naomi, one has to unlearn the reflexive acceptance of book titles, or any interpretive framing device, as neutral. One has to unlearn an unthinking acceptance of dominant trajectories within the history of interpretation as necessarily normative. Why? Because there is an older woman in the picture who cannot be seen, or heard, if we are constantly being directed to the outlines of the younger woman.

FOR FURTHER STUDY

LaCocque, André. *Ruth: A Continental Commentary*. Minneapolis: Fortress, 2004.

Lapsley, Jacqueline E. *Whispering the Word: Hearing Women's Stories in the Old Testament*. Louisville, KY: Westminster John Knox, 2005.

Pressler, Carolyn. *Joshua, Judges, and Ruth*. Westminster Bible Companion. Louisville, KY: Westminster John Knox, 2002.

Sakenfeld, Katharine Doob. *Ruth*. Interpretation. Louisville, KY: John Knox, 1999.

———. *Just Wives? Stories of Power and Survival in the Old Testament and Today*. Louisville, KY: Westminster John Knox, 2003.

25. For the most part it is not clear when the titles were added to biblical books, and so it is with the book of Ruth. The possible later addition of the title does raise interesting questions about the relationship between title and book: the title itself becomes an explicit interpretive act that shapes all future readings of the book.

9

Wisdom and the Feminine in the Hebrew Bible

LINDA DAY

During one particular course I was teaching, a seminar on wisdom literature, at the conclusion of each class period one of my students rushed out the door as quickly as he possibly could. I could not understand why Robert was in such a hurry to leave class. Most all of the students hung around for a while, continuing to hash over the topics of that day's class or chat about their upcoming plans as they leisurely gathered books and belongings. Robert was one of the more talkative and friendly students in the class, frequently ready with a thoughtful question or comment during class discussions, so his haste seemed out of character. One day I asked him, "What's the rush?" He replied, "Judge Judy comes on at four o'clock. I've got to get home to watch Judge Judy." Though vaguely recognizing the name, I had never watched the television program. After this encounter, I decided that I needed to check her out, and discovered that she is an articulate, strong-minded, and intelligent woman who displays a quick wit. As she determines rulings, she often provides lessons in personal responsibility, proper behavior, and prudent life choices to plaintiff and defendant alike. I became impressed at how Robert had implicitly made a connection between the qualities of ancient wisdom that we were studying in class and their embodiment in a real-life person. Judge Judy, along with oth-

This essay is dedicated, with great admiration and affection, to Katharine Doob Sakenfeld. Kathie is, without question, a "wise woman" of our time, manifesting academic wisdom and practical wisdom both in all she undertakes.

ers like her, reflects the type of women's wisdom found throughout the biblical tradition.

Wisdom literature is primarily represented in the biblical tradition by five books: Proverbs, Job, and Ecclesiastes (also known as Qoheleth) in the Hebrew Bible; and Wisdom of Solomon and Sirach (also known as Ben Sira or Ecclesiasticus) in the Apocrypha. Yet elements of wisdom can also be detected in many biblical psalms, narratives, and even some prophetic texts. Wisdom thought incorporates a variety of content and literary forms, but common elements include an interest in the order of the universe and its creation, a concern for the education of young persons, the cultivation of virtues that will allow one to cope successfully in life, and a desire to understand some of the mysterious aspects of human existence.

Given the general androcentricity of the Hebrew Bible, there exist somewhat surprisingly strong associations of the wisdom tradition with the feminine. In this essay I briefly explore some of these connections. We see such representation most readily, I believe, in certain female biblical characters who reflect wisdom in various, and often similar, ways.

EVE, THE SEEKER OF WISDOM

The link between wisdom and women comes early on in the biblical tradition; we need go no further than the second chapter, to the figure of Eve. Eve, as we all know, has not always been viewed positively. Though scant attention is paid to her and Adam throughout the remainder of the Hebrew Bible, she has captured the imagination and reaped the scorn of many from the turn of the era up to our own day as the creature in the garden who is gullible, easily led astray, and responsible for the downfall not only of her mate but of the entire human race.[1] Yet, over a century ago, Elizabeth Cady Stanton argued that "the unprejudiced reader must be impressed with the courage, the dignity, and the lofty ambition of the woman. . . . Compared with Adam she appears to great advantage through the entire drama."[2] Then early in the modern feminist movement, Phyllis Trible's influential reading of

---

1. For an excellent collection of samplings of interpretations throughout the centuries, see Kristen E. Kvam, Linda S. Schearing, and Valarie H. Ziegler, eds., *Eve and Adam: Jewish, Christian, and Muslim Readings on Genesis and Gender* (Bloomington: Indiana University Press, 1999); also Pamela J. Milne, "Eve and Adam: Is a Feminist Reading Possible?" *Bible Review* 4, no. 3 (June 1988): 12–21, 39.

2. *The Woman's Bible* (Boston: Northeastern University Press, 1993), 24–25. Originally published in 1895 by New York European Publishing Company.

the second creation story elucidated the possibility of a more egalitarian and positive understanding of this character.[3]

In addition to such advantageous qualities, Eve may also well be understood as a seeker of wisdom. It is first important to note that Gen 2–3 includes the terminology and motifs of traditional wisdom thought. The tree of life that God plants (2:9) branches out through the book of Proverbs, where it is likened to various positive attributes (11:30; 13:12; 15:4), but most significant is how the tree of life reflects wisdom herself (3:18). Indeed, there is a strong connection in ancient Near Eastern, and possibly even Israelite, iconography of trees and snakes with goddesses.[4] The second tree, the one that figures more prominently in the narrative, similarly represents wisdom thought, for it is "the tree of the *knowledge* of good and evil." The term "good and evil" functions in a holistic sense, as a merismus representing a totality of mature understanding. Furthermore, though the Hebrew term used to describe the snake (*'ārûm*) is often rendered with a negative connotation by biblical translations ("crafty," "shrewd," "cunning"), it is actually a term from the wisdom corpus, in which it is used as a positive descriptor for practical wisdom. Designating a sensible, prudent, resourceful, or clever person, it is frequently contrasted with the foolish or simple individual (cf. Prov 12:16, 23; 14:15, 18; 27:12). Snakes themselves are seen to represent understanding in the ancient world; recall, for instance, Jesus' admonition in the New Testament to be "wise as serpents" (Matt 10:16; cf. also Prov 30:18–19).

In the scene in Gen 3:1–6, Eve both exhibits wisdom and seeks greater wisdom. Her intelligence and inquisitive nature become especially clear in comparison with the actions of the man. A "belly-oriented"[5] creature, he does not speak during this scene, and his sole action is unquestioning obedience to the woman. Eve is the one who speaks with authority and single-handedly represents the couple. The fact that the serpent uses plural second-person verbs indicates the man's inclusion in the gathering, but he allows the woman to reply for him.

---

3. "A Love Story Gone Awry," in *God and the Rhetoric of Sexuality* (Overtures to Biblical Theology; Philadelphia: Fortress, 1978), 72–143. For a helpful synopsis of some of the most significant feminist interpretation of this story, see Alice Ogden Bellis, *Helpmates, Harlots, and Heroes: Women's Stories in the Hebrew Bible* (Louisville, KY: Westminster John Knox, 1994), 45–66.

4. Lyn M. Bechtel, "Rethinking the Interpretation of Genesis 2.4b–3.24," in *A Feminist Companion to Genesis* (ed. Athalya Brenner; Sheffield: Sheffield Academic Press, 1993), 77–117, here 86–90; Phyllis A. Bird, "Genesis 3 in Modern Biblical Scholarship," in *Missing Persons and Mistaken Identities: Women and Gender in Ancient Israel* (Overtures to Biblical Theology; Minneapolis: Fortress, 1997), 174–93, here 183–87; see also the essay by J. J. M. Roberts and Kathryn L. Roberts in this volume.

5. In Trible's terminology ("A Love Story Gone Awry," 113).

Theologically astute, Eve is able to engage in rational and thoughtful conversation. The clever serpent, one might argue, chooses the cleverer of the two humans with whom to converse. Eve exhibits good reasoning abilities, weighing out the benefits and drawbacks of the information she observes. An independent thinker who does not mindlessly follow instructions, she reinterprets the tradition, that is, what stands for common wisdom in the garden (not to eat the fruit because bad things will happen). Not repeating it verbatim, Eve elaborates and adds her own interpretation (3:3 vs. 2:16–17).[6] Moreover, she is able to identify and distinguish differing qualities—the physical, the aesthetic, and the cerebral—of a concept (v. 6). Altogether, Eve is a smart lady.

Yet she yearns to be smarter. The guiding force behind Eve's conversation and her ultimate decision is her desire for wisdom, for greater understanding, and the serpent appears to know about this desire. Rather than trying to tempt her with immortality (that is, to eat fruit from the tree of life), the serpent tempts her with the fruit that she truly craves, the fruit of the tree of knowledge. What Eve wants is for her eyes to be opened, to be able to see with divine understanding (v. 5). The order in which the three attributes of the fruit are presented (first as good for food, then as pleasant to look at, and finally to make one wise; v. 6) suggests that its final attribute, that the fruit conveys wisdom, is what tips the balance and convinces her to disobey the divine decree. The Hebrew verb here is *śākal,* which suggests more than mere knowledge of a subject but the gaining of insight and comprehension. The reference to "seeing" (the verb *rāʾâ*) and to the tree as "good" (*ṭōb*) reflects the terminology of Qoheleth, the quintessential wisdom teacher who continually observes the world by seeing, then evaluates what is good. Thus, the hope of gaining greater wisdom is the plank of the argument that finally convinces Eve. Like a wise one who desires the fruit of righteousness, she takes from the tree (Prov 11:30) and joins those who avidly pursue Woman Wisdom (for instance, Prov 3:13–26).

Throughout this encounter, Eve displays a considerable degree of courage. Not even death will deter her; though threatened with it, she remains unafraid (v. 3)—or perhaps, becoming wise is so important to her that she will risk death to attain it. We can observe how this woman "is willing to take risks. She is comfortable with the lack of closure. She does not know what is going to happen. Obviously, neither

---

6. This detail may exhibit theological overtones as well, intimating at the holiness of the tree (as suggested by Trevor Dennis, *Sarah Laughed: Women's Voices in the Old Testament* [Nashville: Abingdon, 1994], 20) and presenting Eve as a better theologian than both the snake and the man.

does God."[7] Indeed, one interpreter even sees Eve as outwitting not only the serpent and the man, but also the deity.[8]

WISE WOMEN, THE DISPENSERS OF WISDOM

The Hebrew Bible is replete with accounts of women who dispense wisdom to others, who advise in various capacities. Some do so in very public and political settings. Though they fall less clearly within a wisdom trajectory narrowly defined, they speak intelligently and authoritatively as they advise kings regarding matters of state. For instance, Huldah functions in the capacity of a prophet (2 Kgs 22:14–20; 2 Chr 34:11–28), Esther advocates as a representative of a minority population (Esth 5:1–8; 7:1–8:8; 9:11–15), and the medium of Endor acts as a consultant of official divination (1 Sam 28:7–25). Other female figures advise in more private settings. Many biblical women provide needed guidance to their husbands, for example, Abigail (1 Sam 25:2–42), Sarah (Gen 16:1–6; 21:1–14), Jezebel (1 Kgs 19:1–3; 21:5–16), Zeresh (Esth 5:14; 6:13), and the unnamed wives of Manoah (Judg 13:2–25) and of Job (Job 2:9). Sons are similarly the recipients of women's private counsel. The mother of Lemuel dispenses wisdom to her son (Prov 31:1–9), as does the martyred woman with seven sons (2 Macc 7:1–42). Some of these counseling mothers may have held the official role in the court of queen mother (Hebrew *gĕbîrâ*) who advised her son, the reigning king, on governmental matters (Athaliah [2 Kgs 11:1–20; 2 Chr 22:1–23:15], Bathsheba [1 Kgs 2:13–25], the Queen of Babylon [Dan 5:1–12]).[9] Women even advise other prominent women; note that the mother of Sisera heeds "her wisest courtiers" (Judg 5:29–30). Such narratives comprise a strong tradition of intelligent, and even outspoken, women that courses throughout the biblical tradition.[10]

7. Danna Nolan Fewell and David M. Gunn, *Gender, Power, and Promise: The Subject of the Bible's First Story* (Nashville: Abingdon, 1993), 31.

8. Ph. Guillaume, "The Demise of Lady Wisdom and of *Homo Sapiens:* An Unwise Reading of Genesis 2 and 3 in Light of Job and Proverbs," *Theological Review* 25, no. 2 (November 2004): 20–38, here 31.

9. For further description of this office, see Nancy R. Bowen, "The Quest for the Historical *Gĕbîrâ*," *Catholic Biblical Quarterly* 63 (2001): 597–618; Susan Ackerman, "The Queen Mother and the Cult in Ancient Israel," *Journal of Biblical Literature* 112 (1993): 385–401.

10. Useful for further investigation into the advising capacities of a variety of biblical women is Silvia Schroer, "Wise and Counseling Women in Ancient Israel: Literary and Historical Ideals of the Personified *Ḥokmâ*," in *A Feminist Companion to Wisdom Literature* (ed. Athalya Brenner; Sheffield: Sheffield Academic Press, 1995), 67–84.

It is against this full and varied backdrop that I highlight four female characters who are aligned especially closely with wisdom: the woman of Tekoa, the woman of Abel, Judith, and Deborah. All provide wise counsel in the public sphere. They are alike in that they work with the top leaders of Israel, provide instruction at pivotal times in the nation's history, and shape the circumstances of the people as a whole. Within the space of a few chapters in the book of 2 Samuel, two otherwise unnamed women are identified with the appellation "a wise woman" (ʾiššâ ḥăkāmâ), a phrase used nowhere else in the Hebrew Bible. Second Samuel 14:1–24 relates how Joab, David's general, sends for a "wise woman" to come from the village of Tekoa to Jerusalem. She acts the part of a mourning woman and tells the king a parable about two sons, which convinces David to allow his son Absalom to return from exile. Following Absalom's revolt, Joab and the army are in pursuit of the defector Sheba and his followers and besiege the town of Abel of Beth-Maacah. A "wise woman" calls out from the city wall to Joab, convincing him to spare the town if she arranges the death of Sheba (2 Sam 20:4–22). An invading army and a town under siege likewise provide the catalyst for Judith's actions. She advises the town leaders, devises a plan to infiltrate the enemy camp, and single-handedly defeats their commander and saves her people. Thrice Judith is described as wise, twice with the Greek term *sophia* ("wise," Jdt 8:29; 11:20) and once with the term *sunesei* ("intelligent, insightful," 11:21). The designation "wise" is not used by the biblical text for Deborah, but her actions nonetheless clearly identify her as a woman who similarly dispenses wisdom in a public setting (Judg 4–5). Deborah is a judge, and the only official so named in the book who acts in the modern judicial sense; she adjudicates disputes among the people of Israel in a "courtroom" that is even known and remembered by her name, "the palm of Deborah" (4:5).

Certain characteristics can be imputed to this type of female wisdom. First, it is quite verbal; all of these women gain success through rhetorical means. Wise in tongue, their speech is adept and persuasive. The wise woman of Tekoa and the wise woman of Abel incorporate elements from the wisdom tradition through their inclusion of proverbs (2 Sam 14:14; 20:18), and the latter goes out to the people, literally, "in her wisdom" (bĕḥokmātāh, 20:22). There is an element of the serpent's clever and resourceful type of wisdom in their speech. What they say is often ambiguous and multireferential, able to be understood in more than a single way. Judith's statements to the enemy general are also filled with double entendre (Jdt 10:11–16; 11:5–12:20), and the wise woman of Tekoa takes on a guise not her own and speaks in parables.[11] Even Deborah's statement about the enemy falling by "the hand of a woman" (Judg 4:9) has an indirect aspect; does she mean herself or Jael?

The wisdom of these women has a strong element of the useful and the practical; it is not wisdom for the academy but for real life. All are problem solvers. A difficulty arises and, with perfect timing, they come forward into the situation and use their intelligence to fix it. Moreover, their courage is remarkable. The problems they solve are military, and they put themselves in the midst of the battle. Deborah leads the troops to war; unarmed, Judith walks straight into enemy territory; and the woman of Abel calls into her presence a man who has just feigned affection only to murder in cold blood (2 Sam 20:8–10).[12] Even the wise woman of Tekoa's conversation with King David is risky and potentially dangerous.[13] All four women have "the ability to speak the right word at the right time, to capture the essence of a situation in a few, but pleasing, words and thereby to redirect the course of events."[14] They are quick thinkers, good talkers, and enterprising actors.

Not only is she herself insightful, this type of wise woman is recognized by others for her intelligence. These women have a reputation for wisdom in the broader community. The town leaders' observations about Judith reflect such recognition: "Today is not the first time your wisdom has been shown, but from the beginning of your life all the people have recognized your understanding" (8:29). These dispensers of wisdom are leaders; they command authority, and their people do as they direct. Barak, along with thousands of warriors, follows Deborah's command to battle (Judg 4:6–16); the townspeople of Abel heed their wise woman's instructions with nary a question (2 Sam 20:22). The locus of the authority of these wise women, however, lies outside the official government and its court in Jerusalem. For instance, the town

---

11. Patricia K. Willey considers in greater detail the nuances, ambiguities, and even convolutions of her speech ("The Importune Woman of Tekoa and How She Got Her Way," in *Reading between Texts: Intertextuality and the Hebrew Bible* [ed. Danna Nolan Fewell; Literary Currents in Biblical Interpretation; Louisville, KY: Westminster John Knox, 1992], 115–31).

12. Moreover, a severed head is the successful result of these three women's military exploits. We might note the thematic connections between the stories of Deborah/Jael and Judith; see Sidnie Ann White, "In the Steps of Jael and Deborah: Judith as Heroine," in *"No One Spoke Ill of Her": Essays on Judith* (ed. James C. VanderKam; Society of Biblical Literature Early Judaism and Its Literature 2; Atlanta: Scholars, 1992), 5–16. Susan Ackerman explores the role of Deborah and other female military heroes in *Warrior, Dancer, Seductress, Queen: Women in Judges and Biblical Israel* (Anchor Bible Reference Library; New York: Doubleday, 1998), 27–88.

13. Willey, "Importune Woman of Tekoa," 117–18.

14. Claudia V. Camp, "The Wise Women of 2 Samuel: A Role Model for Women in Early Israel?" in *Women in the Hebrew Bible: A Reader* (ed. Alice Bach; New York/London: Routledge, 1999), 195–207, here 199.

of Tekoa was a good ways south of Jerusalem, Abel of Beth-Maacah was in the furthermost northern part of Israelite territory, and Bethulia is a fictional name representing a small village in the hill country. It may well be the case that the title "wise woman" indicated an official role in the early history of Israel, a tribal or village leader connected with the governance as well as the education of the town.[15] Perhaps the more rural, outlying populations held greater openness to women's leadership than centralized Jerusalem and its monarchy. Yet the status and authority of these women are acknowledged not only by the inhabitants of their villages but also by high priests, generals, kings, foreign nations, and even the celestial realms (cf. Judg 5:2–18; Jdt 15:8–10; 16:21–25).

An intriguing, though allusive, connection among these accounts is the imagery of motherhood. The phrase "a mother in Israel" occurs only twice in the Hebrew Bible, but both times in these stories, in reference to Deborah (Judg 5:7) and to the city of Abel (2 Sam 20:19). Moreover, the wise woman of Tekoa does not use maternal language but actually takes on the persona of a mother, grieving the misfortunes of her sons. Yet the biblical text does not indicate that any of these women are actually themselves mothers with children, nor even that they are married. (Judith is widowed and refuses remarriage.) The maternal quality of Eve, "the mother of all living" (Gen 3:20), is here taken up metaphorically.

WOMAN WISDOM, THE EMBODIMENT OF WISDOM

In the biblical wisdom literature, the figure of Woman Wisdom figures prominently. Woman Wisdom is presented as the personification of wisdom itself. Named simply "Wisdom" (Hebrew *Ḥokmâ*, Greek *Sophia*), this quality is characterized as a female being. Outside of one passage in the book of Job (Job 28:1–28), in the Hebrew Bible Woman Wisdom appears throughout the first nine chapters of the book of Proverbs. A dramatic and highly complex figure, she dons the persona of prophet, hostess, disciplinarian, and lover. Proverbs, interestingly enough, features women at its beginning and its conclusion. Woman Stranger, Woman Wisdom's counterpart, also plays an important role in chapters 1–9, and the final chapter comprises a mother's instructions to her royal son (31:1–9) and a poem describing the actions and attributes of

15. See ibid.

a worthy woman (31:10–31).[16] The figure of Woman Wisdom is taken up and enhanced throughout the wisdom books in the Apocrypha, including various places in Sirach (where she is often identified with the Torah), Baruch, and 2 Esdras, but it is in the Wisdom of Solomon (chaps. 6–10) in which her pervasive character is emphasized and she is further epitomized as spirit, divine consort, and savior.[17]

Surely one of the most startling features about Woman Wisdom is her intimate connection with God. Only God can completely understand her; try as they might, humans are simply unable fully to do so (Job 28:1–28). Living with God, Woman Wisdom is "a breath of the power of God . . . a pure emanation of the glory of the Almighty . . . a spotless mirror of the working of God" (Wis 7:25–26; also 7:7; 8:3; 9:4). More than an intermediary between the human and the divine, personified Wisdom "brings a sense of the divine presence and closeness to *all* of creation that is simply unequalled."[18] She represents God in the earthly realm. As YHWH, the deity of grand actions, is distant, abiding in heaven, Woman Wisdom is active on earth; her approachable demeanor, in addition to her very presence, represents divine proximity in a uniquely immanent fashion to human beings.

In the action of creation, God and Woman Wisdom are joined. Some passages present her as actively creating the world, for instance, Prov 3:19; 9:1, Wis 7:22. Other passages depict her as God's very first act of creation, before earth or heavens, for instance, Wis 9:9; Sir 1:4–10; 24:1–12. The well-known poem in Prov 8 is ambiguous regarding Woman Wisdom's precise role in creation. In verse 22, the Hebrew verb *qānâ* can mean "to create," "to acquire," or "to possess"; and in verse 30, the rare noun *ʾāmôn* can indicate either a little child or a master architect. Thus, is she a beloved daughter whom YHWH creates, playing in the brand-new universe, or a collaborator who has previous existence, bringing necessary skills to the task of creation? Given the Hebrew poets' love of ambiguity and wordplay, perhaps the statements allude to both possibilities. In any event, Woman Wisdom's participation in creation remains constant. Apparently, God needs her presence to create properly.

---

16. A female perspective can also be detected in passages in Prov 1–9 that, on the surface, appear predominantly male-oriented; see Athalya Brenner and Fokkelien van Dijk-Hemmes, *On Gendering Texts: Female and Male Voices in the Hebrew Bible* (Leiden/New York/Cologne: Brill, 1993), 113–30.

17. All of these books are of course distinct, with unique emphases and characteristics, but for the purposes of this essay I consider together their statements about Woman Wisdom.

18. Roland E. Murphy, "The Personification of Wisdom," in *Wisdom in Ancient Israel: Essays in Honour of J. A. Emerton* (ed. John Day, Robert P. Gordon, and H. G. M. Williamson; Cambridge: Cambridge University Press, 1995), 222–33, here 232, emphasis original.

Woman Wisdom is the embodiment of created life itself. She brings immortality and long life, boasting, "Whoever finds me, finds life" (Prov 8:35; 3:16; Wis 6:18–19; 8:13). The "tree of life" in the original garden has now become Wisdom herself (Prov 3:18; Sir 24:13–22). Eve, also, is a giver of life, "the mother of all living," for the name Eve (ḥavvâ) reflects ḥayyâ, "life" (Gen 3:20). She, like Woman Wisdom, is a co-creator with God; note her exclamation at the birth of Cain, "I have created a man with YHWH's help!" (the same verb qānâ linguistically links her statement to Wisdom's exclamation of her own history vis-à-vis YHWH in Prov 8:22). Both of these female figures, in representing wisdom, also represent life itself; female wisdom is presented as nothing less than the very essence of existence. In the words of Claudia V. Camp, a foremost feminist scholar of the wisdom materials, "[t]he transcendent otherness to which the metaphor Woman Wisdom refers is life in all its relationality, with people, nature and God."[19]

Like other wise female biblical figures, Woman Wisdom is good with words. To catch people's attention, she raises her voice and calls out to all who would listen; her speech is compelling, and it represents truth and righteousness (Prov 8:6–9). The text highlights her verbal acuity, for an astute reader will note the great number of terms designating speech in Prov 1:20–33 and 8:1–24. The voice of Woman Wisdom is an extension of the divine voice; she brings the authority and power of God's voice to the public square. Hers is first a message of reproof, mincing no words in the chastisement of those who do not heed her voice (Prov 1:20–23). But it is also a message of hospitality, seeking people out, drawing them in, and urging them to eat and drink their fill (Prov 9:1–6; Wis 6:12–16; Sir 24:19–22).[20]

Woman Wisdom is everywhere, "pervading" and "penetrating" all places (Wis 7:24). In the universal realm, she traverses the highest heaven to the deepest abyss, violent oceans and all earthly territories (Sir 24:3–7). And in the human realm, she sets up her soapbox everywhere— city gates, country hills, roadways, street corners, city walls, marketplaces. She inhabits many realms. Yet though pervasive, she can also be elusive. Playing hard to get, she does not always make herself available,

19. "Woman Wisdom as Root Metaphor: A Theological Consideration," in *The Listening Heart: Essays in Wisdom and the Psalms in Honor of Roland E. Murphy, O. Carm.* (ed. Kenneth G. Hoglund, Elizabeth F. Huwiler, Jonathan T. Glass, and Roger W. Lee; Journal for the Study of the Old Testament Supplement Series 58; Sheffield: JSOT Press, 1987), 46–76, here 65. See also her classic *Wisdom and the Feminine in the Book of Proverbs* (Sheffield: Almond, 1985).

20. For a helpful analysis of the various forms and functions of discourse in Proverbs, see Carol A. Newsom, "Woman and the Discourse of Patriarchal Wisdom: A Study of Proverbs 1–9," in *Gender and Difference in Ancient Israel* (ed. Peggy L. Day; Minneapolis: Fortress, 1989), 142–60.

and her admirers must put in hard work and prove their devotion (Job 28:12–22; Sir 6:18–26). Both the public and the private are her domain, and indeed, she resembles the image of the worthy woman of Prov 31 in her ability to move easily between them. Able to mediate, the figure of Woman Wisdom suggests that the proper place for female wisdom is in all types of human relationships.[21] As Kathleen M. O'Connor observes, "The Wisdom Woman appears abruptly in . . . all places where crowds gather, where people come together to transact daily commerce and legal dealings in the ancient cities. In the thick of life at its shabbiest and most exciting, in the routine of daily marketing and in the struggles of ordinary people to survive—it is there that the Wisdom Woman extends her invitation."[22]

In attempting to determine the proper category in which to classify Woman Wisdom, scholars have experienced difficulty.[23] Did the ancient authors intend to present her as a mere literary device, a literary fiction? Or does she represent a divine being, a goddess? And if a goddess figure, does she have non-Israelite origins, reflecting the Sumerian Inanna, the Egyptian Maat, or the Greek Isis? If we consider her generally to be a personification of the attribute of wisdom, as is most commonly done by interpreters, we must also agree with Roland E. Murphy that there is no other comparable personification in the Hebrew Bible, one who actually speaks for YHWH.[24] And if we consider her to be a metaphor for God, we must agree with Camp that this metaphor goes beyond symbolic representation to carve out conceptual space in our real exis-tence (a "root metaphor" in her terminology).[25] Perhaps the movement in ancient Israelite religious belief away from the recognition of god-desses to a single male god led either to the disappearance of her divine status,[26] or enhanced it as a result of a continuing need for female divine imagery.[27] Multifaceted, clearly Woman Wisdom defies a simple under-

---

21. Camp, "Woman Wisdom as Root Metaphor," 55.

22. *The Wisdom Literature* (Messages of Biblical Spirituality 5; Wilmington, DE: Michael Glazier, 1988), 70.

23. For discussion of the range of options for classification, see Michael S. Moore, "'Wise Women' or Wisdom Woman? A Biblical Study of Women's Roles," *Restoration Quarterly* 35 (1993): 147–58; Judith M. Hadley, "From Goddess to Literary Construct: The Transformation of Asherah into Ḥokmah," in *A Feminist Companion to Reading the Bible: Approaches, Methods and Strategies* (ed. Athalya Brenner and Carole Fontaine; Sheffield: Sheffield Academic Press, 1997), 360–99; O'Connor, *Wisdom Literature*, 82–85.

24. "Personification of Wisdom," 222.

25. "Woman Wisdom and the Strange Woman: Where Is Power to Be Found?" in *Reading Bibles, Writing Bodies: Identity and The Book* (ed. Timothy K. Beal and David M. Gunn; London/New York: Routledge, 1997), 85–112, here 95–96.

26. Bernhard Lang, "Lady Wisdom: A Polytheistic and Psychological Interpretation of a Biblical Goddess," in *Feminist Companion to Reading the Bible*, 400–423.

27. Hadley, "From Goddess to Literary Construct"; see also her "Wisdom and the Goddess," in *Wisdom in Ancient Israel*, 234–43.

standing. Most likely, this figure worked on the hearers and readers of the biblical works in which she is embedded on a variety of levels simultaneously—and she continues to do so.

IMPLICATIONS OF FEMALE WISDOM IMAGERY
FOR CONTEMPORARY WOMEN

Scholars have considered the influence of biblical wise women on the experiences of real-life women in history. It is quite possible that the biblical tradition both reflects the lived experiences of real women and the social roles they held, and empowered historical women and the society in which they lived.[28] In addition, in recent years the concept of wisdom has become an interpretive lens frequently employed by scholars, biblical interpreters and theologians alike.[29]

In contemporary society there are many real-life women who fill the role of "wise woman." We do not need to look far to see the wisdom of the Judge Judys, as well as the Sandra Day O'Connors, the Maya Angelous, the Madeleine Albrights, and the Ellen Goodmans of our day. Such women are not afraid to express themselves, even if what they say is not conventional or proper. Their examples remind us that along with a sharp mind comes a wise tongue (or pen!), and that speaking one's mind requires particular courage. Yet our modern wise women still remain, to a surprising degree, on mainly the local level—the town mayor, the president of the school board. Sadly, they are now only slightly more likely to be on the floor of the Senate in Washington or a corporate boardroom on Wall Street than they were in the royal administration of King David.

The yearning for wisdom and understanding might well inhabit us all. A friend once gave me a coffee mug that bears the slogan "Smart women thirst for knowledge." The phrase expresses, I believe, the same Catch-22 facing Eve and others who would seek wisdom. One has first

---

28. For example, Carole R. Fontaine, "The Social Roles of Women in the World of Wisdom," in *Feminist Companion to Wisdom Literature,* 24–49; Hal Taussig, "Wisdom/Sophia, Hellenistic Queens, and Women's Lives," in *Women and Goddess Traditions in Antiquity and Today* (ed. Karen L. King; Studies in Antiquity and Christianity; Minneapolis: Fortress, 1997), 264–80; Camp, "Woman Wisdom and the Strange Woman."

29. Note, for instance, Patricia O'Connell Killen, *Finding Our Voices: Women, Wisdom, and Faith* (New York: Crossroad, 1997); Grace Ji-Sun Kim, "The Grace of Sophia and the Healing of Han," *Toronto Journal of Theology* 18 (2002): 129–41; Susan Cady, Marian Ronan, and Hal Taussig, *Wisdom's Feast: Sophia in Study and Celebration* (San Francisco: Harper & Row, 1989); Elizabeth A. Johnson, *She Who Is: The Mystery of God in Feminist Theological Discourse* (New York: Crossroad, 1993); Elisabeth Schüssler Fiorenza, *Wisdom's Ways: Introducing Feminist Biblical Interpretation* (Maryknoll, NY: Orbis, 2001).

to be smart even to know to desire greater knowledge—or perhaps the converse is more apt, that one's very action of trying to gain wisdom identifies her as already possessing a fine intelligence. The wisdom tradition elevates the learning process itself. In our contemporary academic climate, with its increasing emphasis on the acquisition of professional skills, wisdom honors those who want to understand broadly. Indeed, it insists that we become lifelong students and asserts that our education will bring us the greatest joy. The different types of biblical wisdom (crafty, resourceful, traditional, rhetorical, and so on) can represent the different intelligences we bring to the task of learning. Surely, we are all students in Woman Wisdom's classroom.

Those of us committed to learning will search for Woman Wisdom until we find her. Yet in doing so, the biblical tradition poses a challenge. The book of Proverbs is extremely male-oriented; it is exclusively young men ("sons") who are addressed. To join those who seek wisdom, women are thereby forced to include ourselves where we have been, by tradition, excluded. We must write ourselves into the text. Modern women's appropriation of this tradition represents an example of how women, when facing the androcentric biblical text—to say nothing of patriarchal religious and social institutions—must make new patterns, must read ourselves into places we were not previously envisioned as inhabiting.

Woman Wisdom, as a personification of the deity, reminds us of the power of metaphorical envisioning. Theologically speaking, she portrays a feminine aspect of the divine: God is like a smart, self-confident, and outspoken woman. The power of human models in the biblical text gives us a glimpse of how we might be (as well as how we should not be). The power of theological metaphors gives us a sense of the divine. Woman Wisdom travels effortlessly throughout the universe, between the divine and the human realms, between the animal and the physical worlds. She illustrates the interconnectedness of all life. Indeed, wisdom is the very tree of life. Her fruit is sweet and satisfying. The serpent is correct: when we eat it, we will not die, but our eyes will be opened to all the possibilities that life holds.

FOR FURTHER STUDY

Brenner, Athalya, ed. *A Feminist Companion to Genesis*. Sheffield: Sheffield Academic Press, 1993.

Brenner, Athalya, and Carol Fontaine, eds. *Wisdom and Psalms: A Feminist Companion to the Bible (Second Series)*. Sheffield: Sheffield Academic Press, 1998.

Camp, Claudia V. "The Wise Women of 2 Samuel: A Role Model for Women in Early Israel?" In *Women in the Hebrew Bible: A Reader*. Edited by Alice Bach, 195–207. London/New York: Routledge, 1999.

———. "Woman Wisdom and the Strange Woman: Where Is Power to Be Found?" In *Reading Bibles, Writing Bodies: Identity and The Book*. Edited by Timothy K. Beal and David M. Gunn, 85–112. London/New York: Routledge, 1997.

McKinlay, Judith E. *Gendering Wisdom the Host: Biblical Invitations to Eat and Drink*. Journal for the Study of the Old Testament Supplement Series 216. Gender, Culture, Theory 4. Sheffield: Sheffield Academic Press, 1996.

Trible, Phyllis. "A Love Story Gone Awry." Chap. 4 in *God and the Rhetoric of Sexuality*. Overtures to Biblical Theology. Philadelphia: Fortress, 1978.

10

"I am Black and *Beautiful"*

The Song, Cixous, and *Écriture Féminine*

F. W. DOBBS-ALLSOPP

"We are 'black' *and* we are beautiful." This phrase closes with a rhetorical flourish one of the early sections in Hélène Cixous's essay "Sorties: Out and Out: Attacks/Ways Out/Forays."[1] As Verena Andermatt Conley notes, here Cixous is "mocking [Sigmund] Freud's statement that describes women as the black continent."[2] Cixous makes clear her debt to Freud earlier when she states that "the 'dark continent' trick has been pulled on" women; the phrasing and use of quotation marks clearly signal the quote (S 68). And she uses the language of darkness ("black," "dark," "night," "shadows," "apartheid," "Africa," "wrapped in veils," and the like) to figure the repression of women throughout these initial sections. Freud's image is patently racist and misogynist, and this the "triply marginalized" Cixous—woman, Jew, and Algerian colonial—

For a generation now, Katharine Doob Sakenfeld has been a leading feminist voice in the academy and in the church, and it is with much pride that I acknowledge how profoundly my own feminist sensibilities have been shaped by her teaching, scholarship, and above all friendship. Indeed, what stands out most for me is how Kathie's feminism shapes her entire orientation to life, and it is this "holism" that I mean to honor most here as I engage the writings and thinking of Hélène Cixous, a holistically oriented feminist. For both Sakenfeld and Cixous, the trajectory of the feminism they chart (in radically different ways) ultimately leads to a better humanism, a better way for women *and* men to navigate the world in which they (we!) find themselves.

1. In Hélène Cixous and Catherine Clément, *The Newly Born Woman* (trans. Betsy King; Minneapolis: University of Minnesota Press, 1986), 69. It also occurs in Cixous's similarly minded though substantially briefer essay "The Laugh of the Medusa," in Elaine Marks and Isabelle de Courtivron, *New French Feminism: An Anthology* (Amherst: University of Massachusetts Press, 1980), 248. Both essays were originally written in the mid-1970s, and they provide my main point of entry into Cixous's oeuvre; references to them are provided parenthetically in the body of the essay, with page numbers preceded by S (for "Sorties") and M (for "Medusa").

2. Verena Andermatt Conley, *Hélène Cixous* (New York/London: Harvester Wheatsheaf, 1992), 37–38. The image itself comes from Freud's (notorious) essay on "Femininity."

can only abhor. But Freud, according to Cixous's reading, tells a certain truth about sexual difference with his image as well, and this Cixous wants to retain. "She chooses not to take the route that denies sexual difference(s)," explains Andermatt Conley, "but to accede to a play of differences that would not turn into oppositions. . . . Cixous intimates that 'black' is a neutral term until it is charged with a negative value in a system of oppositional hierarchies."[3] Hence, what Cixous does so effectively is to retain the important notion of sexual difference(s) informing Freud's image while charging the image itself with positive (instead of negative) value. She achieves this by borrowing language from the Song of Songs: "I am black and beautiful" (1:5). Though Cixous acknowledges taking shortcuts through her reading of the (Hebrew) Bible (S 73), biblical language and allusions abound in her work. As is the case with Freud's statement, phrasing and quotation marks sign Cixous's linguistic debt. But here, too, the sense and tone she gives to the phrase jibe well with its use in the Song; in fact, Cixous's reading of the Song offers an illuminating gloss on this biblical line.

Like Cixous, the Shulammite[4] embraces a negative perception that nonetheless tells a particular truth and transforms it into a positive symbol of self-identity. What is at issue in this line is the Shulammite's unique beauty. A luminous and ruddy complexion was stereotyped as the normative image of health and beauty for the day (cf. 1 Sam 16:12; 17:42; Song 5:10; Lam 4:7).[5] In contrast, the Shulammite's skin is dark, blackened, as we are told, from prolonged exposure to the hot Mediterranean sun as she works in the vineyards (1:6). In 1:5 the Shulammite names her blackness, classifying herself among things that are black (e.g., the tents of Kedar), and then defiantly and most affirmatively pronounces this blackness beautiful. The syntax of the Hebrew is equivocal. The Vulgate's reading of the phrase as "black am I, *but* beautiful," for example, has good warrant, but a conjunctive reading ("I am black and beautiful") is grammatically just as viable, and, as Cixous's emphatic "*and*" shows, is just as capable of capturing the line's defiant

---

3. Ibid., 37–38.

4. "The Shulammite" appears in 7:1 as a designation for the otherwise anonymous female lover whose voice dominates the Song. There is as yet no consensus among scholars as to the etymological understanding of this Hebrew term (*haššûlammît*). The presence of the definite article (*ha-*), however, shows that it is not a personal name, and whatever the term's literal meaning, it is surely intended to allude both to "the Shunammite" (*haššûnammît*) woman of 1 Kgs 1:15 and to Solomon (*šĕlōmōh*), who is often evoked in the Song (1:1; 3:7, 9, 11; 8:11, 12).

5. This stereotype, of course, must ultimately be heard against the backdrop of the ancient Near East, whose basic ethnic stock would have tended toward peoples of darker hair and skin pigments. Further, it appears to privilege an image of beauty that is projected most prominently through the lens of elite culture, since only elite (e.g., royal) men and women would not have needed to work outdoors for prolonged periods of time, and therefore they would not have been as susceptible to sunburn and tanning.

tone and better expresses the Shulammite's unreserved affirmation of her blackness.[6]

In appropriating the line, Cixous clearly expands its scope, both in terms of voice ("we") and content (encompassing issues beyond beauty, such as gender, sexuality, and race). Yet these expansions are very much in the spirit of the original Hebrew text. There can be little doubt that the voice of the Shulammite that we hear in the Song, which is raised here so defiantly (though playfully) against one set of cultural prejudices, were it recontextualized (as it is in Cixous's reading), would similarly sing out against other prejudices. In fact, one may even argue, following Ellen Zertal Lambert,[7] that insofar as beauty "on the outside is intimately bound up with who one is on the inside" and thus touches on every aspect of our embodied lives, the extension of the Shulammite's voice to question other cultural wrongs committed against our embodied selves—patriarchy and misogyny, anti-Semitism and genocide—is even embedded thematically within the biblical text. But this begins to move away from the initial point I want to make here, namely, that Cixous uses the language of blackness in Song 1:5 to counter and redeem the language of darkness she inherits from the psychoanalytic discourse of Freud.

It is not too surprising that Cixous read the Song and even appropriated some of its language.[8] More intriguing is the insight that this gives about the Song's larger sensibilities, namely, that in important ways the Song realizes the kind of *écriture féminine,* or "feminine writing," that Cixous calls for in "Sorties" and "The Laugh of the Medusa." Cixous herself acknowledges that there have always been poets (even male ones) "capable of loving love and hence capable of loving others and wanting them, of imagining the woman who would hold out against oppression and constitute herself as a superb, equal, hence, 'impossible' subject, untenable in a real social framework" (M 249; cf. S 98). My claim is that the poet of the Song is such a poet. In the brief remarks that follow, I offer some initial thoughts toward this larger thesis, taking the poem in Song 1:5–8—the larger context out of which Cixous's "black and beautiful" language comes—as my chief textual point of reference. The line of argument pursued is both deductive and constructive in nature. The constructive element is crucial as it is only in the act

---

6. The construal of this line has long been a point of debate among scholars (see Marvin H. Pope, *The Song of Songs* [Anchor Bible 7C; New York: Doubleday, 1977], 307–18) and both translation possibilities (contrastive or conjunctive) have positive elements about them. In the end, however, the problem is one of translation. The Hebrew conjunctive (*waw*) may be understood either way.

7. As cited in Wendy Steiner, *Venus in Exile* (Chicago: University of Chicago Press, 2001), 218.

8. Cf. Andermatt Conley, *Hélène Cixous*, 61, 97.

of bringing Cixous into conversation with a reading of the Song that the latter's affinities with the former can be recognized. One happy consequence of this reading strategy is to open up interpretive pathways into the Song that are pregnant with untapped political, philosophical, and even theological possibilities and relevances. For Cixous, writing (and reading) are always inherently political acts, capable of questioning cultural and social practices, staging crises, inventing new possibilities. "If there is a somewhere else that can escape the infernal repetition, it lies in that direction, where *it* writes itself, where *it* dreams, where *it* invents new worlds." "That," exclaims Cixous, "is writing" (S 72). The Song's "unflagging, intoxicating, unappeasable search for love," especially when sighted through Cixousian eyes, I argue, gives us a paradisal "somewhere else"—a writing!—that is vital enough to matter, to transform how we relate one to another, the same and the other; it gives us, that is, an *écriture féminine*. But first, a brief overview of the little poem (or fragment of a poem?) in 1:5–8.

Song 1:5–8

I am black and beautiful,
   O daughters of Jerusalem,

Like the tents of Kedar,
   Like the curtains of Salmah!

Do not look (down) on me that I am black,
   That the sun has gazed at me.

My mother's sons were angry with me,
   They set me as guard of the vineyards,
   But my vineyard I did not guard!

Tell me, you whom I love so,
   where do you graze,
   where do you bed down your flocks at noon?

Or else I'll become like one who wraps herself up
   Among the flocks of your companions.

If you do not know,
   O most beautiful among women,

Then go on out on the tracks of the flock,
   And graze your kids
   Among the shepherds' camps!

This poem breaks into two main sections, verses 5–6 and verses 7–8. The first section is composed of three couplets and a closing triplet and features the voice of the female lover, the Shulammite. It opens with the Shulammite addressing her girlfriends (literally, "the daughters of Jerusalem") and extolling the beauty of her sun-darkened skin: "I am black and beautiful!" (v. 5). The tone is light and playful. The Shulammite appears to be having a bit of fun with what she knows would otherwise be taken as a negative characteristic, emboldened by the assuring knowledge that she and her blackness are loved by another (who addresses her as "most beautiful of women," v. 8). The boast, then, is the healthy braggadocio of one newly in love and eager to share her happiness.

This sense of playfulness is underscored to good effect by the puns and wordplays that abound in the first section of the poem. For example, in the very first word, *šĕḥôrâ*, "black," which is to be derived etymologically from *šāḥar*, "to be black, dark," there is an allusion via the homograph *šāḥar* "to look for, search" to both the "looking" that goes on in 1:6—the girlfriends are implored not to "look down on" (*rʾh*) the Shulammite's black skin that has been "gazed" (*šzp*) upon by the sun— and the "seeking" that is the subject of verses 7–8 (cf. Prov 7:15). In verse 6, the Shulammite explains her exposure to the hot Mediterranean sun as a consequence of her brothers' anger, which prompted them to set her as a "guard" in the vineyards. The Hebrew phrase *niḥărû-bî*, "they were angry with me" (from the verb *ḥārâ*) may also be read as "they burned against me" (from the verb *ḥārar*; cf. Ps 102:4), playing on the scorching look of the sun that burns the skin. The section ends by playing on the literal and figurative meanings of "vineyard" in the Song. The vineyard, garden, or field is the conventional locale of lovemaking in the Song and throughout ancient Near Eastern love poetry. In the Song, however, the vineyard (or garden) is also used as a figure for the Shulammite herself (especially 4:12–5:1; 6:2). It is the latter on which the final line in verse 6 turns: if she was set to "guard" (*nōṭērâ*) the family's literal "vineyards" (*hakkĕrāmîm*), her own more figurative "vineyard" (*karmî šellî*) she has not "guarded" (*lōʾ nāṭārtî*)—this last bit said, no doubt, as a happy boast, which also tells us that the poem's initial line is in no way demurring.

The second section of the poem features the teasing banter of two lovers and comprises two stanzas, each having a triplet and a couplet and the two together forming an inclusio (triplet:couplet::couplet: triplet). The unannounced theme is the search for love that both so achingly desire but neither will admit (at least outwardly). The Shulammite speaks first in a mock pout, wondering where her lover (here imagined as a shepherd) grazes his flocks that she may join him during the afternoon siesta. She begs him to tell her, lest she be forced to wander among his companions' flocks "as one wrapped up." Again the choice of diction is playful. The Hebrew verb *rā'â* ("to feed, graze") is used elsewhere in the Song to refer to the man's enjoyment of sexual pleasures (5:1; cf. Prov 30:20), and it does not take too keen of an imagination to pick up on the double entendre in the verb *rābaṣ,* "to lie down." The precise reference of the term normally glossed as "to wrap up oneself" (*'ōṭĕyâ*) is uncertain, though most scholars take a cue from Gen 38:14–15 and assume that the tease refers to the Shulammite having to disguise herself like a prostitute in order to find her lover. The boy stands his ground, replying that if she truly does not know— and of course he implies that she *does* know—then she should go right ahead and graze (*rĕ'î*) her kids among his companions' flocks. She, too, is imagined as a shepherd, but "kids" may be intended also to refer more figuratively to the girl's breasts (cf. 1:14), as with the "gazelles" and "fawns" in 4:5 and 7:3. The boy thus returns her teasing threat of attracting other lovers in a kind of tit for tat: go ahead sell your wares, then!

* * *

From the start Cixous refrains from defining *écriture féminine* too closely: "It is impossible to *define* a feminine practice of writing, and this is an impossibility that will remain, for this practice can never be theorized, enclosed, coded" (M 253). Indeed, an openness to difference and to the unknown is at the very heart of how Cixous sees and engages the world, and thus the last thing she wants is to close off prematurely any unforeseen possibilities for "an/other writing."[9] Yet, as she continues, this hesitancy to define "doesn't mean" that a feminine writing "doesn't exist." It most certainly does. As Ian Blyth and Susan Sellers have seen, though Cixous stops short of offering a restrictive definition of *écriture féminine,* she does nonetheless "give various hints and suggestions about the nature of *écriture féminine.*"[10] I take up several of these "hints and suggestions" as a way of measuring (some of) the Song's Cixousian affinities.

9. Susan Sellers, *Hélène Cixous: Authorship, Autobiography and Love* (Cambridge: Polity, 1996), xi.
10. Ian Blyth and Susan Sellers, *Hélène Cixous: Live Theory* (New York/London: Continuum, 2004), 19.

IN THE AFFIRMATIVE

Cixous writes in the affirmative. She asserts life: "What is feminine (the poets suspected it) affirms: . . . and yes I said yes I will Yes, says Molly (in her rapture), carrying *Ulysses* with her in the direction of a new writing; I said yes, I will Yes" (S 85).[11] This "yes" does not ignore death, as Cixous acknowledges, "We live, we write starting from death." "But," she says, and this is the crucial bit, "I am not expecting death. . . . For me, . . . if there was a first end, a 'beginning,' it was a yes, a smile, two recognizing each other. Me: life flows towards life. Between life and life there is an unknown passage."[12] This affirmative nod toward life not only shapes the themes and topics that routinely appear in Cixous's writing, but it infects the very way she writes, her tone, the enlivening electricity that courses through her diction and syntax. Her wordplay and many puns, convoluted syntax, unconventional use of capitalization, and privileging of nonlinear ways of thinking all bring life to the reading experience, inscribe the very vitality by which she means to counter death (by leaving no space for it) and "to win grace."[13]

The Song is the Bible's foremost inscription of an abundant and fully lived life. In our poem, this embrace of life animates the Shulammite's opening exclamation, "I am black and beautiful" (v. 5), and inspires her exploration of the "tracks of the flocks" in verse 8, the "unknown passage" between "life" (hers) and "life" (his). The image of the lush and verdant vineyard in verse 6, which shimmers brilliantly against both the black backdrop of the poem's early verses (vv. 5–6) and the dusty brown tracks habitually traveled by Mediterranean shepherds and featured in the later lines (vv. 7–8), is one of the Near East's most potent symbols of life. In the Song's rendition, the vineyard also functions to reclaim for human habitation the lost paradise of the Bible's primordial garden, Eden—and thus the Song is in a very real way the original story of paradise regained, a quintessential Cixousian theme.[14] But as with Cixous, this poem's affirmation of life is given as eloquently and as effectively in its light and playful tone (the zealous boasts and teasing flirtations of those newly in love) and the play of its language

11. Cf. Andermatt Conley, *Hélène Cixous*, 11–12; Abigail Bray, *Hélène Cixous: Writing and Sexual Difference* (New York: Palgrave Macmillan, 2004), 67–70.

12. Hélène Cixous and Mireille Calle-Gruber, "Inter Views," in *Hélène Cixous, Rootprints: Memory and Life Writing* (London/New York: Routledge, 1997), 82.

13. Hélène Cixous, "Coming to Writing," in *Coming to Writing and Other Essays* (Cambridge, MA: Harvard University Press, 1991), 3.

14. Cf. Sellers, *Hélène Cixous*, 63–64.

(puns, sound play, and the like). It is in and through such lyric gestures that poetry "opts for the condition of overlife," as Seamus Heaney says.[15] Both Cixous and the Song raise their voices to sing of a life brimming with possibility and happiness.

(WRITING) THE BODY

"Woman must write her body," says Cixous (S 94). Her entire project presupposes an alternative way of writing (thinking)—"an/other writing" as Sellers aptly glosses it—to the masculinist (phallogocentric) discourse that otherwise has dominated and shaped Western critical thought. This "other writing" begins with the body. After all, "We are sentient beings," notes Cixous—beings, that is, whose every interaction with the world beyond our skin is mediated through our skin. Historically, however, the body has been mostly neglected in the West, given the mind/body dualism that pervades its philosophical tradition(s). Cixous contends that it is woman, being "more body than man is" (S 94, 95), who has suffered more adversely from this dichotomous way of thinking: "We have turned away from our bodies. Shamefully we have been taught to be unaware of them, to lash them to a stupid modesty; we've been tricked into a fool's bargain" (S 95). Therefore, Cixous's charge to write the body means to underscore and to celebrate human embodiment and to urge women (and men!) to allow their bodies to inform their ideas and to "pay attention to all the nonverbal, unconscious, instinctual drives and sensations" of the body.[16] Indeed, to write from female bodily experience for Cixous is nothing short of re-creating the world.

The Song presents us with just such "an/other" world, one where the healthy celebration of the human body and an embodied sexuality is thoroughgoing and plain for all to see. The language of these poems frequently intends to evoke and to open onto the various bodily senses —smell, touch, taste, sound, sight. There is even a quite literal (if still highly figured) writing of the Shulammite's body in verse 6 ("my *vineyard* I did not tend"), and it is most definitely not tied to "a stupid modesty." Far from it. On this topic ancient Near Eastern conceptions of humanity were thoroughly holistic; no mind/body split here. This is important for readers of the Song (and other biblical literature) to keep

---

15. Seamus Heaney, *The Redress of Poetry* (New York: FSG, 1995), 158.
16. Blyth, *Hélène Cixous,* 33.

in mind, as there is a tendency, especially when reading in translation, to overspiritualize. So when we encounter, for example, even such a seemingly straightforward phrase in English translation as "you whom my soul loves" (šeʾāhăbâ napšî) in verse 7, we would do well to read as if Cixous were looking over our shoulders and exhorting us not to be "tricked." Both of the Hebrew terms used here are far more holistic than are their usual English glosses. Thus a more fitting (if overly prosaic) rendering of the phrase would be something like "you whom I cherish and want with every bit of me," though spoken with the plain simplicity of "you whom I love." But the main point is that the Song and Cixous are thinking along very similar lines and that the image of wholeness projected through the figure of the Shulammite anticipates and is compatible with the mind/body holism extolled by Cixous.

LOVE AND LAUGHTER

Any engagement with Cixous, even one so brief as this one, requires at least a passing glance at the theme of love (and especially romantic love), which is a central concern in so much of her writing. For Cixous love is above all an opening to the other, which, she says, is everything: "there's nothing without the other."[17] It "is about receiving the strangeness of the other without being threatened by the difference; it is about a fidelity to the other, the passion of wonder, an openness to the unknown, the unthought."[18] But most important, it is all this while also wanting "the two, as well as the both, the ensemble of one and the other," an ensemble that honors the self as well as the other. It is a relationship of two beings and the "third body" they create in their exchanges "in-between." The "relationship between beings that alone merits the name of love," writes Cixous, involves real exchange, "a recognition of each other," "the intense and passionate work of knowing," each taking "the risk of other, of difference, without feeling threatened by the existence of an otherness," and each "delighting to increase through the unknown that is there to discover, to respect, to favor, to cherish" (S 78). As Abigail Bray notices, there is a tendency in much poststructuralist thought to imagine the other as an idealized

17. Ibid., 104.
18. Ibid., 75.

horizon empty of particular historical and social content.[19] Cixous's privileging of the love relationship as the premier locale for encountering the other offers a powerful corrective to this tendency. Not only does the other become imaginable as a real, flesh-and-bone individual, but by attending to the agency and reality of the self (as well as that of the other), Cixous imagines a way of encountering otherness that respects difference and makes space for both subjects in the relationship: "The loving to be other, another, without it necessarily going the route of abasing what is the same, herself" (S 86).

Such a thinking of the other (ethics) through love has obvious appeal for any critically engaged reading of the Song, the West's primordial lyric celebration of romantic love between two people. In verses 5–8, love as such is not really a topic of focus, though it does provide the backdrop against which the poem demands to be read. This is especially evident in verses 7–8. Here we overhear the two lovers teasing one another—nicely counterpointing the girls' gossip in verses 5–6. Mutuality (of an asymmetrical variety where difference is respected) is one of the hallmarks of the Cixousian loving relationship, and it also is what distinguishes the Song's portraiture of love more generally.[20] The mutuality is made manifest not in what is said but in the way of the saying, in the poem's form of discourse, dialogue. Conversation, "speaking to," and as Cixous so often stresses, "listening," is the mode (par excellence) of ethical discourse, a linguistic gesture through which life, respect, and otherness is imputed to an other and the possibility for real exchange is created. The Song's use of dialogue (here in the lovers' trade of teasing barbs), then, carries with it ethical implications and contributes significantly to what shapes the Song into a genuine "duet."[21]

In verses 7–8 we also glimpse the Shulammite's willingness to risk for the other (later in the sequence the risk will be paid with a very real beating [5:7]). But the aspect of love I want to accent is its delight, its laughter, its need at times to be utterly frivolous and so unnecessary. Vital to Cixous's outlook—and why, I suspect, that love features so prominently in her thinking—is her allowance for superabundance, uselessness, and waste (S 93). Laughter (literally and figuratively) and play (linguistic and otherwise) fill the pages of her writing. Life is not

19. Ibid., 76.
20. Michael Fox, *The Song of Songs and the Ancient Egyptian Love Songs* (Madison: University of Wisconsin Press, 1985), 304ff.
21. Cixous and Calle-Gruber, *Rootprints,* 17.

always serious, even for one who, like Cixous, is only too aware of her "luck," of her "being born in Algeria" and a little too late, or else, she says, "I would anonymiserate eternally from Auschwitz" (S 71). The talk we overhear in verses 7–8 is in the end very silly, the teasing chitchat of two young lovers—perhaps they are sitting alone together somewhere under a tree, passing the lazy afternoon hours—and thus easily dismissed. And yet, Cixous reminds us, we very much need such times of silliness and frivolity, "taking the time a phrase or thought needs to make oneself loved, to make oneself reverberate" (S 93). The Song is filled with figured laughter, delight, and happiness. We should expect nothing less of paradise in a garden of love, and we should cherish and nourish their presence in our own lives.

Finally, I note the great variety of loving couples who populate Cixous's writings—licit, illicit; heterosexual, homosexual, bisexual; living women and men all—as a reminder that the Song is but one instantiation of love's story. Its celebration of a particular love between one man and one woman ought not to be read as a monolithic definition of love, but rather should open us up to the wonder and good of love wherever, whenever, and among whomever it may be found.

L'ÉCRITURE FÉMININE

There is much more to say about Cixous's notion of *écriture féminine*, even with regard to the small poem in Song 1:5–8. But the few themes herein explored may suffice to give a sense ("hints and suggestions") of what Cixous means by *écriture féminine* and of how the Song achieves a version of this "feminine writing." Both of the major senses Cixous attaches to the adjective "feminine" in her ever-fluctuating usage aptly characterize the Song as feminine (then and now). First, and most transparently, the term "feminine" isolates the sex-specific experiences of being a woman—biological, libidinal, imaginary. Cixous writes "toward women" "as a woman." Indeed, "being a woman" is primary and, as she says, "determines me absolutely."[22] Thus, at one level a feminine writing is a writing of, about, for women. If there is any book of the Bible that qualifies as feminine in this sense it is the Song of Songs. It is the voice of a woman, the Shulammite, that dominates this poetic sequence. She literally has the most lines, and it is her voice that both

22. As quoted in Lynn Kettler Penrod, *Hélène Cixous* (London: Prentice Hall, 1996), 5.

opens and closes the sequence and that readers find the most compelling. The language of the Song presents another version of femininity with the grammatically feminine forms that abound as nowhere else in the Bible. The variety of sexuality most prominently on display throughout the sequence also may be described historically and culturally as feminine—a diffuse *jouissance,* nonteleological, evocative, passionate, innocent, interiorly and relationally oriented.[23] And some have even speculated that the Song was authored by a woman.[24]

If always rooted in anatomical or biological sex ("sexual difference"), the term "feminine" also and ultimately signifies for Cixous a different approach to the other, a way of "keeping alive the other" that opposes patriarchy—or as she calls it, "phallo(go)centrism" (M 249; S 79, 81, 83, 86). That is, the word "feminine" ultimately carries for Cixous larger ideological connotations. As such, it is a qualifier of sexual difference applicable to both women *and* men. In fact, she makes a point of using masculine and feminine so as "to avoid the confusion man/masculine, woman/feminine: for there are some men who do not repress their femininity, some women who, more or less strongly, inscribe their masculinity. Difference is not distributed, of course, on the basis of socially determined 'sexes'" (S 81). Hence, her program of a feminine writing is open to, inclusive of, and producible by males as well as females, even though Cixous believes that it is currently easier (for historico-cultural reasons) for women to write and think the feminine. Ultimately, the trajectory of her thinking leads through the feminine to a "better human": "always . . . coming from sexed, marked, different places; and then, in a certain place . . . the difference gives way to . . . what awaits us all: the human."[25] This is a mature feminism, a feminism that never loses sight of the woman's cause or the vital importance of sexual difference but also dares to implicate itself on behalf of all humanity, women and men too—"Isn't it evident that the penis gets around in my text, that I give it a place and appeal? Of course I do. I want all. I want all of me with all of him. . . . But I do desire the other for the other, whole and entire, male or female" (M 262). This is a feminism that, as a male, I too can finally own and in which I can flourish.

23. See Jerrold S. Cooper, "Enki's Member: Eros and Irrigation in Sumerian Literature," in *Dumu-E2-Dub-Ba-A: Studies in Honor of Ake W. Sjöberg* (ed. Hermann Behrens et al.; Philadelphia: University Museum, 1989), 87–89; "Gendered Sexuality in Sumerian Love Poetry," in *Sumerian Gods and Their Representations* (ed. Irving Finkel and Markham Geller; Groningen: STYX, 1997), 85–97; Gwendolyn Leick, *Sex and Eroticism in Mesopotamian Literature* (London/New York: Routledge, 1994), 21, 58.

24. E.g., S. D. Goitein, "Women as Creators of Biblical Genres," *Prooftexts* 8 (1988): 23–27.

25. Cixous and Calle-Gruber, *Rootprints,* 19.

This second and more ideologically engaged sense of the term "feminine" also appropriately characterizes the Song, which so obviously both shares certain sensibilities with Cixous and stands in opposition to the dominant masculinity of its day. Of course, to what manner of use the Song's feminine ideology would have been put in its own time is a harder question to answer. It may well be that it served to reinforce very traditional values.[26] But even were that true, it says nothing about how we contemporary readers of this biblical love story may choose to deploy it. The present and future remain ever open. Our responsibility is to make of them what we desire. What Cixous says of parenting is applicable to our thinking through of the "feminine writing" that is the Song of Songs: "No, it's up to you to break the old circuits. It will be the task of woman and man to make the old relationship and all its consequences out-of-date; to think the *launching* of a new subject, into new life, with defamilialization" (S 89).

FOR FURTHER STUDY

Cixous, Hélène. "The Laugh of the Medusa." In *New French Feminism: An Anthology.* Edited by Elaine Marks and Isabelle de Courtivron, 245–64. Amherst: University of Massachusetts Press, 1980.

———. "Sorties: Out and Out: Attacks/Ways Out/Forays." In *The Newly Born Woman,* by Hélène Cixous and Catherine Clément. Translated by Betsy King, 63–132. Minneapolis: University of Minnesota Press, 1986.

———. *Coming to Writing and Other Essays.* Cambridge, MA: Harvard University Press, 1991.

Exum, J. Cheryl. *Song of Songs.* Old Testament Library. Louisville, KY: Westminster John Knox, 2005.

Fox, Michael. *The Song of Songs and the Ancient Egyptian Love Songs.* Madison: University of Wisconsin Press, 1985.

Grossberg, Daniel. "Song of Songs." Chap. 2 in *Centripetal and Centrifugal Structures in Biblical Poetry.* Atlanta: Scholars, 1989.

---

26. Cf. Leick, *Sex and Eroticism,* 67–68.

11

Job's Wife

C. L. SEOW

The unnamed wife of Job has only one line in the entire Joban drama. According to the Hebrew text, she says, literally, "You are still holding fast to your integrity. Bless God and die!" (Job 2:9). The word "bless," though, may be read in opposite ways. It may be taken at face value, or it may be understood as a euphemism, meaning "curse." Assuming the latter meaning, interpreters through the ages have roundly condemned Job's wife as an unthinking fool, an irritating nag, a heretic, a temptor, an unwitting tool of the devil, or even a personification of the devil himself.

Such a negative view of Job's wife was promulgated by the four "doctors of the church"—Ambrose, Augustine, Jerome, and Gregory the Great—and followed by most interpreters, both Jewish and Christian. Ambrose surmised that the devil destroys everything Job possesses, except his tongue (so that he might blaspheme) and his wife (so that she might tempt him to do so). She is, Ambrose thought, a temptor in the mold of Eve (*Patrologia latina* [PL] 16, cols. 698–99). In similar fashion, Augustine explained that God permits the devil to leave Job's wife unharmed because God knows through whom "Adam" would be tempted—the Woman (PL 36, cols. 660–62). The story of Job and his wife is like that of Adam and Eve, Augustine elaborated, except that Adam succumbs to the persuasion of Eve, while Job, the New Adam,

It is a pleasure to offer this essay in honor of my teacher, colleague, and friend, Kathie Sakenfeld, from whom I have learned far more than I can remember.

does not fall to the devil's ruse through the Woman (PL 35, cols. 2006–7). Hence, Augustine famously called Job's wife "the Devil's helper." Jerome, too, developed this analogy but added a contrast between Eve—the old and the new Eve coalesced in one—and the Virgin Mary, the former leading one out of paradise, the latter leading one to heaven (*Corpus Christianorum: Series latina* [CCSL] 46, col. 193).

Other interpreters who follow this trajectory constitute a veritable "who's who" in the history of early Christian exegesis, including John Chrysostom, Hesychius of Jerusalem, Aphrahat, Caesarius of Arles, and Gregory the Great. This exegesis is seen in early Christian iconography as well. The most elaborate exposition of this view is in Gregory's *Moralia in Iob*, in which he posited that the Adversary tests human beings in two ways: through suffering, but also, and more subtly, through persuasion. Failing to break Job through the earlier calamities, therefore, the Adversary "returns to Eve" (CCSL 78, cols. 444–45). As the snake in the garden of Eden stirs Eve to speak perversely, so the Adversary causes Job's wife to speak perversely. Having lost in open combat, therefore, the Adversary attacks Job surreptitiously through his new weapon—her tongue. Gregory's *Moralia* is without question the single most important commentary on Job in the Middle Ages, exerting an influence on virtually all Christian exegesis of the book.

Such negative perceptions of Job's wife have remained prevalent throughout history. In medieval mystery plays, known from the eleventh century onwards, Job's patience is set over and against his wife's supposed impatience, and she is typically cast in liturgical dramas as a shrew and a fool. The nefarious impact of such renderings must not be downplayed. In the twentieth century it is evident in the thoroughly misogynistic interpretation of Austrian painter and playwright Oskar Kokoschka. Jilted by his lover, Alma Mahler, the widow of the renowned Viennese composer, Kokoschka portrays Job's wife in his play *Job* (1917) as a femme fatale, a lover to the devil and a tool used by him to destroy Job. For the initial performances of the play in Dresden and Berlin, Kokoschka reused a poster previously painted for his *Mörder, Hoffnung der Frauen*, a poster that shows a grotesque upper body of a woman (now representing Job's wife), her neck mutilated and her head tilted to the right, but her hands still stubbornly clutching the body of another in front of her. The artist's misogyny is manifest, too, in a lithograph showing Satan throwing the woman out a window onto Job below. Even worse, Kokoschka commissioned a life-sized doll made to look just like his lost lover, a doll that he, in a drunken fit, decapitated, smashing a bottle of red wine over its head. All this derived from an interpretation of that singular line that Job's wife speaks!

Alongside such readings, however, there are alternate representations that together constitute a dissenting "minority report," as it were.[1] This minority report has largely been overlooked, thus skewing her place in the history of interpretation and reception. Indeed, the negative view of Job's wife has been so dominant that even the positive portrayals have typically been read negatively. This essay considers two pieces of art in which Job's wife is portrayed positively.

DÜRER'S "JABACH ALTARPIECE"

One of the most famous scenes of Job and his wife was painted by Albrecht Dürer in the early sixteenth century on the two side panels of the so-called "Jabach Altarpiece."[2] Commissioned by Dürer's patron, Friedrich the Wise, the Elector of Saxony, during a time when the region was plagued by deathly epidemics, Job was the subject of choice because he was widely regarded in that era as a protector from the plague and a patron saint of the afflicted. And Friedrich was, by all accounts, extraordinarily afraid of diseases.[3]

On the left panel, Job is seated with his eyes closed, his face resting on his left hand, his elbow resting on his knee, while his right arm is on his thigh, his right hand dangling despondently. His sores are visible, but he seems resigned. His wife is standing to his left, pouring a bucket of water on him. The scene is clearly continued on the right panel, since the train of her dress continues therein, as do the horizon and background scenery. The right panel also shows two musicians, one playing a wind instrument and the other a little drum. The drummer's face looks remarkably similar to Dürer's own, as one sees in his many self-portraits,[4] suggesting that the artist has painted himself into the scene.

---

1. Already in the Septuagint Job's wife is given an expanded role. There she gives a long speech in which she reminds Job of her share in the suffering that tragedy brings to her family and, instead of telling Job to curse God, she tells him to "say something" to God. A very similar view is evident in the pseudegraphical work *Testament of Job*, where she is presented as a faithful wife who does everything she can to support Job and, as in the Septuagint, only tells Job to "say something" to God. The portrayal in the *Testament of Job* was influential in Jewish and Islamic interpretations. In some Islamic legends, for instance, Job's wife is called Raḥma, the term in the Qur'an for divine compassion as manifest through human agents, including Jesus and Muhammad. Indeed, she is portrayed as the earthly agent of divine help for Job.

2. The left panel is now in the Städelsches Kunstinstitut in Frankfurt am Main. The right panel is in the Wallraf-Richartz Museum in Cologne. For a convenient image of the two pieces together, see http://www.wga.hu/frames-e .html?/html/d/durer/1/04/1jabach.html.

3. Erwin Panofsky, *Albrecht Dürer* (2 vols.; Princeton, NJ: Princeton University Press, 1948), 1:93.

4. See Joseph L. Koerner, *The Moment of Self-Portraiture in German Renaissance Art* (London/Chicago: University of Chicago Press, 1993), *passim*; Jan Biaostocki, *Dürer and His Critics* (Baden-Baden: Valentin Koerner, 1986), 91–143.

Heinrich Wölfflin proposed some time ago that the scene is of Job being relieved of pain by water and soothed by music.[5] That position has been eloquently defended recently by Samuel Terrien, who points to a similar convergence of the motifs of melancholy and the presumed therapeutic effects of water and music in a lithograph by Dürer.[6] Others who are not so sanguine, however, follow the dominant view in imputing malice to Job's wife. The musicians in the scene, though, are no doubt positive. The drummer—who so strikingly resembles Dürer himself—and his colleague are bringing comfort to Job with their talents. They are what friends should be to those who suffer, not like the friends of Job as portrayed in the biblical book. On this point most critics seem to agree. Job's wife, however, does not receive such favorable consideration by critics. She is, one interpreter suggests, not "a compassionate woman but rather a contrary woman who scolds her husband, and Dürer intended to contrast the friendly spirit of the musicians with the spite of Job's wife."[7] Yet there is no reason whatsoever to assume any discontinuity within the picture.[8] There is certainly no sign of hostility on her face, as all interpreters agree, and the judgment that she is upbraiding her husband is belied by the fact that her mouth is closed. The portrayal of her is, in fact, that of a gentle woman. Just as the musicians provide comfort for her husband through their music, she pours water on him to soothe him or to cleanse him of his pus and worms. Her act is born not of malice but of compassion. If Job's wife wishes for death for Job as an end to his suffering, it is not out of wickedness and blasphemous intent but out of compassion for the one who suffers beyond human ability to tolerate. She does not, after all, say, literally, "curse God," but rather "bless God," as the Vulgate, the basis of all the vernacular Bibles of that time, has it.

Among Jewish exegetes in the medieval period, it was considered a viable option to take the imperative ("bless") at face value. Indeed, Joseph Qimḥi reported in the twelfth century that there were some

5. Heinrich Wölfflin, *The Art of Albrecht Dürer* (trans. Alastair and Heide Grieve; London: Phaidon, 1971), 137.

6. See Samuel Terrien, *The Iconography of Job through the Centuries: Artists as Biblical Interpreters* (University Park: Pennsylvania State University Press, 1996), 139–45.

7. Zefira Gitay, "The Portrayal of Job's Wife and Her Representation in the Visual Arts," in *Fortunate the Eyes That See: Essays in Honor of David Noel Freedman in Celebration of His Seventieth Birthday* (ed. Astrid Beck et al.; Grand Rapids: Eerdmans, 1995), 521.

8. Nor need one imagine a contrast between these panels and the putative middle portion, as does Anzelewsky, who sees the Joban scene as a counterpoint to the center piece, which he believes to be a scene with the Virgin Mary (Fedja Anzelewsky, *Dürer: His Art and Life* [trans. Heide Grieve; New York: Alpine, 1980], 112–13). If these were, indeed, side panels, the original must have been sawn in two for that purpose. In any case, if the putative middle piece is, indeed, of the Virgin Mary, these panels may in fact be continuous with that piece, suggesting that Job's wife was in fact showing mercy to Job, thus prefiguring the Virgin. All that, however, is pure speculation, since no one can be sure if there was a center piece and, if so, what it contained.

who explained that Job's wife is suggesting that Job's affliction might overwhelm him, perhaps leading him to blaspheme or otherwise sin.[9] So why not bless God faithfully and then ask to die rather than to sin? He should die faithful rather than be pushed by his afflictions to sin! Joseph himself demurred, however, noting that Job rejects her advice. Moses Qimḥi, Joseph's son, also confirmed that there were those who thought that the imperative should be taken literally, for Job's wife means for him to bless God for the evil that they suffer and then, after-wards, to ask to die.[10]

It is difficult to demonstrate, of course, that Dürer was acquainted with Jewish views on Job's wife in this period, although it is clear that the Christian humanists were familiar with Jewish exegesis and that the writings of the Qimḥi family were quite influential in Germany in the fifteenth and sixteenth centuries. What is certain is that Dürer knew the work of Johann Grüninger, who printed the *Biblia Germanica* in 1485. Dürer, in fact, visited the latter's workshop in Strasbourg in the 1490s and may even have used some of Grüninger's woodcuts as mod-els for some of his own work.[11] So it is not insignificant that among the woodcuts of the Grüninger Bible is one of Job and his wife, in which she stands close behind her husband, her left hand gently placed on his shoulder as if comforting him, her head tilted in a gesture of solidar-ity.[12] This picture has an analogue in the German Bible printed in 1483 by Anton Koberger of Nuremberg, the godfather and mentor of Dürer.[13] Koberger had apparently used the woodcuts in Heinrich Quentell's Bible of 1479, a Bible that Dürer also used.[14] In short, three Bibles familiar to Dürer—those of Quentell, Koberger, and Grüninger—all have positive illustrations of Job's wife.

Most significant, Durer was familiar with *Le livre du chevalier de La Tour Landry*, a fifteenth-century work by the French writer Geoffrey de La Tour Landry that portrays Job's wife in a mostly positive manner.[15]

9. Joseph Qimḥi in *Tiqwat Enosh* (ed. Israel Schwartz; 2 vols.; Berlin, 1868; reprint, Jerusalem, 1970), 1:188–89. For all its problems, this remains the only published edition of Joseph Qimḥi available. I thank Alan Cooper for pointing me to these texts.

10. Moses Kimḥi, *Commentary on the Book of Job* (ed. Herbert Basser and Barry D. Walfish; South Florida Studies in the History of Judaism 69; Atlanta: Scholars, 1992), 6* [in Hebrew]. Cf. *Tiqwat Enosh*, 1:150.

11. Albrecht Dürer, *Woodcuts and Woodblocks* (ed. Walter L. Strauss; New York: Abaris, 1979), 153, 159, 183.

12. See Albert Schramm, *Der Bilderschmuck der Frühdrucke* (23 vols.; Leipzig: Hiersemann, 1920–1943), vol. 20, pl. 15, fig. 88.

13. The Burke Library of Union Theological Seminary in New York City, Anton Koberger, *Biblia Germanica* (1483), fol. 251.

14. Schramm, *Der Bilderschmuck der Frühdrucke*, vol. 8, pl. 113, fig. 447. See Dürer, *Woodcuts and Woodblocks*, 153.

15. Geoffrey de La Tour Landry, *Le livre du chevalier de La Tour Landry, pour l'enseignement de ses filles. Pub. d'après les manuscrits de Paris et de Londres* (ed. M. Anatole de Montaiglon; Paris: Jannet, 1854). The relevant portion on Job's wife is on 159–61.

The work continued to be immensely popular in western Europe, as evident in the fact that at least twenty copies of the French text are extant. In this version, Job's wife brings him food by which he is sustained. Under temptation by the devil, she asks her husband if it is not better for him to die, since he is no better off otherwise. Yet she never tells him to blaspheme and he never rebukes her. The narrator, in fact, holds her up as a good woman as Job is a good man.[16] This popular tale was translated into English in 1484 and into German in 1493.[17] The German edition was illustrated by forty-six woodcuts, most of which by none other than Dürer![18] So there can be no doubt that Dürer knew of the minority report on Job's wife.

LA TOUR'S "JOB AND HIS WIFE"

A similarly positive view of Job's wife is suggested in a painting by Georges de La Tour in the seventeenth century.[19] Without knowing its precise subject matter, art critics used to think that the painting could be titled "Saint Peter Delivered from Prison by an Angel,"[20] and they generally agreed that the woman in it is an angel or at least a woman of great compassion, tenderly nursing a pitiful man.[21] All that changed in 1935, however, with the identification of the scene with the book of Job, first by Jean Lafond,[22] who pointed to the broken pot at Job's feet as presumably being broken for a shard with which to scrape him-

16. A similar point is made in the writings of the fourteenth-century German mystic Herrmann von Fritzlar, who characterized Job's wife as a model of a supportive and loving wife, a wife that other men long to have. See Franz Pfeiffer, ed., *Die deutscher Mystiker des vierzehnten Jahrhunderts: Herrmann von Fritzlar, Nicholaus von Strassburg, David von Augsburg* (Göttingen: Vandenhoeck & Ruprecht, 1907), 233, lines 26–27; Karl Reissenberger, ed., *Das Väterbuch aus der Leipziger, Hildesheimer und Strassburger Handschrift* (Deutsche Texte des Mittelalters 22; Berlin: Weidman, 1914), vv. 37098–99, 37385.

17. See, respectively, M. Y. Offord, ed., *The Book of the Knight of the Tower Translated by William Caxton* (London/New York/Toronto: Oxford University Press, 1971), 110–11; and Ruth Harvey, ed., *Der Ritter vom Turn* (trans. Marquand vom Stein [1493]; Berlin: Schmidt, 1988), 174–75.

18. Panofsky, *Albrecht Dürer*, 1:28–30. For the woodcuts, see *Die Holzschnitte zur Ritter vom Turn (Basel 1493)* (introduction by Rudolph Kautzsch; Strassburg: Heitz & Mündel, 1903).

19. Philip Conisbee, *Georges de La Tour and His World* (Washington/New Haven, CT: National Gallery of Art/ Yale University Press, 1996), 94, pl. 65. For a convenient image, see http://www.bergerfoundation.ch/Home/ high_latour.html.

20. Charles Sterling, *Les peintres de la réalité: L'Orangerie des Tuileries* (Paris: Édition des Musée Nationaux, 1934), 47.

21. André Phillipe, *Musée Départemental Des Vosges: Catalogue de la Section des Beaux-Arts, Peintures, Dessins, Sculptures* (Épinal: Musée, 1929), 66–67; W. R. Valentiner, "An Erroneous Callot Attribution," *Art in America* 20 (1931): 114–21; Paul Jamot, "Le Réalisme dans la peinture Française du XVIIe siècle," *La Revue de l'art ancien et moderne* 68 (1935): 69–76; R. Longhi (1935) *apud* Pierre Rosenberg and Francois Mace de L'Epinay, *Georges de La Tour: Vie et ouvre* (Fribourg: Office du Livre, 1973), 151.

22. Jean Lafond, "Tableau de Georges de la Tour au musée d'Épinal. 'Saint-Pierre délivré' ou 'Job et sa femme'?" *Bulletin de la Société de l'histoire de l'art Française*, 1935, 11–13.

self, and then in a lengthier article by Werner Weisbach the following year.[23] When the painting was exhibited in Paris in 1937, it bore the title *Job raillé par sa femme* (Job Mocked by His Wife), a label that sealed the fate of Job's wife.[24] Henceforth, the saving "angel" of earlier critics was transformed into the domineering and unkind wife, and her facial expression and left-hand gesture, hitherto thought to be tender and loving, are now seen as glaring and derisive. To Benedict Nicholson and Christopher Wright, therefore, she is "a Lady MacBeth of a Wife," whose arm is "hovering like a threat above her husband's head."[25] Wright would later add that she is depicted here "as a termagant and Job himself is seen as a pathetic old man helpless against his wife's unthinking tirade."[26]

The composition in the Job piece is reminiscent of several other paintings in La Tour's oeuvre. Job's wife here, in fact, resembles the Virgin Mary in *The New Born Child*[27] and in *The Adoration of the Shepherds*,[28] their dresses being similar in color and style. At the same time, Job's wife is also like St. Irene in *St. Sebastian Tended by St. Irene Holding a Lantern* and *St. Sebastian Tended by St. Irene Holding a Torch*,[29] in which, dressed like the Virgin Mary, Irene performs her act of compassion. Job himself resembles St. Sebastian in the two paintings; he is naked except for the loincloth, just like St. Sebastian. Job's wife in the Joban painting looks down at the suffering Job, as St. Irene looks down at the suffering Sebastian, and she holds a light in her right hand, just as Irene holds a light in her right hand in one of the two. The flame from her candle is not flickering at all, and a constant light in La Tour's iconography is, according to Stuart McClintock, always positive: "It can symbolize the presence of Christ and/or one's steadfast faith."[30] Yet it is Job's wife who holds the flame, and not Job. In any case, the connections between the painting of Job and his wife and the two of St. Irene with St. Sebastian can hardly be coincidental. Job is often associated

23. Werner Weisbach, "L'histoire de Job dans les arts: A propos du tableau de Georges de La Tour au muse d'Épinal," *Gazette des Beaux-Arts* 78, no. 2 (1936): 103–12.

24. See *Chefs d'oeuvre de l'art français, 1937* (2 vols.; Paris: Palais national des arts, 1937), 1:122. So the painting has widely been called "Job Mocked by His Wife." More recent exhibits, however, have tended to proffer the less committal title *Job et sa femme* (Job and His Wife), a title that signals a reconsideration of the interpretation of Job's wife.

25. Benedict Nicholson and Christopher Wright, *Georges de La Tour* (London: Phaidon, 1974), 33.

26. Christopher Wright, *Georges de La Tour* (London: Phaidon, 1977), 8.

27. Ibid., 122, cat. 27. This association was made already by Louis Gonse in his *Les Chefs-D'Oeuvre des Musés de France: La Peinture* (Paris: Société Française D'éditions D'Art, 1900), 129.

28. Wright, *Georges de La Tour*, 120, pl. 73.

29. Ibid., 130–31, pls. 78, 79.

30. Stuart McClintock, *The Iconography and Iconology of Georges de La Tour's Religious Paintings (1624–1650)* (Studies in Art and Religious Interpretation 31; Lewiston/Queenston/Lampeter: Edwin Mellen, 2003), 102.

with St. Sebastian in iconography, both of them being considered pro-
tectors from the plague and patron saints of those who suffer.[31]

Admittedly, such a view of Job's wife would have been contrary to
convention and popular perception of her in the biblical story. Yet La
Tour has been known to go against the grain in his interpretation of
biblical stories. In his *St. Thomas*,[32] for instance, he does not paint the
story about Thomas's doubt, as in John 20:19–29, and as other painters
have tended to do.[33] On the contrary, La Tour depicts Thomas as a
faithful man, his face strong and resolute and his left hand grasping a
well-worn Bible, pointing beyond the biblical moment, the moment of
doubt, to another time when even the doubter has become full of faith.
So, too, La Tour imagines Job's wife not in the biblical moment, as it
were, but in her moment of compassion for her husband—she, indeed,
holding before the sufferer a steadfast light.

RECONSIDERING THE BIBLICAL ACCOUNT

The contradicting perspectives on Job's wife prompt the interpreter of
the biblical text to return and reread it. Arguably the most intriguing
question remains the significance of the term "bless" in the brief speech
of Job's wife. Should it be taken at face value to mean "bless," or is it a
euphemism for "curse"?[34] Or is it, perhaps, intentionally ambiguous
and cannot be decided one way or another?[35] The imperative does echo
the Adversary's words in 2:5. Yet neither Job nor his wife is supposed to
know that; unlike the reader, neither is supposed to be aware of the
conversation between God and the Adversary. Moreover, in the first test
of Job, the Adversary had predicted that Job would "bless" God (1:11),
meaning the term euphemistically, but it turns out that Job did literally

---

31. St. Sebastian is typically seen with one or several arrows piercing him and this, too, is reminiscent of Job, who speaks of God's arrows piercing him (Job 6:4). Diseases are likened to arrows flying about (Job 5:7).

32. Conisbee, *Georges de La Tour and His World*, 71, cat. 13.

33. See Von Gert von der Osten, "Zur Ikonographie des ungläubigen Thomas Angesichts eines Gemäldes von Delacroix," *Wallraf-Richartz-Jahrbuch* 27 (1965): 371–88.

34. Elsewhere in the prologue, the Hebrew verb *bārak* occurs five more times, sometimes clearly euphemistically (1:5, 11; 2:5), sometimes clearly literally (1:10, 21). The former is sometimes assumed to be a euphemism to the scribes, who supposedly emended the text from *qālal* ("to curse"), where *nāʾaṣ* ("to revile"), or the like, because they could not bring themselves to say literally "curse God." Yet the scribes did tolerate literal terms for the cursing of the deity, as evident in Ps 10:3, where *nāʾaṣ*, "revile," is used alongside *bārak*, "bless" (but see 2 Sam 12:14), and in Exod 22:27 and Lev 24:10–23, where *qālal*, "curse," is used of blasphemy. The Hebrew manuscripts are, in any case, unanimous in all the occurrences of *bārak* in Job. To be sure, Syriac does *translate* the euphemistic sense of *bārak* in some cases, as the Peshitta does, but that does not reflect a *Vorlage* different from the Masoretic Text.

35. See Tod Linafelt, "The Undecidability of ברך in the Prologue to Job and Beyond," *Biblical Interpretation* 4 (1996): 154–72.

bless God's name (1:21), precisely what the Adversary had *said* but not what he had *meant* (1:21). The reader knows this, but Job does not. The play on the verb "bless" in its literal and euphemistic senses is part of the narrator's art, and the reader must, in the words of Carol A. Newsom, "negotiate its meaning."[36] Considering the narrator's semantic play, the reader cannot be too sure if Job's wife is echoing what the Adversary said (to bless God) or what the Adversary meant (to curse God). Even those who argue for the literal meaning of the imperative concede, of course, that Job must understand his wife's "bless" euphemistically, for he rebukes her for what she says. Still, whether or not she means the euphemistic sense remains an open question, and the omniscient narrator provides no clue as to how the reader should take it. The tension between human interiority and outward expression, first broached in 1:5, continues to be played out.

Furthermore, the open question about the intention of Job's wife leads one to wonder if Job's rebuke to her might not, in fact, be ironic.[37] He rebukes his wife for what he thinks is outrageous counsel. Yet the vitriol of his own speeches to follow, beginning with his malediction in the next chapter, is certainly no less outrageous, and he will himself long for death to end his suffering, arguably the intent of his wife in the first place. An ironic reading of Job's retort to his wife may be corroborated by the conclusion of the narrator that "in all this, Job did not sin with his lips" (2:10). The curious qualification "with his lips," not found in the conclusion of the first test of Job (1:22), subtly raises the question of human interiority that the narrator first posed in Job's own recognition that his children may have "blessed" (the antiphrastic meaning of the term) God in their hearts (1:5). So some Jewish interpreters have raised the possibility that Job may not have sinned with his lips, but his thought might have been otherwise,[38] or that he had not sinned with his lips *so far*, but may yet do so later.[39] There is no denying that words of Job's wife do echo the Adversary's prediction in 2:5. At the same time, though, her initial words—"you still hold on to your integrity"—echo God's confidence in Job: "he is still holding fast to his integrity" (2:3).

There are only six forms in the Hebrew of her brief speech, three of them echoing God and three echoing the Adversary. Job's wife gives

---

36. Carol A. Newsom, "The Book of Job," *The New Interpreter's Bible* (12 vols.; Nashville: Abingdon, 1996), 4:346.
37. I owe this suggestion to Alan Cooper (private communication), who is inclined to take Job's wife's "bless" literally and Job's pious response as ironic.
38. So Targum Job, *ad loc.*; Raba quoted in *b. Baba Bathra* 16a; Rashi.
39. So Ibn Ezra, *Miqra'ot Gedolot, ad loc.*

voice on earth, therefore, to the celestial exchange, giving Job access that he would not otherwise have to God's affirmation along with the Adversary's doubt. As a character, Job's wife is a minor figure in the Joban drama, having only this one line in the entire book.[40] She is neither hero nor villain. Her function in the book is, rather, a literary and theological one: to present before mortals a theological dialectic. How a human being like Job responds to that dialectic is another question altogether. It is a question pursued throughout the book, a question with which the reader must grapple.

FOR FURTHER STUDY

Astell, Ann. "Job's Wife, Walter's Wife, and the Wife of Bath." In *Old Testament Women in Western Literature*. Edited by Raymond-Jean Frontain and Jan Wojcik, 92–107. Conway: University of Central Arkansas Press, 1991.

Besserman, Lawrence L. *The Legend of Job in the Middle Ages.* Cambridge, MA: Harvard University Press, 1979.

Perraymond, Myla. *La figura di Giobbe nella cultura paleocristiana tra esegesi patristica e manifestazioni iconografiche.* Studi di antichità cristiana 58; Vatican City: Pontificio Istituto di Archeologia Cristiana, 2002.

Perry, Mary Elizabeth. "Patience and Pluck: Job's Wife, Conflict and Resistance in Morisco Manuscripts Hidden in the Sixteenth Century." In *Women, Texts, and Authority in the Early Modern Spanish World*. Edited by Marta V. Vicente and Luis R. Corteguera, 91–106. Hampshire: Ashgate, 2003.

Terrien, Samuel. *The Iconography of Job through the Centuries: Artists as Biblical Interpreters.* University Park: Pennsylvania State University Press, 1996.

---

40. So Victor Sasson, "The Literary and Theological Function of Job's Wife in the Book of Job," *Biblica* 79 (1998): 86–90.

PART THREE

Issues

12

Image and Imagination

Why Inclusive Language Matters

CHRISTIE COZAD NEUGER

Over the past forty years, almost every book and article emerging out of a feminist theological perspective has addressed in some way the issue of language and imagery for God. Over the past thirty years, books and articles on new biblical translations and on creating liturgical resources have increasingly spoken to the language and imagery used for people and God. There is wide-ranging debate expressed within this body of literature. These debates span from arguments that we need to maintain the biblical "he" for people because the Bible sets up male dominance for a good reason;[1] to commitments that biblical language about people needs to change in order to reflect changing cultural norms, but biblical language for God is revelatory in ways that prohibit changing it;[2] to challenges to the theological idolatry of exclusive male language for God and proposals that new language and imagery be used for God.[3] Why has this issue become so important to theologians and religious leaders? And why does the debate continue?

I would like to express my appreciation for Katharine Doob Sakenfeld's extraordinary scholarship in feminist biblical interpretation and for her collegiality and friendship over the years.

1. Wayne Grudem, "Do Inclusive Language Bibles Distort Scripture? Yes," *Christianity Today,* October 27, 1997, 30.

2. Grant Osborne, "Do Inclusive Language Bibles Distort Scripture? No," *Christianity Today,* October 27, 1997, 33–38.

3. Cynthia Snavely, "God Language: Expanding Image, Expanding Concept," *Journal of Religion and Theological Information* 6 (2003): 55–68.

THE NATURE OF LANGUAGE

Part of the answer to these questions has to do with the different ways in which people understand the nature of language. For many people, language is primarily seen as a tool to be used for the expression and exchange of ideas. In this context, language is generally seen as a given, something that has been generated in a culturally specific, yet neutral, manner and serves a primarily descriptive function. Yet increasingly, consensus has built around the idea (and this is by no means a new idea) that language itself is constitutive. In other words, the way we develop and use language serves a creative function—language creates the world we encounter through it. To say it even more strongly, language works to create the world in which we live, and we create language that describes that reality. This is part of the dynamic character of both language and culture. As Penelope Eckert and Sally McConnell-Ginet state, "Language is the primary means through which we maintain or contest old meanings and construct or resist new ones."[4]

Yet this balance of continuity and change, as implied in the above quote, is not neutral. The way we maintain, shape, and change language is related to how we choose, as a culture, to name our beliefs, values, and norms. Amongst the wide variety of experiences and meanings that exist in a culture, some of those experiences and meanings are given priority. As John West, Donald Bubenzer, and James Robert Bitter suggest:

> When one knowledge-position is inferred with more power than others, it becomes dominant and is sometimes referred to as the truth. Dominant knowledge positions are mostly maintained by claims to established and accepted practices, processes that generate and constitute proof of the dominant position. . . . Because dominant narratives focus on the maintenance of power, the processes that support these stories serve two functions: (a) to reinforce and maintain themselves, and (b) to eliminate or minimize alternative stories and explanations.[5]

Such prioritizing means that there are many experiences, perspectives, values, and problems that are kept from finding their way into the

---

4. Penelope Eckert and Sally McConnell-Ginet, *Language and Gender* (New York: Cambridge University Press, 2003), 6.

5. John West, Donald Bubenzer, and James Robert Bitter, eds., *Social Construction in Couple and Family Counseling* (Alexandria, VA: American Counseling Association, 1998), xi.

dominant knowledge-positions of the culture. These experiences either become invisible or become defined by the dominant cultural discourses as deviant and problematic. In an increasingly postmodern world in which we recognize diversity and diverse perspectives as valuable and truth-bearing, many believe that these dominant discourses, which parade as Truth while they block out experiences that contradict them, need to be deconstructed. It is in the midst of this context that the debate about inclusive language and imagery for biblical translation and liturgical resources takes place.

PSYCHOSOCIAL ISSUES

It is important to take a few moments to look at the psychosocial issues around gender-inclusive language. Although by 1971 the Oxford English Dictionary had declared the generic "man" obsolete[6] (as have many publishing and educational guidelines), it continues to be used in many of our secular and religious institutions. Its sustained use may represent a lack of awareness of both the confusion and the inaccuracy of using the same word to represent an entire group while it also represents a specific portion of that group. Or it may represent a commitment to maintaining the kinds of unequal power relationships between men and women in our culture that are both represented and constituted by this kind of pseudo-generic terminology.

Language generates imagery. Imagery is more powerful, more lasting, and more integrative than are concepts; moreover, we use imagery to store that which is most fundamental in our knowledge systems. When proponents of "generic" male language justify its usage, they do so by claiming that "man" includes "women." Although by this time most of us can see the flaws in this kind of thinking, we also have concrete data that demonstrate those flaws. For example, in 1972 researchers from Drake University performed a study with three hundred college students who were asked to select magazine and newspaper pictures that would best illustrate the listed chapters for a sociology textbook being prepared. Half the students were given chapter titles that used "generic" language (political man, industrial man, etc.), and the other half were given chapter titles like "political behavior" or "industrial life." As Casey Miller and Kate Swift report:

---

6. Letty M. Russell, "Inclusive Language and Power," *Religious Education* (Fall 1985): 584.

Analysis of the pictures selected revealed that in the minds of students of both sexes use of the word "man" evoked, to a statistically significant degree, images of males only, filtering out recognition of women's participation in these major areas of life, whereas the corresponding headings without "man" evoked images of both males and females. In some instances the differences reached magnitudes of 30 to 40 percent.[7]

Similar studies have been repeated over the years with other age groups and with similar results. The conclusion must be that when the language of generic "man" is used, the thoughts and images that are formed tend to be of men and not of women. Thus, when we use "generic" male language for humanity, women and women's lives, accomplishments, experiences, values, perspectives, and power are made invisible and, to a large degree, lost. This may seem just a fluke of language—that we began to use "generic" man in our language in some sort of innocence of both the gender implications and consequences. Yet at one point in time the English language exclusively used separate words for "woman," "man," and "humanity." As the language developed in dialogue with a patriarchal culture, one word began to stand for both women and men and also to represent the male gender specifically. As Ann Bodine has documented, in the late nineteenth century in England, "prescriptive grammarians instituted 'he' and 'man' as the 'correct' forms for gender-indefinite referents" (generic terms), suggesting that men were the more normative human (men were strong, women were weak)."[8] The development of the "generic" in English was not an accident. These decisions about language and the continuing use of male-oriented language take place in a culture in which men and men's perspectives are more highly valued than those of women.

A GENDERED CULTURE

We live in a world in which gender is a central organizing category. Moreover, gender, from babyhood through late adulthood, carries with

---

7. Casey Miller and Kate Swift, *Words and Women Updated* (San Jose: iUniverse.com, 1976/2000), 24.

8. Candace West, Michelle Lazar, and Cheris Kramarae, "Gender in Discourse," in *Discourse as Social Interaction* (ed. Teun A. van Dijk; London: Sage, 1997), 2.

it a set of rules, structures through which those rules are enforced, and consequences for following the rules and for breaking them. There are "dominant gender narratives," or gender discourses, within the culture that shape the way we form our personal, familial, and social core narratives and that have major influence on how we make meaning in our lives. Of course, these dominant cultural gender narratives have different kinds of power and influence depending on other cultural particularities like race and class.

Nevertheless, in our dominant U.S. culture, there is a powerful narrative strand that suggests that certain people are more valuable than others. People are subtly and blatantly ordered in a hierarchy of value based on various essential (defined more or less by birth) qualities like skin color, ethnicity, sex, able-bodiedness, intelligence, sexual orientation, and physical appearance. The combination of these factors guides our placement in the value hierarchy to a large degree. The cultural narrative or dominant discourse is the story (and stories) that implicitly and explicitly defines and prescribes this hierarchy and shapes individual, familial, and societal compliance to it. Obviously, this is not as much of a mechanical or deterministic process as I have made it sound. Many factors influence how individuals and institutions internalize and live out dominant cultural discourses. Nonetheless, the narrative about who we are as individuals and as subgroups of humanity powerfully shapes attitudes and behaviors. Gender is one such narrative.

This gender narrative has personal and cultural consequences, including the persistent wage gap between men and women (and between Euro-American women and women of color), continued (and increasing) abuse of women by male partners, and an epidemic of depression among women. Ongoing media messages (advertising, entertainment, and educational) still persistently show men as actors and women as objects. Our language and image systems contribute to these personal and cultural injustices. As Eckert and McConnell-Ginet state, "Our survival does not depend on males wearing blue and females wearing pink; humans are a reflective species and we can talk to each other. The continual differentiation of male and female serves not to guarantee biological reproduction, but to guarantee social reproduction—to reaffirm the social arrangements that depend on the categories male and female."[9]

9. Eckert and McConnell-Ginet, *Language and Gender,* 34.

THEOLOGICAL IMPLICATIONS
OF LANGUAGE AND IMAGERY

Language and imagery that are seen to be given divine approval raise the stakes in the engagement with these issues of gender justice. Some biblical scholars, church leaders, and congregants still believe that "generic" male language for human beings should be used in biblical translations and liturgical formulation. Those who hold this belief seem to do so for one of two reasons. Either they believe that the language of the Bible is specifically inerrant and that male domination over women is divinely inspired and revealed in biblical language, or they believe that the issue of gender in language is trivial or faddish. Some of the anti-inclusive language literature also expresses fear that if church leaders "cave in" to the feminist demands about language, pretty soon the core tenets of Christian faith will also be challenged and risk collapse. A sense of doctrinal gatekeeping seems to drive some of the opposition to making human language in the Bible more inclusive. As Katharine Doob Sakenfeld notes, however, in her helpful survey of feminist perspectives on biblical interpretation, "Among feminists, there remains scarcely any debate about the importance of gender-inclusive human language as part of the overall process of societal change toward more inclusive social and religious structures."[10]

When we turn to look at language for God, though, we come to a much more controversial topic. Sakenfeld continues, "The question of how to speak of the God in whose image male and female are created is more difficult, especially for Christian feminists who are heirs to the trinitarian formula."[11] Trying to formulate language and imagery for God is immensely challenging. God, by definition, is beyond all human language. When we seek to name God, we are attempting to describe our relational experiences of the divine. The most effective ways to do that are through metaphorical, analogical, and poetic language, languages that point beyond themselves to the mystery that can never be described. Human attempts to contain and name God, to capture and control mystery, are at grave risk of idolatry; yet it is the nature of metaphors and analogies to lose their tentative and iconoclastic qualities over time. When this happens, we end up trying to hold on to that which is transcendent and to totalize that which cannot be fully grasped.

10. Katharine Doob Sakenfeld, "Feminist Perspectives on Bible and Theology: An Introduction to Selected Issues and Literature," *Interpretation* 42 (1988): 13.
11. Ibid., 13.

Many would suggest that this is what has happened to the naming of God as Father.

There is broad consensus that God is not biologically male, yet the dominant language and imagery for God reflect maleness. Letty M. Russell notes, "The writings in the Bible took shape in a variety of cultures, but they were all patriarchal and it is not possible either to expect or desire the original manuscripts to reflect sex-inclusive language."[12] Yet, Russell asks, does biblical authority rest on unchanging language and text? Many would suggest that it is more helpful to rest biblical authority on the timeless and persistent themes that emerge throughout the Scriptures, themes like hospitality for those who are traditionally excluded, a relationship with the living God, and the centrality of justice making. These themes inform the rest of our look at gender-inclusive language and imagery through the categories of idolatry, kyriarchy, and injustice.

Idolatry

According to Miller and Swift:

> Nowhere are the semantic roadblocks to sexual equality more apparent or significant than in the language of the dominant organized religions. This is ironic but not surprising. Religious thinkers are forced to depend on symbols, particularly on metaphors and analogies, to describe and communicate to others what is by nature indescribable except in terms of human experience. The symbols are not intended to be taken literally but to point beyond themselves to a reality that can only be dimly perceived at best.[13]

The primary language through which we can begin to reveal our experience of the Holy is that of symbol, metaphor, and image—the language of the imagination. Many experiences of the divine are too big for words and touch us at so many levels that we can only encounter the experience through our imaginations.

Images, be they intellectual, emotional, or physical, are developmentally prior to words for human beings. Many of our earliest memories and knowledge are stored in image form. In addition, images have

---

12. Russell, "Inclusive Language and Power," 587.
13. Miller and Swift, *Words and Women Updated,* 76.

an integrative ability; they pull the thoughts, feelings, and intentions of the experience together in such a way that the encounter is received as a whole. And that wholeness resists deconstruction. Its power resides in the fullness of the experience. Thus images are often the vehicle of encounter with the divine, for individuals and communities. We tend to express and preserve those kinds of encounters through symbol (a meaningful, articulated image) and metaphor. Much of our biblical language for God is expressed in metaphor. One might say, then, that imagination becomes the playground on which we meet God.

A metaphor is a vehicle through which to compare one image to another. In a metaphor, as contrasted with a symbol, there is both similarity and dissimilarity implied in the comparison. As Sallie McFague states in her book *Metaphorical Theology,* "One critical difference between symbolic and metaphorical is that the latter always contains the whisper, 'it is and it is not.' A metaphorical perspective does see connections, but they are of a tensive, discontinuous and surprising nature."[14] This tensive, surprising quality keeps us from being able to collapse the metaphor with the experience being described. When we use metaphor to describe our encounter with the divine, we always have the "is not" to keep us from turning the experience of the divine, which is always partial, into an idol.

In a similar way, when we are exposed to new metaphors for the divine, we, as individuals and communities, are invited to expand our experiences and ideas about God. We may be appalled or we may be delighted, but either way the metaphorical challenge urges us to encounter the divine mystery in a new way, to test out whether this metaphor may bring an unexpected opening to an encounter with God. And new metaphors that reflect an experience with God serve an iconoclastic function. They deconstruct the totality of previous descriptions of God. They refuse to allow us to describe God totally, and thereby they refuse to allow us to domesticate and contain God. With new language, we are held accountable for our tendency to create graven images rather than to live with the ambiguity and mystery that is God. The God who is described in Exodus as "I am who I am, I will be who I will be" (Exod 3:14) serves as a warning to the idolatry of a fixed image or a dead metaphor.

Dead metaphors are those that have lost their "is and is not" quality such that they now only portray the "is." There is no space left between

---

14. Sallie McFague, *Metaphorical Theology: Models of God in Religious Language* (Philadelphia: Fortress, 1982), 13.

the word and that toward which it is trying to point. Rita Gross, speaking out of a Jewish context, writes, "Although it is often ignored, the attitudinal 'as if' or 'as it were' is fundamental to the religious enterprise. If the 'as if' changes to 'it is,' if what is focused on is the metaphor instead of what it points to, religion becomes idolatry . . . for a poverty of religious imagination characteristic of the contemporary milieu makes many people idolaters today. They simply block out of their consciousness the metaphorical nature of religious language and become addicted to the linguistic conventions, the signs and tools of religious discourse."[15]

Kathleen Hughes, a Roman Catholic scholar, gives an example of how dead metaphors can function powerfully as both oppressive and idolatrous when she tells the story of a meeting at the Vatican to discuss inclusive language proposals for English liturgy:

> A representative of the Congregation for the Doctrine of Faith stated, "The angry, irritated and resentful women of the United States are systematically attempting to change the gender of God." His words hung in the air, most of us were astonished. A representative of the highest doctrinal body in the Church was suggesting that God had a gender. How had this conviction formed in him? I submit that it was probably because of the power of words to shape reality. I suspect that language that regularly, consistently, and exclusively referred to the God of our Lord Jesus Christ in masculine terms led this man actually to conceive of God as masculine, as gendered.

She concludes the story by noting that a colleague leaned over to her and whispered John Wesley's words, "The human heart is a perpetual factory of idols."[16]

It is necessary, in order to defeat the human tendency toward idolatry, to continue to generate new images and metaphors for the God-human relationship. McFague suggests that this requires a renewed commitment, as individuals and communities, to contemplation and prayer. She suggests that it is only through spiritual practices that we will defeat our tendency to rely on dead metaphors to express our religious convictions.[17]

---

15. Rita Gross, "Female God Language in a Jewish Context," in *WomanSpirit Rising: A Feminist Reader in Religion* (ed. Carol Christ and Judith Plaskow; San Francisco: Harper and Row, 1979), 169.

16. Kathleen Hughes, "Inclusive Language Revisited," *Chicago Studies* 35 (August 1996): 117.

17. McFague, *Metaphorical Theology*, 5.

Kyriarchy

Kyriarchy is a term, coined by Elisabeth Schüssler Fiorenza, to describe that which is broader than, but includes, patriarchy. It is an interlocking structure of "lordship" that supports and renders operational the hierarchy of valuing described earlier. Kyriarchy is a way to talk about how biblical language tends to justify hierarchical rule by those who are granted cultural power over those who are not. The model of hierarchical rule becomes a problem in and of itself when the primary metaphors for God are those of a ruler. Satoko Yamaguchi suggests, "Because God is kyrios (lord-like), lords and powerholders are god-like. . . . What is at stake here is the transformation of this kyriarchal world into the ekklesia of wo/men."[18] This critique of biblical language opens up the awareness that, while mutuality and community are core religious values, they are undercut by a primary image for God as the One who rules over all.

Nancy Victorin-Vangerud, in her book *The Raging Hearth: Spirit in the Household of God,* suggests that it is important to expand our understanding of the Trinity away from the centrality of the Father God over the other two figures of the godhead. She proposes that Christianity's emphasis on the first person of the Trinity, who rules over the "household of God," has a major impact on the formation of both our human families and the church family. The ruling nature of the Father God in the Trinity, she says, supports the notion that parents (especially fathers) should rule over their children and clergy (often "fathers") should rule over their congregants. Using the story of Pentecost (Acts 2:1–41), she invites us to consider as a model for human community today the role of the Spirit in bringing together diversity while still respecting difference. Her privileging of the Spirit aspects of the Trinity provides a more helpful, nonhierarchical model for the kind of diverse community we experience in this postmodern world and offers a vision for a mutuality not available in the traditional prioritizing of the male-identified, first person of the Trinity.[19] As Arlene Wallace Gordon states, "No one cultural perspective should dominate (in our language about God), but rather each culture should be seen as contributing

18. Satoko Yamaguchi, "Father Image of G*d and Inclusive Language: A Reflection in Japan," in *Toward a New Heaven and a New Earth: Essays in Honor of Elisabeth Schüssler Fiorenza* (ed. Fernando F. Segovia; Maryknoll, NY: Orbis, 2003), 200.

19. Nancy Victorin-Vangerud, *The Raging Hearth: Spirit in the Household of God* (St. Louis: Chalice, 2000).

beliefs, values, practices, and achievements that are equally valuable."[20] There is much at stake when our primary images and metaphors equate God with a white, male ruler because it contributes to a culture in which white male rulership is seen, at the least, as normative and, at the worst, as divinely sanctioned.

Justice

The above issues, of course, lead us to a consideration of justice. When primary metaphors for God collapse the distance between the image and the reality, then whatever name we have given to God in the metaphor becomes our God. When that name has explicit anthropomorphic qualities, like whiteness, maleness, and hierarchical rule, then those qualities become godlike in both our images and our doctrines. Rebecca Chopp puts the matter succinctly: "Patriarchy is revealed not simply as a social arrangement nor as individual acts of cruelty toward women on the part of men, but rather as a deep spiritual ordering that invades and spreads across the social order—through individual identity, to social practices, to lines of authority in institutions, to cultural images and representations."[21]

Issues of naming are crucial to justice making. Questions arise, such as, Who has the right to name? What does it mean to name? How do we name the unnameable? The power of naming, especially naming God, continues to be a high-stake task for the theological enterprise. As early as 1980, a World Council of Churches study group, representing seventeen countries, wrote, "We have discovered that an almost exclusively male image of God in the Christian tradition has helped cause the affirmation of male, white, Western superiority and has led to a sense of inferiority of women and of people from non-Western cultures."[22]

When women are not reflected in the divine image, it becomes difficult for them to find the Holy in themselves. Mary Daly's statement is widely acknowledged: "If God is male, then males are God."[23] Women

20. Arlene Wallace Gordon, "If I Speak in the Tongues of Angels: Has Language Done Irreparable Damage to African Americans?" *Church and Society,* November/December 1998, 34.

21. Rebecca Chopp, *Saving Work: Feminist Practices of Theological Education* (Louisville, KY: Westminster John Knox, 1995), 56.

22. "A Report of the World Council of Churches," *Ecumenical Review* 33, no. 1 (January 1981): 77.

23. Mary Daly, *Beyond God the Father: Toward a Philosophy of Women's Liberation,* With an Original Reintroduction by the Author (Boston: Beacon, 1985), 19.

are "not God." In the words of Rosemary Radford Ruether, "Women no longer stand in direct relation to God; they are connected to God secondarily, through the male."[24] The rights and privileges of a cultural patriarchy, with all its negative consequences for women and children, are bestowed upon men by virtue of their God-likeness. There are significant justice issues in the oppression and marginalization of women that get reinforced through our dominant God imagery and language.

The core critiques of idolatry and irrelevance proposed by many feminist theologians have more recently been joined by those of male theologians considering the religious concerns of men. In a book edited by Richard Holloway, a variety of male theologians respond to issues of sexism in the church both as these issues affect women and also as they negatively impact men. Images of God that combine authority, power, rationality, protectiveness of others, kingship, dependability, righteous anger, maleness, and fatherhood have a formative and normative and harmful impact on definitions of manhood and masculinity.[25] These issues of religious language and the social construction of gendered relationships negatively impact the well-being of all.

The question still remains, though, of what kinds of images and metaphors might we hope to generate as a way both to enhance our access to the divine and to deconstruct a kyriarchal culture. Yamaguchi reports that pronouns for God in Japan are neutral. Yet God is still seen in masculine terms because of all the other imagery that unconsciously informs our understanding of God. She warns that neutral imagery of God will tend to "fill in" with masculine connotations so that it is necessary to generate female metaphors for God as well. We know that God is not gendered as such, but female metaphors will help to deconstruct the male imagery that has been totally descriptive of God. Yamaguchi also suggests that:

> we need to expand inclusive language for G*d to the dimensions of ethnicity, class, sexual orientation, and further particularities of human embodiment, all of which are created in the image of G*d. Such an action is not meant to valorize all the diversity engendered by kyriarchal oppression, but to see the image of G*d embodied in each person, even in the variety of exploited or distorted situations, so that we can clearly see our structural selves, which are against G*d's creation.[26]

24. Rosemary Radford Ruether, *Sexism and God Talk: Toward a Feminist Theology* (Boston: Beacon, 1983), 53.

25. Philip Sheldrake, "Spirituality and Sexism," in *Who Needs Feminism? Men Respond to Sexism in the Church* (ed. Richard Holloway; London: SPCK, 1991), 91.

26. Yamaguchi, "Father Image of G*d and Inclusive Language," 223.

CONCLUSION

We are at a point in our corporate theological journey where the critiques of idolatry, kyriarchy, and injustice have to be taken seriously as we engage in the process of knowing and naming our relationships with each other and with God. Our awareness that the religious language we use participates in constructing our world mandates careful attention to the importance of inclusivity, mutuality, and accountability. Elizabeth A. Johnson makes a crucial point when she states, "The way a faith community speaks about God indicates what it considers the highest good, the profoundest truth, the most appealing beauty. This language, in turn, molds the community's corporate identity and behavior as well as the individual self-understanding of its members. . . . The symbol of God functions. It is neither abstract in content nor neutral in effect, but expresses a community's bedrock convictions."[27]

We must hold on to the commitments that are at the heart of our tradition, those of love, justice, and mutuality, in our language for each other and for God. We must stay aware that our language has very real effects on the lives of people and communities, and that it really does matter how we name one another and God. And we need persistently to be aware that language for God is always partial and tentative, pointing toward the Holy Mystery even as we seek to name the power of our relationships with God.[28]

FOR FURTHER STUDY

Aldredge-Clanton, Jann. *In Whose Image: God and Gender.* Rev. ed. New York: Crossroad, 2000.

Chopp, Rebecca. *The Power to Speak: Feminism, Language, God.* New York: Crossroad, 1989.

Daly, Mary. *Beyond God the Father: Toward a Philosophy of Women's Liberation.* 2nd ed. Boston: Beacon, 1993.

Johnson, Elizabeth A. *She Who Is: The Mystery of God in Feminist Theological Discourse.* New York: Crossroad, 1993.

Segovia, Fernando E., ed. *Toward a New Heaven and a New Earth: Essays in Honor of Elisabeth Schüssler Fiorenza.* Maryknoll, NY: Orbis, 2003.

27. Elizabeth A. Johnson, "A Theological Case for God-She: Expanding the Treasury of Metaphor," *Commonweal,* January 29, 1993, 11–12.

28. I would like to thank Mitzi Ellington for her assistance in gathering research for this article.

13

Rupturing God-Language

The Metaphor of God as Midwife in Psalm 22

L. JULIANA M. CLAASSENS

A central issue in feminist theology regards the question of God-language, or how to speak about God in ways that do justice to the belief that both male and female are created in the image of God. Therefore, both male and female metaphors should be used in our theological artic- ulations. Feminist theologians like Phyllis Trible, Johanna van Wijk-Bos, and Elizabeth A. Johnson have provided us with thought-provoking and inspiring examples of imagining God in new and creative ways.[1] All of these theologians reclaim female imagery for God by lifting up images in Scripture and tradition that have not yet been fully utilized in the past (e.g., Deut 32:13, 18; Num 11:11–15; Isa 42:14; 45:9–12).

However helpful these treatments are in identifying this important issue, a number of challenges still confront feminist theologians in their quest to speak of God in a way that moves us beyond a narrow patriarchal understanding. One such problem is that there are relatively few female images in the biblical traditions compared to the many male- oriented metaphors with which they share narrative space. The question facing feminist theologians who have chosen to stay in the Judeo- Christian tradition is how to use these voices constructively and cre- atively. Toward this task, a first step would be to affirm that these minor

---

1. Elizabeth A. Johnson, *She Who Is: The Mystery of God in Feminist Theological Discourse* (New York: Crossroad, 1992); Phyllis Trible, *God and the Rhetoric of Sexuality* (Overtures to Biblical Theology; Philadelphia: Fortress, 1978); Johanna W. H. van Wijk-Bos, *Reimagining God: The Case for Scriptural Diversity* (Louisville, KY: Westminster John Knox, 1995).

voices are not necessarily insignificant. Rather, as this article shows, the female imagery we find for God in Scripture, although small in amount, plays a definitive role in furthering our speech about God. As we will see, it is exactly these voices that generate dialogue and contribute to the formation of new meaning—often by rupturing traditional formulations about God—which may have the effect of expanding our understanding of God. The challenge is to take these traditions, which still may have been underdeveloped at the time, and utilize them afresh.

In this challenge, the thought of the Russian literary theorist Mikhail M. Bakhtin provides us with helpful perspectives on the way God-language functions in Ps 22.[2] Psalm 22 presents a good example of the struggle involved in finding adequate God-language when traditional metaphors seem insufficient. Within this process, it is significant that we encounter one of the few instances in the Psalms where a female image for God is used. In Ps 22:9–10, we find the provocative image of God as midwife when the psalmist proclaims: "Yet it was you who took me from the womb; you kept me safe on my mother's breast. On you I was cast from my birth, and since my mother bore me you have been my God." I argue that although this female image constitutes a relatively small occurrence in light of the other metaphors used for God, it fulfills an important function in the context of Ps 22—particularly in the way the believer experiences God in this time of crisis. In addition, this female image provides us, as readers, an incentive to broaden and even transform our overall image of God.

This article was conceived in the spirit of the valuable lessons I have learned from my mentor and friend, Katharine Doob Sakenfeld. Her attention to voices from the margins, which is evident in her commitment to reading from a different social location than her own, has taught me about the importance of paying special attention to those voices that at first glance may not be the most evident. Moreover, as an international scholar from South Africa who is learning how to move between worlds, I have found in Professor Sakenfeld a wonderful example as she gracefully glides among her various roles as teacher,

---

2. For a more elaborate discussion of the work of Mikhail Bakhtin as it relates to biblical theology cf. L. Juliana Claassens, "Biblical Theology as Dialogue: Continuing the Conversation on Bakhtin and Biblical Theology," *Journal of Biblical Literature* 122 (2003): 127–44. It is true that Mikhail Bakhtin favored the novel as the space where true polyphony can occur. Bakhtin even states that poetry cannot be polyphonic in the true sense of the word ("Discourse in the Novel," in *The Dialogic Imagination: Four Essays,* ed. Michael Holquist; trans. Caryl Emerson and Michael Holquist [Austin: University of Texas Press, 1981], 286–87). Nevertheless, his principles on dialogue can fruitfully be applied to the Psalms; one can clearly detect in the Psalms how earlier voices are reused in a new context (cf. Herbert Levine, "The Dialogic Discourse of Psalms," in *Hermeneutics, the Bible, and Literary Criticism* [ed. A. Loades and M. McLain; New York: St. Martin's Press, 1992], 146–47).

scholar, administrator, pastor, and church leader in the United States as well as abroad.

THE POWER OF MINOR VOICES

One of the major contributions of Bakhtin's work is his emphasis on dialogue, and particularly his desire to hear all voices equally. Bakhtin first identifies this tendency in relation to the work of Fyodor Dosto-yevsky: "He heard both the loud, recognized, reigning voices of the epoch, that is, the reigning, dominant ideas (official and unofficial), as well as voices still weak, ideas not yet fully emerged, latent ideas heard as yet by no one but himself, and ideas that were just beginning to ripen, embryos of future worldviews."[3]

From his engagement with Dostoyevsky, Bakhtin derives a literary theory that has profound implications for life. It is beneficial to notice different voices not only in novels. Feminist theologians and other groups suffering oppression have helped us understand the necessity, in life itself, to be sensitive to different voices—particularly those who have been silenced in the past. It is exactly this point that makes Bakhtin so attractive for feminist interpreters. A feminist dialogics allows voices to stand next to each other without being merged or drowned out.[4] More-over, this point is particularly helpful for our understanding of the role of female language in theological discourse. As I have noted, the num-ber of female images that are used for God is relatively small indeed. But these voices are essential, for they help to facilitate dialogue. Bakhtin teaches us that when an idea comes into contact with other ideas, what he calls "alien thought," new meaning is born. He says, "The idea begins to live, that is, to take shape, to develop, to find and renew its verbal expression, to give birth to new ideas, only when it enters into genuine dialogic relationships with other ideas, with the ideas of others."[5] Thus, it is exactly the unlikely voice, or the unexpected thought, that is respon-sible for new insight and transformation.

We see something of this at work in the psalm's use of a female image for God as midwife in verses 9–10. Although one could rightly describe

3. Mikhail M. Bakhtin, *Problems of Dostoevsky's Poetics* (ed. and trans. Caryl Emerson; Theory and History of Lit-erature 8; Minneapolis: University of Minnesota Press, 1984), 90.

4. Karen Hohne and Helen Wussow, "Introduction," in *A Dialogue of Voices: Feminist Literary Theory and Bakhtin* (ed. Karen Hohne and Helen Wussow; Minneapolis: University of Minnesota Press, 1994), xii.

5. Bakhtin, *Problems of Dostoevsky's Poetics,* 88; "Discourse in the Novel," 284.

this image, in terms of Bakhtin's description, as not yet fully emerged or as an idea in its embryonic state, this metaphor fulfills an important role in the psalmist's thought process of figuring out who God is in those times when things no longer make sense.

Psalm 22 starts out with a cry of anguish. The psalmist deeply feels the absence of God, and cries out, "My God, my God, why have you forsaken me?" (v. 1). This cry of desolation already suggests something of the inner struggle at work throughout the rest of the psalm. The psalmist is trying to reconcile the personal nature of her relationship ("my God") with her current experience of God's hiddenness and absence.[6]

In the rest of the poem, the psalmist is in dialogue with voices of the past and present as she is trying to recall who God is, using numerous metaphors to describe God throughout the space of the psalm. God is said to be holy (v. 3), the liberator God (vv. 4–5, 8, 20–21), God of the ancestors (v. 4), God as king (v. 28), and God as midwife (vv. 9–10). These metaphors all constitute different ways of imagining the deity—some more traditionally than others.

Within this dialogue we see something of what Bakhtin describes as the dynamic process of moving from speaking in the voices of others to finding one's own voice. Bakhtin shows how, within discourse (e.g., the writings of Dostoyevsky on which Bakhtin bases his theory), one finds a distinctive move from voices that are "authoritatively persuasive" to voices that have become "internally persuasive."[7]

This notion is powerfully illustrated in Ps 22. In her anguish, the psalmist tries all kinds of metaphors to help her out of the pit of despair in which she finds herself. In this dialogue, the psalmist uses the words of others when she begs the God of the ancestors, the liberator God, the God of holiness to save her. Even the voices of those who mock the psalmist, which are introduced in the direct speech quoted in verse 8, invoke this more traditional understanding of God when they parody the ancestors' confidence in a God who saves.[8]

The question is whether these metaphors, which could be considered traditional descriptions of God (or in Bakhtin's words, "authoritarian discourse") always work. We see in verse 6 that even after evoking these traditionally cherished voices of the past, the psalmist draws a

---

6. Although the psalmist was most likely a man, for the purpose of this paper I use the female pronoun in an attempt to be sensitive to inclusive language.

7. Bakhtin, "Discourse in the Novel," 342–43; *Problems of Dostoevsky's Poetics,* 195.

8. Ellen F. Davis, "Exploding the Limits: Form and Function in Psalm 22," *Journal for the Study of the Old Testament* 53 (1992): 97.

sharp contrast between her own experience and the authoritarian voices that have been handed down to her. In the beginning of verse 6, the psalmist uses the phrase "But I." This introduces an outpouring of words of despair (vv. 6–7). The psalmist utters her anguish, using words that describe her shame of being dehumanized (note the description in v. 6, "I am a worm, and not human," and the verbs "despise," "scorn," and "mock")—this in contrast to the ancestors who were not put to shame (v. 5). The psalmist draws a further contrast between her own experience and that of the ancestors when she uses the verb "to trust" three times in verses 4–5 for the relation between her ancestors and God. Her perception of the ancestors who trusted and were saved is contrasted with her own experience of a God who is absent and is not liberating her from her suffering.

Peter C. Craigie calls this a contradiction between theology and experience.[9] At present, the psalmist seems to be questioning the effectiveness of the authoritative voices of the past (theology), with regard to her current experience of being in a dark pit of despair. Ellen F. Davis rightly notes that the previous symbolic system proves to be hopelessly inadequate in the current situation. She argues that the psalm needs a new kind of speech, speech that moves "toward the creation of a new symbolic order capable of encompassing the vastly expanded territory of the psalmist's experience."[10]

This new kind of speech is dramatically illustrated in the radical transformation from the absolute despair the psalmist is experiencing (vv. 2–21) to a renewed hope for the future (vv. 22–31), so much so that some scholars have suggested that this psalm originally consisted of two separate psalms. Most scholars now believe that the psalm is a unified composition that provides a powerful example of moving from lament to praise. I argue that this new vision of the future that grows out of lament is related to the dynamic process of moving from the voices of others to finding new symbols of hope, or in Bakhtin's words, transforming the authoritarian discourse of the past into an internally persuasive discourse. It is only when God-language has become internally persuasive that the psalmist can begin to imagine a transformed future. Within this process, the female image of God as midwife (vv. 9–10), which otherwise could be considered a less dominant voice, provides the

---

9. Peter C. Craigie, *Psalms 1–50* (Word Biblical Commentary; Waco, TX: Word, 1983), 199; Patrick D. Miller, *They Cried to the Lord: The Form and Theology of Biblical Prayer* (Minneapolis: Fortress, 1994), 114.
10. Davis, "Exploding the Limits," 97, 99.

first signs of this type of internally persuasive speech that breaks open the traditional formulations about God.

GOD AS MIDWIFE

The image of God as midwife occurs in verses 9–10 as part of a motivational clause, similar to the motivational clause in verses 3–5 in which the psalmist provides reasons for asking God to help. But there is a distinctive difference between the content of these two clauses. John S. Kselman describes this difference in tone in terms of the transition that occurs from "our fathers" (v. 4) to "my mother" (vv. 9–10); from the voices of the community to the individual's own experience.[11] In contrast to the traditional voices of the ancestors, we see how the motivational clause in verses 9–10 is marked by personal, intimate language that describes the psalmist's own experience of God as present from the moment she drew her first breath. The psalmist addresses God with the pronoun "you," saying that it was God who assisted at her birth, who drew[12] the psalmist out of her mother's womb and who kept her safe on her mother's breasts. From that moment, she was cast upon God, whom she boldly calls "my God." Verses 9–10 end with the confident statement of faith, "You are my God," altering the initial cry of despair in verse 1 ("My God, my God, why have you forsaken me?") into a declaration of trust.

It is significant to note that right after this metaphor of God as midwife (vv. 9–10), one finds the first petition in which the psalmist begs God not to be far away from her (v. 11). This petition is repeated (v. 19), with the added request to God to save her from her situation (vv. 20–21). These two petitions form an inclusio, framing the honest and painful expression of the suffering currently endured by the believer. Immediately following the second petition, the psalm moves into a dramatic transformation (vv. 22–31). It thus seems that this road to transformation is introduced by the move from the traditional voices of the fathers to the personal experience of the speaker, in which the female image of God as midwife plays a central role. This progression reiterates Bakhtin's point of the power of the minor voice to bring about new insight.

---

11. John S. Kselman, "'Why Have You Abandoned Me?' A Rhetorical Study of Psalm 22," in *Art and Meaning: Rhetoric in Biblical Literature* (ed. David J. A. Clines et al.; Journal for the Old Testament Supplement Series 19; Sheffield: JSOT Press, 1982), 184, 194; cf. also Miller, *They Cried to the Lord*, 114–15.

12. The etymology of the Hebrew verb *gōḥî* is uncertain. Most scholars, though, retain the meaning "drew from the womb" (Craigie, *Psalms 1–50*, 196).

So, what connotations would this image of God as midwife—which plays such a central role in the movement from despair to a hopeful future—have? First, in light of the fact that women often died in childbirth (e.g., Rachel [Gen 35:16–19]), the midwife fulfilled a very important function in those situations when people deeply experienced the fragility of life, in those moments when death and life tend to intersect.[13]

The use of this metaphor in the context of Ps 22 is based on the belief that God is the opener and closer of the womb (cf. Gen 29:31; 30:22; 1 Sam 1:5–6). To assign the function of a midwife to God is to profess that God is in control of life and death. It is to implore God to bring about life in the midst of a situation of death (note the description in vv. 17–18 of the psalmist being almost a skeleton whose bones can be counted and whose possessions are divided among others). Elsewhere in the Psalms, the image of the "pit" or "Sheol" is often used to describe suffering similar to that experienced by the psalmist in Ps 22. So, for instance, one finds in Ps 40:2 the expression that God draws the psalmist up from the pit (see also Ps 30:3). Evoking the connotations of a midwife who draws a baby from the womb, thereby bringing life to a child who would have died together with its mother if she stayed in the womb, the psalmist pleads with God to bring about life in her own situation of suffering and despair so strong that it is close to death. In conjunction with her prayer for deliverance in verses 20–21, the speaker pleads with God to deliver her life.[14]

It is significant that, in verses 20–21, the psalmist once more uses the traditional metaphor of God as deliverer. But now this metaphor no longer constitutes the authoritarian voices of others; rather, it has been reclaimed by the psalmist to become internally persuasive. It seems that it is through the employment of the female image of God, as a midwife who delivers, that the psalmist can use in her prayer of deliverance the more traditional metaphor of God as savior.

Furthermore, it is important to note that this image of God as midwife occurs in the midst of suffering and despair. The image is not a magic cure. Right before and right after this metaphor, one finds in-depth descriptions of the physical and psychological anguish the psalmist is experiencing. The psalmist speaks of her pain of being persecuted.

13. The danger of childbirth is evident from the high mortality rate among females in their childbearing years. Carol L. Meyers points out that, whereas men's life expectancy in biblical times was around forty years, women's life expectancy was closer to thirty years of age ("The Roots of Restriction: Women in Early Israel," *Biblical Archaeologist* 41 [1978]: 95).

14. The power of the midwife to bring about life out of death is vividly illustrated in the story of the two midwives in Exod 1, in which the two women, Shiprah and Puah, play a central role in the birth of a nation.

Using a series of animal metaphors (bulls in v. 12, a lion in v. 13, dogs in v. 16), she describes the feeling of being threatened, surrounded, or trapped by whatever circumstances are responsible for her situation. We further see how the psychological anguish the psalmist is experiencing leads to severe physical symptoms. This reaches a climax in verse 14, where the psalmist describes in rich, figurative language how she feels like water being poured out, how her bones are separated and her heart is melting like wax.

But in the midst of this despair we see maternal imagery evoked to describe the need for consolation—like little boys and girls in pain run to their mothers and fathers. In this regard, Phyllis Trible notes how in Ps 22 the "divine and the maternal intertwine."[15] She shows how verses 9–10 make a close connection between God and the mother. In verse 9, it is God who places the psalmist on the breasts of her mother. But Trible notes that the end of verse 9 and the beginning of verse 10 contain two "parallel prepositional phrases whose meanings converge. 'Upon the breasts of my mother' leads directly to 'upon you.' Subject has become object; divine midwife has become divine mother. To be kept safe upon the breasts of the mother is to be cast upon God from the womb."[16]

It thus seems that even if the internally persuasive image of God does not immediately provide relief, it attests to the important realization that God is present in the midst of pain. Wendy Farley has written extensively about the divine compassion that causes God to enter into suffering. This characteristic of God is evoked in the psalmist's repeated petition, "Do not be far away." But Farley rightly points out that God is not only "the benevolent but impotent deity who 'suffers with the world.'" Rather, "divine compassion is . . . a radical love that offers liberating power" to overcome the forces of chaos that are responsible for suffering in the world.[17]

One could thus say that the image of God as a midwife who works in conjunction with the nurturing mother to care for the psalmist is evoked to describe God's presence in the midst of the reality of suffering. Nevertheless, in verses 19–22 the psalmist asks God not only to be present but also to change her situation. This twofold function of God's nurturing presence and God's saving power is captured in the metaphor of God as midwife—a minor voice that gives rise to new insight and provides a new way of imagining God.

---

15. Trible, *God and the Rhetoric of Sexuality*, 38.
16. Ibid., 60. Cf. also Kselman, "'Why Have You Abandoned Me?'" 176–77.
17. Wendy Farley, *Tragic Vision and Divine Compassion: A Contemporary Theodicy* (Louisville, KY: Westminster John Knox, 1990), 113.

VISIONS OF THE FUTURE

In verses 22–31, the psalmist sings a song of thanksgiving in the perfect tense, giving expression to the unwavering belief that God's deliverance is so certain that one can sing of it as if it has already occurred. Within this transformation it is remarkable that the psalmist is no longer singing only of her own deliverance. Using ever-widening circles, the speaker, who was formerly isolated, now proclaims in the midst of the congregation of Israel a new image of God. Using only personalized language, the psalmist reuses old images to provide a new vision that extends far beyond her own personal situation to the congregation of Israel, to foreign nations, to unborn generations, and even to the dead.

Within this new understanding of God, we see a vision of justice in a transformed world where the poor (or afflicted) will have enough to eat (v. 26; cf. also 1 Sam 2:5; Luke 1:53). It is a vision in which God will rule over all the nations, in which people around the earth will acknowledge God, thus proclaiming something of the universal perspective that refuses to claim salvation for only the self.

This vision of God that is both open to the future and also has implications for others relates to the central perspective in a feminist theological reimagining of God, that is, what Mary Grey calls "God as our passion for justice." She says that what is needed to counter the "staticness of the traditional images of God" is a "dynamic image of a God who not only 'hears the cries of the poor' (Ps. 72:12–14), but whose compassion and active solidarity transform the unjust situation."[18]

Such an image of a God who is committed to a transformed world forms a central aspect of feminist theologians' endeavors to critique ideologies and resist oppressive structures. Moreover, in terms of our objective of taking a female image for God and utilizing it afresh, it is significant that the female image of God as midwife who acts as deliverer and comforter culminates in an image of divine justice. This is a good reminder that our new images for God should always contain an element of justice—particularly as God-language can easily become dangerous if claimed exclusively for the self. We should always remember that the liberated could well become the oppressor of tomorrow, and the comforted the coldhearted.

Finally, it is important to note that the psalmist's vision of transformation ends with the hope that future generations will continue to pro-

---

18. Mary Grey, *Introducing Feminist Images of God* (Sheffield: Sheffield Academic Press, 2001), 45.

claim God's deliverance (vv. 30–31). The psalm's conclusion reflects Bakhtin's understanding that the viewer is also a participant in the ongoing dialogue. Every reader continues to respond to the voices of past, and through this process gives new meaning and finds new accents in what has been handed down.[19] This is also true with regard to God-language. We have the obligation to continue the dynamic process of making the traditional voices of others our own by finding new ways of speaking about God that are more suitable for our time. These new images could well be found in the minor voices within the tradition and Scripture, which can be picked up and appropriated anew. Such a transformation corresponds with an important quality of a feminist dialogics, which does not want only to detect the minor voices within a dialogue, but also to find ways to strengthen and expand these voices.[20] It is exactly these voices that may be responsible for surprisingly new insights that broaden our understanding of God, providing us with language that may be more suitable for the times we are facing.

FOR FURTHER STUDY

Grey, Mary. *Introducing Feminist Images of God*. Introductions in Feminist Theology. Sheffield: Sheffield Academic Press, 2001.

Johnson, Elizabeth A. *She Who Is: The Mystery of God in Feminist Theological Discourse*. New York: Crossroad, 1992.

Kwok Pui-lan. *Asian Feminist Theology*. Introductions in Feminist Theology. Sheffield: Sheffield Academic Press, 2001.

Oduyoye, Mercy Amba. *Introducing African Women's Theology*. Introductions in Feminist Theology. Sheffield: Sheffield Academic Press, 2001.

Schüssler Fiorenza, Elisabeth, ed. *The Power of Naming: A Concilium Reader in Feminist Liberation Theology*. Maryknoll, NY: Orbis, 1996.

Trible, Phyllis. *God and the Rhetoric of Sexuality*. Overtures to Biblical Theology. Philadelphia: Fortress, 1978.

Wijk-Bos, Johanna W. H. van. *Reimagining God: The Case for Scriptural Diversity*. Louisville, KY: Westminster John Knox, 1995.

19. Bakhtin, *Problem of Dostoevsky's Poetics,* 18; "Discourse in the Novel," 282. We see something of this dynamic process at work in the future use of Ps 22 itself. It is significant that v. 1 becomes Jesus' prayer on the cross, attesting to the evangelist's conviction that the movement from lament to future hope is exemplified in the event of Jesus' crucifixion and resurrection (cf. Davis, "Exploding the Limits," 104).

20. Suzanne Rosenthal Shumway, "The Chronotype of the Asylum: Jane Eyre, Feminism, and Bakhtinian Theory," in *Dialogue of Voices*, 155.

14

Yahweh's Significant Other

J. J. M. ROBERTS

KATHRYN L. ROBERTS

The discovery of the early-eighth-century Israelite inscriptions at Kuntillet ʿAjrûd[1] and the late-eighth-century Judean inscription at Khirbet el-Qôm[2] mentioning Yahweh and his Asherah (ʾšrth) has reopened the old debate about the status of Yahweh's love life. Since Asherah is the name of a well-known Canaanite goddess, these inscriptions raise the question of whether, contrary to the received biblical tradition, Israelite popular religion in the period prior to the Deuteronomistic reforms[3]

It is with great pleasure that we dedicate this study to Kathie, on the one hand, my fellow student, colleague, and friend, and on the other hand, my teacher, mentor, and friend. The principled, patient, and measured clarity of Kathie's life and scholarship has been an inspiration to us both.

1. Kuntillet ʿAjrûd is a site in the Sinai about sixty-four kilometers south of Kadesh-Barnea. It was apparently a way station for travelers, including Israelites from the northern monarchy. The relevant inscriptions read as follows: ". . . longevity, and may they be sated . . . be granted by [Y]HWH of Teman and by [his] Ashera[h and] may YHWH of (the) Te[man] favor . . ."; "Say to Yahil[yah] and to Yawʿasa and to [. . .] I hereby bless you by YHWH of Samaria and by his Asherah"; "[S]ays Amaryaw (Amariah): 'Say to [my] lord, "Are yo[u] well? I hereby bless you by [Y]HWH of Teman and by his Asherah. May he bless and keep you and may he be with my lord"'"; and ". . . by YHWH of (the) Teman and by his Asherah . . . all that he asks from the Gracious God, . . . and may YHWH give to him according to his desires." See F. W. Dobbs-Allsopp, J. J. M. Roberts, C. L. Seow, and R. E. Whitaker, eds., *Hebrew Inscriptions: Texts from the Biblical Period of the Monarchy with Concordance* (New Haven, CT/London: Yale University Press, 2005), 277–98, and the extensive literature cited there.

2. Khirbet el-Qôm is located in Judean territory about thirteen kilometers west of Hebron and about nine kilometers east-southeast of Lachish. The relevant inscription, found in a tomb, reads as follows: "Uriah the rich commissioned it. Blessed was Uriah by YHWH, and from his enemies by his (YHWH's) Asherah he has delivered him. (Written) by Oniyahu . . . by his Asherah . . ." See ibid., 405–19, esp. 408–14.

3. The Deuteronomistic reforms were a series of religious reforms that grew out of a theological movement that began in the north and emphasized the Mosaic covenant and the theological ideas now incorporated in the book of Deuteronomy. The first state-sponsored attempt to carry out such a reform, however, took place after the fall of the northern monarchy under the southern or Judean king, Hezekiah, in the years between his accession in 715 BCE and Sennacherib's Assyrian invasion of Judah in 701 BCE. Hezekiah suppressed worship in the local shrines, or high places, with their accompanying cultic apparatus, and forced the population to go up to the temple in Jerusalem to perform their sacrificial worship of Yahweh. The local shrines were often built on prominences under a sacred tree or

attributed to Yahweh, the god of Israel, a goddess as his wife or significant other. In the hierarchically arranged, family-oriented world of ancient Near Eastern polytheism, most male deities were associated with a particular goddess as a wife or female companion. Since Yahweh emerges out of that polytheistic past, and since the prophets and the Deuteronomistic Historian(s)[4] constantly complain of Israel's tendency to fall back into polytheistic practices, one might expect that there would be some trace of an earlier female consort.

For such a consort, the figure Asherah would be an ideal choice.[5] Asherah is the later form of the Ugaritic divine name Athirat.[6] Athirat is a mother goddess who serves as the main consort of the god El in the Ugaritic mythology, and who is characterized as the creator of the gods. Since Yahweh either arose from or was very early identified with El, it would seem natural for him to retain El's consort, and since the "sons of God" (Gen 6:2, 4; Job 1:6; 2:1) or "the sons of Elyon" (Ps 82:6; Elyon was also identified with Yahweh early in Israelite history) belong to Yahweh, one might have expected Yahweh to retain their mother, Asherah.

GODS AND GODDESSES IN THE OLD TESTAMENT

A reconstruction of such an earlier stage of Yahweh's life from the biblical record is problematic. Whether due to an editorial policy influenced by the later Deuteronomistic religious reforms or to a much earlier aversion to the acknowledgment of sexuality in its deity, the preserved biblical text is reluctant to name any goddesses, even the goddesses of other peoples. It is less timid when it comes to foreign male deities. The Old Testament mentions quite a number by name: the Babylonian gods Merodach (who is also referred to as Bel, Isa 46:1; Jer 50:2; 51:44), Nebo (Isa 46:1), Nergal (2 Kgs 17:30), and the deified stars Sikkut (Amos 5:26) and Kiyyun (Amos 5:26); the Philistine god

---

trees and were marked by altars, objects known as Asherahs (see below), and stone stela or pillars known as *matstsebah* (plural *matstseboth*). In his state-enforced centralization of worship at the temple in Jerusalem, Hezekiah destroyed these local shrines and their cultic objects, especially the altars, Asherahs, and *matstseboth*. Hezekiah's reform was reversed by his successor Manasseh, but a final and more thorough Deuteronomistic reform was reinstituted by the later king Josiah during the years 628–609 BCE.

4. The Deuteronomistic Historian(s) is a designation for the editor or editors who imposed on the earlier sources preserved in the books of Deuteronomy through 2 Kings (excluding Ruth) a common theological viewpoint based on the theology of Deuteronomy.

5. See the discussion of this goddess in John Day, "Asherah," *The Anchor Bible Dictionary* (New York: Doubleday, 1992), 1:483–87.

6. This name also appears as Ashratum in a Hittite version of a Canaanite myth and as Ashirta in the name of the king of Amurru, Abdi-Ashirta.

Dagon (Judg 16:23; 1 Sam 5:2–5, 7; 1 Chr 10:10); the Ammonite god Milcom (1 Kgs 11:5, 33; 2 Kgs 23:13); the Moabite god Chemosh (Num 21:29; 1 Kgs 11:7, 33; Jer 48:7, 13, 46); the Hamath god Ashima (2 Kgs 17:30); and the Canaanite or Phoenician god Baal. The deified sun (Shemesh) and moon (Yareah) are also mentioned (Deut 17:3; 2 Kgs 23:5, 11; Jer 8:2), though it is unclear whether they were drawn from a foreign pantheon. Only three goddesses are named: Asherah, Astarte, and the Queen of Heaven (Jer 7:18; 44:17–19, 25); but the title "Queen of Heaven" is most likely only an epithet for either Asherah or Astarte.

Of these two, Astarte (or Ashtoreth), who corresponds to the earlier Canaanite Athtart, a sex goddess similar to Anat, is always characterized as a foreign deity. Every biblical occurrence of Astarte in the singular is further specified as "Astarte the god of the Sidonians" (1 Kgs 11:5, 33) or as "Astarte the abomination of the Sidonians" (2 Kgs 23:13). The plural Astartes (or Ashtoroth) appears to be a generic term for foreign goddesses. It is used in parallel with "the foreign gods" (ʾĕlōhē hannēkār, 1 Sam 7:3) and "the Baals" (habbĕʿālîm, Judg 10:6; 1 Sam 7:4; 1 Sam 12:10).[7] Unless it is a textual error for the Astartes, the occurrence of the feminine plural "the Asherahs" (hāʾăšērôt) in Judg 3:7 also appears to serve as a generic term for foreign goddesses.[8]

In contrast, it is not so clear that Asherah, when used in the singular, always refers to a foreign goddess. One could make a case for the Phoenician provenance of the Asherah whose 400 prophets[9] were present alongside the 450 prophets of Baal over against Elijah, the prophet of Yahweh, at the contest between Yahweh and Baal on Mount Carmel (1 Kgs 18:19). After all, Ahab's Phoenician wife, Jezebel, seems to have been the patron of these cultic personnel. Such a foreign background is less self-evident in 2 Kgs 23:4, where Josiah is reported to have removed from the temple of Yahweh in Jerusalem all the vessels that had been made for Baal, for Asherah, and for all the host of heaven.[10] Baal, "Lord," was an early epithet for Yahweh that continued to be used unre-

---

7. This plural use of the Baals is also to be regarded as a generic expression for referring to foreign male deities; it is doubtful that it serves as a more restricted designation for specific forms of Baal.

8. The other occurrence of the feminine plural in 2 Chr 33:3 is probably a textual error for the masculine plural asherim, since it appears to refer to the cultic objects normally designated by that form.

9. Some scholars delete the reference to the four hundred prophets of Asherah as a later gloss, since, unlike the prophets of Baal, these prophets of Asherah are not mentioned again at the conclusion of the contest. Even if it is a gloss, the glossator clearly understood Asherah to be a goddess parallel to the male deity Baal.

10. "Host of heaven" is a generic designation for the sun, moon, and stars, all of whom were regarded as divinities in ancient Near Eastern polytheism. In Israelite Yahwism, these once-independent deities were reduced to dependent members of Yahweh's heavenly army, and a standard epithet for Yahweh was Yahweh of Hosts, referring to Yahweh as the creator or commander of these heavenly beings.

flectively to refer to Yahweh[11] with little criticism until the time of Hosea, who complained about the usage (Hos 2:18–19 [English 2:16–17]). Nor do the "host [$\bar{saba}$'] of heaven" necessarily refer to foreign astral deities, since a very common epithet for Yahweh throughout the biblical period, from premonarchical Shiloh to postexilic Malachi, was "Yahweh of hosts" ($\bar{seba}$'$\bar{ot}$). A foreign origin for "the host of heaven" is no more necessary than is a foreign origin for Moses' Nehushtan, which Hezekiah in his earlier reform removed from the Jerusalem temple as idolatrous (2 Kgs 18:4). Traditional Israelite and thoroughly Yahwistic cultic objects or practices could, in the course of time, come to be regarded as idolatrous and no longer religiously acceptable.

THE MEANING OF ASHERAH

Before one can speak to the issue of Asherah as a native Israelite goddess, it is first necessary to sort through the other meanings of the word "Asherah" as it is used in the Old Testament. The masculine plural form of this word, *asherim,* is used in a number of contexts to refer to wooden cult objects often associated with stone stela, or *matstseboth,* both of which were customarily found near the altar in the local sanctuaries of the previous inhabitants of the land. According to the Deuteronomic law, the invading Israelites were to break down these former inhabitants' altars, smash their stone stela, cut down their *asherim,* and burn their carved images (Deut 7:5; 12:3; cf. Exod 34:13). Unlike the practice of the previous inhabitants of the land, the Israelites were not to plant for themselves an Asherah of any tree beside the altar of Yahweh their God which they built for themselves, nor were they to set up stone stela, or *matstseboth* (Deut 16:21). This text seems to indicate that an actual living tree could be planted to serve as an asherah beside an altar (cf. Judg 6:25–30). John Day, among others, rejects this conclusion and argues that the *asherim* were always nonliving, stylized wooden poles representing trees, but his arguments do not strike us as compelling.[12] He argues that the use of the Hebrew verb '$\bar{a}\dot{s}\hat{a}$, "to make," in connection with these cult objects, shows that it could not refer to planting a living tree, but that is a very fragile argument. Since one can "make" gardens and parks by planting trees in them (Eccl 2:5), why could one not

11. See Jeffrey H. Tigay, *You Shall Have No Other Gods: Israelite Religion in the Light of Hebrew Inscriptions* (Harvard Semitic Studies 31; Atlanta: Scholars, 1986), 14.

12. Day, "Asherah," 483–87.

"make" an asherah by planting a tree to serve that purpose? Isaiah, who objected to both *asherim* and adonis gardens (Isa 17:8, 10–12), announces judgment on both phenomena in an oracle that implies that the *asherim* could be actual trees:

> You[13] will be ashamed of the oaks that you desired,
> And embarrassed by the gardens that you chose;
> For they will become like a terebinth whose leaves wither,
> And like a garden which has no water.
> The strong (oak)[14] will become like tow and its product[15] like
>   a spark,
> And the two of them will burn together with no one to quench
>   (them).[16]
>
>   (Isa 1:29–31)

Although Isaiah does not use the term "asherim" in this oracle, the objectionable oaks in this oracle can hardly be anything other than *asherim*, and if so, then *asherim* could consist in living trees.

Day also objects that since some texts speak of their *matstseboth* and *asherim* as being on every high hill and under or by every green tree (1 Kgs 14:23; 2 Kgs 17:10; Jer 17:2), the *asherim* must be distinct from these actual living trees. That argument is far from convincing. Just as a prominence seems to have been the ideal place for a "high place" (*bamah*), so under or by a green tree seems to have been the ideal place to set up an altar and *matstseboth*. One can hardly avoid the suspicion that, despite the awkwardness in the formulation, the green tree served in these local high places, at least originally, as the Asherah.

Nevertheless, there are some passages where the Asherah appears to be a stylized, apparently carved, wooden pole rather than a living tree. Ahab made the Asherah (1 Kgs 16:33), and it continued to stand in Samaria during the reign of Jehoahaz (2 Kgs 13:6). Manasseh undid the previous reform of Hezekiah, who had cut down the Asherah (2 Kgs 18:4),[17] made Asherah or an Asherah as Ahab had done (2 Kgs 21:3), and placed this carved image (*pesel*) of the Asherah in the temple in

---

13. Reading the second person with the following verb forms. The causal particle and the third person verb form were introduced by the editor as a feeble attempt to link this independent oracle to the preceding material.

14. The only other occurrence of this adjective is in a comparison based on the strength of oak trees (Amos 2:9).

15. I.e., the produce of the garden and the oak planted as an asherah will both burn up.

16. This is the authors' translation.

17. It is unclear where this object stood—on the high places outside the temple complex or in the temple like the following pole-mounted bronze serpent.

Jerusalem (2 Kgs 21:7), from where Josiah later removed and burned it (2 Kgs 23:6). This was hardly a living tree. Maachah, the mother of Asa, is also reported to have made an abominable image (*mipleṣet*) for the Asherah, which Asa cut down and burned (1 Kgs 15:13). Moreover, the Chronicler, though a late source, clearly associates the Asherah with carved, graven, or cast images (2 Chr 33:19; 34:3, 4, 7). In these passages, the term "asherah" comes close to serving simply as a proper name for the goddess Asherah, but it doesn't appear to be quite that simple. Most occurrences of Asherah in the singular include the definite article ("the"),[18] and proper names, including divine names, normally do not have the article in Hebrew. The names of the male deities mentioned earlier never occur with the article, with the exception of Baal and the deified sun and moon, but the latter two hardly count, since the biblical writer may simply be referring to the natural phenomena being misused as objects of worship. Why the difference in treatment between the proper names of foreign male deities, or Yahweh for that matter, and the Asherah?

This evidence suggests that one take another look at the negative assessment of the Asherahs in the Old Testament. There is a recurring complaint in the Deuteronomistic literature that the Israelites had abandoned their God by building for themselves local high places with their own altars, stone stela or *matstseboth*, and *asherim* (1 Kgs 14:23; 2 Kgs 17:10; Jer 17:2). The kings Hezekiah (2 Kgs 18:4) and Josiah (2 Kgs 23:4–15) are praised for doing away with these objectionable cultic practices in their reforms. Similarly negative comments about *matstseboth* and *asherim* (Mic 5:12–13) and altars and *asherim* (Isa 17:8; cf. 1:29–31) appear in the eighth-century prophets (cf. Hos 3:4; 10:1–2).[19] Despite the Gideon story in Judg 6:25–30,[20] we cannot date this aversion to local altars, stone stela, and *asherim* much earlier than the eighth century.

No such aversion is reflected in the stories of the ancestors, Moses, or Joshua. Abraham built an altar at Shechem near the oak of Moreh (Gen

18. The exceptions are 2 Kgs 17:16; 21:3; 23:15; 2 Chr 15:16; cf. the feminine plural in 2 Chr 33:3.

19. Amos's reference to "the shame of Samaria" (NRSV Ashimah of Samaria, Amos 8:14) is probably also an allusion to the Asherah of Samaria (cf. David Noel Freedman, "Yahweh of Samaria and His Asherah," *Biblical Archaeologist* 50 [1987]: 248–49).

20. The Gideon story is set in the premonarchical period of the Judges, sometime in the eleventh century BCE, long before the Deuteronomistic reforms. Yet the story has Gideon destroying the altar to Baal and cutting down the Asherah beside it just as the Deuteronomistic reformers wanted the later Judean kings to do. There is a serious question whether this account is actually an early tradition or an anachronistic projection into the past of much later theological concerns.

12:6–7), and he built another altar by the oaks of Mamre at Hebron (Gen 13:18). He planted a tamarisk tree in Beersheba and called there upon the name of Yahweh El Olam (Gen 21:33). Jacob set up a *matstsebah* to mark the place at Bethel where God had appeared to him in a dream (Gen 28:18–22; 35:14), and he set up another *matstsebah* to mark the site of his treaty with Laban—a site on a height where he also built an altar and where the parties to the covenant ate a covenant meal (Gen 31:45–54). When Moses made the covenant at Sinai, he set up twelve *matstseboth* on the occasion to represent the twelve tribes of Israel (Exod 24:4), and later Joshua followed the same practice at the sanctuary at Gilgal (Josh 4:1–9, 19–24). Moreover, when Joshua made or renewed the covenant between Yahweh and Israel at Shechem, he set up a large stone stela (*ʾeben gĕdôlâ*) under the oak (*ʾēlleh*) in the sanctuary of Yahweh (*miqdaš* YHWH); that is, there was a sacred tree or asherah beside the *matstsebah* (Josh 24:26). Even if the biblical writer does not use the terms "high place" (*bamah*), *matstsebah*, or "asherah" in this account, and even though this author does not explicitly mention the altar at this open-air sanctuary, clearly the sanctuary at Shechem had all these elements. Later, Abimelech made a covenant with the lords of Shechem at this same oak of the stone pillar or *matstsebah* at Shechem (Judg 9:6).

In the Deuteronomistic History, Samuel celebrated a sacrifice and the following communal meal with Saul at a local high place (*bamah*, 1 Sam 9:12–25), and Saul on returning home met a band of prophets coming down from the high place at Gibeath-elohim (1 Sam 10:5, 10). The Deuteronomistic Historian is clearly upset that it was at the high place at Gibeon where Solomon had his famous dream (1 Kgs 3:2–3), but no trace of such qualms is to be found in the older source that the Deuteronomistic Historian was editing (1 Kgs 3:4–15). The Deuteronomistic Historian is also disturbed that even the good Judean kings from the period before Hezekiah did not remove the high places (1 Kgs 15:14; 22:44; 2 Kgs 12:4; 14:4). But the Deuteronomistic Historian's religious criteria for judging these kings seems clearly anachronistic. These kings did not remove the high places dedicated to Yahweh with their altars, *matstseboth*, and *asherim*, because the Deuteronomistic law against these institutions had not yet been formulated. In their day these were perfectly acceptable sites for the worship of Yahweh, and their altars, *matstseboth*, and *asherim* were perfectly acceptable cultic equipment for the worship of Yahweh. What happened, then, in the eighth century to change the attitudes of strict Yahwists?

THE DEMISE OF ASHERAH

We return to the question of the relationship between Asherah, the goddess, and the stylized wooden pole or living tree. Since these wooden objects, living or not, served a religious function in a temple or open-air sanctuary near the altar, and since they are designated by the same name as the goddess, the identity in nomenclature and cultic function suggest a direct connection such as that between a goddess and her symbolic representation. A comparison between the figure of a goddess, naked from the waist up with prominent breasts, shown with each hand feeding a goat standing on either side of her,[21] and the figure of a stylized tree with wild goats in the same position, feeding from either side of it,[22] suggests that the stylized tree served as the nonhuman symbolic representation of the mother goddess Asherah. Such stylized trees appear as one of the cultic symbols represented on the embossed bronze bowls found stacked in a storeroom at ancient Calah (Nimrud), the Assyrian capital during the reign of Tiglath-Pileser III. These bronze bowls were apparently taken by the Assyrians as booty or tribute from Syria and Palestine sometime between Tiglath-Pileser's western campaigns and early in the reign of Sargon II before he moved the capital to Dur-Sharruken (ca. 740–716 BCE).[23] Some of these bowls have four-winged beetles among their iconographic symbols. Y. Yadin was convinced that this symbol was the royal emblem of the Judean kings of the time, and therefore argued that the bowls bearing it were the tribute or booty from a Judean king, a conclusion that he saw strengthened by the presence of inscribed Hebrew on some of the bowls in the collection.[24] One bowl, which we photographed while it was on display in the Berlin Museum, has the four-winged beetle in its center and at points on its two outer rings, but it also shows on the two outer rings the stylized tree, bracketed on either side by a pole-mounted winged serpent, or *saraph* (plural *seraphim*), each facing away from the tree in a protective role, and beyond each saraph there is a deer approaching the tree. These pole-mounted winged serpents are the closest thing we possess to a contemporary portrayal of the Nehushtan that stood in the temple of Jerusalem until Hezekiah's reform in 715 BCE (2 Kgs 18:4;

---

21. James B. Pritchard, ed., *Ancient Near Eastern Texts Relating to the Old Testament*, 2nd ed. (Princeton, NJ: Princeton University Press, 1969), 160, fig. 464.
22. Pirhiya Beck, "The Drawings from Horvat Teiman (Kuntillet ʿAjrud)," *Tel Aviv* 9 (1982): 7, fig. E.
23. R. D. Barnett, "Layard's Nimrud Bronzes and Their Inscriptions," *Eretz Israel* 8 (1967): 1–7* + Pl. I–VIII.
24. Y. Yadin, "A Note on the Nimrud Bronze Bowls," *Eretz Israel* 8 (1967): 6*.

cf. Num 21:9) and probably constituted the raw material for Isaiah's vision of the seraphim (Isa 6:2; cf. Isa 14:29; 30:6). The presence of such cultic symbols on royal Judean bowls suggests that such symbolic representations of Nehushtan and Asherah were both perfectly acceptable in Judean Yahwism prior to Hezekiah's reforms.

There is one caveat, however. The divine name Asherah never appears as the divine element in any Israelite or Judean personal name, either in the biblical onomasticon or in the onomasticon of preexilic Hebrew inscriptions,[25] which is odd if the goddess were widely worshiped in preexilic Israel as a distinct divine being. By analogy with the popularity of such feminine divine elements as Ishtar in women's names from Mesopotamia, one would expect to encounter at least some feminine names with Asherah as the divine element.[26] Yet there is no evidence of that phenomenon. This may suggest that in Israel, even before the Deuteronomistic reforms of Hezekiah and Josiah, the independence of the original Canaanite goddess had been severely restricted when absorbed by militant Yahwism.

Two shifts appear to have transpired. On the one hand, Asherah appears to have been reduced to an aspect, manifestation, or hypostatic presence of Yahweh. This is a phenomenon known in both Mesopotamia and Canaan. A culture occasionally reduced other gods to a simple manifestation of its major deity. Thus Adad, the storm god, could be seen as just Marduk in his manifestation in the storm. Athtart could be referred to as "the name of Baal," that is, as a manifestation of Baal, and the goddess Tannit could be referred to as "the face/presence of Baal," that is, as a hypostatic presence of Baal.[27] The famous inscriptions from Khirbet el-Qôm and Kuntillet ʿAjrûd never refer to Asherah in her own right; the reference is always to Yahweh and his Asherah, as though Asherah had no existence or life apart from Yahweh.

The second move appears to have been a restriction of the symbolization of Yahweh's Asherah to a nonhuman, arboreal, or imitation arboreal form. One might even suggest that the pre-Deuteronomistic offense of Maachah consisted precisely in daring to shape her representation of

25. Tigay, *You Shall Have No Other Gods*, 13. Many Hebrew names consist of a divine name, sometimes shortened, and another element, e.g. Abi-yah, "My father is Yah(weh)," or Jo-nathan, "Ya(h)w(eh)-gave." The study of Hebrew personal names, then, is one way of ascertaining what gods were popular among the general population of Israel and Judah.

26. In the Canaanite personal names attested at Ugarit and in the El Amarna archives, one encounters the goddesses or epithets of goddesses Adattu, Ashartu, Ilat, Ushkharah, ʿAnat, Baʿalat, Kasharat, Labʾit, Nikkal, Nana, Shapash, Shala, and Talaya (see Frauke Gröndahl, *Die Personennamen der Texte aus Ugarit* (Studia Pohl 1; Rome: Pontifical Biblical Institute, 1967), 78–85.

27. Cf. *Hebrew Inscriptions*, 289.

Asherah in too human a form.[28] The same may be true of the image of Asherah that Manasseh put in the temple (2 Kgs 21:7). Eventually the threat of separating Yahweh's Asherah from Yahweh and giving her an independent anthropomorphic form led to the rejection of any representation of this feminine aspect of Israel's deity. The presence of a sacred tree or a pole stylized as a tree in nonanthropomorphic form became just as unacceptable near the altar as any anthropomorphic representation of Asherah, and eventually even any explicit acknowledgment of this feminine aspect of Yahweh was prohibited as a result of the Deuteronomistic reforms.

FOR FURTHER STUDY

Keel, Othmar, and Christoph Uelinger. *Gods, Goddesses, and Images of God in Ancient Israel*. Minneapolis: Fortress, 1998.

McCarter, P. Kyle, Jr. "Aspects of the Religion of the Israelite Monarchy: Biblical and Epigraphic Data." In *Ancient Israelite Religion: Essays in Honor of Frank Moore Cross*, edited by Patrick D. Miller Jr., Paul D. Hanson, and S. Dean McBride, 137–55. Philadelphia: Fortress, 1987.

Mettinger, Tryggve N. D. *No Graven Image? Israelite Aniconism in Its Ancient Near Eastern Context*. Coniectanea Biblica, Old Testament 42. Stockholm: Almqvist & Wiksell, 1995.

Miller, Patrick D. *The Religion of Ancient Israel*. London/Louisville, KY: SPCK/Westminster John Knox, 2000.

Niditch, Susan. *Ancient Israelite Religion*. New York: Oxford University Press, 1997.

Smith, Mark S. *The Origins of Biblical Monotheism: Israel's Polytheistic Background and the Ugaritic Texts*. Oxford: Oxford University Press, 2001.

28. Tryggve N. D. Mettinger has convincingly argued that Israel's aniconic animosity toward anthropomorphic representations of the deity is quite early (*No Graven Image? Israelite Aniconism in Its Ancient Near Eastern Context* [Coniectanea Biblica, Old Testament 42; Stockholm: Almqvist & Wiksell, 1995]).

15

Women, Violence, and the Bible

NANCY R. BOWEN

The title of Phyllis Trible's landmark book *Texts of Terror*[1] broke the silence and revealed the secret: the Bible is not a safe space for women. Subsequent titles such as *Lethal Love*[2] and *Battered Love*[3] further documented the fact that the biblical text is replete with tales of violence against women. The attention given by feminist biblical scholars to the topic of violence against women in the Bible often reflects their concern with real-world violence against women in contemporary society.[4] Feminist scholars uncover ideologies that support violence against women in the biblical text, to demonstrate that the same dynamics exist today.[5] Modern women know that their experiences of violence echo what they find in the biblical text. This intersection between the stories of biblical women and women today is evident in this reflection

---

This work is in honor of Katharine Doob Sakenfeld, who has created a safer space for a generation of women biblical scholars.

1. Phyllis Trible, *Texts of Terror: Literary-Feminist Readings of Biblical Narratives* (Overtures to Biblical Theology; Philadelphia: Fortress, 1984).

2. Mieke Bal, *Lethal Love: Feminist Literary Readings of Biblical Love Stories* (Bloomington: Indiana University Press, 1987).

3. Renita Weems, *Battered Love: Marriage, Sex, and Violence in the Hebrew Prophets* (Overtures to Biblical Theology; Minneapolis: Fortress, 1995).

4. Katharine Doob Sakenfeld (*Ruth* [Interpretation; Louisville, KY: John Knox, 1999]) gives attention to how the interpretation of Ruth contributes to violence against women in Asian contexts.

5. The intersection between the biblical text and domestic violence has been of particular concern. See Pamela Cooper-White, *The Cry of Tamar: Violence against Women and the Church's Response* (Minneapolis: Fortress, 1995); Naomi Graetz, *Silence Is Deadly: Judaism Confronts Wife Beating* (Northvale, NJ/Jerusalem: Jason Aronson, 1998); Linda Day, "Rhetoric and Domestic Violence in Ezekiel 16," *Biblical Interpretation* 8 (2000): 205–30; Susan Brooks Thistlewaite, "Every Two Minutes: Battered Women and Feminist Interpretation," in *Feminist Interpretation of the Bible*, 96–107 (ed. Letty M. Russell; Philadelphia: Westminster, 1985); Weems, *Battered Love*.

on Zipporah's abandonment (Exod 18:2) and Miriam's leprosy (Num 12:1–15) by one of my students. "Miriam had questions and concerns. She spoke out and was severely punished, by God no less. What does this say to women who want to voice their concerns? This would seem to strengthen a man's use of authority, if not violence, to silence a woman. And with Zipporah, Moses, the great one, after being saved by his devoted wife, simply dismisses her and the kids when they have turned around for him! Gee, where have I seen that story before?!"[6]

My aim in this essay is to consider some of the various intersections between women, violence, and the Bible. In the first section I provide a map of such intersections, which is an important step in order to continue to break the silences and reveal the secrets of the ways in which the Bible is not a safe space for women. Based on our own experience, we name the violence of the text, whether it is explicit or implicit. An ethical response to biblical violence requires naming it, for only then can we take responsibility for resisting it. What to do about it is the focus of the second section. There I ponder what those of us who engage with this text as a matter of faith and who advocate for the liberation of women might do about the violence. The intersection of the biblical text with faith and life today requires a discussion of ethics, theology, and appropriation. What is presented is not comprehensive, but is rather is to serve as a framework for discussion. There are undoubtedly intersections missed, issues and texts not addressed, and other possible frameworks.[7]

In order to discuss the various intersections of violence, women, and the Bible, it is helpful to begin with a brief definition of violence. "Violence is the extreme application of social control. Usually understood as the use of *physical force*, it can take a *psychological form* when manifested through direct harassment or implied terroristic threats. Violence can also be *structural,* as when institutional forces such as governments or medical systems impinge upon individuals' rights to bodily integrity, or contribute to the deprivation of basic human needs."[8] Many persons understand violence in primarily physical terms—something that harms the body. But as this definition makes clear, there are other levels of violence. "Violence

---

6. Joanna McClelland, in a reflection paper for a class on women in the First Testament. Used by permission. I use the terms "First Testament" and "Second Testament" throughout for reference to the Old and New Testament, respectively. See James A. Sanders, "First Testament and Second," *Biblical Theology Bulletin* 17 (1987): 47–49.

7. For example, see Luise Schottroff, Silvia Schroer, and Marie-Theres Wacker, *Feminist Interpretation: The Bible in Women's Perspective* (trans. Martin and Barbara Rumscheidt; Minneapolis: Fortress, 1998), 153–60.

8. Laura L. O'Toole and Jessica R. Schiffman, eds., *Gender Violence: Interdisciplinary Perspectives* (New York: New York University Press, 1997), xii.

now includes such phenomenologically elusive categories as psychological, symbolic, structural, epistemic, hermeneutical, and aesthetic violence."[9] Regardless of the level at which it occurs, therefore, the use of force to control, resulting in harm, is the essential character of violence.

INTERSECTIONS OF WOMEN, VIOLENCE, AND THE BIBLE

The primary intersection occurs within the Bible in stories that recount physical acts of violence *against* women. Unfortunately, there are too many examples of this. Some stories of physical violence, including death and dismemberment, are Lot's wife (Gen 19:26), Chozbi (Num 25:7–8, 15), the Levite's concubine (Judg 19), and Jezebel (1 Kgs 21:23; 2 Kgs 9:10, 33–37). Two subcategories deserve particular mention. One is the killing or abduction of women during war, which includes legal (Deut 21:10–14) and narrative (Num 31:9, 17–18; Josh 6:21; 8:25; Judg 21:8–24) texts. The other subcategory reflects the numerous stories of sexual violence against women, such as Hagar (Gen 16:1–4), Bathsheba (2 Sam 11:4), and Tamar (2 Sam 13:11–14). These and similar stories highlight the central intersection of women, violence, and the Bible, namely, depictions of the use of physical force against women, resulting in bodily harm.

An intersection that is often overlooked is biblical accounts of physical violence committed *by* women. The most direct examples are Jael (Judg 4:17–22) and Judith (Jdt 13:6–10). Sometimes women's violence occurs at a distance. The woman's hand may not directly hold the sword, but her actions are a proximate cause of violence. Examples include Delilah's deal to deliver Samson to the Philistines (Judg 16:4–22); Jezebel's (ab)use of royal power to bring about the death of Naboth (1 Kgs 21:7–15); and Esther's manipulation of Ahasuerus, which leads to the deaths of 75,800 Persians and the ten sons of Haman (Esth 8:8; 9:13). Violence by women also appears in stories that evince levels of physical and psychological violence *between* women, such as Sarah and Hagar (Gen 16:1–9; 21:9–10), Hannah and Penninah (1 Sam 1:6–7), and the two mothers forced into cannibalism (2 Kgs 6:24–29). No con-

9. Beatrice Hanssen, *Critique of Violence: Between Poststructuralism and Critical Theory* (Warwick Studies in European Philosophy; New York: Routledge, 2000), 9 (quoted in Cheryl B. Anderson, *Women, Ideology, and Violence: Critical Theory and the Construction of Gender in the Book of the Covenant and the Deuteronomic Law* [Journal for the Study of the Old Testament Supplement Series 394; London: Clark, 2004], 10).

sensus among feminist biblical interpreters is apparent as to how to assess women's use of violence. Should we celebrate them as examples of women's (em)power(ment), or critique them as evidence of the constraints of patriarchy?

Yet another intersection implicates the biblical God in women's victimization. Too often, the role of the deity in stories of violence against women is absence. God is silent when it comes to the violence against Dinah, Jephthah's daughter, the Levite's concubine, Bathsheba, or David's daughter Tamar, to name just a few examples. This divine silence implicitly justifies the violence.

Even worse, God is often presented as the perpetrator of violence; for instance, Linda Day demonstrates the disturbing similarities between the profile of a wife batterer and the characterization of God in Ezek 16.[10] Many women today shudder at the image of God as a batterer. Yet many would also claim that they experience God as a deity who abandons them in the midst of violence or who feel that the violence they experience is in some way divinely ordained. The biblical God may be totally foreign to a woman's experience of the Divine—or all too familiar. The metaphorical violence of a jealous husband against his wife in the prophetic literature (Hos 1–3; Jer 2–3; Ezek 16, 23)[11] illustrates the use of violence in "extreme application of social control." When relationships are hierarchically structured, control of the structure becomes central. The superior person in such a relationship interprets any deviation from the norm on the part of the subordinate person as getting out of control or not knowing her place. The solution is to (re)assert control over the subordinate, often through physical violence. In the Bible, both the covenant relationship between Israel and YHWH and the marriage relationship between a man and a woman are conceived as hierarchically structured. Women are presented as sexually subordinate to men and men's control of sexual reproduction, just as Israel is subordinate to YHWH's control. These two hierarchical relationships meet in the prophetic imagery of Samaria and Jerusalem as YHWH's wife. The cities are symbolized as an unfaithful wife who has deviated from the hierarchical norm of sexual fidelity. YHWH, as

---

10. Day, "Rhetoric and Domestic Violence."

11. On this issue, see the essays in parts 1 and 2 of *Feminist Companion to the Latter Prophets* (ed. Athalya Brenner; Sheffield: Sheffield Academic Press, 1995); Day, "Rhetoric and Domestic Violence"; J. Cheryl Exum, "The Ethics of Biblical Violence against Women," in *The Bible in Ethics: The Second Sheffield Colloquium*, 248–71 (ed. John W. Rogerson, Margaret Davies, and M. Daniel Carroll; Journal for the Study of the Old Testament Supplement Series 207; Sheffield: Sheffield Academic Press, 1995); Weems, *Battered Love;* Gale Yee, *Poor Banished Children of Eve: Woman as Evil in the Hebrew Bible* (Minneapolis: Fortress, 2003), esp. chaps. 5 and 6.

husband, therefore "justifiably" punishes the wife (Samaria/Jerusalem) in order to (re)assert control. Punishment includes such acts of violence as being stripped naked (Hos 2:3; Ezek 16:39; 23:26); public exposure or mockery (Hos 2:3, 10; Ezek 16:37, 57; 23:10, 29), mutilation (Ezek 23:25, 34), gang rape (Ezek 16:40), stoning (Ezek 16:40; 23:47), and death (Ezek 16:40; 23:10, 47). Not only violent, this imagery is frequently classified as pornography in feminist writings because it involves objectification, domination, pain, and degradation.[12] The marriage metaphor also intersects with psychological and structural violence. Even the threat of violence becomes psychological abuse when it is used as a means of control. Moreover, hierarchical relationships are structurally violent insofar as the superior requires force to ensure the subordination and subjugation of the inferior in order to maintain the hierarchy.

Structural violence against women is present not only in metaphors but also throughout the Bible. The biblical text has its origins in the patriarchal contexts of antiquity. "Patriarchy refers to the systems of legal, social, economic, and political relations that validate and enforce the sovereignty of male heads of families over dependent persons in the household."[13] Patriarchy constitutes a form of structural or systemic violence against women by using the force of ideology and social structures in ways that harm women by failing, for example, to consider that women have the right of autonomy, including the right to construct culture, to control property, to maintain bodily integrity, to make their own decisions, and to express their own views.

Phyllis Trible observes, "It is superfluous to document patriarchy in Scripture."[14] Nonetheless, it is important to name some of the manifestations of patriarchal violence against women in the Bible. Women's roles and status are primarily restricted to the family as daughter, wife, mother, and widow. Women especially are not granted sexual autonomy. Women do not decide whom to marry; instead, a man "takes" a wife. When occasionally a woman is characterized as a subject who acts autonomously, for example, Tamar (Gen 38) and Ruth, their cases are always exceptional. The potential for autonomy arises from their position outside of patriarchal norms, during the moment when they are free of male con-

---

12. See, for example, T. Drorah Setel, "Prophets and Pornography: Female Sexual Imagery in Hosea," in *Feminist Interpretation of the Bible* (ed. Letty M. Russell; Philadelphia: Westminster, 1985), 86–95. This imagery appears in the Second Testament in the destruction of the Whore of Babylon in Rev 16:1–19:2.

13. Rosemary Radford Ruether, "Patriarchy," in *Dictionary of Feminist Theologies* (ed. Letty M. Russell and J. Shannon Clarkson; Louisville, KY: Westminster John Knox, 1996), 205.

14. Phyllis Trible, "Depatriarchalizing in Biblical Interpretation," *Journal of the American Academy of Religion* 41 (1973): 30.

trol. In the end, however, their actions are intended to normalize their position within the patriarchal structure, to become once again wives under male control and eventually the mothers of sons. Once that normalization is accomplished, these women cease to be actors.

Male determination and control of legitimate sexual activity is clearly evident in biblical legal materials. For example, adultery is defined as a violation not against the woman but against another man, when a man has sex with a woman engaged to or married to another man (Deut 22:22; Lev 20:10; cf. Deut 5:18//Exod 20:14 and Deut 5:21//Exod 20:17). In an examination of laws in the Book of the Covenant and the Deuteronomic Law that expressly construct gender differences, Cheryl B. Anderson argues that these laws construct gender as male dominance and female subordination. Using modern feminist legal theories, she argues that such laws support male dominance because they systematically favor males and oppress females, have a negative effect on women, and embody only male experience—all indicators of structural violence.[15]

Patriarchy is further evident in the restriction of women's participation in Israelite religion. Women are entirely absent from the prescriptions of religious activity in the legal materials, most notably the priesthood (Exod 28; Lev 6:8–7:38; 8:1–9:24; 16:34), and they are restricted to the margins of cultic life in roles such as singers (Exod 15:20–21; Judg 11:34; 1 Sam 18:6) and mourners (Jer 9:17; Ezek 32:16). Although women occasionally appear in legitimate religious roles, such as prophet (Exod 15:20; Judg 4:4; 2 Kgs 22:24), their religious activity is mostly viewed by biblical writers as illegitimate and dangerous (e.g., 1 Kgs 15:13; 2 Kgs 23:7; Jer 7:18; Ezek 13:17–23; Neh 6:14).

Violence against women, at many levels, can therefore be documented *in* the biblical text. Another intersection of women, violence, and the Bible is violence *by* the text, when the Bible is used as a weapon against women, especially to enforce subordination and to suppress the feminine. The many ways such violence has taken place in the history of interpretation is beyond the scope of this essay. One example, however, is the interpretation and privileging of certain texts to restrict women's participation in leadership roles in Christian traditions, particularly to prohibit women's ordination.[16] First Timothy 2:11–12 and

---

15. Some of the laws she examines include injury to a pregnant female (Exod 21:22–25), exclusion from cultic participation (Exod 23:17; Deut 16:16), rape of a betrothed virgin (Deut 22:23–27), and levirate marriage (Deut 25:5–10) (*Women, Ideology, and Violence*, 36–50, 66–100).

16. Elisabeth Schüssler Fiorenza (*In Memory of Her: A Feminist Theological Reconstruction of Christian Origins* [New York: Crossroad, 1983], 43–60) provides critical analysis of a number of ways in which this has occurred.

1 Cor 14:33–35 are invoked as authoritatively prohibiting women from preaching, despite the fact that the Second Testament often depicts women who speak wisely and commandingly, including a woman who instructs Jesus (Mark 7:24–30). The argument is made that women are to be silent because they are subordinate to men.[17] Therefore, to assume a position of authority over a man is a violation of patriarchal hierarchy and is not to be tolerated.[18] These texts, and traditional interpretations of them, function not only to restrict women's participation in Christian liturgy but also to sustain the systemic violence of patriarchy.

Gender bias in interpretation is another example of violence against women by the text and its interpreters. In addition to whatever gender bias exists in the biblical text, many commentators (typically men, but also some women) read their own prejudices and stereotypes back into it in ways that function to reinforce women's subordination. One way this happens is when readers consider the text to be more patriarchal than it actually is. For example, in her reading of Gen 2–3, Trible documents ways in which the text actually resists traditional patriarchal interpretations used to justify women's subordination.[19] Another form of bias in interpretation is when female characters are traditionally viewed in sexual terms even when such language is absent from the text. For instance, Jezebel is described as a "whore" even though she is portrayed as sexually faithful to Ahab. Most commentators assert that Tamar "intends" to act as a prostitute when she goes out to meet Judah, even though the narrative does not reveal her intentions. Furthermore, in the story of Bathsheba and David (2 Sam 11), the text provides no information regarding Bathsheba's feelings or the significance these events had for her. She never speaks. Her only voice is a message to David to inform him that she is pregnant. The language of the text suggests violence against her. David "saw" her, "took" her (this detail is obscured in the NRSV translation), and "lay" with her.[20] David, as male and king, is dominant and active; Bathsheba, as female, is subordinate and passive. She is the victim of David's abuse of his royal power. Yet she is tradi-

---

17. Women's subordination is supported by interpretations of Gen 2–3 in 1 Tim 2:13–15 and subsequent interpretations that symbolize Eve as evil. Phyllis Trible (*God and the Rhetoric of Sexuality* [Overtures to Biblical Theology; Philadelphia: Fortress, 1978], 73) provides a partial list of the specific ways in which Gen 2–3 has been interpreted to support female submission.

18. In addition to the 1 Corinthians and 1 Timothy references, see also Eph 5:22–24; Col 3:18; 1 Pet 3:1–7.

19. Trible, *God and the Rhetoric of Sexuality,* 72–143.

20. Identical language is used of Shechem in regard to Dinah. He "saw" her, "took" her, and "lay" with her (Gen 34:2).

tionally portrayed as a harlot, temptor, and adulterer.[21] In other words, she is a "bad" girl, blamed for David's violence against her.

Examples of all of these intersections could be multiplied; the cumulative effect is horrifying and disturbing. We see how violence against women lies at the heart of "sacred" Scripture, the "Holy" Bible. If a feminist perspective includes resistance to violence against women, then are we to resist the Bible?

READING ETHICALLY

These intersections raise profound ethical and theological issues, including the connection between patriarchy and violence against women. Anderson argues that the inherent violence of the male-dominant/female-subordinate gender paradigm makes actual violence against women more likely.[22] Indeed, many studies have demonstrated the intertwining of the Bible, sexual violence, and patriarchal gender constructs.[23] In a relationship of dominance and subordination, the use of violence is accepted as a necessary means of maintaining order in the hierarchy. Insofar as the Bible views men in a hierarchical position over women, and insofar as this view is considered to be divinely ordained, this has real consequences for real women. There is a causal connection between biblical views on the subordination of women and actual violence against women. Feminist readers of the Bible are troubled that violence against women is justified in the Bible, in society, and even in churches and synagogues. In the current culture of violence against women, for anyone who advocates liberation for women, including liberation from violence, biblical interpretation becomes an urgent ethical issue.

So what are those who are concerned for the spiritual and physical well-being of women today to do with the Bible? Numerous feminist interpreters suggest strategies for reading biblical texts that resist violence and promote women's well-being. Readers can find helpful proposals in the works of J. Cheryl Exum,[24] Cheryl A. Kirk-Duggan,[25]

---

21. J. Cheryl Exum ("Bathsheba Plotted, Shot, and Painted," *Semeia* 74 [1996]: 37–73) documents similar distorted interpretations in film and paintings.

22. Anderson, *Women, Ideology, and Violence;* see esp. 101–10.

23. See, for example, Joanne Carlson Brown and Carole R. Bohn, eds., *Christianity, Patriarchy, and Abuse: A Feminist Critique* (New York: Pilgrim, 1989); and Cooper-White, *Cry of Tamar.*

24. J. Cheryl Exum, "The Ethics of Biblical Violence Against Women," in *Bible in Ethics,* 265–69.

25. Cheryl A. Kirk-Duggan, *Refiner's Fire: A Religious Engagement with Violence* (Minneapolis: Fortress, 2000), 136–59.

Elizabeth Schüssler Fiorenza,[26] and Trible.[27] Feminists are acutely aware that the text that oppresses women is the very same text in which women often find liberation. They seek to identify dynamics that may critique, disavow, or contradict violence against women which also exist within the text, and to appeal to these other dynamics in ways to promote women's well-being. For instance, many have found warrant for women's liberation in the story of the liberation of the Hebrews from slavery in the book of Exodus. Rahab's nonviolent negotiation with the spies counters the violence against the Canaanites. The female figure of Wisdom in Proverbs, imaged as Sage and Lover, provides potential for nonviolent and nonhierarchical images of God and the divine-human relationship. Tamar's decision to take action on her own, and not at the behest of any male, reflects women's struggles today to act as subjects rather than be acted upon as objects. We might even argue that the inclusion of Ecclesiastes' nonconformist theology within the canon can be the basis for arguing for the inclusion of feminist theology within the canons of Christian and Jewish theology. These and other texts do not create some "pure" canon within the canon. In fact, all of these examples are imbedded in texts that exhibit various levels of violence. Yet they also contain dynamics that allow readers to challenge biblical violence.

Another strategy is to read the biblical text in the manner of confession. These difficult texts should be proclaimed and taught within faith communities. They should be treated not as paradigms to follow, though, but as part of our heritage from which to turn away in repentance as we confess that they reveal to us the sins of sexism, violence, and patriarchy. Another way of saying this is to advocate reading the biblical text as a mirror of identity. What we see in the Bible are stories that tell us that when we demonize the Other (whoever that might be), the result is the theological justification of violence and destruction. When we see this dynamic in the text and critique it, we can then consider how contemporary situations also reflect similar dynamics and critique them. Having confessed that these are our sins, we can then repent and turn to another way.

Some women (and men) may decide that the Bible will ultimately never be a safe space for them. These readers may determine that, for the sake of their own safety, their authentic choice must be to reject a relationship with the Bible. This step is like the therapeutic decision of

---

26. Schüssler Fiorenza, *In Memory of Her,* 32–33; and *Bread Not Stone: The Challenge of Feminist Biblical Interpretation* (Boston: Beacon, 1984), 60–61.

27. Trible, *Texts of Terror,* 3.

an abused child to cut off relations with her parents or of a wife to end a marriage with an abusive husband. It is a type of "principled a-theism, which acknowledges that God exists without choosing to be in a relationship with the divine."[28] Such a position might be seen as being "post biblical." These persons might also need to seek out other expressions and communities of faith than those identified as Christian or Jewish. Others who choose to remain in relationship with the Bible, however, must accept that they have a right to make this determination, without being coerced by threats of hell or arguments that their perception is flawed.

For those who do choose to stay in relationship to the Bible, one way to create a safer space is by enlarging the understanding of canon to include nonbiblical texts that inspire and authorize women and men in their struggle against violence and oppression. A feminist liberationist approach would also call for expanding the definition of "text" to include other media besides print. The search for messages that disavow violence, delineate nonsexist and nonpatriarchal traditions, and contradict the male-dominant/female-subordinate gender paradigm at the root of much violence should be limited neither to the Bible nor to "texts." These might form the basis of a Third Testament[29] that, whether authorized or not by religious judicatories, would function in some sense as Scripture—a guide for who we are and how we are to live as God's people. The writings of Amy Tan, Alice Walker, or Margaret Atwood, or the music of Sweet Honey in the Rock, might well serve as some contemporary "canonical" texts.

One way to add to the canon is through midrash. Midrash is a form of interpretation that creates new stories based on biblical stories.[30] In Judaism, rabbis used this approach, which was often done by utilizing the gaps in the biblical narrative, in order to make the text yield laws and teachings not apparent in a surface reading of the text. Feminist interpreters can also engage in midrash with a feminist hermeneutic. We can retell biblical stories of women and violence in ways that critique the violence and promote egalitarian, nonhierarchical paradigms

---

28. Kimberly Parsons Chastain, "The Dying Art of Demon-Recognition: Victims, Systems, and the Book of Job," in *Power, Powerlessness, and the Divine: New Inquiries in Bible and Theology* (ed. Cynthia L. Rigby; Atlanta: Scholars, 1997), 174–75.

29. See n. 7.

30. Contemporary examples of midrash include Steven Spielberg's movie *The Prince of Egypt* (1998); Anita Diamant, *The Red Tent* (New York: St. Martin's, 1997); Norma Rosen, *Biblical Women Unbound: Counter-tales* (Philadelphia: Jewish Publication Society, 1996); Carol Lakey Hess, *Caretakers of Our Common House: Women's Development in Faith Communities* (Nashville: Abingdon, 1997), 26–29.

for how to live. "Tamar's Story" is one midrashic effort to suggest new pathways to liberation from violence.

TAMAR'S STORY (GENESIS 38)

"Ben zonah," Tamar swore softly. "Every year at sheep shearing I am angry all over again."

Her friend Rebekah mumbled inarticulate syllables that indicated she was listening. She didn't really need to respond. Tamar's reminiscence was a well-rehearsed litany. It would spill forth whether Rebekah responded or not.

"It seemed like a good match," Tamar continued. Although Tamar was looking at her, Rebekah knew that Tamar wasn't seeing her, but past her to the memory. "Er's father was wealthy and respected. And Er himself seemed like a prize. He was *so* good-looking. My father wasn't the only one negotiating a bride price. But that's all I knew about him—his image." Tamar's wistful voice turned as hard as the desert landscape outside the door. "I thought I had won, only to discover how much I had lost. Thank God for veils. No one could see that I didn't weep when he died."

Rebekah knew that, of course. Friends often know more than family. She also knew how badly Er had beaten Tamar. Handsome Er was also unfaithful Er. His own pursuit of other lovers made him imagine that Tamar might do likewise. And so he feared that Tamar might dishonor him, even though Tamar had done nothing to warrant that fear. Because he could not control his own desires he controlled Tamar instead. He justified his abuse by telling her that it was to teach her to not so much as to look at another man. More than once Rebekah had rubbed healing ointment on Tamar's bruised breasts.

"I still don't know why Judah did nothing." Tamar's voice intruded into Rebekah's own recollections. "Of course I know why he didn't." Bitterness edged her words. "Judah is incapable of concern for anyone other than himself. As long as Er's behavior didn't directly affect him, he tolerated it. And then the business with Onan."

Tamar stopped speaking because for a moment she couldn't continue. Rebekah watched Tamar fight for control of her voice. "I thought it was a terrible idea. Onan had always resented that he was not first-born. Judah always ignored him. He and Seth were both invisible to Judah. I could see what was coming. Onan finally had a way to take revenge on Er and Judah. But no one cared about my point of view."

Tamar turned and looked at Rebekah. "It would have been to my benefit to inherit Er's estate and go my own way. But no one cared about my benefit, either. I went along with this foolish plan anyway because I felt trapped by responsibility. I had left my father and mother and joined myself to this household. Didn't I owe Er a son? And it was tradition." Her eyes reflected her question. "How do you resist tradition?"

Her next words make Rebekah's skin tingle as though a lightning bolt had struck nearby. "Well, we know how well that turned out."

She looked out the doorway to check on the twins. They were busy chasing each other around the oak tree.

"It was actually a relief to go home after that, though I didn't know what was going to happen next. Father was making vague curses about boils and itch and madness.[31] Mother kept weeping. It was exasperating that everyone seemed to think that all this was *my fault*. How could it be my fault that Er and Onan died? Why wasn't it their fault or God's fault? I was just trying to do what everyone thought I should do—be a good daughter and a good wife."

Tamar stopped speaking again. In the pause Rebekah's own thoughts again wandered. Rebekah ached for her friend, as she ached for so many women. How thankful she was to have someone with whom to share the burdens of life. The last time they had met, it had been Rebekah pouring out her grievances. Rebekah lived with a guild of healers and prophets of God. Her parents had protested, but with two sons and another daughter to care for, it was more token than genuine. Rebekah knew that, without husband and sons, she faced an uncertain future. But she also knew that God had called her to her work. She had never understood why she was forced to choose between family and calling. Why couldn't she choose both? But what sent her running to Tamar for consolation was the knowledge that no matter how gifted she was as a healer or how clearly she discerned God's word, she would never be the "father" of the guild. That position of honor was given only to men. From childhood Rebekah had been taught that God rewards righteousness.[32] Well, if righteousness equalled following tradition or following God's call, then few women reaped any reward. That righteousness was as rewarding as chasing after wind. Could there be another way?

The faint sounds of bleating sheep intruded into Rebekah's musings. The sound also prompted Tamar to continue her litany. "Then came that day. I knew something had to change, so I decided to take matters

---

31. Deut 28:27–28.
32. E.g., Gen 15:18; Ps 18:20; Prov 11:18.

into my own hand. I really didn't have a clear plan when I set out to Enaim. I think what I hoped was that elders would be gathered at the gate and that I could appeal to them to force Judah either to release me from the family or to marry me to Selah.[33] Not that either of those were really what I wanted, though by then I hardly knew what I wanted. But it seemed better than the void I was in."

A boyish shriek filled the air at this dramatic moment. Tamar and Rebekah rushed out. Zerah had thrown Perez's sandals up in the tree, and one of them remained stuck on a branch, out of a ten-year-old's reach. Perez was loudly protesting this indignity. A long stick solved the problem, and an apology and some fresh milk mixed with honey quickly restored peace.

"Some wine, Rebekah?" Tamar asked as they returned to the house. "Whatever is good to you," Rebekah answered. It wouldn't have made any difference if she had refused. It was always at this point in the story that Tamar brought wine, as though she needed it to fortify herself for the telling. Or to dull the pain. Or perhaps both.

"There was no one more surprised than me when Judah thought I was a prostitute. It was like a dream. Even as he was lying with me I was wondering if one of my father's curses had worked, that Judah didn't recognize me. How could he not recognize someone he had seen every day for years? Afterwards it came to me that the reason he didn't was because the needs or wants or desires of anyone else are invisible to Judah. He couldn't see *me*. He saw only what *he* wanted and desired, and what he wanted and desired was intercourse. So that's what I gave him."

Tamar gazed into her wine, maybe to see in its depths the wisdom she thought she lacked. "Everyone thinks that I set out to seduce him, Rebekah, even though that was the furthest thing from my mind. Everyone also thinks that I tricked him. But he deceived himself. It wasn't me. To this day I don't know why I agreed to his ridiculous proposition."

Tamar took a drink and held the wine in her mouth for a moment, savoring its taste, perhaps also savoring that moment. "But what I do know is this. There weren't any *good* decisions, Rebekah. God knows that to remain as a widow in my father's house, to marry Selah, or to try to find another husband willing to marry a woman who's already known men were no better choices than what Judah presented me with. But at least, Rebekah, this was *my* choice. I made *my own* decision. And

33. Deut 25:5–10.

that's what made the difference. It had proved impossible to live with the decisions others made for me." She smiles as Zerah and Perez run in, clamoring for dinner. "And although perhaps it's not ideal, I find it much easier to live with my own choice."

The long shadows of the oak tree are another reminder that the day will soon end.

"I had better go, Tamar," Rebekah said, rising from her seat. She sighed, "The guild members are going to think I've run away from my responsibilities."

Tamar hugged her friend close. "Thanks for listening to me remember again, Rebekah. It helps that you know my story. I keep thinking that there has to be another way. I pray for the day when men will be able to recognize that women are not just wives and mothers, and when women will be able to make their own choices and decisions about their lives. Maybe someday I won't have to retell my story because there will be a different story to tell."

"Amen," Rebekah whispered, "Amen."

FOR FURTHER STUDY

Anderson, Cheryl B. *Women, Ideology, and Violence: Critical Theory and the Con-struction of Gender in the Book of the Covenant and the Deuteronomic Law.* Journal for the Study of the Old Testament Supplement Series 394. London: Clark, 2004.

Brenner, Athalya. "Some Reflections on Violence against Women and the Image of the Hebrew God: Prophetic Books Revisited." In *On the Cutting Edge: A Study of Women in Biblical Worlds.* Edited by Jane A. Schaberg, Alice Bach, and Esther Fuchs, 69–89. New York: Continuum, 2003.

Camp, Claudia V., and Carole R. Fontaine, eds. "Women, War, and Metaphor: Language and Society in the Study of the Hebrew Bible." *Semeia* 61 (1993).

Kirk-Duggan, Cheryl A., ed. *Pregnant Passion: Gender, Sex, and Violence in the Bible.* Semeia Studies 44. Atlanta: Scholars, 2003.

Washington, Harold C. "Violence and the Construction of Gender in the Hebrew Bible: A New Historicist Approach." *Biblical Interpretation* 5 (1997): 324–63.

Yee, Gale. *Poor Banished Children of Eve: Woman as Evil in the Hebrew Bible.* Minneapolis: Fortress, 2003.

16

The "Biblical View" of Marriage

CAROLYN PRESSLER

As debate over "family values" and "gay marriage" rages both in churches and in the larger society, we have read and heard much about the "biblical pattern of marriage." According to this view, the Bible presents a clear, homogenous ideal of marriage as the union of two individuals, one male and one female, blessed by the church and sanctified by God. Some conservative churches hold that the newly married couple establishes a nuclear family, of which the man is the head.[1] A broader range of Christians evoke the "biblical view" of marriage as one man and one woman to oppose extending the legal rights that marriage accords heterosexual couples to those in committed same-sex relationships.[2]

This essay builds on work done for a paper commissioned by the Joint Committee for Ministry to and with Gay and Lesbian Persons, their Families, and Friends: A committee of the Minneapolis- and St. Paul–Area Synods of the Evangelical Lutheran Church in America for a working group discussion on marriage entitled "What Is God Doing with Marriage," held on April 23, 2005, at Augsburg College, Minneapolis. It is dedicated with love and gratitude to Katharine Doob Sakenfeld, who, as my dissertation advisor, gently and incisively guided my first forays into the subject of women, marriage, and the family in the Older Testament, and who remains a dear friend, beloved mentor, and wonderful conversation partner.

1. Perhaps the most widely publicized appeal to the "biblical pattern of marriage" took place in 1998, when the Southern Baptist Convention revised its faith and message statement to include the requirement of "wifely submission." It states: "A wife is to submit herself graciously to the servant leadership of her husband even as the church willingly submits to the headship of Christ." The paragraph on the family describes marriage as the union of one man and one woman ordained by God (http://www.sbc.net/bfm/bfm2000.asp#xviii). A resolution passed by that denomination in 2003 clarifies their conviction that the nuclear family is integral to the biblical pattern: "The biblical vision of the family is obscured further by current attempts to redefine the family itself and to marginalize the importance of the nuclear family" ("On Kingdom Families," June 2003 [http://www.sbc.net/resolutions/amResolution.asp?ID=1125]).

2. Others define the "biblical pattern of marriage" even more exclusively. See Ron DuPreez, "The God-given Marital Mandate: Monogamous, Heterosexual, Intrafaith," *Journal of the Adventist Theological Society* 10, no. 1–2 (Spring-Autumn 1999): 23–40.

Such use of the Scriptures clearly demonstrates Katharine Doob Sakenfeld's assertion that "biblical interpretation is a political act, an act with consequences for the church and the world."[3] Invoking biblical authority to require "wifely submission" directly counters feminist interpreters of Scripture, who, as we noted, bring to the biblical text an "awareness of women's subordination as unnatural, wrong . . ." (11, citing O'Connor). Invoking the "biblical pattern of marriage" to oppose "gay" marriage is—or should be—of equal concern to feminist biblical interpretation, which takes as one of its goals the flourishing of all women, including those who are lesbians, and which seeks justice for persons oppressed not only by sexism but by all the interlocking forms of oppression.[4]

Appeals to the Bible to legitimize patriarchal and heterosexist practices raise methodological issues that may be for feminist interpreters as significant as the substantive issues. How can and how should the Bible function in modern (or postmodern) ethical reflections—in this case, about marriage? Is it possible both to embrace the Bible and to reject its patriarchal and heterosexist depictions of marriage? Many of us, biblical scholars as well as laypersons, have a tendency to approach our work with biblical interpretation around ethical issues topically. Concordance in hand, we identify specific texts that treat a given issue (in this case, marriage) and look to those texts for models or, at least, for indications of the parameters of ethical behavior. In this essay I argue that questions about the nature of marriage in general, and about the morality of wifely submission or same-sex marriage in particular, cannot be resolved by turning to the Bible, seeing what various texts say on the topic of marriage, and going out and doing likewise. Such an approach to using the Bible in ethical reflection fails to take the Scriptures seriously enough. It ignores (1) the multiplicity of voices existing within the canon, (2) the distance between the circumstances addressed by the ancient Israelite or the Newer Testament authors and our own times, and (3) the varying authority of different kinds of biblical texts.

3. "Feminist Biblical Interpretation," *Theology Today* 46 (1989): 164.
4. Seen from the perspective of this professor of biblical interpretation, the argument that we must conform to the biblical view of marriage as the union of one man and one woman is rather ironic—even amusing. According to the biblical stories, Jews are the descendants of Jacob and his two primary wives and two slave wives—one man and four women. Christians, meanwhile, are the followers of one who was born, by the Spirit, to a young unwed mother—one woman and no man.

THE BIBLE SPEAKS WITH MANY VOICES

Older Testament

The Older Testament does not offer a single view of marriage, much less a single view of the family. Biblical Hebrew does not have a noun "marriage" or a verb "to marry"; it rarely uses terms that explicitly refer to marital status ("husband" or "wife").[5] Instead, the texts speak of a man "taking" or "having" a woman. Nor do the texts contain a definition or description of the institution. The Older Testament does recognize a variety of possible more or less formal legal conjugal relationships, including the following.[6]

> Normatively, at least as far as one can discern by studying biblical laws, a girl in her early or mid-teens could expect to be "taken" as "the woman" of a man, perhaps in his twenties or early thirties who, by paying her father a *mohar,* or "bride wealth," assumed authority over her. It is not clear how the ancients viewed the bride wealth. I am skeptical of interpretations that treat the *mohar* as the purchase price of a girl, or the wife as the property of her husband. The free wife is not chattel, per se. She has some rights. More likely, the *mohar* compensated the girl's family for the loss of her labor; alternatively, it may have been a nest egg held for the woman by her family in case she was widowed or divorced without cause. Bride wealth did establish the husband's legal claim to the young woman. After the bride wealth was paid, for another man to have sex with the girl was considered adultery. The bride probably brought a dowry with her into the marriage, though its size and nature would depend on her family's relative wealth (see Judg 1:15).

> A girl whose family could not afford to give her a dowry might become a man's concubine, that is, a secondary wife. Such a marriage was legitimate but low in status, and divorce—that is, the dismissal of the woman—was correspondingly simple.

---

5. The phrase *bĕʿûlat baʿal,* literally "mastered by a master," occurs twice in the Older Testament, both times in texts having to do with adultery, in order to be very clear that the woman is married to another man. The terms *baʿal* (master) and *ʾādôn* (lord) are used in the sense of "husband" slightly more frequently.

6. These patterns emerge from a study of Pentateuchal laws and related narratives. For a fuller discussion of these texts, see my *The View of Women Found in Deuteronomic Family Laws* (Beihefte zur Zeitschrift für die alttestamentliche Wissenschaft; Berlin: de Gruyter, 1993); and "Wives and Daughters, Bond and Free: Women in the Slave Laws of Ex 21:2–11," in *Gender and Law in the Hebrew Bible and the Ancient Near East* (Journal for the Study of the Old Testament Supplement Series 262; ed. Victor Matthews, Bernhard Levinson, and Tikva Frymer-Kensky; Sheffield: Sheffield Academic Press, 1998), 147–72.

Extremely poor parents[7] might be forced to sell their daughter as a slave wife to a man who might keep her for himself, assign her to his son, or, presumably, give her to a slave. The girl became a slave, not a free wife, but she did have certain rights.[8]

A girl whose community was conquered could be taken as war spoil. Numerous narratives describe Israelite warriors as taking women and/or children as booty, a practice well documented in the cultures surrounding Israel. Deuteronomy includes a law that provides a way for an Israelite man legally to marry such a captive, should he wish to do so (21:10–14). The law attempts to prevent him from enslaving her if he should tire of her.

According to a practice referred to as "levirate marriage," if a man shared land with a married brother who died childless, he was obligated to take the widow as his own wife; their first son was considered the dead man's child and heir (Deut 25:5–10).

In all of these cases, the woman might be her husband's only wife, or she might be one of numerous concubines, primary wives, and slave wives. That is, a man might have many wives of various sorts if he could afford them, though a woman might have only one husband. Citing the lack of reference to polygamy in the creation stories, earlier commentators tended to insist that the Older Testament sets forth monogamy as the ideal.[9] Many of Israel's founders and heroes, however, including Abraham, Jacob, Gideon, and David, are depicted as polygamous.[10] Moreover, the Deuteronomic laws assume that a man might have more than one wife (Deut 21:15–18). The Older Testament, therefore, does not appear to present a single form of marriage as ideal.

In the Older Testament, "marriage" is less a matter between two individuals and more a union of two families. Among the upper classes,

---

7. The text refers to a father selling his daughter as a slave-wife. Legal contracts from surrounding cultures indicate that widows not only could sell their children into slavery but, in fact, were more likely to be so impoverished or indebted that they were forced to do so ("Wives and Daughters," 167 n. 49).

8. The purchased daughter's status is debated. Some commentators have argued that she had all the rights of a free married woman. The law, however, is couched in language of slavery, not of marriage. She is an ʾāmâ (handmaid), not an ʾiššâ (wife), and, if dismissed, she is "sent away," not divorced. See Pressler, "Wives and Daughters."

9. From the statements that God created humankind male and female (Gen 1:27) and that "therefore a man leaves his father and his mother and clings to his wife, and they become one flesh" (Gen 2:24), commentators have asserted that the ancient Israelites viewed marriage between one man and one woman as the ideal. There is no question in my mind that ancient Israel and the early churches understood marriage as heterosexual. Ancient science had no knowledge of diverse sexual orientations any more than it had knowledge that the earth was round rather than flat. It is a mistake, however, to view these texts, which express two of many biblical views of marriage, as proof of the Older Testament ideal. Nor should they be read exclusively as indicating that marriage is intended only for reproduction (Gen 1:26–28) or only for relationship (Gen 2:4b–25).

10. Nor was polygamy confined to ancestors and to the royal family, as some have argued. Elkanah, husband of both Hannah and Peninnah, was a commoner (1 Sam 1:2).

households sought alliances that would increase their power and their property. The vast majority (90–95 percent) of Israelites and Judahites were subsistence farmers. For them, marriage arrangements would have been determined by what was most likely to help the household survive.

The family was patrilineal and patrilocal. That is, the household and lineage were defined in terms of the husband, not the wife. The young bride would normally join her husband's family household, a multi-generational group headed by her husband's father and his primary wife.[11] Other adult sons and their families, widowed or divorced adult daughters, and, if the household was sufficiently wealthy, slaves, indentured servants, resident aliens, or other landless or indigent persons would have been part of the group. For the majority of Israelites who were rural farmers, the household was also the workplace. Marriage, then, was less a matter of individuals than of households, and less about emotions than about economics. Leo G. Perdue's definition of marriage in ancient Israel seems on target: "In essence, marriage was an economic arrangement between two households, normally within the same kinship structure, to ensure their viability and to strengthen their solidarity and sense of cooperation."[12] In any of its forms, marriage was a decidedly secular matter. No priest was involved; there was no blessing ritual, though several biblical and extrabiblical texts suggest there might have been hearty parties!

Newer Testament

In contrast to biblical Hebrew, the Greek of the Newer Testament does have words for "marriage" and for "giving or being given in marriage." Like the Older Testament, however, the Newer Testament neither presupposes nor mandates a single definitive form of marriage. Some of the diverse forms of Israelite and Judahite marriage appear to continue into the Common Era.[13] In contrast to the Older Testament, the Newer Testament seems to presuppose that monogamy is generally normative.

11. Archaeologists have found compounds consisting of a few dwellings clustered around a common courtyard. This material evidence that Israelites lived in extended or compound families supports the biblical depiction of the *bēt ʾāb,* the "father's house." The classic article on archaeology and the family is Lawrence Stager's "The Archaeology of the Family in Ancient Israel," *Bulletin of the American Schools of Oriental Research* 260 (1985): 1–35.

12. "The Israelite and Jewish Family: Summary and Conclusions," in *Families in Ancient Israel* (Leo G. Perdue, Joseph Blenkinsopp, John J. Collins, and Carol Meyers; The Family, Religion, and Culture; Louisville, KY: Westminster John Knox, 1997), 171.

13. The Newer Testament presupposes Israel's Scriptures, taking for granted its various laws and explicitly naming those things that are distinctive.

Polygamy was not outlawed, though, until the rule of Emperor Theo-
dosius I, who declared it illegal among the Jews in the late fourth century CE.[14] Documents found in the region of the Dead Sea show that
polygamy was practiced well into the second century CE.[15] Levirate
marriage (whereby a man marries his deceased brother's widow) was
also known in the Common Era (Matt 22:23–33=Mark 12:18–27=
Luke 20:27–40). Beyond these exceptional cases, the practice of marriage among Jesus' audiences and followers, and then later in the early
churches, probably depended on several factors. These included the
social class of the families, whether the girl's family was urban or rural,
whether it was Jewish or Gentile, and, if Jewish, the extent to which it
was influenced by Greco-Roman practices. Marriage continued to be a
matter of economics and legal rights more than of emotions or religion.
As in preexilic Israel, the new wife joined her husband's household,
which comprised not only a multigenerational network of relatives by
blood and marriage, but also, for the wealthy, slaves and their families,
clients, and others. Both rural and urban households were workplaces
or businesses as well as domiciles. As in ancient Israel, marriage was a
secular, not a religious matter. No priests, presbyters, or deacons were
involved in the contract between the bride's family and the groom or
his agent.

That is not to say that marriage and family ethics were irrelevant to
the Newer Testament authors. According to the Gospels, Jesus strongly
affirmed the commandment prohibiting adultery, extending it to prohibit divorce and to warn against (intentionally?) lustful thoughts. Paul
permits divorce under certain circumstances but rules out remarriage if
one's divorced spouse is still living. Apart from the prohibitions of adultery and divorce, which are fairly consistent, attitudes toward marriage
and the family in the Newer Testament are strikingly diverse. Paul's view
of marriage is one of concession. It is preferable to marry than to burn
with passion, but those who can do so would be better off remaining
single. In light of the expected imminent return of Jesus, any change in
marital status is a distraction from the urgent task of saving as many
as possible before the end (1 Cor 7:1–40). In contrast, the author of

---

14. Josephus, a Jewish historian writing in the first century CE, noting that Herod's sons had multiple wives, writes
that "it is our ancestral custom that a man have several wives at the same time" (*Ant.* 17.14; *BJ* 1.477; quoted by John
J. Collins in "Marriage, Divorce, and Family in Second Temple Judaism," in *Families in Ancient Israel,* 121). Collins
also notes that the Mishnah allows men who can afford it up to five wives (*m. Ketub.* 10.5; *m. Ker.* 3.7). As Collins
writes, however, "it would be a great mistake to take the Mishnah or the Talmud as a normative description of Jewish life in the period before the fall of Jerusalem" (105).

15. See Nahal Hever, "Babatha's Ketuba," *Israel Exploration Journal* 44 (1994): 75–101.

1 Timothy ascribes a salvific—and sexist!—dimension to marriage and family. Women "will be saved through childbearing" (1 Tim 2:15).

Carolyn Osiek elaborates conflicting attitudes toward marriage and the family in the Newer Testament. On the one hand, a number of texts undergird the patriarchal family dominant in Roman culture, commanding wives to submit to their husbands and husbands to love their wives (Eph 5:21–6:9; 1 Pet 2:13–3:7; 1 Tim 2:8–15; Titus 2:2–10). On the other hand, numerous sayings and acts attributed to Jesus have a distinctly antifamilial tone. The Gospel of Mark, for example, depicts Jesus rejecting the demands of his relatives with the words, "Whosoever does the will of God is my brother, sister, and mother." Or again, in Luke, he answers women who bless his mother, "Rather, blessed are those who hear the word of God and keep it." Osiek understands the contrasting views as two different ways in which the early churches answered the basic question: "does discipleship consist of the promotion of harmonious relationships within recognized social structures . . . or does it consist in the jolting challenge that overturns and rejects our most cherished human relationships . . . ?"[16]

This sketch of diverse forms of marriage and contrasting attitudes towards marriage and family found in the Older and Newer Testaments does not, of course, answer the question of what marriage should look like for modern people of faith. It does, however, challenge claims that there is a single biblical view of marriage, and highlights how little biblical basis there is for the view of marriage as a religiously sanctioned, unchanging institution defined by the private relationship between two individuals, one woman and one man to whom the woman must submit.

CULTURAL DIFFERENCES

The reader will already have noticed that in all its various forms, marriage in ancient Israel and the early churches was very different from marriage in twenty-first-century North America. Ancient marriage, in its myriad forms, was not a private matter between two individuals but an arrangement between two households for their survival and benefit. The couple joined in marriage did not together form a nuclear family

16. Carolyn Osiek, "The Family in Early Christianity: 'Family Values' Revisited," *Catholic Biblical Quarterly* 58 (1996): 7–8. Rosemary Radford Ruether identifies the same tension and raises similar questions about the biblical basis for the conservative Christian understanding of the "biblical view of the family" in her article "An Unrealized Revolution," *Christianity and Crisis* 43 (1983): 399–404. Ken Stone has briefly developed an argument similar to my own in "Can Biblical Scholarship Shed Light on the 'Same-Sex Marriage' Debates?" *Chicago Theological Seminary Register* 91, no. 3 (2001): 17–22.

as the basic unit, but joined the man's extended family, a household that included both kin and unrelated persons, and that was typically headed by the groom's father, not the groom. Marriage was an economic and legal affair; no religious official played any role in the matter for several centuries after the formation of the church. Both the Older and Newer Testaments depict marriage as thoroughly hierarchical and patriarchal.[17]

These differences ought not to surprise us. In several ways, the circumstances that shaped marriage in ancient Israel and the early churches were extraordinarily different from the circumstances that mark our culture. Two such differences, the importance of which can hardly be overstated, are noted here. First, the majority of the population in ancient Israel and in the Greco-Roman period struggled to eke out a living barely sufficient to survive. The prescribed roles of various family members, the pressure to bear children who quickly became part of the family's labor supply, and any marital decisions (whose daughter to choose for one's son; to whose son to give one's daughter) were all shaped by the pressures to survive. What would help the rural family raise enough crops, sheep, and cattle to make it through the dry season? What would help the urban family produce and sell enough goods to keep going? Families in the United States often struggle financially— but not often at the same subsistence level, and as a society we are immeasurably more affluent.

Underpopulation is the second major factor that sets ancient Israelite society at a great distance from our own. The life expectancy of people throughout biblical times was very low, barely half that of modern Westerners.[18] Infant mortality was very high. Some scholars believe that only one-half of Israelite babies lived past puberty; others think this estimate is overly optimistic, that parents could expect to raise only one out of three children to adulthood. In many ways, therefore, Israel struggled to survive as a community.

17. Note that the "pattern" of marriage and the family that emerges from the biblical texts may differ from actual practice. The texts reflect the perspective of a small, privileged sector of Israelite society. Although some biblical traditions likely originated with women or with rural men, all of them were heavily edited by upper-class, urban males and reflect their experiences, interests, and ideals. Carol Meyers, drawing on biblical texts, archaeological findings, and social anthropological studies of preindustrial agrarian families, suggests that in practice among the great majority of the population who lived as subsistence farmers in rural areas, the roles of women and men were much more egalitarian than the biblical texts might suggest. Women were most involved in child care, gardening, caring for small animals, and preparing, preserving, and distributing food and clothing, tasks that carried power and required a high level of skill in the subsistence economy of ancient Israel. She convincingly argues that women, rather than being subordinate and submissive to their husbands, were interdependent farm partners ("The Family in Early Israel," in *Families in Ancient Israel*, 1–47; see also her *Discovering Eve: Ancient Israelite Women in Context* [New York: Oxford University Press, 1988]).

18. Among the rural poor majority in ancient Israel, life expectancy for a man was barely forty years; because of the dangers of childbirth, women's life expectancy was around thirty years.

Under these circumstances, and especially for the poorer families who composed most of the population, personal fulfillment and happiness were not major considerations. Marriage was not primarily about romance or companionship, although biblical texts do recognize those dimensions.[19] It was about families helping each other produce and reproduce—about bread and babies. The biblical emphasis on reproduction needs to be understood in that context. Maximizing the number of children born to the community was a matter of survival. Numerous biblical injunctions, from abstaining from sexual intercourse during the woman's menstrual period, to exempting men from military obligations during their first year of marriage, to the tiny handful of negative biblical references to homosexuality, appear to be shaped by this concern.[20]

The contrast with modern Western cultures is obvious. Our problem is not underpopulation but overpopulation. Practices and restrictions that were necessary in ancient cultures in order to maximize the number of births have become liabilities for twenty-first-century Western cultures. Moreover, increased affluence means that, as a culture, we have the luxury of caring about personal happiness. Historically, churches have ascribed a dual purpose to marriage: companionship as well as the birthing and nurture of children.[21] Over time, the relative emphasis given to these two goals has shifted, with increased emphasis now placed on companionship.

CENTER VERSUS PERIPHERY

It is simply not possible to find a single pattern of marriage in the Bible that we may then apply to our lives. There are too many different views of marriage in the Bible, and the distance between the social and familial contexts that shaped those views and modern Western culture is too great.

19. Concern for personal well-being and emphasis on relationship rather than child-rearing seems to underlie the second creation story in Gen 2:4–25. See especially v. 18, "Then Yahweh God said, 'It is not good that the man [or the human] should be alone; I will make him a helper as his partner.'"

20. There is no direct biblical prohibition of lesbian sex, which perhaps comes into view in Rom 1:26 as one of many examples of unrighteous Gentile behavior. (In Hellenistic thought, "natural" sex referred to penetration of the subordinate partner by the dominant one. Anything else was thought to be "unnatural." Some Newer Testament scholars therefore believe that Rom 1:26 could refer to a woman who engaged in heterosexual acts from an "unnatural" position—that is, anything but a missionary position.) The relative absence of concern about lesbian sexual acts probably in part reflects biblical androcentrism; women are generally less visible than men in the Scriptures. In part, it also reflects the science of the day, which assumed that sperm contained the complete baby, in miniature, and must not be wasted. The woman's role was simply incubation. Lesbian sex, therefore, would not have been seen as the terrible waste of potential life represented by male-male sex.

21. For instance, churches do not hesitate to bless the marriage of a heterosexual couple past child-bearing age, or of a woman who has had a hysterectomy to a man who has had a vasectomy. For discussion of companionship as the Protestant view of the primary purpose of marriage, see J. Robert Williams, "Toward a Theology for Lesbian and Gay Marriage," *Anglican Theological Review* 72 (1990): 134–57.

Few if any, even among the most conservative Christians, would argue that our families should begin paying bride wealth to establish patriarchal civil unions between one man and as many women as he can afford!

Some might argue that since all the varying patterns of marriage suggested by biblical texts depict marriage as heterosexual, and overwhelmingly if not unanimously portray it as patriarchal, we must conform to these consistent themes. That is, the Bible presents a pattern of marriage in the aggregate. Methodologically, those who make such an argument run up against a problem; the various texts having to do with marriage portray other consistent characteristics at odds with the conservative ideal. Marriages in ancient Israel and Palestine were patriarchal and heterosexual; they also

— Were secular, rather than a matter for church or synagogue.
— Were between two households, not between two individuals.
— Made the couple part of an extended family. The nuclear family had so little independent significance that there is no word for it in biblical Hebrew or Koine (biblical) Greek.
— Required chastity of the wife but, in the Older Testament at least, did not require the husband to be sexually faithful to his wife.

One cannot uncritically accept some common threads as normative while ignoring others. Moreover, all such themes must be understood within their cultural contexts, which differ so greatly from our own. This is not to say that we should ignore specific biblical texts about marriage. To engage in such study is to enter into conversation with the ancient community whose practices and ideals may raise important questions, offer helpful challenges, and provide insights into our own. For example, the biblical texts related to marriage may offer a useful critique of the prevalent individualistic notion of marriage in our culture. They suggest the need for a broader set of relationships to support commitment and help the family remain economically viable, and they assert the importance of fidelity to nurturing commitment and love. But all biblical texts or themes—and all contemporary practices—are subject to critique in light of the deepest theological values of the faith community, values that are informed by central biblical dynamics and in dialogue with experience,[22] reason, and the traditions of the church.

22. As Choon-Leong Seow writes, the Bible itself affirms the role of experience and science in theological and ethical reflection. Its wisdom tradition "recognizes that there are truths that do not come from special revelation" ("A Heterotextual Perspective," in *Homosexuality and Christian Community* [ed. Choon-Leong Seow; Louisville, KY: Westminster John Knox, 1996], 21).

As James B. Nelson eloquently writes, serious ethical reflection on the role of Scriptures in our thinking about marriage must shift the debate from the periphery to the Bible's center.[23] That is, as we turn to the Bible as a source for ethical reflection, we must identify the great overarching biblical principles, values, and stories that can serve as our theological plumb lines, by which to measure not only our own decisions and actions but also less central, less persistently enduring biblical views.[24] Since Martin Luther and John Calvin, Protestant churches have acknowledged that biblical texts have varying degrees of authority; some are more central and some more peripheral. To take an obvious example, the story of Elisha setting bears on little boys who taunt him (2 Kgs 2:23–24) has relatively less authority than the great central stories of God delivering Israel at the sea or of Jesus' crucifixion and resurrection. Similarly, the various and changing injunctions in the legal collections of Exodus through Deuteronomy (e.g., to stone disobedient sons to death) have less binding authority than the demonstrably repeated and enduring words of the Ten Commandments.[25]

Rosemary Radforth Ruether, in her classic *Sexism and God-Talk,* articulates a prophetic liberating tradition as a central biblical dynamic that, in correlation with women's experience, she identifies as her theological norm. She identifies four dimensions to this prophetic liberating principle: "(1) God's defense and vindication of the oppressed; (2) the critique of dominant systems of power and their powerholders; (3) the vision of a new age to come in which . . . God's intended reign of peace and justice" overcomes "the present system of injustice"; and "(4) the critique of . . . religious ideologies and systems that function to justify and sanctify the dominant, unjust social order."[26] From my perspective as one who teaches the Older Testament, I resonate with Ruether's articulation of the call for justice sounded throughout the Hebrew Scriptures in its laws, prophecies, hymns and stories, and manifest in Jesus' life and

---

23. "Relationships: Blessed and Blessing" (http://www.ucc.org/justice/pdfs/emr15.pdf).

24. For an excellent discussion of the weighting of biblical materials in relationship to same-sex relationships, see Patrick D. Miller, "What the Scriptures Principally Teach," in *Homosexuality and Christian Community,* 53–63. In his essay about feminist interpretation in this volume, Miller points to the "law of love" as key to critiquing patriarchy both in the Bible and in our modern relationships. The "law of love" stands against biblical arguments for "wifely submission."

25. Although I have neither the room in this essay nor the expertise to do so, our reflections marshaled also need to take into account the long and varied history of Christian ethical thinking about marriage. Considering that history seriously would involve looking at the expandability and adaptability of biblical mores—for example, the expansion of the biblical understanding of fidelity to include not only the husband's exclusive claims over his wife's (or wives'?) sexuality but also the wife's comparable claims. It would have to take seriously the considerable evidence marshaled by historians that the church was not involved in marriage until the ninth century at the earliest, the shift away from emphasizing procreation to emphasizing companionship, and the greatly changing understandings of gender and male-female relationships.

26. Rosemary Radford Ruether, *Sexism and God-Talk: Toward a Feminist Theology* (Boston: Beacon, 1983), 24.

teaching. As the prophet asks, "What does Yahweh require of you but to do justice, and to love kindness, and to walk humbly with your God?" (Mic 6:8).

Good biblical interpretation is not a matter of going to particular verses or chapters, tearing them out of context, wadding them up, and shooting them like bullets at others. Good biblical ethical reflection does not seek to identify the forms of Israelite and Greco-Roman social institutions and apply them as binding over our lives. Sound biblical ethical reflection is a matter of responding with all of our best reasoning ability and with humble love to the great story of the God who creates in lavish abundance and who loves all that God creates with welcoming, justice-seeking, life-giving passion.

FOR FURTHER STUDY

Osiek, Carolyn. "The Family in Early Christianity: 'Family Values' Revisited." *Catholic Biblical Quarterly* 58 (1996): 1–24.

Pressler, Carolyn. *The View of Women Found in the Deuteronomic Family Laws.* Beihefte zur Zeitschrift für die alttestamentliche Wissenschaft. Berlin: de Gruyter, 1993.

Purdue, Leo G., Joseph Blenkinsopp, John J. Collins, and Carol Meyers. *Families in Ancient Israel.* The Family, Religion, and Culture. Louisville, KY: Westminster John Knox, 1997.

Seow, Choon-Leong, ed. *Homosexuality and Christian Community.* Louisville, KY: Westminster John Knox, 1996.

PART FOUR

Intersections

17

Feminist Interpretation and Biblical Theology

PHYLLIS A. BIRD

For most Christians, particularly those of Protestant or Evangelical heritage, "theology" is biblical theology, and the Bible is a theological book. In fact, throughout most of the Christian era, theologians were biblical scholars and biblical scholars were theologians.[1] With the rise of modern historical study of the Bible, however, biblical theology became a separate discipline or subject within the field of biblical studies. This essay explores the relationship between this specialized form of biblical scholarship and feminism.[2]

Two observations guide our exploration and determine the shape of the discussion. First, the subject of biblical theology has been contested since its origins, with ever-new attempts to define its nature and aims. In some periods and circles it has been viewed as the essential core of biblical studies and the crown of the discipline; in others it has been deemed an illegitimate child, incompatible with scientific biblical scholarship, to be banned from the discipline. Yet biblical theology has played a critical role in the history of modern biblical scholarship and has informed countless preachers, teachers, and theologians. It has

---

1. Jewish biblical interpretation has a distinct, and equally complex, history in relationship to theology. One of the new features of contemporary biblical theology is interaction between Christian and Jewish biblical scholars, drawing upon their distinct theological traditions (see below).

2. See also my broader essay "Old Testament Theology and the God of the Fathers: Reflections on Biblical Theology from a North American Feminist Perspective," in *Biblische Theologie: Beiträge des Symposiums "Das Alte Testament und die Kultur der Moderne" anlässig des 100. Geburtstags Gerhard von Rads* (ed. Bernd Janowski, Michael Welker, and Paul Hanson; Altes Testament und Moderne 14; Münster: LIT, 2005), 69–107.

also experienced a resurgence in recent years, with a flurry of new publications and a broadened arena of engagement, including significant Jewish participation.

Second, the entire history of the subject, including the most recent period of expanding boundaries and debate, has been marked by a glaring absence of women and an apparent lack of feminist interest—a neglect made more striking by the fact that the first major work of feminist Old Testament interpretation was offered as a contribution to biblical theology.[3] The relative absence of women[4] from the discipline of biblical theology has occurred during a period in which feminists and feminism have made profound and far-reaching changes in the field of theology[5] and had substantial impact on many areas of biblical studies, forging new fields (such as feminist hermeneutics and women in the biblical world) and penetrating deeply into others (such as literary, rhetorical, and ideological criticism).[6] But large areas of traditional biblical scholarship seem little touched, including the field of biblical theology, where tomes can be written, reviewed, and debated with minimal involvement of feminist scholars or interaction with feminist scholarship.

A few examples from the field of Old Testament[7] theology will serve to illustrate the current state of the discipline.[8] A 1992 anthology designed to represent "the flowering of Old Testament theology" in the past century contained selections from twenty-five authors, of whom only one was a woman (Phyllis Trible).[9] Revised and updated in 2004 to reflect the revival of activity in the field, the new edition includes nine new authors among a total of twenty-eight, but Trible remains the

3. Phyllis Trible, *God and the Rhetoric of Sexuality* (Overtures to Biblical Theology; Philadelphia: Fortress, 1978), with its precursor, "Depatriarchalizing in Biblical Interpretation," *Journal of the American Academy of Religion* 41 (1973): 30–48.

4. I do not equate "woman" with "feminist," but where women are not present, feminist perspectives are rarely represented or seriously engaged.

5. A shift that is reflected by Uwe Gerber's 1987 publication *Die feministische Eroberung der Theologie* (The Feminist Conquest of Theology) (Munich: Beck).

6. See especially the essays by Kathleen M. O'Connor, Patrick D. Miller, Beth LaNeel Tanner, and Nyasha Junior in this volume.

7. I use the expression "Old Testament" as the traditional Christian designation. There is no common term for the Scriptures shared by Christians and Jews when they are viewed from within the two traditions that hold them sacred, although "Hebrew Bible (HB)" is now widely used in academic and interreligious contexts. When the dual religious claims on this corpus are accented, I use the compound "Old Testament/Hebrew Bible"; I substitute "biblical theology" for "Old Testament theology" when referring to the general idea or category of work.

8. Biblical theology generally takes the form of either Old Testament theology or New Testament theology. This chapter focuses on the theology of the Old Testament/Hebrew Bible, which presents distinct problems and accounts for the majority of scholarly activity.

9. Phyllis Trible, "Feminist Hermeneutics and Biblical Theology," in *The Flowering of Old Testament Theology: A Reader in Twentieth-Century Old Testament Theology, 1930–1990* (ed. Ben C. Ollenburger, Elmer A. Martens, and Gerhard F. Hasel; Winona Lake, IN: Eisenbrauns, 1992), 448–64.

sole female.[10] The same gender profile is replicated in recent collections of essays relating to biblical theology.[11] But the pattern of minimal female representation is not confined to publications, which typically lag behind current activity; it also characterizes the professional meetings of biblical scholars and teachers as they present and critique their latest work. At the 2000 meeting of the Society of Biblical Literature (SBL), the major association of biblical scholars in North America, the large audience assembled for a discussion of James Barr's *The Concept of Biblical Theology*[12] virtually mirrored the all-male panel on the platform. And although the Theology of the Hebrew Scriptures Section of the Society of Biblical Literature (which organized the panel) was chaired through most of the 1990s by a feminist scholar (Alice Ogden Bellis), who sought to encourage women's participation, her seven-year effort found little response.[13] It would appear that feminists have a problem with biblical theology, but where does it lie—and is this the whole picture?

One could argue that the relatively recent entry of women into the field of biblical scholarship has meant that few feminist biblical scholars have the range and depth of exegetical experience needed to write the kind of encompassing Old Testament theology that has characterized past efforts in the field. Among Old Testament scholars, Phyllis Trible alone seems to possess the necessary experience, as well as interest, to produce—or at least conceive—such a work, but she has no obvious followers in this enterprise. The evidence above suggests that conversation between feminists and biblical theologians is not taking place. But if the discipline of biblical theology appears to hold little interest or priority for feminist biblical scholars, this does not mean that feminists have no interest or engagement in theological interpretation of the Bible. It is rather to be explained by the nature of the discipline and the history of

10. Ben C. Ollenburger, ed., *Old Testament Theology: Flowering and Future* (Winona Lake, IN: Eisenbrauns, 2004). The disproportion is even greater in Gerhard F. Hasel's *Old Testament Theology: Basic Issues in the Current Debate*, 4th ed. (Grand Rapids: Eerdmans, 1991). An initial survey of the forty-three-page bibliography reveals fewer than ten recognizable female names among well over four hundred authors, and only two of these specifically deal with biblical theology or hermeneutics. Trible's name does not appear.

11. See, for example, the 1997 festschrift for Rolf Knierim, entitled *Problems in Biblical Theology* (ed. H. T. C. Sun and K. L. Eades; Grand Rapids: Eerdmans), whose twenty-five contributors are all male. Additional examples are noted in Bird, "Old Testament Theology," 82.

12. James Barr, *The Concept of Biblical Theology: An Old Testament Perspective* (Minneapolis: Fortress, 1999).

13. In 1993 Bellis was the first woman to serve on the steering committee of the section and was its chair from 1995 to 2000. Although her efforts to increase women's participation began to bear fruit in later years, she acknowledges the resistance of women to present papers in the section, as well as the failure of the section to address feminist concerns (personal communication, July 23, 2001). The 2004 Society of Biblical Literature meeting showed increased participation of women in the audience as well as on the panel that reviewed John Goldingay's *Old Testament Theology*, vol. 1, *Israel's Gospel* (Downers Grove, IL: InterVarsity, 2003). The panel included two women.

theology and biblical studies in North America, as well as the complex
relationship of feminism to theology and the Bible. Some feminists,
responding to the theological legacy of biblical patriarchy, want to cut
theology free from the Bible, or at least from the Old Testament, while
others want to cut the Bible free from theology. For those feminists who
(still) view the Bible as a source of continuing theological claims, the
discipline of biblical theology has offered little promise. Preoccupied
with debate over its own identity, it has shown little awareness of the
issues that are paramount for feminists.

A QUESTION OF IDENTITY

The question of identity, purpose, and aims stands at the heart of ongoing debate concerning the subject of biblical theology. Put simply,
What is it? and Who needs it?[14] The term itself is ambiguous. It can
refer on the one hand to a theology based on the Bible, or in accord
with the Bible—a constructive and normative work (that is, a formulation of what the Bible compels us to believe). But it can also refer to the
theological ideas contained within the biblical texts, as historical affirmations of faith, described without normative claims (that is, a description of what the biblical writers believed).[15] The latter sense has
generally prevailed in biblical studies, but the boundary between historical and constructive understandings has never been absolute.[16]
Shifting over time, it has left uncertainty about the legitimacy and goals
of the discipline and, as specialization drives them ever further apart,
whether it is primarily a concern of theologians or biblical scholars.

Biblical theology was born with the rise of modern historical study
of the Bible. Historical criticism attempted to read the biblical texts
against the background of the times in which they were written, as
ancient literary documents that shared the language and thought forms
of other writings of their day. It distinguished the views of the biblical
text and its authors from the dogmatic (doctrinal) interpretation of the
church, which had made the Bible subservient to church doctrine. The
idea of a biblical theology distinct from dogmatic theology was first

14. See Bird, "Old Testament Theology," 72, 98–102.
15. Brevard S. Childs, *Biblical Theology of the Old and New Testaments: Theological Reflections on the Christian Bible* (Minneapolis: Fortress, 1993), 3.
16. In practice, the ways of defining biblical theology have not been limited to these two types. Thus Barr (*Concept of Biblical Theology*, 5–17) identifies six different definitions.

articulated by Johann Philipp Gabler in his inaugural lecture as professor of theology at the University of Altdorf (in Germany) in 1787. In
his oration "On the Proper Distinction between Biblical and Dogmatic
Theology and the Specific Objectives of Each," Gabler emphasized the
distinct nature of the two forms of theology with respect to their
sources, methods, and aims—giving priority to biblical theology. Dogmatic theology, he argued, is normative and prescriptive; its task is to
formulate and teach what was to be believed. Although it uses the
Bible, it also depends on philosophy and church tradition. In contrast,
biblical theology is historical and descriptive; its task is to give a "true
and accurate description of the religion of the Bible in its various periods and contexts."[17] It is concerned with what the biblical authors
believed in their own times. But Gabler added a further aim to the task
of biblical theology: the ultimate goal of its description is to formulate
a pure biblical theology, understood as "a systematic presentation of
God's eternal truths or the unchanging ideas found in the Bible which
were valid for all times."[18] Thus, in Gabler's view, the descriptive enterprise is to serve a normative end. Therefore, biblical theology in its original conception embodied a tension between descriptive and normative
aims that underlies its entire subsequent history.

What triumphed in the following century, the 1800s, was the historical and descriptive effort, offering new insight into the religious world of
ancient Israel and the early church, and highlighting the striking similarities of biblical beliefs and practices to those of surrounding peoples. It
increasingly took the form of histories of the religion of Israel and early
Christianity, rather than theologies. A backlash occurred in the early
1920s, during which scholars rejected the descriptive approach and
stressed a theocentric (God-centered) reading and the uniqueness of biblical faith. Some Old Testament scholars attempted to combine a historical treatment of Hebrew religion with a systematic presentation of "the
timeless truth of OT revelation"; others rejected a twofold approach.[19]

From 1933 through 1938, Walther Eichrodt published a three-
volume *Theology of the Old Testament* that he organized around the idea of
covenant as the center of Old Testament theology, emphasizing that the
idea derived from the Old Testament itself (rather than from Christian

17. John H. Hayes and F. Prussner, *Old Testament Theology: Its History and Development* (Atlanta: John Knox,
1985), 63, cited by Barr, *Concept of Biblical Theology*, 62.
18. Cited by Barr, *Concept of Biblical Theology*, 62.
19. Otto Betz, "Biblical Theology, History of," in *The Interpreter's Dictionary of the Bible* (ed. George Arthur But-
trick; New York/Nashville: Abingdon, 1962), 1:433–35.

dogma) and tied the Old Testament and New Testament together.[20] A new flowering of biblical and Old Testament theology followed, with a variety of attempts to integrate affirmations of timeless truth revealed in the Bible with recognition of the historical nature of the revelation. It climaxed with the publication of Gerhard von Rad's two-volume *Old Testament Theology* in 1957 and 1960, which rejected Eichrodt's notion of a center and his method of systematic synthesis as alien to the Israelite mental world as well as to the Old Testament's own presentation of the faith of Israel.[21] Von Rad argued that the theological witness of the Old Testament takes the form of a *Heilsgeschichte* (saving history), and the task of an Old Testament theology must be to retell that history. Thus it must have a historical form—not as a history of Israelite religion, but rather as a sequential presentation of the Bible's theological witnesses to God's action in history.[22]

Few new attempts at writing an Old Testament theology were made in the period immediately following von Rad's work, though the biblical theology movement, which had flourished in North America in the 1940s and 1950s, continued into the 1960s. This movement, which promoted a Bible-centered approach to theology, was grounded in the churches (especially Presbyterian) rather than the academy, and it found expression in programmatic works, word studies, and journals (such as *Theology Today* and *Interpretation*) rather than in biblical theologies. Despite its impact in the churches, the movement had little lasting effect on biblical studies as an academic discipline. Throughout the 1970s and 1980s, biblical theology as traditionally conceived was in decline, though works of Old Testament theology continued to be written, mostly in Europe. In the Society of Biblical Literature, participation in the Old Testament Theology Section was so low in 1982 that its termination was anticipated.[23] But it did not terminate, though it changed its name, as new activity began to manifest itself, in new places and in new directions.

THEOLOGY AND ACADEMIC STUDY OF THE BIBLE IN NORTH AMERICA, 1960–1990

One factor in the crisis of biblical theology in North America was a dramatic growth in biblical and religious studies that accompanied the

---

20. English version: Walther Eichrodt, *Theology of the Old Testament* (2 vols.; trans. J. A. Baker; The Old Testament Library; Philadelphia: Westminster, 1961, 1967).

21. English version: Gerhard von Rad, *Old Testament Theology* (2 vols.; trans. D. M. G. Stalker; New York: Harper & Row, 1962, 1965).

22. Ibid., 435; Barr, *Concept of Biblical Theology*, 32–37.

23. See Bird, "Old Testament Theology," 78.

establishment of religious studies programs in state colleges and universities, thereby "freeing" study of the Bible from the exclusive domain of theological seminaries and church-related institutions. In public institutions and private universities that had severed church ties, the Bible was taught alongside other religious traditions and writings, without claims to authority. As biblical studies was cut loose from the church, the profile and program of the Society of Biblical Literature was transformed by an expanded base and orientation toward a broader public.[24] The Society of Biblical Literature has been, since its origins, a significant determiner of what is occurring in the field of biblical studies. It is therefore useful to consider what participation in it reflects about the state of biblical theology and of feminist interpretation. By the late 1960s scholarly interpretation without theological presuppositions or aims had become the accepted norm in the Society, and suspicion or rejection of theological interests continued to define the general ethos during most of the following decades. But new developments in the 1980s and 1990s brought a widening of interest in theology under the banner of hermeneutics,[25] as well as renewed vigor in the "classical" field of Old Testament theology.[26]

Increasing numbers of women in the Society of Biblical Literature and a small African American presence led, in the 1970s and 1980s, to the formation of program units concerned with the particular hermeneutical interests of these groups. These units emphasized the role of experience and religious tradition as well as culture in interpretation of the Bible. The growing force of postmodernism, with its rejection of the ideals of objectivity and distance (associated with historical criticism), fostered interest in the subjectivity and social location of the interpreter, while increasing globalization encouraged efforts of contextual interpretation. Religious identity could resurface in this pluralistic milieu at the same time that the theological imperialism of supposedly neutral historical scholarship was denounced. The question "Whose Bible is it anyway?" was being raised from a number of different directions, including that of Jewish interpretation.[27]

Of the various new interests, it was Jewish perspectives, rather than feminist concerns, that impacted biblical theology in the academy. The

24. Ernest W. Saunders, *Searching the Scriptures: A History of the Society of Biblical Literature, 1880–1980* (Society of Biblical Literature Centennial Publications 8; Chico, CA: Scholars Press, 1982).

25. The term "hermeneutics" signifies the activity and theory of translating biblical ideas and affirmations into contemporary idiom, in order to produce (or reveal) a message that speaks to current needs.

26. Bird, "Old Testament Theology," 77–78.

27. See Philip R. Davies, *Whose Bible Is It Anyway?* (Journal for the Study of the Old Testament Supplement Series 204; Sheffield: Sheffield Academic Press, 1995).

Old Testament Theology Section changed its name in 1995 to Theology of the Hebrew Scriptures; in 1996 it featured a panel on Jewish and Christian interpretation; and in 1998 it added a Jewish cochair. But although one of the two Jewish panelists in 1996 was a woman (Tikva Frymer-Kensky), feminist interests and feminist participation remained largely invisible.[28] It would appear that "biblical theology," however defined, has been viewed by feminists as alien or infertile ground. Clearly the center of their work was elsewhere.[29] Yet the feminist silence has not been total, though the single prominent voice was not sounded in the Old Testament Theology Section of the Society of Biblical Literature.

PHYLLIS TRIBLE'S OVERTURES FOR
A FEMINIST BIBLICAL THEOLOGY

Trible's essay in *The Flowering of Old Testament Theology*, entitled "Feminist Hermeneutics and Biblical Theology," is excerpted from a 1989 article in the journal *Theological Studies*.[30] She begins with an overview of feminism and then sketches the history of biblical theology to a climax in 1933–1960, a period framed by the works of Eichrodt and von Rad. Beginning in the early 1960s, she sees the discipline as being in decline, with few new works and none dominating the field. Yet she maintains that the subject had "grown through experimentation," identifying "conversation between sociology and theology, discussion of canon, and development of bipolar categories for encompassing scriptural diversity" as elements of this growth. "More broadly," she concludes, "biblical theology [had] begun to converse with the world."[31] It is in this expanded conversation with the world that she situates her feminist approach to the subject, setting it over against a two-hundred-year history which she summarizes as follows:

> First, biblical theology (more often OT theology) has sought identity, but with no resolution. . . . Second, guardians of the discipline have fit a standard profile. They have been white Christian males of European or North American extraction, educated in seminaries, divinity schools, or theological faculties. Third, overall, their interpretations have skewed or neglected matters not congenial to a

28. See n. 13 above and Bird, "Old Testament Theology," 78–81.
29. Bird, "Old Testament Theology," 82–85.
30. Thus her original audience was theologians rather than biblical scholars.
31. Trible, "Feminist Hermeneutics," 453.

patriarchal point of view. Fourth, they have fashioned the discipline in a past separated from the present. *Biblical theology has been kept apart from biblical hermeneutics.*[32]

Trible's emphasis is on the final point. It is the separation of biblical theology from hermeneutics that she wishes to challenge as a feminist, joining feminist critique to challenges coming from many other directions.[33] With this emphasis on hermeneutics, she surveys the state of feminist hermeneutics and feminist biblical studies before turning to the task of envisioning a feminist biblical theology. Though not yet ready to write one, she declares that the time is ripe to make "overtures." Arguing that "feminists do not move in the world of Gabler, Eichrodt, von Rad, and their heirs," she begins her sketch of a feminist alternative by identifying three points of contrast with the "classical discipline." First, a feminist biblical theology will be "primarily constructive and hermeneutical, not just descriptive and historical." Second, because the discipline belongs to diverse communities, it is "neither essentially nor necessarily Christian." And third, "No single method, organization, or exposition harnesses the subject."[34]

The first step of her feminist theology is exegesis, "the *descriptive* and *historical* task . . . [of] explor[ing] the entire picture of gender and sex in all its diversity," a step she illustrates by examples from her earlier studies. Her second step is constructive and hermeneutical: envisioning the contours and content of a "theology that subverts patriarchy."[35] Rejecting the systematic-covenant model of Eichrodt and the tradition-historical model of von Rad, she chooses for her focus the "phenomenon of gender and sex in the articulation of faith." Six tentative proposals provide content to this step. A feminist theology, she suggests, would begin with Gen 1–3, "explore the presence and absence of the female in Scripture," reflect theologically on Israelite folk religion (including worship of the Queen of Heaven and the relationship between Yahweh and Asherah), expose idolatry by showing how the language for God "guards against a single definition" or final statement of faith, defend the altering of words and meaning in wrestling with patriarchal language, and consider the question of authority as critical for biblical theology. Centering authority in readers and appealing to

---

32. Ibid., 454 (emphasis added).
33. Ibid.; cf. Bird, "Old Testament Theology," 87.
34. Trible, "Feminist Hermeneutics," 458.
35. Ibid., 458, 464.

Deut 30:15–20, she suggests that "feminism might claim the entire Bible as authoritative, though not necessarily prescriptive."[36]

A FEMINIST FUTURE FOR BIBLICAL THEOLOGY?

Trible's overtures whet our appetite for the work she envisions—to take its place alongside the models she rejects, as an alternative theological reading of the Hebrew Scriptures, and an invitation to other reassessments, including other feminist approaches.[37] What distinguishes the theology she envisions from those of her male forerunners and colleagues is not simply her choice of gender analysis as its key, but her recognition that the "blessing" sought from the text (or its Subject) comes only through struggle, because it is bound in patriarchal language and structures. With every other feminist theologian, Trible knows the Bible as a source of pain as well as promise. Insisting on the promise, she demands a hermeneutic, and a theology, that acknowledges the pain.

Thus far, Trible stands alone in proposing a feminist biblical theology, but she is not the sole feminist engaged in the activity of biblical theology. Feminist theological reflection has found expression in a variety of forms of biblical scholarship, as well as interpretive efforts outside the academy. Feminist biblical theology is found in commentaries and word studies, exegetical essays and studies of selected problems, themes, and images. It is also found in sermons and Bible studies, by laywomen as well as biblical scholars. One of the distinguishing features of feminist biblical scholarship is its awareness of a larger sisterhood of interpreters, from which it draws insight and impetus for its work and to which it is accountable. Much of the feminist biblical interpretation described elsewhere in this volume is deeply theological, whatever its particular subject or concern. Whenever feminists address biblical texts with questions of truth and justice, they are engaging in biblical theology.

Among Old Testament/Hebrew Bible scholars, the honoree of this volume, Katharine Doob Sakenfeld, stands out as one who has consistently incorporated theological reflection informed by feminist sensitivity into her writings.[38] To name other names runs the danger of

---

36. Ibid., 462–64.
37. See Bird, "Old Testament Theology," 88–107.
38. See the listing of Sakenfeld's publications at the end of this volume. Although some titles immediately signal a theological concern (e.g., "The Problem of Divine Forgiveness in Numbers 14" and "Feminist Perspectives on Bible and Theology"), theological insights enrich many other works, including her recent *Just Wives? Stories of Power and Survival in the Old Testament and Today.*

identifying a limited group of scholars as "feminist biblical theologians" when many more are engaging issues of biblical theology. In addition, feminist biblical scholars who are not directly involved in theological interpretation—and may have no theological interests—have contributed greatly to our understanding of the theology of the Old Testament/ Hebrew Bible through their studies of female figures, images, and metaphors; women, cults, and deities in the biblical world; and gender constructions and literary theory.[39]

A major reason for the relative invisibility of women in circles of biblical theology is that other subjects have had greater immediacy and urgency for women entering a male-dominated profession. Much of feminist contribution to biblical scholarship has been cultivated in groups with specifically feminist interests and agendas. But the structures that have served to stimulate and support feminist scholarship have also served to isolate feminist discussion from the larger debate, especially in traditional subjects, such as Old Testament theology.[40] In light of this pattern, we may ask, What will it take for feminist contributions to move from the ghetto of feminist studies into the "mainstream"—or for the "mainstream" to realize that it is only a current in the turbulent waters of the discipline? Whatever the contributions of feminists to theological reflection on the Old Testament/Hebrew Bible, the challenge of feminist engagement with a biblical theology that attempts to comprehend the full witness of the Old Testament/Hebrew Bible (or the Bible as a whole) remains. If feminists are not participants in the ongoing discussion and production of such works, how will their insights and critique be incorporated?

Trible has caught the attention of the "mainstream" of biblical theologians—by standing outside it and critiquing it. Other, less visible feminist scholars have worked within the tradition, willing to claim the heritage of Gabler and von Rad, if not (yet) to make overtures for a feminist biblical theology.[41] Whatever form their efforts may take and in whatever direction the discipline may move, feminists will insist that a biblical theology that fails to address the androcentric distortions and patriarchal skewing of the Bible's theological witness cannot be true to its historical testimony or to its contemporary readers.

---

39. See Bird, "Old Testament Theology," 84–85.

40. On the tensions in women's scholarly commitments and agendas, see Adela Yarbro Collins, "Introduction," in *Feminist Perspectives on Biblical Scholarship* (ed. Adela Yarbro Collins; Society of Biblical Literature Biblical Scholarship in North America 10; Chico, CA: Scholars Press, 1985), 3–5.

41. For suggestions of alternative approaches, see Bird, "Old Testament Theology," 93–95.

FOR FURTHER STUDY

Bird, Phyllis A. "Biblical Authority in the Light of Feminist Critique." In *Missing Persons and Mistaken Identities: Women and Gender in Ancient Israel,* 248–64. Overtures to Biblical Theology. Minneapolis: Fortress, 1997.

Camp, Claudia V. "Feminist Theological Hermeneutics: Canon and Christian Identity." In *Searching the Scriptures.* Vol. 1, *A Feminist Introduction,* 154–71. Edited by Elisabeth Schüssler Fiorenza. New York: Crossroad, 1993.

Ollenburger, Ben C., ed. *Old Testament Theology: Flowering and Future.* Winona Lake, IN: Eisenbrauns, 2004.

Trible, Phyllis. "Five Loaves and Three Fishes: Feminist Hermeneutics and Biblical Theology." *Theological Studies* 50 (1989): 279–95.

18

Feminist Interpretation for the Laity

FREDA A. GARDNER

Feminist biblical interpretation is, and indeed has been since its beginnings, a gift to the church. Interpreting Scripture and theology and life from a feminist perspective first entails seeing, reading, analyzing, hypothesizing, and predicting through the eyes, experiences, and voices of women of many colors, cultures, and ages. Then we can offer the results to women and to the church at large as vehicles of God's ongoing revelation to humankind. Yet no matter what the dictionary might say, to some people feminism still implies feisty, loud, radical females who cringe if you refer to them as girls. Therefore, the challenge before anyone who would introduce or continue to employ feminist language and interpretation is often considerable.

Katharine Doob Sakenfeld entered the academic and scholarly world when feminism was more of a conviction than a reality. There were still miles to go before any significant portion of the population would see women as a whole as invested both with certain characteristics and with inalienable rights—characteristics that were still to be tested against the valued (read "male") traits of each society, and rights which forever had been ascribed to only men and not yet to the whole of humankind. That she had proven her intellectual gifts as equal to, and often surpassing, those of her fellow male students could not be disputed, but success in the graduate world did not automatically translate into admiration and appreciation in the academic world. She, like others of her generation and of previous generations, had to win the respect that was often automatically bestowed on her male counterparts.

Careful, caring, and cautious forays into feminist interpretation in the early days of the feminist movement were initiated through seminal books and bolstered through experiments behind closed doors by conference attendees who encouraged one another to take risks with new standards and new possibilities for criticism. Regrettably, they were the recipients of often scathing rebukes for taking seriously what many deemed too frivolous for academe. Survivors of such experiences began to write and then to speak, when invited to by the outside world, about the need for clarity of language and for new insights into age-old interpretations. Over time, as women entered the academic arena, they found in each other allies, comforters, and provocateurs who encouraged one another to keep on in what was increasingly becoming more significant than the merely political and was more essential to life than "playing the games" necessary for gaining public approval.

Outside the world of the academy, women, who had only in the past two or three decades been allowed to share leadership roles in the church, were of two minds: either they were eager or they were reluctant to present a woman's way of being an elder, deacon, or other-named church leader. North American Protestant churches had held the line in support of male dominance for so long that many members of the church, both male and female, were hesitant, if not stubborn, about doing things differently or asking questions about church governance or biblical interpretation. Actions and language that deviated from custom were often laughed at or trivialized, if not condemned, as the cause of what was seen to be wrong with the life, worship, and teaching of the church. Changes in the language used for God, even that supported by the imagery and language found in Scripture, threatened both men and women who felt that the alterations rocked the very foundations of their faith or, conversely, that they were not worthy of any serious consideration. For many, there was no rationale for change that could assuage their fears that such new concepts and new ways of acting would bring down the very foundations of Christian belief.

Into such conflicting feelings and attitudes came women brave enough and secure enough either in themselves or by virtue of their positions to test the waters. They began to reach out to the multitudes of women who had been carefully taught to discredit themselves and their experiences, and to those who had quietly begun to speak up and speak out about their own senses of call and their own gifts, which they began to hope might be used in the church in opportunities heretofore designated "for men only."

Some biblical scholars began to teach from overlooked texts, having mined the Bible in its original languages and ancient circumstances for tales of women's inclusion in Scripture. The names of women long left unrecognized came into view, and their stories were lifted up for what words of truth might be perceived in them. For many women this was the first cautious step into self-recognition, a foretaste of the realization that, like those biblical women, they had gifts and callings worthy of pursuit. Yet for every woman who came to know herself as a daughter of God, there were others who felt unfaithful, selfish, or foolish when they found new meaning in Scripture. And so defenses were mounted and protected. Nonetheless, by the time Katharine Sakenfeld was promoted to full professor and delivered the mandatory lecture to her peers, she had colleagues on both sides of the aisle who listened with respect. As she dealt with the daughters of Zelophehad (Num 27:1–11), the focus of her address, some persons became aware—perhaps for the first time—that there might be more in a text than had always been thought or imagined.

In the early stages of the feminist movement, scriptural interpretation often included nothing more than the lifting up of overlooked or superficially treated passages in which women have a minor, or even a central, role. Yet any assertion that God might be engaging in self-revelation through the words or actions of a woman was often met with disbelief. Moreover, for many white North Americans, the possibility that African American, Latina, or Asian American women might read certain passages differently from the way they did also came as a revelation. Soon women from Asia, Africa, and Latin America also challenged the presumed "universality" of white women's perspectives. Katharine Sakenfeld, in her book *Just Wives?* encourages a global perspective as she engages women from a variety of cultures to bring their own contexts and values into interaction with familiar texts to the benefit of all and, undoubtedly, the discomfort of some.[1] As Walter Brueggemann reminds us, all interpretation is done within a historical context and necessitates reconsideration in the ever-changing times of our lives.[2]

---

1. Katharine Doob Sakenfeld, *Just Wives? Stories of Power and Survival in the Old Testament and Today* (Louisville, KY: Westminster John Knox, 2003).

2. Walter Brueggemann, Brian K. Blount, and William C. Placher, *Struggling with Scripture* (Louisville, KY: Westminster John Knox, 2002).

FRAMEWORKS FOR TEACHING AND LEARNING

It is one thing to come to new insights, but another thing to make them available to the larger world—that is, to teach. To consider doing that with the words, thought patterns, and language of Scripture, along with our own cultural perspectives, is both thrilling and daunting. Given, however, that feminist perspectives can come as a challenge, or even a threat, to many people, it is important to introduce them with care, compassion, and pedagogical awareness. And it goes without saying that, at all times and in all circumstances, teaching the laity has to be something more than mere speaking at them.

Parker J. Palmer offers a helpful framework for such teaching. A foremost scholar of education theory, Palmer has defined teaching as creating a space in which obedience to truth is practiced.[3] Paraphrasing this idea, perhaps we might back up a step to say that the teacher's task is to create a space where truth can be known. Such truth is not a fact or a set of presuppositions, but rather something that emerges from the activity of pedagogy and grasps the learner with its implications of greater insight into things that matter. Palmer suggests three characteristics of the space wherein truth can be known and obedience to it practiced: openness, boundaries, and hospitality.[4] These three characteristics are not unknown to many who do or would teach, but they are often overlooked or deemed inconsequential when considered over against the import of the scriptural passages to be explored.

Openness

First the result of intentional activity on the part of the teacher/leader, openness requires that someone act to remove impediments to learning, obstacles both internal and external. Historically, good teachers have almost always paid attention to such external factors as room temperature, room size, blocked vision, and the like. What many have paid little or no attention, however, are the internal factors, that is, what both teacher and learners bring into the space. One of these fac-

3. Parker J. Palmer, *To Know as We Are Known: A Spirituality of Education* (San Francisco: Harper & Row, 1983).
4. Ibid., 71.

tors is fear: fear of being revealed as ignorant, fear of being belittled or categorized, fear of a teacher's authority or of exhibiting behavior that might affect one's future with the group or at the job, fear that some may not take the class seriously and may therefore make one's own interest questionable. One example of just such a fear can be seen in people who hesitate to take a Bible class in the church because it seems to them that everyone else knows exactly where to find Joshua or Ephesians. No one bothers to tell them that there is a table of contents in every Bible, and we can still be good Christians even if we resort to using it.

Openness connotes a receptivity to, as we say, "the truth that seeks to be known." This is especially relevant for teaching that is focused on God's self-revelation and is underlain by the conviction that God is primarily concerned with having truth emerge and become a living thing in the life of the learner. Such understanding is not something to be merely read but then deemed irrelevant or insignificant to the business of living; it is to be lived.

Boundaries

Every space needs boundaries. We know that for a child to grow well, boundaries are necessary. Without them children are at risk, always potential victims of their own fears or misinformation. For many young people, the questions are: What are the limits which, if I cross them, I will be out . . . outside the love, care, and respect of my family or my peers? What if I go too far? How far can I go and still be loved and considered a worthy part of this group? Adult learners, not only children, also need such boundaries.

If there are no limits, if teachers—alone or with the class—set none, then learners will flee when the going gets tough. They will remove themselves literally by not attending, or figuratively by feigning indifference, by faking illness, or through sarcastic belittling. These are all ways that students can say either "I'm not here" or "What we are doing is worthless." People also flee, in one way or another, because the truth hurts or challenges. If no boundaries have been set, if rules of engagement that encourage openness and forswear embarrassing or ignoring another have not been established and practiced, fight or flight are the students' only choices.

Hospitality

Palmer further reminds us that a learning experience, whether intended or happenstance, can become tense and potentially painful. Thus hospitality in learning is essential. The practice of hospitality allows for the discomfort of truth, whether we are approaching something for the first, third, or forty-third time. Today we expect everything in an instant, at least in the North American context. Those who teach are not immune to this expectation, and neither are parents and other leaders; almost every teacher has said, "If I've told you once, I've told you a hundred times," or "We went over all that last week; why must we do it again?" Even though we know about multiple intelligences and recognize that people learn in different ways and are best taught through different methods, and even though we realize that people bring different gifts to the process, we sometimes berate ourselves and others if we or they seem to be deliberately "not knowing."

THE REWARDS AND CHALLENGES
OF FEMINIST BIBLICAL INTERPRETATION

If these matters seem important for teaching in general, the stakes are yet higher when it comes to teaching Scripture. Here we are dealing with God's words to us, with long-held and long-honored words and meanings. Even for those who know little of the actual teachings of Scripture or of the previous interpretive work done across hundreds of years, the Bible itself has an aura that suggests that what is read should be seen as final and that how it has been interpreted should be considered the last word. Those for whom the contents of Scripture have been a mystery, or who have made a protective peace with portions that cannot be understood or believed, may be the most adamantly opposed to any contemporary interpretation.

Feminist biblical scholars have been engaged for more than three decades in ascertaining what constitutes feminist interpretation and to what ends it is employed. Those questions are not irrelevant to the laity, yet neither are they foremost in the minds of more than a relative few. Using feminist interpretation to critique patriarchy can raise questions for some about the apparent dishonoring of long-known and well-admired male biblical figures. If feminist interpretation is used to question the authenticity of certain portions of Scripture, it can threaten both strong and tenuous attachments that are felt to be the foundation of faith.

The Presbyterian Church (U.S.A.) has embarked on a program known as "Reading through the Bible." Many who have chosen to undertake this program have been challenged by serious questions which, as we struggle through the Old Testament, are easy both to become focused on and stopped by, for instance, "How could God do that to those people?" or "Why do we need to know those old rules which have no place in life today?" Understood as an ongoing call to God's people to discern for their time what God is saying about life and the living of it, and the values that resonate with God's intent for humankind, biblical interpretation is a mystery to many. Such an under-standing suggests that in sermons, in new-member and confirmation classes, and, indeed, in every form of education, interpretation needs to be lifted up as essential preliminary and foundational content. If the laity are to broaden both their attention and their convictions in order to con-sider from new perspectives what God is doing in their lives today, they must first and then consistently be encouraged to understand the mean-ing and role of Scripture in the lives of the church and of the individual.

Such understanding necessitates knowing who is speaking for God or about God, and who is not included in the biblical text. Analogies from daily life can help us recognize that not all people see or value things in the same ways. What is "in" for one group of teenagers, for example, may be swept away by the experiences of a high school in another part of the country or in a different culture. The highest and most cherished goals for family life in one culture may at first be seen as less significant than those found in one's own group, but examina-tion may reveal that others' values raise a question about one's own pri-orities. The quality of life and relationships among those with little of the world's goods may jar the prerogatives of a consumer society. For example, we can consider the devotion to one another of the lost boys of Sudan, a group of young orphaned refugees who, forced from their homes, traveled together through the vast African wilderness. Their fierce allegiance to one another's survival and well-being may illumine how little "love your neighbor" has come to mean to the many of us who push aside statistics about the poverty and racism that infect our own society. Stories that reinterpret the biblical text or make starkly clear how we have read Scripture in a way that affirms our own choices can therefore be shared in many contexts that do not bear the explicit title of "Interpretation of Scripture."

Although teaching feminist interpretation of Scripture has unique possibilities and pitfalls, it is not unlike introducing anything new to a particular group. The challenge for the introducer, be it pastor, religious educator, leader of a woman's group, or committed church member, is choosing the appropriate means for this introduction and being ready to accommodate the group receiving the new information and perspective. There are those who advocate the "drop the person off the dock and s/he will learn to swim" method—that is, total immersion—but it hardly seems fit for the task of seeing Scripture in a new light. At the very least it is important to recognize and name the fears that the hearers and learners might hold. Statements like "This will sound different to you and may even be hard to hear, and that is a very normal reaction" or "This may sound quite different to you from what you are used to, but I invite you to be aware of any new ideas or insights that might appear as you listen" can allow listeners to hear with an open mind instead of becoming self-defensive. Even those students who display no great knowledge of Scripture may have more than a few cherished Bible stories or passages that are the foundation of their sense of their own faith.

It is easy to imagine that, for some people, learning that a particular woman in Scripture is not a mere hearer of the word but, in fact, a doer of the word may shake a well-developed and carefully guarded self-identification or, for men, a sense of privilege, ownership, and even domination. Even to learn of the crucial roles played by biblical women who are generally buried in stories that appear to have only to do with men is a shock to many and may occasion panic as the learner is challenged to reorganize what has, seemingly forever, been assumed to be the whole truth. A biblical account told from the perspective of the women involved rather than the men can be more upsetting than we might expect it to be in the twenty-first century. It is unsettling to the man whose identity is posited on the supremacy of male perspective, knowledge, and action. But it can also be unsettling to the woman who has settled into the role of "second best" even though she appears to have a voice and opinion on some matters. We see such discomfort in women who are reluctant to accept a call to be an elder and in men who are reluctant to take on a teaching role in the church, perhaps because of long-held presuppositions about what women and men should be doing. Having one's "rules to live by" questioned by another culture's basic beliefs about life is a jarring experience for people, and it is a gracious gift to offer them help to stay rather than to flee.

For women, to realize that God's intent holds all people accountable to live in a way that is often at cross purposes with personal desires or cultural values can be more of a challenge than many persons are ready to face. If I am implicated in God-become-human Jesus' teachings, I am then to read Scripture as descriptive of my life and of the life I have been called to live. In the North American context, the messages of the Bible often come as a clarion call for us to be at odds with what we so easily value. Feminist interpretation may force white, privileged women to look with new eyes on their sisters who are not so privileged because of their skin color, because of their lack of formal education, or because they do not have the kind of wealth that allows for gracious sharing with little cost to one's own lifestyle. Indeed, this might become an occasion for a woman to harden her own well-fought-for ways of existing in a still male-dominated world. For men, hearing previously unheard voices and being introduced to new perspectives on "taken-for-granted" interpretations may lead them to experience mild or serious shake-ups of their own foundations of faith and living. Confronting the word from God will evoke all the protective devices we have all so carefully honed in defense of what is most comfortable to believe and act on.

Yet fear is not the sole, nor even necessarily the predominant, response of laypersons to feminist interpretation. As women find role models and validation of concerns long harbored, their excitement grows. New insights into what it means to be a daughter of God and a female disciple of Jesus Christ may bring similar new insights to men as they encounter the wider implications of discipleship and the possibilities for sharing such discipleship with women. The further awareness of a new solidarity among women that comes from hearing long-silenced voices wrestling with the word of God from contexts long ignored by most other women might allow us to see what indeed we have been called to be. Feminist biblical interpretation feels like a breath of fresh air or a taste of living water for many women who have harbored, protected, or buried their sense that God's intent for humankind does, in fact, include women. Likewise, men may be encouraged to look at their own cultural, ethnic, and gender contexts for implications for a different, perhaps more challenging, understanding of what it is to be a disciple today.

The teacher therefore must help the learners to face their fears and anger, and to see them for what they are. The recognition that, in the theological affirmation "God so loves the world," the "world" includes those who see and experience life in ways very different from one's own may present a challenge to examine the choices, allegiances, and motivations that give shape to one's own life of discipleship. If it is hard for a poverty-stricken parent to imagine the life of the affluent parent whose children never know hunger and have no end of the culture's gadgets, then it is equally hard for affluent persons to imagine that those who live in poverty read with different eyes the biblical teachings about daily living and hold their readings before us in discomforting realism. Feminist interpretation, like that of liberationist theology, must be embedded in a context rich in prayer and forgiveness, a context of confession and ongoing support for what new insights demand from those who hear and see the challenge of discipleship in new ways.

In this task the teacher, of whatever title or in whatever context, must know that she or he is moving onto holy ground with any group of learners, must see in the other the image of God, must be the first to admit to fears and the urge to flee from truth. That teacher must create an arena of love, justice, and goodwill for those who may be wounded and for those who may be lifted up by new truths (or old truths reshaped). Those who have long been silenced by the rule of the majority must find space that will welcome their contrary-to-custom interpretation of Scripture and must know that they will not be cast out for expressing it before others. Feminist biblical interpretation is a challenge to everyone's status quo and, with revelation that others have heard God's voice in different ways, it requires the honest claiming of what is liberating and what is daunting, all performed in trust that the community will hold together as the struggle to see and act continues.

FOR FURTHER STUDY

Harris, Maria. *Women and Teaching: Themes for a Spirituality of Pedagogy.* New York: Paulist, 1988.

Hess, Carol Lakey. *Caretakers of Our Common House: Women's Development in Communities of Faith.* Nashville: Abingdon, 1997.

Moore, Mary Elizabeth Mullino. *Teaching as a Sacramental Act.* Cleveland: Pilgrim, 2004.

Palmer, Parker J. *To Know as We Are Known: Education as a Spiritual Journey.* Rev. ed. New York: HarperCollins, 1993.

Peters, Rebecca Todd. "Decolonizing Our Minds: Postcolonial Perspectives on the Church." In *Women's Voices and Visions of the Church: Reflections from North America,* ed. Letty M. Russell, Aruna Gnanadason, and J. Shannon Clarkson, 93–110. N.p.: World Council of Churches, 2005.

Pohl, Christine. *Making Room: Recovering Hospitality as a Christian Tradition.* Grand Rapids: Eerdmans, 1999.

19

What I Have Learned from My Sisters

PATRICK D. MILLER

Although my siblings, Belle and Mary, belong to the list of sisters I have in mind in the title of this essay, I use the term more broadly than that, much as we have used the term "brothers"—often inclusively, of course!—to speak of our relationship with other persons, whether actually kin to us or not. My point is not to switch from "brothers" to "sisters" as an all-inclusive term, but to recognize from the start that whatever perspective I have gained on feminist interpretation and women's issues has come from women who are kin to me, my colleagues in the ministry and teaching, and women whose writings and speeches have influenced and guided my thinking. One could make a case that all learning originates in the impact of persons who teach, but I am especially aware of that in the ways my mind has changed and I have learned to think and speak differently in light of women's experience and its interpretation by my sisters.

Feminist interpretation has its roots deep in the long history of the women's movement. In its simplest and broadest form, it has to do with reading the Bible in a way that is attentive to the place of women in the text and the world of the text, what is said about them and by them,

---

Among my sisters in the church and the academy, no one has done more to inform my thinking and teach me about these matters than Katharine Sakenfeld, through her writings on feminist interpretation, her own interpretation of biblical texts, and especially through years of teaching and working with her at Princeton Theological Seminary.

what is done to them and what they cannot do.[1] The impact of feminism on me began with discovering the significance of language and the oppressive and liberating possibilities in the way we speak. So I begin with that issue, which is one on which both the church and the secular world have made much progress but whose significance should not be lost in the process. Then I turn to reflect on the specific impact of feminist interpreters on my reading and understanding of biblical texts.

Growing up in the South, I learned early on about the negative power of language as I was taught not to use racist speech.[2] What I had no clue about, however, was that standard, universally accepted ways of speech could hide the culture and the church's subordination and oppression of women as much as the failure to give them a vote or to ordain them to the ministry. The oppressive character of our modes of speaking has been much more subtle and often accepted by women as easily as men. My growing awareness of this very large issue is identifiable by looking back at some of my writings where I am now painfully aware of the easy and constant use of male language to speak of both women and men as well as the standard use of male imagery and pronouns to speak of God.[3] Beginning in the mid-1970s that changes radically. Henceforth, the use of male language to speak generally of human beings or of God disappears.[4] Thus, both personal experience and the interpretive task lead me to suggest that attention to the place of women in Scripture begins with a sense of the role that language plays, which cannot be separated from the more hermeneutical issues.

LANGUAGE AND COMMUNITY

Language is such an elementary part of our life that we hardly give any thought to it, certainly not in comparison to its importance in our lives. It is like breathing. Most of the time we speak and hear with little

---

1. There are, of course, more complex and indeed more sophisticated ways of describing feminist interpretation, as may be seen in the essays in this volume as well as in the work of Sakenfeld and many other women interpreters.

2. That early learning was only partial, for all around me I heard terms that were racist referring to African Americans, though I did not recognize the fact at the time.

3. For example, in a 1969 essay on the notion of the land in the book of Deuteronomy, I use male language to refer to human beings ten times in the first twenty-five lines, ironically in an opening discussion of racism and matters of economic justice ("The Gift of God: The Deuteronomic Theology of the Land," *Interpretation* 23 [1969]: 451–65). I entitled a 1971 essay on worship in the Old Testament "'Him Only Shall You Serve'" ("'Him Only Shall You Serve': Reflections on the Meaning of Old Testament Worship," *Andover-Newton Quarterly* 11 [1971]: 139–49).

4. There are two exceptions to this generalization. One is simply the fact that I sometimes slip into old habits and overlook what I now regard as linguistic mistakes. The other is my use of the term "Lord" to speak of God, a practice that continues to be a matter of debate among feminists and others.

thought to the complexity, uniqueness, and miracle of language, to the astonishing fact that in a matter of a few hours each of us will utter hundreds of new sentences that have never been spoken before, that we can put words together and say new things without ever having learned them. More than any other feature, language distinguishes the human from all other creatures in the natural order. There are moments when the significance of language rises before us, for example, when a baby begins to talk or when we are in a country where everyone speaks a language we do not understand. In the latter case, all sorts of things are said, heard, and done around us, and none of it makes sense. We do not know what is going on because we do not have the language.

Such moments as these bring to awareness what more serious analysis confirms: language is at the very center of our existence, making life possible. As much as anything, language transforms existence from the bestial to the human. Indeed, it opens up access to the divine, for whom one of the primary categories of our understanding and appropriation is "word," indeed word made flesh. Several features of language come into play as one asks about the role of language in regard to the way we think and speak about women, and more particularly about women and Scripture.

Language communicates. That is what it is designed to do, and that is in fact what happens. Language says what we think and feel, or it communicates and conveys ideas, attitudes, and perceptions whether or not they are intended. This may be obvious, but it is quite important. It does not work to say, "When I say 'man' or 'he,' I mean it generically to include both men and women, so that is what one should hear and receive." What in fact one hears and receives is a focus on men/males because that is what is said in a language perfectly capable of speaking about and distinguishing males and females.

For ages we got away with such claims because we created little conscious pain. There was a general consensus that the male terms would often serve to incorporate the female, that male terminology could be generic as well as gender oriented. The effect of this usage was much subconscious pain, as well as continuing linguistic support for hiding and subordinating women and communicating that males are the primary and dominant category.

Language has power. To revise a familiar childhood saying, "Sticks and stones may break my bones, but words can *really* hurt me." We know this to be true. Even growing up in a highly segregated society where racism was pervasive, I knew there were words beyond the pale, words that had tremendous power to inflict pain. But it is not just certain words that have power. Rather, all language has such ability. One thinks of the potency of words of evaluation, how praise and criticism can affect the way we and others regard ourselves and act. Consider the power of expressions like "I'm sorry," "Thank you," or "I love you." There is no such thing as neutral words without power. We fooled ourselves into thinking that ordinary nouns and pronouns have such neutrality. Inattentive to the power of all language, I would not use an obscenity or ethnic slur that puts down persons, but I was indifferent to everyday language that, as it is used, can have the same effect.

Language changes. A truism in linguistics, language change is something all of us encounter. It is why new translations are created, new dictionaries compiled, handbooks of grammar and syntax revised regularly. The elimination of masculine words—nouns and pronouns—as a mode of speaking generically of both women and men is one of the most profound changes in the history of the English language. It has reduced the way we use language to subjugate. In the process, it has changed reality. Or at least language and reality have interacted with each other in the last decades to enhance the place of women in all realms of life.

Whatever the secular world may do—and it is often ahead of the church—the changes to our language are a matter of justice, community, and pastoral care. Language is a matter of *justice* because, in giving dominant place to the male, our language has served to undergird and support countless ways women have been afflicted and treated unjustly and unfairly in a community that knows justice is one of the cornerstones of the universe and righteousness is the very name of God. It is a matter of *community* because there is no real possibility of unity, fellowship, and common spirit where many in the community hear themselves left out and are in fact subordinated to others, not temporarily or for reasons of function—there are legitimate subordinations—but permanently and because they are women. Christian community is created out of the reality that in Jesus Christ there is neither bond nor free, Jew nor Greek, male nor female. We are all one in Christ. But we cannot claim that oneness if in what we say over and over we do not include all members of the community. And language is a matter of *pastoral care* because in the Christian community pain and suffering are neither to be inflicted nor to be ignored.

The question of our language use impinges on three areas having to do with interpreting and speaking about the Bible. The first of these is the necessity of speaking and writing in ways that do not use male language to incorporate women, whatever the subject of our speech. The significance for handling Scripture lies in the fact that we fail to communicate either accurately or without hurt unless our mode of speech and writing tends to gender matters properly. That is as true for writing, preaching, teaching, and conversation about the Bible as it is for any other topic. Happily, the necessary changes have been widely accepted and practiced. For instance, many publishing houses now have clear policies supporting inclusive language style.

The second area is our language and speech about God. That is more complicated and is still under debate, though once again feminist scholarship and writing has taken us a long way.[5] There are several aspects to this issue. It starts not so much from speech practices or the language of Scripture as it does from the significant and necessary tension between the claim that God is God and not a human being and the belief that God is nevertheless to be conceived, known, and spoken of in personal categories. In every respect God is both personal and gender free. That is an important claim of Christology, where the maleness of Jesus has always been a testimony to the incarnation of God in human flesh, not in male gender.[6] In like fashion, some of the most common and important traditional male terms for God and for Jesus reflect ways of speaking but do not carry theological claims within them. Thus to speak of God as "father" has always been understood as parental language even as the christological term "son" refers to the parent/child relationship. In neither case is anything inherently gender-specific. On the contrary, it is crucial to make sure that gender specification is not indicated. With the changes in language in our time, the issue is heightened. As we have learned not to use masculine language generically, theological terminology has to move in the same direction. Exclusive and insistent use of masculine language to refer to the deity is potentially a violation of the commandment against idolatry. The Deuteronomic form of the Second Commandment clearly has in mind not only worship of false gods and making idols of other gods, but also human creation of images of the true God (Deut 4:10–18). In our

---

5. One of the things I have learned from my sisters is that the degree of seriousness of the problem of our language about God is not measured by the number of persons who are sensitive to the issue. This number continues to grow in both academic and church contexts, though, I suspect, more among women than men.

6. I can still remember the powerful effect of seeing on the front page of *The New York Times* a picture of Edwina Sandys's bronze sculpture *Christa*. It is a crucifix, but the body on the cross is that of a woman. Few pieces of art have had such a profound and permanent effect on my theology as this one, even though I have never seen the actual sculpture.

time, such images are more likely to be conceptual and theological than plastic and sculpted. So I have come to see the following:

> When the male image serves to make us think we can really see God or becomes a requirement for our language and conceptuality, then it becomes an idol. Change, in the form of breaking the idol, opening up restricted and narrow conceptions of the transcendent One, is imperative. To think and speak of God as female, she, her, mother may be a form of obedience to the commandment. Every image or word for God, however beloved it may be, is subject to theological critique because it is by definition inadequate and penultimate.[7]

The third area of language change toward affirming recognition of the place and role of women is in the work of translating the Bible. It is in some respects the most controversial and sometimes the most difficult area in which to effect language change.[8] To do so means to be both faithful to the text and faithful to the women who are in and around the text and addressed by it. Because we are dealing with a fixed and sacred text, the matter is always subject to strong feelings and opinions. The spate of contemporary translations, however—many of which have theological agenda and perspectives[9]—and the possibility of varied translation principles operating among the different translations allows for the possibility of translations that do not perpetuate gender-specific language where gender reference is not a part of the intention of the text. Yet the matter of intention is where the debate begins and does not really end. We are dealing with an ancient text whose meaning a translation is designed to open up as fully as possible but also with a sacred text whose meaning is found in the way it addresses the contemporary community of faith. It is a document that is highly patriarchal in explicit ways that cannot be erased by translation moves; it is also a text whose translation may enhance that patriarchal dimension or diminish it. So, for example, the expression "Son of Man," one of the key New Testament terms for Jesus, miscommunicates when the Greek is translated with the usual masculine words "son" and "man." It is likely that the term for "son" here means "belonging to the category of" and that the term for "man" here connotes a human

---

7. Patrick D. Miller, "Theses on the Gender of God," *Haelan* 6 (1985): 5.

8. I have discussed these matters, particularly in regard to my involvement in the work of the NRSV Translation Committee and the Inclusive Language Lectionary Committee, in two earlier essays: "The Inclusive Language Lectionary," *Theology Today* 41 (1984): 26–33; and "The Translation Task," *Theology Today* 43 (1987): 540–45.

9. For examples of explicit theological perspectives in some translations, see Miller, "The Translation Task," 543.

being. A translation such as "the human one" would communicate more clearly the force of the term than the traditional translation, which in some ways appears to be literal but is not.[10] The critique that the *Inclusive Language Lectionary* violates the original meaning or what the authors intended is easy to make, but it ignores the complexity of the translation task as well as the varied purposes toward which translation may aim.[11] Elsewhere I have summarized the issue as follows:

> Translation is therefore inevitably an interpretive enterprise. It is and must be carried out within a hermeneutical circle: both the circular relationship between part and whole and the circle that incorporates the text, the translator/interpreter, and the audience/situation. At the same time, it is *not* the case that anything goes, any more than that is true at any level of interpretation. In any interpretive enterprise, plausibility and acceptability by a wider audience are necessary controls. There are boundaries, and these are narrower, generally, for translation than for other levels of interpretation. . . . But as an act of interpretation, translation requires a debate rather than the assumption of self-evident truth about right and wrong, good and bad translation decisions.[12]

INTERPRETATION

The paragraph I have just quoted points to the heart of the matter. Feminist interpretation is a matter of hermeneutics, one that has become quite complex in the best sense of the term, that is, rich and varied, not narrow and predictable in its outcomes. Of all the things that I have learned in this regard, the most memorable, enduring, and influential is the significance of context and experience for the work of interpretation.[13] A variety of my own experiences have shaped my awareness of the way in which one's location and what happens in the process of reading texts and simply living in community can teach and direct, indeed significantly *change,* the way one reads and understands the biblical text.

10. See the comment of Jack D. Kingsbury: "In translating this title, one can perhaps capture its force in Mark's story by rendering it as 'this man' or 'this human being'" (*The Christology of Mark's Gospel* [Philadelphia: Fortress, 1983], xii).

11. For some of the issues involved in the way we understand Scripture as both ancient text and contemporary word, see Sandra M. Schneiders, "Church and Biblical Scholarship in Dialogue," *Theology Today* 42 (1985): 353–58.

12. Miller, "The Translation Task," 541–42.

13. Attention to social location is not a concern of feminist interpretation alone, but that is where I have been most profoundly conscious of its significance.

For me the shaping contexts appeared early on. When the *Inclusive Language Lectionary*[14] was first published, each member of the committee received five copies. I kept one copy for myself and, in a kind of instinctive response, gave the other copies to the four persons who had influenced me the most to think about language, about its potential for creating or destroying community, and especially the limited, excluding, and thus ultimately oppressive character of a language system that is shaped by masculine terms. Those four persons were my wife, Mary Ann; my two sisters, Belle and Mary; and my mother, Lila. That distribution of the *Lectionary* reflected the fact that my life has been significantly involved with and impacted by intelligent, active, secure, whole women who have been a primary relational community. These women have not been—in their own minds or in the minds of others—absorbed into a male ethos, although each has lived and worked in intimate relationships with men. To live in relation to them is to be highly aware of women qua women and also of the individuality, creativity, and personality of each woman. They have taught me *indirectly* to think of, to be conscious of, women on their own terms, whether in my classroom, among my colleagues, or in the pages of Scripture, and thus they have helped to place the category and experience of women on a par with that of men. These women have also taught me *directly* as they have spoken rationally and intelligently about the effects of a mode of speech that claims to be gender-free and inclusive but always uses male terms, never female, to express the inclusiveness. They have raised questions about my writing and language, especially pushing me to go further, not to be intellectually and theologically timid. In the process, they have argued carefully and sensibly, not simply proposing extreme and off-putting positions.[15]

The years of work on the New Revised Standard Version Committee[16] presented a constant exercise in having to think and translate so that the text was accurately conveyed while its patriarchy, and often the particular patriarchy of traditional translations, was not ignored and was countered where it could be done legitimately. Because that translation unfolded over about two decades, it was possible to see a process of change as members of the committee became more attentive to the place of women in the text or the way in which translations unnecessarily excluded them. The impact of interpretive context was

---

14. See n. 18.

15. There are many other women who fit this mold and are a part of the community that has taught me how to speak and read Scripture, not least, of course, the honoree of this volume.

16. See n. 18.

particularly sharp as I saw one of our members who fought for a more inclusive mode of speech in the new translation, often referring to some of his women students and the issues they raised, lose interest and in fact begin to shift back to traditional noninclusive language as he moved into retirement and out of contact with his students and their questions and probes.

The thoughtful insights of my own students were a guiding beacon during the 1970s when I began to become aware of women's issues and their significance for interpreting the Bible. A conference planned by women in the seminary community of which I was a part—students, wives of faculty members, and other women—gently pushed those of us on the faculty to engage the issue, to look at women in Scripture and how they are portrayed and how the texts about them are interpreted. It is not an accident that my own writing and speaking began to break out of its noninclusive modes of speech during this time. The teacher was being taught by women who themselves were learning as they went.

I thought these matters were settled and worked out in my mind when I was asked to take the place of a colleague as the liaison between the NRSV Committee and the Inclusive Language Lectionary Commit-tee.[17] Because the NRSV Committee was taking a more conservative approach to the issue of inclusive language—not attempting to deal with God language at all, for example—the National Council of Churches appointed a committee to prepare a translation of the common lection-ary that would provide a translation where language for God and human beings is fully inclusive.[18] I still recall going through the committee's work to that point during a daylong train ride to my first meeting, react-ing often with surprise and sometimes scholarly hostility—even though I was supportive of the enterprise—and making notes to correct the many errors I saw in what had been proposed. It was only as members of the committee explained their decisions and as I listened to and reflected on their analyses and rationale, and especially as I tried to take the assignment seriously and worked with these women and men, that I came to appreciate the care with which the committee had worked and

17. Beginning in the late 1940s, there was a gradual movement away from the standard King James Version of the Bible, which had been used by churches literally for centuries, toward more contemporary translations. The transla-tion that led the way was the Revised Standard Version (RSV), a translation prepared over a number of years by a committee under the auspices of the National Council of Churches (NCC). In the 1970s, the NCC asked this com-mittee to engage in necessary revision to bring the translation up to date. A number of persons were added to the committee over a period of time, and in 1989 a much revised form of this translation appeared with the title New Revised Standard Version (NRSV). During the same period of time, another committee, appointed also by the NCC, was asked to translate the texts that make up the common lectionary used by many denominations and churches to be completely inclusive in its language about human beings and about God.

18. The committee's task included attending to language that functioned negatively or oppressively to ethnic groups.

the way in which linguistic and theological sensitivity were brought together to produce a truly inclusive and defensible translation.

Beyond this critical role of experience and context, of relationships and location, I have learned at least the following things about and from feminist interpretation. First, the experience of women and the community of sisters is not merely ideology. It is a legitimate hermeneutic and functions for many persons as a criterion for judging Scripture and what it has to say to us. Katharine Doob Sakenfeld has put the matter sharply and pointedly: "The place of women's experience (and the proper definition of 'experience') in appropriating the biblical witness is in my view the central issue around which feminist discussion of approaches to biblical authority revolves."[19] She quotes Elisabeth Schüssler Fiorenza as seeing the locus of revelation "not in texts but in Christian experience and community."[20] That is largely on target, in my judgment. I would suggest it is better put not so much as alternative choices but the interaction of texts with Christian experience and community. When my sisters have turned to the texts of Scripture, their insights have been indeed revelatory.[21] I can share in those insights, discern and appropriate the truth they have discovered, but I do not bring their experience and context to that discernment and so must receive it from them.

Second, recognizing the particularity of women's experience and the community of women does not, however, mean that men are unable to attend to what the Bible says about women and to learn from those texts. Feminist criticism is a way into the biblical texts, an angle of vision, a perspective opening up dimensions of the text that may remain hidden, mute, or unidentified. As with any mode of criticism, it is important that there be persons who engage in its practice in a wholehearted fashion, developing models of approach and identifying the many issues involved and the possibilities and problems posed by such a critical method. The essays in this volume belong to such efforts. I do not identify myself as a feminist critic in this sense any more than I perceive myself as a form critic. Yet, as it is necessary to attend to the issues and methods of form criticism once one has learned how that helps in reading and interpreting texts, so also the ways into the text arising out of feminist interpretation belong to any serious effort to read and interpret Scripture. Feminist hermeneutics is a particular critical method, in some

---

19. Katharine Doob Sakenfeld, "Feminist Perspectives on Bible and Theology: An Introduction to Selected Issues and Literature," *Interpretation* 42 (1988): 6–7.

20. Ibid.

21. That does not mean that either the experience or the hermeneutic is outside the possibilities of criticism. All interpretation, of course, is open to criticism. To acknowledge this fact, however, does not vitiate the interpretive gains that women's experience offers to all interpreters of Scripture.

ways much richer and more complex than other critical methods. At the same time it is an aspect of all good interpretation. I have not, nor have many of my male colleagues, recognized this as thoroughly as needs to be the case.

Third, feminist biblical interpretation especially has taught me the need for both a hermeneutic of suspicion and a hermeneutic of retrieval. Much of feminist interpretation is a proper and powerful hermeneutic of suspicion, questioning the text, identifying its patriarchy and oppression of women, resisting its power to effect such ways of being and acting in the contemporary culture and the church. Especially for male interpreters and those of us for whom the authority of Scripture is a fundamental assumption and principle of interpretation and theology, suspicious or questioning reading of Scripture is so necessary and valuable that we must fight to overcome the inherent resistance to such readings that our context and assumptions may create in us. The hermeneutic of retrieval cannot come before the problems of the text have been identified. It is, however, a necessary next step if the biblical text is to be appropriated in any helpful or authoritative manner for the community of faith. It may be that some texts have to be set aside. Yet much of the time, our interpretations are aimed at apprehending the text as a word to the contemporary community. If that is the case then interpretation will need to find what matters in the text, genuinely retrieving it rather than setting it aside.[22]

Fourth, it is difficult to appropriate the texts without a critical principle that enables judgments to be made, discrimination among texts, and decisions about what is normative and controlling and what is to be rejected. Indeed, one may operate with more than one critical principle. Rosemary Radford Ruether's "prophetic principle" serves to challenge every text or interpretation of a text that creates an oppressive outcome.[23] The critical principle comes from within Scripture itself, as should all such norming claims. I would assume that the gospel is itself a norm by which all texts and all interpretations are judged. Do they effect God's will to set free the oppressed, to bring good news to sinners, the weak, and the dying? So also the long-standing principle of interpreting Scripture by Scripture means that any text and any reading is to be seen in light of the whole of Scripture and so subject to critique,

---

22. For a fine example of such hermeneutics of retrieval, see Jacqueline E. Lapsley, *Whispering the Word: Hearing Women's Stories in the Old Testament* (Louisville, KY: Westminster John Knox, 2005). Her specific form of this is labeled a "hermeneutic of trust."

23. Rosemary Radford Ruether, *Sexism and God-Talk: Toward a Feminist Theology* (Boston: Beacon, 1983), 20–46.

modification, and even rejection in light of the larger picture presented by the whole. The traditional hermeneutical guidelines known as the rule of faith and the rule of love continue to serve well in a feminist reading of Scripture as judgments and priorities are made. The rule of faith, which asks for the coherence of any interpretation with the church's tradition, comes under some question in feminist interpretation as classical ways of reading Scripture are indeed part of the problem the church inherits. When such conflict occurs, the rule of love may be the necessary hermeneutical tool for judging, and indeed for rethinking, the rule of faith. If the texts and our interpretations of them do not enhance the love of God and the love of neighbor, then both are to be relativized.[24]

THE COMMUNITY OF WOMEN AND MEN

Ultimately, the community that reads the Bible is a community of both women and men, more specifically, women and men together. We may read the texts on our own. Feminist interpretation is attentive to the place of women in the text and arises from the experience and place of women in our world. Yet few texts tell the story of women alone. If there are many fewer texts directed to men only than we may have once thought, there are also few texts directed simply to women. The community of faith is finally not gender-specific. It is made up of men and women who live and die together, who work and play and love together, whose life is intertwined by their very being male and female. The beginning of Scripture makes this point squarely and confronts us with an anthropology of man and woman, one that is clearly aware of gender particularity and just as clear that from creation on, woman and man are here together.[25] The human story as represented in Scripture

---

24. One of the more helpful interpretations of the rule of love is the following:

> Any interpretation of Scripture is wrong that separates or sets in opposition love for God and love for fellow human being, including both love expressed in individual relations and in human community (social justice). No interpretation of Scripture is correct that leads to or supports contempt for any individual or group of persons either within or outside of the church. Such results from the interpretation of Scripture plainly indicate that the rule of love has not been honored. This rule reminds us forcefully that as the rule of faith and life, Scripture is to be interpreted not just to discover what we are to think or what benefits we receive from God in Christ, but to discover how we are to live.

(*Presbyterian Understanding and Use of Holy Scripture and Biblical Authority and Interpretation* [Louisville, KY: Office of the General Assembly, 1992], 20.)

25. Although marriage is clearly one of the basic relationships between men and women, it is only one of the many ways that women and men live together in this world. Nor should these comments be construed as condemning same-sex committed relationships, a subject that I have treated in "What the Scriptures Principally Teach" in *Homosexuality and Christian Community* (ed. Choon-Leong Seow; Louisville, KY: Westminster John Knox, 1996), 53–63; reprinted in Patrick D. Miller, *The Way of the Lord: Essays in Old Testament Theology* (Forschungen zum Alten Testament 39; Tübingen: Mohr Siebeck, 2004), 286–96.

is, in its most fundamental character, a story of the community of men and women.

All of that is by way of suggesting that the context of interpretation is not simply our individual and communal experiences as women or as men but the community of women and men that was created by God and remains both the way we live—for better or worse—and a way of conceiving the church. Implicit in that claim is a hermeneutic that seeks not simply to look at the place of women in the text but at the way in which women and men live in community and what we may learn from that.[26] To illustrate this point, let me turn briefly to a set of biblical stories of men and women in community.

Abigail, Michal, Bathsheba, and David

Beautiful and wise, Abigail has a mean and ill-behaved husband, Nabal, who stupidly insults David (1 Sam 25). Abigail is sharper than her husband and immediately perceives the danger in his actions. Quickly and aggressively, she plans and acts to offset the danger. Abigail does not turn to her husband automatically. When his stupidity threatens the household, she moves on her own to appeal to David but does not tell her husband. David perceives her judgment and shrewdness, and grants her request. Indeed, he is so impressed that he woos her for his bride after Nabal dies at God's hand. Abigail accepts his proposal with alacrity. She has advanced her position significantly, taking initiative to protect herself and control her destiny, refusing to be so caught in a social system that the stupidity and churlishness of her husband must be accepted. She acts to affect her fate and does so successfully.

In love with David (1 Sam 18:20), Michal protects his life, helping him escape from her father's attempt to kill him, willing even to risk deceiving her father to do so (1 Sam 19:11–17). She is depicted as a lover; sharp, cool, and clever in a dangerous situation; spiteful and willing to reprove her husband even though he is king (2 Sam 6:16–23). Yet she is also a pawn in the affairs of her father and husband. Saul uses

---

26. I have sought to uncover such a way of reading the initial chapters of Genesis in an essay titled "Man and Woman: Toward a Theological Anthropology," in *Reading from Right to Left: Essays on the Hebrew Bible in Honour of David J. A. Clines* (ed. J. Cheryl Exum and H. G. M. Williamson; Journal for the Study of the Old Testament Supplement Series 373; London: Sheffield Academic Press, 2003), 320–28; reprinted in Miller, *Way of the Lord*, 310–18. The impact of feminist interpretation is evident when this essay is compared with an earlier small monograph, *Genesis 1–11: Studies in Structure and Theme* (Journal for the Study of the Old Testament Supplement Series 8; Sheffield: JSOT Press, 1978). The later essay provides some of the background and presuppositions of the case study that is presented here.

her desire to marry David as the opening scheme for David's death. He later gives her to another man when her husband, David, is in hiding. David gets her back, primarily to cement his claim to Saul's throne, and does so even when the story clearly indicates she has established a new and happy relationship within her second marriage and home (2 Sam 3:12–16). So in this story of the interrelationship of women and men, the woman's love and her shrewd behavior is consumed as she becomes a pawn in the political affairs of men. No wonder the last word we hear about Michal is that she despises David. The loving, clever, daring wife has become spiteful and resentful.

Bathsheba is the beautiful woman as sex object, victim of the adulterous lust of David. And as is often the case—for example, the massacre that results from the rape of Dinah (Gen 34)—the victimizing of woman or violence toward woman leads to even more violence, in this case the murder of Bathsheba's husband Uriah (2 Sam 11). So even for the "man after God's own heart" (1 Sam 13:14), male power can and does abuse the woman and treat her as a thing to be taken. The story does not end there, of course. The violated woman whose identity is given almost entirely in relation to her husband—her name is mentioned only twice in the story—goes on to become the bearer of the promise through her child Solomon. And the nearly nameless one becomes more clearly identified as she asserts herself in behalf of her son Solomon's claim to the throne (1 Kgs 1–2).

So what does one make of these stories of David with Abigail, Michal, and Bathsheba? Several things should be noted. David is in many respects a model figure in the biblical tradition—the one after God's own heart, the shaper and definer of the Davidic kingship out of which the whole messianic theology takes shape, the author of psalms, which, as David's songs, are meant to have a universal appeal as David becomes a kind of representative person who "experiences the full range of human emotions."[27] What the stories of David and these women reveal, however, is that a community of women and men is not created under male power even when the male is of exemplary character. In such a situation, women are not persons with whom one lives in a community of mutuality and cooperation but rather are things to be taken. The great sin of the exemplary one is a sin against a woman and its ongoing rippling effects.

Even in this situation, however, the women are not merely passive tools in the hands of the dominant male. They are efficient, clever, and

27. Brevard S. Childs, *Introduction to the Old Testament as Scripture* (Philadelphia: Fortress, 1979), 521.

cool, as well as beautiful. They act with daring to protect their own interests and those of their husband and children. Even under male control, they are capable of shaping destiny.

From the David stories it becomes clear that a dimension of the failure of kingship in ancient Israel was the failure of the king to establish justice and equity between men and women, beginning with his own actions. The anticipation of a messianic age that will overcome that failure is an anticipation of one whose rule of *šālôm* and *ṣĕdāqâ*, of peace or well-being and righteousness, will indeed be just what those terms indicate—a reign of harmony and wholeness and diminishing hostility between men and women as well as between nations, the establishment of a right relationship among neighbors, that is, among women and men. The new humanity that God's rule is to bring and for which God's people hope and pray encompasses a new community of women and men.

FOR FURTHER STUDY

Gench, Frances Taylor. *Back to the Well: Jesus' Encounters with Women in the Gospels.* Louisville, KY: Westminster John Knox, 2005.

Hardesty, Nancy. *Inclusive Language in the Church.* Atlanta: John Knox, 1987.

Johnson, Elizabeth A. *She Who Is: The Mystery of God in Feminist Theological Discourse.* New York: Crossroad, 1992.

Lapsley, Jacqueline E. *Whispering the Word: Hearing Women's Stories in the Old Testament.* Louisville, KY: Westminster John Knox, 2005.

Newsom, Carol A., and Sharon H. Ringe, eds. *Women's Bible Commentary with Apocrypha.* Rev. ed. Louisville, KY: Westminster John Knox, 1998.

Ruether, Rosemary Radford. *Sexism and God-Talk: Toward a Feminist Theology.* Boston: Beacon, 1983.

Sakenfeld, Katharine Doob. *Just Wives? Stories of Power and Survival in the Old Testament and Today.* Louisville, KY: Westminster John Knox, 2003.

Tennis, Dianne. *Is God the Only Reliable Father?* Philadelphia: Westminster, 1985.

Wren, Brian A. *What Language Shall I Borrow? God-Talk in Worship: A Male Response to Feminist Theology.* New York: Crossroad, 1989.

The Accomplishments
of Katharine Doob Sakenfeld

COMPILED BY SARAH ZHANG

BIOGRAPHY

Erudite yet nonjudgmental, sensitive but not sentimental, Professor Sakenfeld is admired by friends, colleagues, and students. The field of feminist biblical hermeneutics owes much to her works, which incorporate not only the sociocultural backgrounds of women's life in biblical times but also perspectives from diverse contemporary contexts. Her seminars and writings concerning the history of premonarchical Israel expertly integrate textual, rhetorical, social scientific, and archaeological resources.

Born in 1940 in Ithaca, New York, Katharine Doob Sakenfeld grew up in eastern Tennessee and Providence, Rhode Island. After graduating from the College of Wooster first in her class, she earned the M.S. in Sociology from the University of Rhode Island, the B.D. from Harvard Divinity School, and the Ph.D. from Harvard University. In 1970 she joined the faculty of Princeton Theological Seminary. Along the line, she has been a guest professor at San Francisco Theological Seminary, the Drew University Theological School, Boston College, and Union Theological Seminary in Dasmariñas, the Philippines. Currently, she serves as the William Albright Eisenberger Professor of Old Testament Literature and Exegesis and the director of Ph.D. Studies at Princeton Theological Seminary.

As a true expert of multitasking, Professor Sakenfeld is also active as an ordained Presbyterian minister in the Presbyterian Church (U.S.A.).

In addition to her commitment to regularly teaching adult education classes, she has served as the Moderator of the Presbytery of New Brunswick and has also functioned as a representative of her denomination to the Consultation on Church Union and to the Commission on the Faith and Order of the National Council of Churches.

At the same time, Professor Sakenfeld has been an esteemed member in the community of biblical scholars. She has served as president of the Biblical Colloquium, and has been named to the editorial boards of the *Journal of Biblical Literature, Theology Today,* and *Word and World.* In the Society of Biblical Literature, she has served as the secretary/treasurer and National Program Committee chairperson, the chairperson of its Nominating Committee, and is currently a member of its Committee on Programs and Initiatives. The society's highest honor was bestowed on her when it selected her to serve as its president for the year 2006–2007.

Professor Sakenfeld handles demands from all corners with a unique combination of intellectual height, professional efficiency, and pastoral warmth. She never fails to amaze all who know her.

BIBLIOGRAPHY OF KATHARINE DOOB SAKENFELD

1970

"Studies in the Usage of the Hebrew Word *Ḥesed*: A Thesis." Ph.D. diss., Harvard University, 1970.

1973

Review of *The Christian Church and the Old Testament,* by Arnold A. van Ruler. *Journal of Ecumenical Studies* 10 (1973): 165–66.

1974

Review of *Exodus,* by Brevard S. Childs. *Theology Today* 31 (1974): 275–78.

1975

"Problem of Divine Forgiveness in Numbers 14." *Catholic Biblical Quarterly* 37 (1975): 317–30.
"The Bible and Women: Bane or Blessing?" *Theology Today* 32 (1975): 222–33.

1977

Review of *Liberating Word,* ed. Letty M. Russell. *Interpretation* 31 (1977): 321–22.

1978

The Meaning of Ḥesed in the Hebrew Bible: A New Inquiry. Missoula, MT: Scholars, 1978.
"Ezekiel 18:25–32." *Interpretation* 32 (1978): 295–300.

1979

"And Sarah Laughed." *Journal of Biblical Literature* 98 (1979): 423–24.
Review of *God and the Rhetoric of Sexuality,* by Phyllis Trible. *Theology Today* 36 (1979): 294–95.

1980

Review of *Blessing in the Bible and in the Life of the Church,* by Claus Westermann. *Interpretation* 34 (1980): 103–4.

1982

"Old Testament Perspectives: Methodological Issues." *Journal for the Study of the Old Testament* 22 (1982): 13–20.

Review of *The Ordination of Women,* by Paul K. Jewett. *Theology Today* 38 (1982): 504–6.

1983

"Feminine and Masculine Images of God in Scripture and Translation." In *The Word and Words: Beyond Gender in Theological and Liturgical Language.* Edited by William D. Watley, 50–60. Princeton, NJ: Consultation on Church Union, 1983.

"Loyalty and Love: The Language of Human Interconnections in the Hebrew Bible." *Michigan Quarterly Review* 22 (1983): 190–204.

1984

Review of *The Bible and Liberation: Political and Social Hermeneutics,* ed. by Norman K. Gottwald. *Princeton Seminary Bulletin* 5 (1984): 251–52.

Review of *Justice and History in the Old Testament,* by Richard Adamiak. *Catholic Biblical Quarterly* 46 (1984): 526–27.

1985

Faithfulness in Action: Loyalty in Biblical Perspective. Philadelphia: Fortress, 1985.

"Theological and Redactional Problems in Numbers 20:2–13." In *Understanding the Word: Essays in Honor of Bernhard W. Anderson.* Edited by James T. Butler, Edgar W. Conrad, and Ben C. Ollenburger, 133–54. Sheffield: JSOT Press, 1985.

"Feminist Uses of Biblical Materials." In *Feminist Interpretation of the Bible.* Edited by Letty M. Russell, 55–64. Philadelphia: Westminster, 1985.

"Law, History and Tradition." *Catholic Biblical Quarterly* 47 (1985): 383–84.

"The Prayer." *Princeton Seminary Bulletin* 6 (1985): 6–7.

Review of *Wisdom Literature and the Psalms,* by Roland E. Murphy. *Princeton Seminary Bulletin* 6 (1985): 45.

Review of *Sociological Approaches to the Old Testament,* by Robert R. Wilson. *Theology Today* 41 (1985): 506.

Review of *Theodicy in the Old Testament,* ed. by James L. Crenshaw. *Princeton Seminary Bulletin* 6 (1985): 45.

1986

"Bread of Heaven." *Princeton Seminary Bulletin* 7 (1986): 20–24.

"Joshua-Judges." With Norman K. Gottwald, Edward Greenstein, Walter Harrelson, and Steve Reid. RSV Project. Standard Video Bible Study Old Testament Series. Kerr Associates. 120 mins. Videocassette.

1987

"Loyalty and Love: The Language of Human Interconnections in the Hebrew
    Bible." In *Backgrounds for the Bible.* Edited by Michael Patrick O'Connor
    and David Noel Freedman, 215–29. Winona Lake, IN: Eisenbrauns,
    1987.
"Till the Heart Sings: A Biblical Theology of Manhood and Womanhood."
    Journal of Biblical Literature 106 (1987): 697–99.

1988

"Zelophehad's Daughters." In *Perspectives on the Hebrew Bible: Essays in Honor
    of Walter J. Harrelson.* Edited by James L. Crenshaw, 37–47. Macon, GA:
    Mercer University Press, 1988.
"Zelophehad's Daughters." *Perspectives in Religious Studies* 15 (1988): 37–47.
"Feminist Perspectives on Bible and Theology: An Introduction to Selected
    Issues and Literature." *Interpretation* 42 (1988): 5–18.
"In the Wilderness, Awaiting the Land: The Daughters of Zelophehad and
    Feminist Interpretation." *Princeton Seminary Bulletin* 9 (1988): 179–96.

1989

"Feminist Biblical Interpretation." *Theology Today* 46 (1989): 154–68.
Review of *An Introduction to the Old Testament: A Feminist Perspective,* by Alice
    L. Laffey. *Anglican Theological Review* 71 (1989): 207–8.
"NRSV: A Standard for Our Time." With Art Cribbs, Robert C. Dentan, Bruce
    M. Metzger, Lydia Talbot, and Arthur O. Van Eck. Kerr Associates. 18 mins.
    Videocassette.

1990

"Who Is My Neighbor?" In *The Church with AIDS.* Edited by Letty M. Russell,
    175–82. Louisville, KY: Westminster John Knox, 1990.

1991

"Accuracy in Biblical Translation." In *What We Say and What We Mean:
    Workshop Models and Materials on Language about God and the People of
    God.* Presbyterian Church (U.S.A.) Women's Ministry Unit. Louisville, KY:
    Women's Ministry Unit, Presbyterian Church (U.S.A.), 1991.

1992

The Oxford Study Bible: Revised English Bible with the Apocrypha. Edited with James
    R. Mueller and M. Jack Suggs. New York: Oxford University Press, 1992.
"Love (OT)." In *The Anchor Bible Dictionary.* Edited by David Noel Freedman,
    4:375–81. New York/London/Toronto: Doubleday, 1992.

Review of *Reformed and Feminist: A Challenge to the Church,* by Johanna W. H. van Wijk-Bos. *Princeton Seminary Bulletin* 13 (1992): 361–62.

Review of *The Feminine Unconventional: Four Subversive Figures in Israel's Tradition,* by André Lacocque. *Critical Review of Books in Religion* (1992): 146–47.

Review of *Compromising Redemption: Relating Characters in the Book of Ruth,* by Danna Nolan Fewell and David Miller Gunn. *Critical Review of Books in Religion* (1992): 130–31.

1993

"New Approaches to Understanding and Study of the Bible." In *American Bible Society Symposium Papers on the Bible in the Twenty-First Century.* Edited by Howard C. Kee, 125–44. Philadelphia: Trinity Press International, 1993.

Review of *The Flowering of Old Testament Theology: A Reader in 20th-Century Old Testament Theology, 1930–1990,* ed. by Gerhard F. Hasel, Elmer A. Martens, and Ben C. Ollenburger. *Interpretation* 47 (1993): 424–26.

1994

Numbers: Journeying with God. International Theological Commentary. Grand Rapids: Eerdmans, 1994.

"Listening to Asian Voices." *Biblical Interpretation* 2 (1994): 363–66.

Review of *Numbers 1–20: A New Translation with Introduction and Commentary. Princeton Seminary Bulletin* 15 (1994): 201–2.

1995

Journeying with God: A Commentary on the Book of Numbers. Edinburgh: Handsel, 1995.

"'Feminist' Theology and Biblical Interpretation." In *Biblical Theology: Problems and Perspectives: In Honor of J. Christiaan Beker.* Edited by Steven J. Kraftchick, Charles D. Myers Jr., and Ben C. Ollenburger, 247–59, 332–34. Nashville: Abingdon, 1995.

1996

"Fences and Neighbors." *Princeton Seminary Bulletin* 17 (1996): 58–63.

"David Weadon: A Tribute (Aug. 8, 1956–Dec. 30, 1995)." *Princeton Seminary Bulletin* 17 (1996): 348–50.

Review of *Women's Visions: Theological Reflection, Celebration, Action,* ed. by Ofelia Ortega. *Theology Today* 53 (1996): 132.

Review of *The New Testament and Psalms: An Inclusive Version,* ed. by Victor R. Gold et al. *Theology Today* 53 (1996): 279–81.

1997

Reading the Bible as Women: Perspectives from Africa, Asia, and Latin America. Edited with Phyllis A. Bird and Sharon H. Ringe. *Semeia: An Experimental Journal for Biblical Criticism* 78 (1997).

"Deborah, Jael, and Sisera's Mother: Reading the Scriptures in Cross-Cultural Context." In *Women, Gender, and Christian Community.* Edited by Jane D. Douglass and James F. Kay, 13–22. Louisville, KY: Westminster John Knox, 1997.

1998

"Numbers." In *Women's Bible Commentary,* ed. by Carol A. Newsom and Sharon H. Ringe, 45–51. Louisville, KY: Westminster John Knox, 1998.

1999

Ruth. Interpretation Bible Commentary. Louisville, KY: John Knox, 1999.

"The Story of Ruth: Economic Survival." In *Realia Dei: Essays in Archaeology and Biblical Interpretation in Honor of Edward F. Campbell, Jr. at His Retirement.* Edited by Prescott H. Williams Jr. and Theodore Hiebert, 215–27. Atlanta: Scholars, 1999.

"Ruth 4, an Image of Eschatological Hope: Journeying with a Text." In *Liberating Eschatology: Essays in Honor of Letty M. Russell.* Edited by Margaret A. Farley, 55–67. Louisville, KY: Westminster John Knox, 1999.

"Social Location in the Hebrew Bible and Hong Kong." *Biblical Interpretation* 7 (1999): 187–91.

2000

"Feminist Reading of the Bible: Problems and Promises." *Bangalore Theological Forum* 32 (2000): 18–27.

"Num 16:27–33, Wives of Dathan and Abiram," "Num 18:11, 19, Daughters of Aaron," "Num 19:22, Person Becoming Purified," "Num 21:29, Daughters of Moab," "Num 21:1, Moabite Women," "Num 26:33; 27:1–11; 36:1–12; Josh 17:3–6; 1 Chr 7:15, Daughters of Zelophehad," "Num 31:9, 15–18, 35, Midianite Women," "Deut 2:34; 3:6, Women (and Men and Children) in Towns of the Amorite Kings Sihon and Og." In *Women in Scripture: A Dictionary of Named and Unnamed Women in the Hebrew Bible, the Apocryphal/Deuterocanonical Books, and the New Testament,* 220–23. Edited by Carol Meyers, Toni Craven, and Ross S. Kraemer. Boston: Houghton Mifflin, 2000.

Review of *Reconstructing the Society of Ancient Israel,* by Paula M. Nutt. *Princeton Seminary Bulletin* 21 (2000): 260–61.

2001

Ruth (Interpretation Bible Commentary). Translated into Japanese. Tokyo, 2001.
Ruth (Interpretation Bible Commentary). Translated into Korean. Seoul, 2001.

2002

"Tamar, Rahab, Ruth, and the Wife of Uriah: The Company Mary Keeps in Matthew's Gospel." In *Blessed One: Protestant Perspectives on Mary.* Edited by Beverly R. Gaventa and Cynthia L. Rigby, 21–31. Louisville, KY: Westminster John Knox, 2002.
"At the Threshing Floor: Sex, Reader Response, and a Hermeneutic of Survival." *Old Testament Essays* 15 (2002): 179–99.

2003

Just Wives? Stories of Power and Survival in the Old Testament and Today. Louisville, KY: Westminster John Knox, 2003.
"Naomi's Cry: Reflections on Ruth 1:20–21." In *A God So Near: Essays on Old Testament Theology in Honor of Patrick D. Miller.* Edited by Brent A. Strawn and Nancy R. Bowen, 129–43. Winona Lake, IN: Eisenbrauns, 2003.

2004

"Why Perez? Reflections on David's Genealogy in Biblical Tradition." In *David and Zion: Biblical Studies in Honor of J. J. M. Roberts.* Edited by Bernard F. Batto and Kathryn L. Roberts, 405–16. Winona Lake, IN: Eisenbrauns, 2004.
"How Hosea Transformed the Lord of the Realm into a Temperamental Spouse." *Bible Review* 20 (2004): 29–35.

2005

General Editor of *The New Interpreter's Dictionary of the Bible.* 5 volumes. Nashville: Abingdon, forthcoming.
Review of *Poor Banished Children of Eve: Women as Evil in the Hebrew Bible,* by Gale A. Yee. *Theology Today* 61 (2005): 582–86.